The World Year Book of Education 1970
Education in Cities

The World Year Book of Education 1970

Education in Cities

Joint Editors:

Joseph A. Lauwerys, D.Sc., D.Lit., F.R.I.C.
Professor of Comparative Education in the University of London

David G. Scanlon, Ed.D.
Professor of International Education, Columbia University

Published in the United States of America by

Harcourt, Brace & World, Inc.

New York   Chicago   San Francisco   Atlanta

ISBN 0-15-598566-3

Printed in 11/12 Bembo (270) in Great Britain by
Hazell Watson & Viney Ltd, Aylesbury, Bucks

The World Year Book of Education 1970

Contents

Section IV **Europe**

Section V **The Near, Mid and Far East**

Editors' Introduction

Our purpose, in this volume, was not to produce yet another book describing various aspects of the 'urban crisis', but to concentrate on the effects of urbanization on education at all levels – an aspect which has, of course, been mentioned explicitly in the literature concerned with problems of urban growth though usually in the context of social problems, town planning, and so on. Although the current and growing problems have increasingly been the subject of intensive national and international study by government departments, local authorities, town planners, architects, geographers and social scientists all over the world, it appears that there is very little published information, at international level, about the effects of urban growth on educational systems and education.

What we have set out to do in this volume, therefore, is to present a comparative study of some general educational problems common to most urban areas and then to see what particular problems arise from different sorts of urban development, for example, the growth of shanty towns, the decay of city centres, the dispersion of the city or the establishment of new towns. The analysis is made more specific by the number of case studies which exemplify particular educational problems arising from different sorts of urban development in different parts of the world.

A study of the contributions in the volume, while revealing similarities both in the development of cities throughout the world and in the educational problems which arise, also shows how complex those problems are. Even in general terms the articles reveal that the solutions in terms of schools to be provided and curricula to be followed have yet to be found. The solutions, in terms of specific countries and the problems unique to them, are even further off.

It may be, of course, that schools can do far less than has been commonly supposed to help in the solution of problems which are social and political rather than educational. Nevertheless, the role of the school is still crucial as one of the main agencies in the task of transmitting attitudes and the social and intellectual skills required of all who live in cities. This task would be easier if there were agreement as to what was desirable and how, in curricular terms, it could be achieved. The present volume, we believe, goes at least some of the way in the analysis of the problems without which solutions cannot be realistically assessed.

The Editors, while endorsing the volume as a whole, do not necessarily support all the views contained in individual contributions.

J. A. Lauwerys
University of London
David G. Scanlon
Columbia University

Joseph A. Lauwerys, D.Sc., D.Lit., F.R.I.C.
Commandeur des Palmes Académiques
Professor of Comparative Education and Dean
of the Faculty of Education, University of London
Visiting Professor of Education in the Sorbonne
Hon. Professor of Education, University of Ankara

Dr Joseph A. Lauwerys retires as Professor of Comparative Education in the University of London at the end of the academic year 1969–70. One of his first tasks when he was appointed to this position in 1947 was to recommend the annual publication of the *Year Book of Education* which had not been published during the war years. Since 1948 he has been the London Joint Editor, collaborating for some years with the late Dr Nicholas Hans in London and from 1953 with Joint Editors from Teachers College Columbia University – Dr Robert King Hall, Dr George Z. F. Bereday and Dr David G. Scanlon. He brought to the immensely important task of strengthening a transatlantic bridge through a joint publication, a wealth of experience and scholarship in Comparative Education. His personal contacts with the Allied Ministers of Education during the war, his influential role in the establishment of Unesco, and his personal and sympathetic knowledge of the U.S.A., enabled him to draw together the strands of an emerging discipline and give to it a new direction. With his collaborators on both sides of the Atlantic and throughout the world, the *World Year Book of Education* has provided more than an annual review of statistical information and some comparative articles. Each year since 1948 a theme has been selected and treated comparatively, often on the basis of a particular social science approach. These volumes have made a substantial contribution to the development of Comparative Education.

In thanking Dr Lauwerys for his long and distinguished contribution to the preparation and publication of the *World Year Book of Education*, we hope that for many years to come we shall have the benefit of his advice and active participation in future volumes.

H. L. Elvin
Chairman, London Editorial Board
R. Freeman Butts
Chairman, New York Editorial Board

Section I: Towards a Theory of Urban Education

1 *Education in Cities*

Brian Holmes

The city like the greater universe is neither hostile nor friendly. It is simply indifferent. Yet like a magnet attracting iron filings it draws people to it in spite of the fact that alienation, anonymity and frenetic activity may be among the consequences of living in the new environment. People move for a variety of reasons. Some come with a clear purpose and hope. Others leave their former homes because life there is hard, dull, hopeless. Others simply drift into a strange new situation. There is abundant evidence to show that the in-migration of people is largely responsible for the unprecedented rate of growth of conurbations. Though high birth rates, low infant mortality and longevity have certainly helped to accelerate it.

In most cases the growth is unplanned and usually uncontrollable. However, some of the reasons why people move to the city are known and the rates at which they move and patterns of urban growth have been studied so that generalizations are possible about some problems of education in big metropolitan areas.

One of the most obvious features of urban growth throughout the world is the rate at which it is taking place. In Chicago, for example, the population has risen from 386,000 in 1900 to 3,700,000 in 1970. Rotterdam's population more than doubled between 1900 and 1960. In the last 150 years the population of the central area of the Ruhr has multiplied 36 times to create a megalopolis. In Rome the increase of the school population is approaching 20,000 per year. In Venezuela the proportion of people living in the countryside or in small towns has dropped from 70 per cent to 30 per cent in the last 30 years. In the same period Durban's population has increased two-and-a-half-fold; Delhi's by over four times; and Manila's growth was almost three-fold in just over twenty years. Rapid rates of growth create more serious problems than does mere size since none of the social services can keep pace with the influx of people. As the density of population rises housing facilities cannot easily be extended. Water, electricity, gas and other services lag behind the needs of the rising number of people. Sewage and waste disposal become problems. Public transport cannot meet the demands of those wishing to use it and private vehicles jam the streets. When old and modern forms of transport come together there arises the kind of chaos described in the article on Calcutta. As for the schools, more and more pupils are frequently accepted although it may be virtually impossible to increase the accommodation. In short all the social services are strained to the limit. Schools are overcrowded, buildings are out of date or non-existent and the rate at which they can be improved falls well behind the rate at which children of school age pour into the city. These population growth rates are in themselves important factors in creating slums and slum schools.

A variety of factors explain the attraction of the big metropolitan area. Some are positive. Capital cities offer opportunities in politics and in the bureaucracy which are unavailable elsewhere. In seaports and inland communication centres commercial activities usually flourish. The industrial city, while not an entirely modern phenomenon, now has unique characteristics and provides a new range of occupations. Cities, whether old or new, are often centres of culture. New York, Tokyo, London, Calcutta and Chicago – for example – are either national or state capitals which offer a whole range of political, economic and cultural opportunities. Consequently they attract several different groups of people.

From small cities and towns may come ambitious, well-trained young men often with their families. They seek political power, professional advancement and more money. Similarly qualified single women are also attracted by these advantages. All these look for comfortable middle class apartments or houses and parents want to make sure that the schools are satisfactory before choosing where they will live. The chances are high that members of this group, provided they are not members of an underprivileged minority, will fit into big city life fairly easily. At the same time, the range of economic opportunities will attract less well-trained, semi-skilled and unskilled workers who may come to the city with or without their families. When they arrive their freedom of choice is restricted by poverty, race and nationality.

Lack of opportunity in the villages and rural areas also 'pushes' people to the urban centres. They are even less free to choose where and how they will live and may well cluster in ghettos. Again their origins may place them at a disadvantage. Many immigrants come from rural areas of other countries. Some are drawn by the prospects of life in a new country. Others seek refuge from political oppression. The seriously disadvantaged among them are those without money or marketable skills who may well not speak the language of the host country. Their religious and ethnic backgrounds are obvious in a new environment which, in general, is neutral but where in face-to-face relationships deep prejudices persist. Members of each of many different in-migration groups will face, and create, their own somewhat unique problems. Educationists are consequently confronted by a range of difficulties for which no panacea exists. Superficially it may seem that the city, neither hostile nor friendly, can cope with some types of newcomer but a deeper analysis is needed of group characteristics and the reasons for the choice of areas where newcomers settle before specific educational solutions can be proposed.

The Growth of Metropolitan Areas

A vast literature is replete with studies showing how cities and metropolitan areas grow. Three patterns are frequently used to describe in general terms what happens. One model of concentric circles points to the growth of new districts in ever-widening zones around a central core. The second, radial-sector, model suggests that cities grow out along the lines of rail and road transport. Third, the multiple-nuclei model draws attention to developments round a number of cores which may previously have been small communities. All three help to explain city expansion patterns. It is evident from the literature that patterns of development within these three models vary considerably and rarely can one of them, by itself, be used to describe migration movements. The conurbations of North America and Europe show processes of growth which are shared by some cities elsewhere. Usually in these continents rural or foreign immigrants move out to the suburbs either along lines of transport or to the next concentric zone, or to nuclei of population outside the metropolitan area. Ambitious, go-ahead promotion hunters may move into villages and small towns within commuting distance further out. Infilling occurs as a result of these processes and a large uninterrupted megalopolis is created. The heart or core of the old city decays, the suburbs sprawl and the smaller communities which once had separate identities lose them. Commuting brings chaos. Business and industry cannot expand and have to be dispersed. Often the old centre is rehabilitated. These processes are widespread but somewhat different patterns occur outside Europe and North America. Characteristic of many Latin American and Asian urban centres is the shanty town for rural immigrants on the periphery of the old city.

While these patterns differ, the old centre and the shanty town on the periphery share the problems previously mentioned and at least one other. Both are transit stops on the way to better jobs and houses for people, many of whom, however, are trapped until cleared out or rehoused by urban renewal or until they accept defeat and return, or are sent back to the villages and countries whence they came. The uncontrolled character of most of these processes is widespread, and attempts to restrict entry into the city centre or shanty town, or to coerce those who come either to return or to accept limitations on their freedom, are often felt to be contrary to the spirit and practice of democratic government. The dilemma is real and cannot easily be resolved since in most countries close control over individual choice is unacceptable. Articles on China and South Africa describe policies designed to prevent the uncontrolled growth of cities.

In this volume no attempt has been made to add to the sociological analysis of processes of urbanization. Case studies, however, show how and under what influences some large and growing cities have developed. Since 1930 Caracas has become a new city of some two million inhabitants as the result of the discovery and exploitation of oil. The government and economy were centralized, jobs became plentiful, attracting foreign workers as well as thousands of *campesinos*. For many years industry has drawn workers to the Ruhr. Many African cities, too, such as Durban and Lagos, have become industrial centres. Tourism is one of the main reasons for the growth of Rome and Udaipur. Haifa, typical of Israel, has received a flood of refugees from Arab countries and Eastern Europe. Many newcomers to Nottingham are from the West Indian islands and the Indian peninsula. Chicago's recent growth has been due in part to the migration of negroes from the Southern States. New York City has received these and immigrants from Puerto Rico and, during the fifties, refugees from Europe. The main patterns of settlement in these cities are described; they fall into the main models referred to. From the viewpoint of educational policy, however, attention is for the most part directed in this volume to problem areas, that is to those points in the city or metropolitan area to which the obviously less advantaged people move.

Rural and Urban Typologies

Nevertheless much research is needed on how city children from well-to-do, stable, and successful homes should be educated. That these children survive and may appear to succeed possibly disguises the fact that the schools of the large conurbation should be transformed if they are to meet demands which have never previously existed. For are not today's schools copies of institutions which served rural and semi-urban societies in the past? Typologies facilitating comparisons of rural and urban life would facilitate the more thorough study of how city schools should prepare pupils for big city life. For example, Talcott Parsons refers to affective, diffuse, particularistic and ascriptive societies in which relationships are dominated by emotions, members perform a range of tasks, and are treated on the basis of their personal qualities or in the light of their subgroup membership, and mobility and promotion depend on their inherited position and qualities. These features characterize the rural society. In urban societies individuals are by and large prepared to forgo short-term benefits for long-term gains and work out their relationships on a rational basis. They have a particular role or roles to perform, they are treated as equals before the law and gain promotion on the basis of achievement. In the nineteenth century, F. Toennies made a distinction between 'communities' and 'societies' and E. Durkheim's concepts were not very different. Karl Marx compared feudalistic and capitalistic industrial societies. More recently L. Wirth has identified the main traits of city life, and R. Redfield has defined a folk society in a way that suggested an ideal polar-type urban society. None of these, or any other available polar models has been specifically used in this volume although any one of them would offer a useful comparative framework. Each author has drawn on his expertise and knowledge to describe the growth of cities, the problems which result and the educational policies followed.

The serious problem areas are created by the arrival of large numbers of people from rural-village backgrounds or foreign countries. Frequently those from abroad move from economically less well developed to more highly developed countries and have, in addition, rural backgrounds. They enter unfamiliar political, economic and social situations. In politics and administration the city is impersonal and the individual is subordinate to the organization. Voting is along party lines rather than for a familiar person. Wealth, racial background and the support of a party machine nevertheless influence any successful search for power. At the same time, achievement is likely to count for more than nepotism in a bureaucracy based upon concepts of equality and rationalism. In some respects then, political institutions of the city are operated on a different set of norms from those in the rural areas. In other matters small community values persist. Economic life is not the same either. The main difference lies in the degree of specificity. In the city each of a great many occupations demands specific, repetitive skills. The city worker performs one task, the final product being the outcome of many interrelated processes. The rural newcomer has frequently been used to performing all the tasks needed to start and complete a piece of work. Again in the large factory interpersonal relations are based on unfamiliar forms of organization. The newcomer may have been used to working alongside members of his family – in the city he cannot. In the village success may have come to him in his job because he was well-known – in the city promotion criteria are based on achievement. Time-keeping, the speedy performance of routine tasks and the acceptance of boredom are important. Men and women compete against impersonal production norms. In the new situation the family helps rather little. Moreover, the immigrant often leaves his large family behind and comes alone to the city. Generally the urban family is a nuclear rather than extended unit. It is more mobile, many of its political and economic functions have been removed, and it is frequently less stable. In the urban family emotions dominate behaviour less, roles are not so diffuse, and success does not depend so much upon inherited qualities. Consequently the rural newcomer faces problems of adjustment in the political, economic and familial aspects of his life. Well-known expectations are unlikely to be fulfilled, and if he is to succeed in his new occupation he must learn new attitudes which are often antithetical to those he brings from his previous environment. For him to acquire these new attitudes is more difficult than to learn new skills. Most theorists of social change have maintained that mores or deeply held sentiments have a permanence that makes adaptation to technological innovations slow. Here the view is held that because the mores of the big city are very different from those of the rural area, village or small town major educational problems arise in rapidly growing conurbations.

At the same time the rural in-migrant lacks the marketable skills of a complex industrial or commercial society. At one time simple literacy – the 3 Rs – was a very important qualification which enabled literate villagers to enter the lower levels of an expanding administration or to obtain a modest commercial job. They could be absorbed in the cities of the first industrial revolution. No longer. Certainly the complex industries of today demand many workers who perform simple, repetitive tasks, but increasingly highly skilled personnel should be able to apply general principles to particular tasks, be flexible in outlook and be capable of learning new skills quickly.

In short, if the newcomers are to fit into industrial life they need a formal education appropriate to the demands, both technical and psychological, made upon them by modern automated industry. Evidently this is one aspect of educational policy which, if given high priority, could meet some major problems facing rural immigrants. Many reform proposals have advocated more vocationally orientated schools but the *World Year Book of Education* of 1968 on 'Education and Industry' showed how intractable are some of the difficulties of educating for modern industry. The education of city children, however, should go far beyond occupational preparation. An exclusive concern with purely vocational training would deny the major aims of educationists. For example, while the solution of economic problems may be extremely important it would be unwise to achieve it at the expense of political stability and social integration. Consequently today the role of the school and adult education in promoting the skills of political participation and social harmony in an urban setting should rightly receive careful attention.

The Role of the School

Can the city school discharge all the functions given to it by John Dewey?

In Chicago Dewey remembered the educative experiences of the rural community in which he had been brought up. Since they could not be replicated in the neutral city, he thought that the school should become, in miniature, the rural environment where children could learn the attitudes and skills of democratic life through active participation and shared experiences. By implication, these attitudes and skills were those which had served the U.S.A. well when most of its population lived in small communities. His solution, therefore, presupposed that successfully inculcated rural attitudes would serve an urban population, but they cannot. In India a policy of Basic Education is justified by the same misapprehension, as more, though still a minority, of its people live in cities and hope to work in developing industries. Soviet polytechnical theory, on the other hand, takes full account of the fact that young people are growing up in an industrial society, assumes that more and more of them will live in big towns and cities and that they will need the moral training appropriate to such a life.

One of the first tasks, therefore, in face of the urban crisis, is to re-assess the most general aims and more immediate goals of an educational system. Should the schools attempt to reconstruct society? Or should they limit their role to the preservation of all that is best in existing society? Should newcomers to the city have their traditional value system strengthened? Or should they be encouraged to abandon inherited values and ways o life for those of the city? Is it the task of the schools to re-formulate the values and attitudes of an urban environment? In short, can education be an agent of social change or is it bound simply to help young people adapt to the institutions of life they find? An even larger question turns on whether or not there exist attitudes and social skills which if adopted would improve the quality of city life.

Few contributors have questioned the worth of traditional value systems. Dr Ianni points out, however, that the practical situation in which many in-migrants find themselves in North America totally denies the values they are encouraged by their teachers to accept. It is very difficult to argue that if and when in the city the values of a rural Christian society have been submerged, their polar opposites are appropriate alternatives. Hate thy neighbour! Never do unto others as you would they should do unto you! Be dishonest! Never comfort the sick! Do not help the needy! And so on. None of these alternatives would appeal to educationists. Yet many such commandments nevertheless find practical expression in the ghettos of the northern cities of the U.S.A. and on the pavements of the swarming cities of India. The differences between what is taught in school and what happens outside cannot fail to impress themselves on young people. If neither traditional rural values nor their antitheses seem satisfactory, what can replace them? This question should be asked even if at the moment there is no obvious answer.

One consequence of this situation is that discussions about the purpose of education not only lack novelty but often seem dangerously complacent and out-of-date. The claims of politics, industry and social class are too frequently couched in terms of situations which for the most part no longer exist. Emphasis is given by some educationists to vocational training to meet manpower needs, including top-level scientists and technologists. Others wish radically to restructure the social class system by reorganizing the schools. Often the relation between education and democracy is conceived in eighteenth or nineteenth century terms. But political, economic and social class theories are at the moment in a state of flux and the certainties of previous generations have given way to doubts about the efficacy of liberal encyclopedist traditions or Marxian alternatives. A more determined search for new normative theories of the 'good and just society' may well arise from the present confusion of thought. The new theories will have to make sense not of rural societies or even the nineteenth century industrial societies but of the sophisticated machine age megalopolis of the twenty-first century. Until such theories emerge the role which education can and should play will remain obscure.

Educational Problems

Some of the main educational consequences of urbanization are relatively easy to see. Overcrowded schools in the centre of a city are a universal phenomenon. An almost total lack of easily accessible educational facilities is not unusual in peripheral shanty towns. One reason why these conditions cannot be improved is that the tax base is small on which money for the slum or shanty town school is raised. Property owners, whether of private domestic living quarters or factories, are not always prepared to pay high taxes or maintain schools. In densely populated areas tax money has to be spread over the education of a great many school age children. The capital expansion of facilities in the crowded city is difficult unless funds are available and rehabilitation schemes are underway. Similarly more overall social planning of shanty towns is a prerequisite to the provision of adequate school buildings. In brief, the finance to meet current and capital costs can rarely be raised in heavily populated areas of the old city or peripheral shanty towns.

The rates at which sections of the population move also affect the quality of education. In slum areas many parents wish to move out as soon as possible and the time their children spend in any one school is often very brief. In the northern cities of the U.S.A., moreover, whole communities within the metropolitan areas may leave one district for another as new immigrants arrive. If the turnover of pupils is rapid so too is that of teachers. Good salaries in the cities may help to stabilize teaching staff but conditions of work do not encourage many to seek permanent careers in the slum schools. The impermanence of the school community is bound adversely to affect discipline and learning. Yet to stabilize the slum school would mean to deny, to many who want to use it, a stepping stone to a better life. Those who move out of the slum are the most energetic and no doubt the ones who can take most advantage of what the slum school has to offer.

This is one of the most serious educational dilemmas. Should the school enable slum children to survive? Should it provide them with skills and attitudes which will enable them to escape? Or should it, as the reconstructionists might suggest, try to rehabilitate the city, and if so in what image? None of these questions can be answered without taking into account short-term educational objectives and long-term goals which may well be contradictory.

At the level of practical educational policy a number of major decisions have to be faced. Among those which are important are included finance, administration, the structure of the school system, curriculum, out of school education and teacher preparation. In the patterns of policies described in this volume, coherence and consistence are rarely found. Policies appear to be based on more *ad hoc* decisions reached as a result of political pressures than on the findings of substantial research. No doubt this state of affairs accurately reflects the magnitude of the problems and the shortage of imaginative solutions. As a generalization, however, it is possible that in the past the main features of the rural and small town school system have been retained in the cities. The size of these schools has grown enormously and their socio-economic context is no longer rural in spite of the fact that many of the in-migrants carry with them rural attitudes. The apparent viability of a rural school system in a suburban environment may frequently disguise the fact that radically different institutions are needed in the cities.

Typically, rural schools are maintained by the local community for its members. Formerly the schools catered for a minority of children except at the primary stages. Secondary education, either in the community or in the nearest larger centre of population, was normally reserved for a selected few. Birth and wealth as well as ability were criteria of selection. Success in school provided opportunities for the few to leave the rural community to seek their fortune in the town or small city. The curriculum was for the most part based on the religious beliefs of the community and centred round carefully selected literature – frequently 'the classics'. The early schools in Europe were Christian and used the Bible and Latin texts. Jews, Moslems and Buddhists have for centuries run schools based on studies of their own sacred texts. The Chinese schools had a more secular tone but Confucian ethics were taught through the classical literature. Such schools were controlled by those who had succeeded in them so that clerical or 'establishment' control was a feature of most school systems up to the nineteenth century. Then it was challenged. Sometimes secular control came in the form of local responsibility. In other countries centralism was introduced early on. In response to the needs of the nineteenth century, national systems evolved in which the national or federal authorities exercised more and more influence over finance, supervision, the curriculum and teacher preparation. Yet the desirability of local participation was retained even in such highly centralized systems as France as well as in the German Länder and in England and, of course, in the fiercely decentralized systems such as the U.S.A. and Canada.

The Administrative Unit

Now the question of the appropriate size of the unit of administrative control is again posed. Strangely, where there is a considerable measure of centralized administration over a large metropolitan schools system as in New York City, the devolution of administration is urged. On the other hand where, as in Manila, much authority lies in the hands of small administrative units in the metropolitan area, the cry is for more centralized control and financing. Do the different circumstances justify such radically different claims?

The traditional arguments are political. States rights has been an issue since the U.S.A. constitution was amended. A fine balance was drawn in the English 1944 Act between Ministry and local authority responsibilities. Recently financial and administrative issues have forced a reduction in the number of local School Boards in the U.S.A. In England the Redcliffe-Maud Committee reported in 1969 on the desirability of creating fewer and larger local authorities. Some years ago in London when the County Council became the Greater London Council and many responsibilities of the old L.C.C. were delegated to local boroughs, the educational unit was retained as the Inner London Education Authority. The satisfaction many teachers experienced working in the authority's school was manifest in their attempts to retain the old large unit. Nevertheless, in most countries professional opinion is divided on questions of national and regional control and local participation. The argument for smaller units seems vague. It is often held that the participation of members of the community served by the schools is vital to the solution of the problems facing city schools. But why? Can local enthusiasm replace professional expertise? And how can local effort make itself effective?

The Plowden Report in England on primary schools recommended that parents should be more actively involved in their children's education and at the same time held that schools in deprived areas should get priority treatment. In contrast New York teachers were called out on strike against community control. Under what circumstances can local participation be effective? Members of the smaller community may well be able to offer advice and tangible support when the image of the school they wish to help is that of a rural school – transplanted, to be sure, into the city environment. Many attitudes of these middle class, successful parents may be particularistic, affective, and ascriptive in their orientation as far as the school and several features of their environment are concerned. Their ability to help depends on whether or not they can keep the school and other social agencies as traditional institutions. The chances of success in the well-to-do suburb where parents can control their environment are far greater than in the overcrowded slum. But in the heart of the old city few institutions – domestic, economic or political – retain their rural characteristics, and disadvantaged parents cannot control their environment. For both groups, however, the stabilization of transplanted institutions is virtually impossible. Because the problems seem less acute, however, middle class professionals may think the solution to urban problems lies in policies which in fact perpetuate rural institutions whereas the evolution of significantly new-type schools is needed. Some of the proposals to build educational plazas which are described in this volume represent creative solutions.

In summary, when in order to solve some of the problems of the urban school participation is urged, it is often on the bases of attitudes appropriate to the rural or folk society in which homogeneity of outlook, together with a strong sense of group loyalty are based on informal but accepted status and traditional, spontaneous and uncritical modes of behaviour. If so, the creation of city institutions facilitating such participation is vital. On the other hand professional educationists are rightly anxious that participation by laymen should not involve a loss in their power. Here we have an unresolved dilemma.

Finance and Disadvantaged Groups

As mentioned above, slum communities are unable, unaided, to raise the money to finance good schools. Studies of Chicago and other U.S. cities show that the suburban schools are much wealthier than those in the old core. To redress this inbalance equalization or additional funds for slum schools are needed. In some countries such as the United Kingdom, national policy is designed to ensure that the amount spent per capita on education throughout the country is roughly the same. Where teachers' salaries are on a national scale, as they often are, one major source of inequality is removed. Nevertheless, everywhere considerable differences exist between the wealthy and the not-so-wealthy schools. Again the financing of private, and particularly religious schools, creates problems. In many countries the private religious schools bear the brunt of educational provision. Frequently politics make it impossible to subsidize these schools to any great extent, notably in the U.S.A. and, until recently, in France. Elsewhere, as in the Netherlands and the United Kingdom, financial support is generous. Without public funds such schools are likely to be old, poorly equipped and staffed by underpaid and sometimes not satisfactorily qualified teachers. Yet without these schools and their devoted teachers many city schools systems would collapse. An example of the dilemma are the proposals made in the U.S.A. 1965 Elementary and Secondary School Act which made federal funds available to schools in communities where family incomes were below a very low minimum. Many such disadvantaged communities are served by Roman Catholic parochial schools. Should they qualify for federal aid in spite of the First Amendment to the Constitution? In any case it is doubtful whether the funds made available are on a sufficiently massive scale to ensure that the slum schools have some chance of being equipped up to the standard of the suburban and small town schools.

As for the organization of the school system, much attention has been paid recently in Europe to its reorganization along comprehensive lines. In the U.S.A. as long ago as the 1840s Horace Mann was arguing that the common elementary school in which children of the wealthy and poor sat side by side was vital to the moral tone of the community. Since 1945 on the grounds of justice and equality there has been pressure in many countries to establish common or comprehensive schools at the second stage of education. The social purpose has been to improve social mobility and reduce sharp social divisions. Little has been said of the ways in which in a vast city the comprehensive school *per se* will achieve its social goals. The city divides the population, the density of which is sufficiently high to fill the school with children largely from one community. In many cases the whole school community is disadvantaged. In fact many comprehensive schools are for the disadvantaged.

Frequently members of the disadvantaged group have not only an inferior socio-economic status but come from foreign countries or from different ethnic and cultural backgrounds. In the U.S.A. the negroes fall into this category; in the United Kingdom Commonwealth immigrants from Africa, Asia and the West Indies. Should policies of forced integration of schools be followed? Differences of opinion exist among the school authorities and leaders of minority groups. The integration of schools by transporting children from one neighbourhood to another has been attempted in some American cities. In England and Wales policy varies. Some local authorities, recognizing the need to mix cultures in school, move the children of Commonwealth immigrants some distance from their homes to ensure that they are educated in multi-racial schools. Other authorities claim that the educational level of immigrant children can be raised more effectively if they are given special attention in virtually segregated classes. On the other hand some black power leaders in the U.S.A. want the schools to promote their own minority culture. Some Commonwealth immigrants in England do not wish to lose their cultural identity and resist integration. Evidently the issues are complex and policies of comprehensivization should be seen in the light of housing policies and the attitudes of minority groups. The ways in which comprehensive schools can solve city educational problems better than other forms of school organization should be carefully considered. The answers are not at all clear.

Vocational Schools and Polytechnical Education

One attractive organizational solution seems to be to increase the number of vocational schools in which young people can be prepared for an occupation. Much has been written about the problems of educating youth for modern industrial life. It has been argued that technological changes are taking place so rapidly that to train effectively for today's world will leave trainees unprepared for tomorrow's job. Such points of view frequently justify an education based on a few principles of great generality from which, to be sure, many implications and applications can be drawn. The problems of generalizing this ability to perform a difficult intellectual task are often ignored. So vocational schools face a number of challenges. If they are strictly vocational in providing young people with the skills of a trade they are felt to restrict opportunities. If the education they provide is based upon general principles – from science and technology – it is frequently thought by pupils to be irrelevant.

Over the years theories have been proposed designed to make education relevant to the economic life of the community without being restrictive. Mr Ghandi's Wardha scheme, which became official government policy as Basic Education after Independence, was made when it was envisaged that the Indian economy would remain largely agricultural and subsistence. Its intention was to provide a sound general education through the vocational activities of a village or rural community. The Second World War accelerated independence and the new government embarked upon a policy of rapid industrialization. Could an education devised for a rural-subsistence economy adequately serve the needs of an industrial society in the throes of urbanization? The thesis advanced here is that such a system of basic education was unlikely to transform the folkways and mores of a rural people to those in harmony with urbanized industrial living.

Soviet experience is also instructive. Educational policy in accordance with Marxian doctrine is overtly geared to the needs of a modern industrial society. Great attention was paid in the past to manpower needs conceived rather narrowly in terms of the numbers of skilled personnel needed at all levels and in all branches of industry, commerce and agriculture. Soviet theoreticians have long realized that this was not in itself enough. A satisfactory education for today's industrial life should involve changes in the outlook of young people towards production and their fellow workers. The age-old dichotomy between manual training and intellectual education should be broken down. These excellent proposals implied radical changes in the mores and the acceptance of a new interpretation of men's relationship to each other. A number of reasons for the difficulties of implementing theory in the U.S.S.R. can be suggested. Perhaps the concepts of modern industry were idealized. No doubt teachers had not been thoroughly prepared for their new tasks. Men brought in from industry to educate young people to respect manual work and understand the place of machines in the factories of today may not have been capable of doing much more than show potential university students how to operate machines. Some new attitudes could be taught but the appeal has been heavily affective by evoking loyalties to an ideology, a class and a nation. Even in the U.S.S.R. the perplexing problems of metropolitan education demand systematic investigation.

Nevertheless, the Soviet analysis is very instructive because it pointed out that the dichotomy between general education and manual instruction lay at the heart of present problems of reform. Too often the content of education and the conceptual frame of reference which determines the way in which it is treated do little to prepare young people to cope with industrial city life. The intellectualism of European education is based upon neo-classical views of society, individuality and ways of knowing which originated in pre-industrialized societies. They were applied with success to education in small cities. Now elitist concepts of society are increasingly challenged and particularly in urban settings. In world declarations and national constitutions all individuals are held to be equal before the law and possessing equal human rights.

But theories of knowledge as old as Aristotle continue to influence the world of education and give rise to curricular theories which might have served autocratic Sparta or democratic Athens reasonably well, but cannot today really meet the needs of the teeming millions in industrial or commercial cities. Perhaps an up-dated liberal arts curriculum might serve a minority of children and vocational training might meet the needs of the masses. Such segregation is less acceptable now, at least politically, than before. Equality is stressed and participation urged.

Pragmatic Solutions

Meanwhile pragmatic theory in the U.S.A. directed the attention of educationists to the need to provide in an industrializing and urbanizing society an education which would help individuals to solve their problems collectively through the exercise of intelligence. Activity methods, learning from experience, projects, problem-centred curricula and the like, were the practical solutions proposed by a succession of progressive educationists in the U.S.A. Both progressive child-centred and social-centred approaches attempted to help young people make sense of and adapt to the changing world of the twentieth century. Many progressive educationists retained a romantic view that America's success was based on the spirit of the frontier. The virtues which helped the descendants of the Mayflower and millions of immigrants to subdue the West and lay the foundations of a dynamic new twentieth century civilization dominate much American thinking. But these were the virtues of a society in which individualism operated in small communities. Can they bring greater stability to the modern cities of the U.S.A.? Where indeed are the stabilizing factors in cities in which movements in and out are on a vast scale? Each day the commuters pour in early in the morning and stream out at night. The theatre crowds drive in. Conventions of business men, professional people, fraternity groups and so on fill vast hotels for a few days. Aircraft land and take off at invertals of seconds rather than minutes. The streets are already hopelessly congested, the skies are becoming so. The transients are part of the moving city. The number of people who live all their life in the same house or street or city grows smaller and smaller. A willingness to accept change is evidently one of the most important norms for survival in a modern city.

Pragmatism seems to provide a theoretical basis on which to build educational theories because it accepts change as one of the striking features of urbanization and implies that problems faced by young people in their environment should constitute the core of a general education. It suggests that in theory proposed solutions should be tested in practice. Finally it maintains that men through the collective exercise of intelligence can anticipate problems and cope with them more successfully.

Progressive educationists accepted the main principles of pragmatism and proposed methods of teaching and curriculum organization in accordance with them. They showed in the Eight Year Study between 1932 and 1940 that a high school curriculum closely geared to college entrance requirements was not essential to success at college. Criticisms of progressive education, fear that European education was 'better' and the pressure of manpower needs provided ammunition for those university professors and others who wanted to return to a curriculum based on the academic or basic disciplines and who wanted to provide accelerated and enriched courses for gifted children. When these movements in the U.S.A. pointed up the startling differences between the education provided for the middle class suburban child and the ghetto urchin, compensatory programmes of education were introduced. They were designed to bring young children from disadvantaged homes up to the level of achievement of their more favoured peers.

The U.S.A. reaction to international competition, and the move away from progressive educational principles of curriculum design are instructive. First because in no country have the problems of the city been studied more intensively. Secondly because nowhere else is there available a widely accepted theory of education which would make it possible to organize schoolwork round the problems of city life. And finally, perhaps in no country is the federal or national government less able than in the U.S.A. to influence and finance the agencies of the welfare state. The sources of hope and the seeds of educational frustration in the U.S.A. deserve careful comparative study. Of special interest is the Model Cities Program which implies that in meeting city problems comprehensive socio-economic planning and adequate finance are needed.

Planning

From England accounts of the way in which the planning of new towns away from the large conurbations may throw light on such proposals. The dispersal of population and the incorporation into overall plans of the educational needs of the community are instructive. But it should be noted that this solution is one which makes it unnecessary to think seriously about the kind of education which could serve a large city. There is little to suggest that educational policy in the new towns is novel – it does not need to be. If national policy checks the flow of people to the centres of high density population; if it slows down the rate of immigration from Commonwealth countries; if in short it inhibits the changes which are the source of urban problems, then radical re-thinking of education may not be necessary.

The South African case studies illustrate how political and social control reduce the magnitude of some problems even if they raise extremely contentious moral issues. Again policy in Communist China is designed, by encouraging movement out of the cities back to the rural areas, to meet the problems of urban growth by preventing it. Neither policy, controlled movement into designated townships nor an organized return to the rural areas, is universally acceptable and where they are not there is an obligation to seek new approaches to education on the basis of research.

The involvement of universities and teacher education institutions in this endeavour is evidently a much advocated trend. Field research into the precise nature of the socio-economic problems is needed, and a clearer understanding of the educational alternatives is desirable. Some analysis is required of the limited functions the school can play in the rehabilitation of the city so that the consequences of such limitations may be anticipated.

Two major needs stand out. First the attitudes appropriate to the non-affective, specific, universalistic and achieving city should be known in detail if schools are to contribute to their acceptance by city youth. Related to the achievement of this task are techniques of changing rural into urban attitudes. The other major difficulty is to devise appropriate new institutions. Some modes of administration and the size of administrative units should be reconsidered. Since the structure of the school system has a direct bearing on the successful adjustment of young people to one or several aspects of city life more research would help. A curriculum geared directly to the specific problems of urban living – in the areas of earning a living, keeping healthy, bringing up a family, participating in civic affairs, and spending leisure time profitably – is probably one of the most urgent reforms. Such a curriculum may have to be based upon information organized into quite new but teachable subjects. Unfortunately the progress in this direction in the U.S.A. has been checked by pressure to revise traditional subjects in the light of manpower needs. Much more research into the content and organization of new teaching subjects is a *sine qua non* of effective policy under present conditions.

One depressing conclusion which emerges from the case studies is that archaic solutions are often offered to modern problems. Evidently enlightened educational policy has little hope of success unless other agencies of social improvement are available; without the support of such agencies – adequately financed and staffed – the schools can hardly succeed. With such support what should the schools attempt? Guidelines to action were proposed at a National Conference on the Educational Dimension of the Model Cities Program held in Chicago.[1] They suggested that (*a*) the urban school should become a centre for community life, (*b*) it should develop closer working relationships with other human service agencies, (*c*) it should provide socially and racially integrated educational experiences, (*d*) it should provide student centred instruction, (*e*) its facilities should become increasingly specialized and differentiated, (*f*) the urban school should establish closer links with universities, (*g*) it must be more accountable for educational outcomes, (*h*) policy decisions affecting the school should be made at the community level, (*i*) the revenue base for the urban school must be expanded, and finally (*j*) the urban school must

---

[1] *Education and Urban Renaissance* edited by R. F. Campbell, Lucy A. Marx and R. O. Nystrand.

offer leadership in making the entire community a positive educative force.

The case studies in this *World Year Book of Education* show how difficult it is, in a variety of circumstances, to translate these principles into practical realistic policies. Central to the thesis of this introduction is that the schools of today are basically rural institutions and that the values which receive the support of many educationists are also those appropriate to a rural community. Often these are based on and have the authority of religion. Many in-migrants bring to the city these or similar values and on the face of it should fit into a school system which tries to bolster them up. The tragic fact seems to be that neither rural attitudes nor rural institutions can operate in a big city without serious personal and social maladjustment.

The dilemmas facing policy formulators are acute. Many of them have been outlined in this volume. The conditions under which they arise have been comprehensively surveyed. Some imaginative solutions have been described. But the impression which remains strongest is that the rates of change from one kind of society to another brought about by the accumulation of technical inventions and the uncontrolled movement of peoples into the urban centres have not been matched by the quantity or quality of research which is undoubtedly needed if imaginative educational solutions are to be found to some of the problems consequent on urban growth.

and the needs for education, as well as those of transportation, government, health and the economy, the whole metropolitan area must be regarded as the unit for investigation.

Schooling in the Metropolitan Setting

When school problems in the city become the topic of public concern, they are rarely *sui generis*, but rather arise from more general conditions: population growth, change in the age composition of communities, economic progress, man-power and finance problems, and so on. Changes in the composition of populations, in social and political ideology, in economic organization, create school problems. The size and density of the urban community, its heterogeneity, its interdependence, the interactions of its human components, and above all, its mobility and changeability – in fact, those features discussed above – are the sources of educational problems and debates in large cities.

From both the local and the global perspectives, three major categories of problems confront the educational observer. First, there are the political and economic issues: who shall run the schools for urban populations? Who shall make which types of decisions? How shall administrative power be distributed between local, regional and national levels of authority? And how is the effort to be planned, financed, and implemented? The second and third groups of problems are more directly pedagogical. One has to do with personnel (students, teachers, and administrators) and calls for responses to the changing populations in the schools of densely-settled areas. The pupil populations of urban schools pose new problems, not only because of numbers, but also because of their backgrounds, aspirations, and competencies. As a concomitant and as a consequence, ought there not be new criteria, new job descriptions and therefore new training programmes for those seeking employment in the schools? And finally, closely associated with the previous set of questions, what of the curriculum, the pedagogical methods and tools, and the patterns of internal school organizations? Are these changing as a response to new conditions? Are changes desirable? What is the relation of such innovations to educational outcomes?

One example of a major current issue in two big cities confirms both the widespread nature of some phenomena and the peculiarity of the local cases. The physical growth of metropolitan centres all over the world, but especially in the more developed countries, has created economic and administrative problems for city school systems everywhere. The decentralization controversy in New York, and the administrative reorganization which London underwent in 1965, are examples of responses to the same kind of pressure. The New York situation is different, of course, in that its current educational problems are as much a function of the United

States' historical problem of segregation of Negroes as of the sheer size of the city. The city has been 'ghettoized' into communities which are either black or white, either poor or reasonably well-off, either inner-city or suburban. Yet, the situation in London has similar features. Growing residential congestion at the centre has, as a result of considerable planning, been controlled, but the flight to the suburbs is evident. The influx of migrants from Asia and the Caribbean has created sizeable culturally, racially, and economically homogeneous enclaves different from the mainstream of the society. The phrase, 'town of villages' takes on a new meaning in today's London, where, as in New York, one moves from one cultural world to another as one moves around the city. In some senses, London's educational problems are unique, for they are part of the national effort to raise standards, adapt and modernize, and to implement a set of social and political principles through reform of school organization and practices. Yet in this, too, there are similarities with the basic considerations in the United States and elsewhere. The precedents and recent developments may differ, but the general process and contingencies are widespread.

When this discussion is extended to other aspects of schooling, the comparability of the two cases becomes sharper. Even though there is a strong precedent in the United States for public participation in educational decision-making and a strong tradition of parental exclusion from this activity in England, neither of the two cities conforms strictly to these principles. Through its appointed Board of Education and its extensive and highly centralized supervisory and administrative machinery, New York has effectively excluded parents and local citizen groups from the type of influence they have enjoyed in other communities in the States. In London, as in New York, the power of a local community to influence school decisions at large or in a district varies, but the relatively high degree of school autonomy and progressiveness of the Educational Committee and its administration have resulted in responsiveness to public demand. As a consequence, despite the differences in national practices and local provisions, London and New York recognize that parents, as well as local and regional administration, must somehow participate in educational decisions in their own cities.

The trend toward homogeneity of local communities within the urban setting creates very special problems for educational thinkers and practitioners. The most serious current issue in the United States and, with local variations, in other parts of the world, is the existence of gross differences in educational facilities, motivation and achievement according to urban sub-culture and residential community within the metropolis. The moral problem is not new; where there is national commitment to a set of democratic principles, such self-perpetuating social injustice cannot be tolerated. The economic and political aspects are generally realized too:

when a given group of people does not fully utilize a society's educational facilities, manpower is wasted and 'social dynamite' is stored up. But the persistence and even the growth of such divisions diminishes the potential made available by urban organization and life. It also threatens the very existence of the city as a social, economic, and political unit and as the nerve centre of the nation.

As a result of 'ghettoization', the student clientele of an urban school may be categorized according to a single label: low income, or any of the recent euphemisms (deprived, underprivileged), immigrant (meaning black, Puerto Rican, Asian, culturally different and racially distinct), middle class. The labels are either socio-economic, racial or religious, and serve as simple indicators of the special nature of the community. It is not yet clearly understood whether it is the empty pocket or the skin colour which accounts for the special nature of a given community and, by extension, of the children in a particular school. What is more generally conceded, however, is that the school institution is often unsuccessful in making the majority of some groups of youngsters productive or even minimally educated and responsible citizens, able to compete on the educational ladder or as adults in the economic society. Where an urban centre has succeeded in providing some measure of schooling for the whole range of its population, an appreciable minority has not been able to profit. In some extreme cases, a complete breakdown has resulted; in others, schools remain open but have abandoned any pretence of operating as educational institutions. Teachers and pupils engage in no productive communication, curriculum is abandoned, the formal school organization has no function except, possibly, to enforce attendance. In addition, the separate components of the school situation – parents, administrators, teachers, pupils – work against, instead of with, one another. As a particular situation deteriorates, the whole educational enterprise is effectively blocked by the actual withdrawal of one or another of these groups (student dropouts, teacher strikes, withholding of funds or other facilities, for example), or by its passivity.

Little agreement exists on the best means of solving the problems of metropolitan schools. Judging from the nature of both the arguments and the proposals, there appears to be little agreement on what the problems are. *Exposés* of the horrific conditions in city slum schools are common in the United States. Radical and romantic nostrums are almost as frequent, reminders of the noble muckraking and progressive spirit of the turn of the century. More money and more devotion are the main deficiencies, as many of these writers see it; but a new curriculum, new teaching means and objectives and a new kind of concern for human relationships are some of the more specific targets. Wide agreement does exist on the need for making curricula more relevant to students, and not only the poor and the urban; and for considering ways of making teaching more effective through the use of new tools (books and educational hardware) and new patterns of organization (grouping practices, student participation in school government).[6] In addition, attention is being given to the question of using adult manpower more effectively, not only by use of teaching machines and other devices, but also by employment of 'para-professionals'. These may be housewives who assist the classroom teacher in several ways, depending upon their competence and desires, possibly marking home-work, more usually distributing and collecting materials, keeping records, more rarely assisting in individual or small-group instruction. The signific-ance of this development is not purely as a school facility. It recognizes the growing trend towards part-time employment of mothers; it also provides sorely-needed job opportunities in a convenient location for poverty areas; and it draws into the schools, as active participants, adults who may otherwise have remained passive outsiders.

If attention tends to be devoted to the school problems of cities in the more advanced countries of the world rather than to the exploding urban communities of South America, Africa, and Asia, it may be due to the ethnocentrism of writers, to which fault this author is no exception. But it is also due to the dearth of systematic and reliable data on the large cities of the undeveloped world and the rapidity with which information becomes obsolete. The economic, social and political problems of 'new' countries are replicated in the educational aspects of their cities. The over-riding considerations are to retain what progress has been made so far in developing educational facilities and to extend at least some minima to the majority of the inhabitants. All the more reason why attention should be given to describing the dimensions of schooling and its urban settings (social, economic, political), to investigating their relationships and identi-fying the special problems of the school and its context in non-Western, under-developed nations. Where resources are scarce and priorities are numerous, planning is paramount and an information base for such planning needs to be created.

Need for Research

It is clear that the problems of metropolitan schools are too important and broad in scope to be left to the educators alone. But they are also beyond any other single group, be they politicians, economists, socio-logists, teachers, or parents. Research on the subject, as well as planning for the future, is the responsibility of and the opportunity for the several

---

[6] Much less attention has been directed at the suburban aspects of metropolitan education (see, for example, Alice M. Miel, *The Shortchanged Children of Suburbia* (New York: American Jewish Committee, Institute of Human Relations Press, 1967), or at the role of the urban wealthy in the schooling (public and private) of the metropolis.

social and behavioural science disciplines, collaborating to share concepts, data, and techniques.

While there is wide agreement that something needs to be done, that more money and facilities are required for schools to serve the urban poor more successfully, and while there is no lack of proposals to solve the problems of big-city schools, little consensus exists beyond this point. Solutions in a given location tend to be piecemeal, *ad hoc* responses to immediate pressures, resting upon no more solid a basis than faith, limited research, and a strong sense of what appears to be politically expedient at that moment. Yet the big cities of the world provide a species of laboratory for the researcher. Comparison could reveal not only the range of educational alternatives offered to deal with the several dimensions and problems of urbanization, but conceivably some evidence as to their outcomes. The experience of large cities, studied systematically and comparatively, may help to clarify the relationships between aspects of schooling and the urban environment in which they occur and even project the possible outcomes of specific measures for the guidance of a particular group of city educational planners.

But much work has to be done before useful investigation can be achieved. There is, first of all, an extraordinary lack of basic information on the subject. Second, there is a noticeable absence of empirical investigation and verifiable results. And third, there is a dearth of useful validated theory on the subject.

Urban sociologists and political scientists have written extensively on urban and metropolitan areas, producing many individual case studies, considerable information on urban composition and organization, and a theory on urban growth and development. Yet the information has been of little value for the educator, or at least it has not yet been utilized. The demographic and spatial dimensions of urban development have been quite fully explored, but little is known with much degree of certainty about those aspects of urban life most relevant to the educator.

In order to achieve an information base for comparative study and understanding, a host of new maps are needed of the cities of the world, maps which depart from the familiar topographical style and offer more than figures of population density and land utilization. They must, in addition, reveal the location of groups of children according to such educationally relevant criteria as parental occupation and educational level, for example, and sub-cultural groupings other than socio-economic. Such maps should also present data on residential patterns over time. The most up-to-date educational details, such as school efforts at innovation, and pupil achievement, are needed to complete the map. With such information, planners may be able to chart the educational needs and obstacles of the future.

But this is only the beginning. Planners also need to know if given administrative devices do in fact have predictable outcomes, whether dispersal of the decision-making process, for example, does in fact lead to amelioration of educational problems in any identifiable respects. They need to know whether there is any relationship between educational expenditure in general and improvement, between certain kinds of expenditure and specific kinds of change. A lengthy list of questions is awaiting investigation, concerning teachers, their selection, preparation and use in the system, and about curriculum and methods. The answers will be insufficient if based merely upon single innovations under specific and limited conditions. But on the basis of systematic, comparative, controlled investigations, some generally valid conclusions may be drawn about schooling and its social context.

One special area is the politics and economics of metropolitan school systems. The political, institutional concomitants of educational innovation may be studied at several levels, from case studies of schools attempting new programmes and policies which cause social and political community repercussions,[7] to the comparative study of power and decision-making in big-city schools.[8] The economic dimensions, too, pose several types of unanswered questions: for example, the relation of a city's over-all educational level to that of the nation, and the significance of comparative disparities; the relation of school production of trained manpower at various levels of skill to the metropolitan and to the national economies; the efficiency of the school system as an economic organization according to the resources available. Here too, then, lies the opportunity to engage in studies which delve beneath description, beyond mere amassing of information.

In short, basic information on the environmental conditions of metropolitan areas and on their educational characteristics are sadly lacking, not only for those nations just beginning to bring schooling to the mass of their populations, but even for the highly developed countries of the world. Furthermore, descriptive and evaluative information on specific educational problems in big cities and efforts to solve them needs to be more widely disseminated. But far more important, such information must be gathered and arranged in such a way as to permit investigation into the connexions between educational and other phenomena. Only on such a basis, will it be possible to lay bare the educational correlates of metropolitan environments.

---

[7] Leila Berg, *Risinghill; Death of a Comprehensive School* (Harmondsworth, Middlesex: Penguin Books, 1968).

[8] Marilyn Gittel and T. Edward Hollander, *Six Urban School Districts: A Comparative Study of Institutional Response* (New York: Frederick A. Praeger, 1968).

Conclusion

Metropolitanism is the life-style of this century. It is already so character-istic of technologically advanced countries that the residents of Paris, London, New York and other urban agglomerations form a trans-national community of the like-minded, with converging beliefs, lives, needs and conditions of existence. Growth of urban centres in the undeveloped world is part of the same general phenomenon, radically altering past forms of behaving and living. The divergencies within the metropolis are sharp, between the various sub-groups such as inner-city and suburban residents, between the urban poor and the propertied, salaried middle class. They are a danger to the organic life of the metropolis and a refutation of its promise for a better life. Yet the separation between schooling and its metropolitan setting appears sharper still: schools 'short-change' the children of affluent suburbanites and of ghetto-dwellers alike, though in different forms, as they serve their immediate communities with greater or less efficiency. They often also seek deliberately to remain above and apart from many aspects of their environment. In physical form as well as function, schools and especially colleges and universities in the city are reminiscent of mediaeval fortresses, turning their backs on the heteroge-neous, vibrant, complex metropolis. Interdependence being the main feature of this modern form of living, the interaction between education and its big-city settings is the priority for research on a comparative basis.

In this essay, the author has attempted to be descriptive rather than prescriptive, and theoretical rather than practical. Not that the intention was to be *im*practical; the purpose has been to set metropolitan-educational problems in some tentative theoretical framework. Only with such a framework is it possible to proceed to investigate some of the specific relationships that link the schools and their educational problems to their settings. And only through systematic testing of general propositions (parts of theories) against the evidence of the real world is there any hope of using insight and understanding to explain.[9] For reality tends to be obscured by the data and the immediacy of problems, and only systematic, comparative, empirical investigation can expose the principles which explain them.

The study of education and of efforts to ameliorate the lot of deprived city dwellers and protected suburbanites is a highly subjective enterprise, prone to ideological bias, political expediency and economic exigencies. By striving for objectivity and clarification which systematic investigation promises, a useful, indeed, a practical contribution is possible.

---

[9] For exposition and examples of this view with special reference to the field of comparative education, see: Harold J. Noah and Max A. Eckstein, *Toward a Science of Comparative Education* (The Macmillan Co., 1969), and Max A. Eckstein and Harold J. Noah (eds.), *Scientific Investigations in Comparative Education* (The Macmillan Co., 1969).

3

The Urban Functions of Educational Institutions

Ruth H. K. Wong

'Cityness', just as 'intelligence', is a theoretical construct. In the main there are three approaches used to conceptualize the city. Miner[1] has summarized them as the following:

(i) the ideal type-constructs such as the *Gemeinschaft-Gesellschaft* contrast of Toennies or the Folk-Urban typology of Redfield;

(ii) the trait-complex approach which characterizes the city in terms of clusters of empirical attributes such as size, density, and occupation of the population;

(iii) the rural-urban continuum of community types.

All these approaches see the difference between the city and other places as one of degree and not necessarily of kind – 'not qualitatively different from the essence of other sorts of communities'.[2]

This chapter, however, will assume the trait-complex approach using multiple criteria as suggested by Sjoberg,[3] who sees 'the urban centre (in contrast to a rural one) as characterized by larger size, higher density and a preponderance of persons engaged in non-agricultural economic activity. These non-agriculturalists must include a group of literate persons.'

This definition is particularly acceptable when cross-cultural comparisons and generalizations are attempted. 'After all, communities in, say, the five thousand to ten thousand population category may differ widely in their social characteristics according to whether they form part of pre-industrial civilized societies, transitional orders or industrial ones'.[4]

It is also the intention to limit the scope of this chapter to the consideration of educational problems and institutions in urban areas within newly emergent countries, which are for the most part transitional societies and have begun on the road to industrialization. They fall into the categories

---

[1] H. Miner, 'The city and modernization' in *The City in Modern Africa* (H. Miner, ed. (London: Pall Mall Press, 1967), p. 3.

[2] H. Miner, ibid.

[3] G. Sjoberg, 'The rural-urban dimension in pre-industrial, transitional, and industrial societies,' *Handbook of Modern Sociology* (Faris, E. L., ed.) (Chicago: Rand McNally and Company, 1964), pp. 130–131.

[4] G. Sjoberg, ibid.

of Level II and Level III countries according to the Harbison-Myers composite index.[5]

The reasons for concentrating on such societies are as follows:

Firstly, most of the world's population is concentrated in newly emergent countries – countries which are not only emerging from a colonial past, but are moving from a pre-industrial past and striving for an industrial tomorrow. A close look at the role educational institutions can play in such developing societies will expose to view the widest possible spectrum of common problems.

Secondly, while it would be interesting to discuss the urban functions of educational institutions in highly industrialized societies, the degree of difference between cities in such societies and those in transitional ones is sufficiently marked to justify a more lengthy treatment than would be possible within the space provided for this paper.

Most cities in transitional societies share certain common traits.

1. Main cities in such societies are largely the creations of various colonial powers which once established them as centres of trade and of political administration. As they were concerned more with the economic returns of settlement, the early colonialist governments deliberately pursued an open-door policy, whereby immigrant races of diverse ethnic and cultural origins were admitted to help quicken the initial pace of development. Slaves were sometimes imported and indentured labour used to counter the unreliability of indigenous labour.

Colonial policy and economic motives helped to foster the growth of a multi-racial heterogeneity of tongues, religions and cultures, which tended to be particularly characteristic of towns and cities. Thus in West Malaysia, for example, the three major races – Malays, Chinese and Indians – are all found in the large towns and urban areas while in large parts of the rural area there is a significant reduction in and an almost total absence of other races besides the Malays. In Guyana, the Indians, who came to the country as indentured labour, dominate the countryside where their forbears were first settled to cultivate the land, while the earlier immigrant Africans (brought in as slaves) and the Chinese have tended to concentrate in the towns, side by side with Indian minorities.

It also happened too commonly in the history of colonies that the various immigrant and indigenous groups kept their separate ways, their social, cultural and economic differences reinforced by a mutually pre-served physical apartness. Cities have their particular quarters for the residence and pursuits of members of each group.

With the status of independence and the advent of industrialization,

---

[5] F. Harbison and C. A. Myers, *Education, Manpower and Economic Growth* (New York: McGraw-Hill, 1964), p. 223.

the various ethnic enclaves could not continue separate and aloof. More especially was it necessary for groups within the city, which generally influenced and dominated the countryside, to demonstrate a unity of purpose which was necessary to support the ideals and goals of nationhood and to make economic progress possible. Thus life in the cities of transitional societies has particular social and political significance. Where the cities have erupted with racial hatred, the progress of the country as a whole has tended to suffer.

2. The urbanization process in transitional societies takes place within the context of a population explosion. As the pace of industrialization gathers momentum, it adds to the problems of crowdedness in that it attracts an inflow of people from rural areas, who are not only drawn by the bright lights of the city, but are also urged by the belief that the city has opportunities to offer for self-advancement, where the land has disappointingly failed them. 'In the less developed countries, incomes from agriculture tend to fall relative to other incomes because (a) population on the land increases more rapidly than food output; (b) new investment is concentrated in industial production and urban development generally; and (c) the prices of primary products in world markets are falling.'[6]

The simultaneous explosion of population and aspiration aggravates the stresses and strains of city life. The structures, most of which belong to a pre-industrial era, can no longer accommodate the many who are born there and the many more who move in. Contact with industrial urban cultures generate other aspirations and demands which heighten the tensions between groups.

3. The transitional society finds its members likewise undergoing a transitional, sometimes almost schizophrenic existence in a search for a new identity. Certain hallowed institutions and values have to yield to new ones. Those who adapt to change easily sever themselves from the past, sometimes almost ruthlessly. The extremely conservative find themselves rejected, an unassimilated element of city life. But the greatest strain devolves on the compromisers.

Take, for example, the social institution of the extended family. Small flats and crowded urban conditions are not really conducive to the continued preservation of such an institution. Yet many a young couple admit the intrusion of aunts, uncles and parents into their homes. Within the narrow confines there is no escape from the daily chafings. The children face an uncertain discipline from plural forms of authority. They tend to become less directed, less restrained.

---

[6] International Labour Office, *Why labour leaves the land: A comparative study of the movement of labour out of agriculture.* G. Sjoberg (Geneva: Switzerland), pp. 209–210.

Louis Wirth[7] pointed out that urbanites meet in highly fragmented roles, that the contact of full personalities is impossible. Contacts are impersonal, superficial, transitory and segmental simply because the number of persons in interaction are too many for anything better.

For those whose way of life has been one of deep attachment to family and clan, what is the best means of initiation into the relative coldness of urban relationships? Or, is there some means whereby the old ties can be preserved in new forms? It has been reported that juvenile delinquency is least pronounced among Chinese communities in American towns and cities. It may be interesting to study to what extent an adherence to familial values has contributed to stability. Such studies will help developing countries to decide which of their traditional values may be retained with profit.

4. The urban-rural dichotomy tends to remain sharply defined, and particularly so where most of the financial resources of the state are deployed into urban development without corresponding developmental changes in rural areas. The conditions which result place an undue burden of effort on the city to multiply financial resources, to provide education, and to generate job opportunities. The labour migration to the city means a neglect of the land and a gradual withdrawal of the wherewithal to support city life. The city has to look elsewhere, and normally at high costs, for sources of supply. A vicious circle is begun whereby the land becomes poorer for want of attention and the city becomes more expensive for lack of sustenance from the source which initially made its development possible.

In the light of the foregoing discussion, it is pertinent to view the functions of urban educational institutions in developing countries as associated with three roles – an integrative role, in which they help to examine, evaluate and preserve the best in the cultures of the various ethnic groups; an innovative role, in which they give leadership in the introduction of new methods and new means for the nurture of human resources and the cultivation and multiplication of material resources; and, finally, a catalysing role in which they promote and accelerate much-needed change.

The Integrative Role of Educational Institutions

Important as it is to developing societies to forge out of people of diverse ethnic origins a single nation, loyal and dedicated to common ideals and goals, the skills and expertise required to bring this about seem singularly lacking. South American Guyana, West African Nigeria, East African Kenya, Asian Burma, Ceylon and Malaysia have all had their problems

7 L. Wirth, 'Urbanism as a way of life,' *Amer. J. of Soc.*, 44, July 1938, pp. 1–24.

over racial issues. It seems particularly apt here to quote (though quite out of context) an excerpt from Millas[8]:

> The old humanist adage 'Man is the measure of all things' loses its meaning more and more if it applies to one human being alone; *all humanity is becoming the measure*. No man today can acquire the rudiments of the whole body of human knowledge, so that the only possible 'measure of things' lies within a system of communication among men who can talk to one another and explain their individual experiences and thoughts.

Paraphrasing this for our present purposes, no single race has the monopoly of excellence and, for a growing world, it is crucial that men communicate their experiences and thoughts for the attainment of a wider perspective to match the widening horizons of human endeavour. The developing countries cannot hope to progress, unless internally this wider perspective of human equality is attained.

Now, educational institutions with tradition and status in developing countries are generally sited in the city, where the population tends to be most heterogeneous in terms of ethnic differences. The links of communication between groups should be forged in these institutions. At the tertiary level, universities should have strong departments of sociology, psychology and political science which should supply a multi-disciplinary approach to the many aspects of race relations, a subject rather too scrupulously avoided, even where these departments exist. At the secondary level, courses of civics, generally recognized as important for the education of good citizens, should not merely stress the correctness of the 'obey-the-law' line. More opportunity should be given to pupils of varying ethnic and cultural backgrounds to compare and discuss differences in codes of acceptable behaviour at home and in society and to select and share what they deem to be desirable values. At the primary level, the content of the curriculum should include folk-lore, songs and dances of all cultural groups in the country. Children should be encouraged to share activities together.

It seems ironical that, while developing countries with race problems frequently deplore the presence of divisive forces and profess a desire for harmony, their leaders unwittingly by-pass the means for achieving the goals of integration. It was considered by university administrators in a certain country, for example, that such disciplines as pertain to the social sciences were of lower priority than those of the natural sciences and commerce, because the return on investment in respect of the former was not visibly evident. Yet they allowed the retention of the traditional

---

[8] J. G. Millas, 'The interplay revealed in history and in practice, and its contribution to a broader humanism', *The Interplay of Scientific and Cultural Values in Higher Education To-day*, IAU Papers, 5 (Paris: International Universities Bureau, 1960), p. 20.

disciplines of history, the languages and law (equally unremunerative and, perhaps, rather over-productive in educated unemployables). It did not occur to them that a re-examination of university curricula was necessary and that, for the very success of technological progress the 'fundamental unity among the different forms of expression assumed by culture in the course of history – science, technique, art, language, behaviour, and so on'[9] should be studied in their essence, that is, the student should *know* this unity not just *about* it so that he may view his own interests and contribution as part of a common endeavour, in which the duties and tasks of others also have a place. More and more the student should be made aware of the social and moral issues of innovative effort in relation to the well-being of the group as a whole, not of self. Actually, few universities in developing countries address themselves to the problems of integration between man and man, between man and environment, between technology and the humanistic tradition. They are as aloof as their Western prototype. Yet, to them, the very area for research is easily available at their doorstep.

There is another aspect of formal education which needs to be mentioned. There is a tendency at both university and secondary school levels to disallow open and objective discussion of any issue with a political or racial content. This seems but to benefit the professional student rebel, while the average student, unchallenged by the problems which obtain in society, remains insufficiently schooled to meet them when they surface into the open.

To prevent quiet disassociation which can be just as inimical as noisy rebelliousness to attempts to integrate and unify, some dialogue must be allowed. Unfortunately tertiary institutions in cities are faced with an increasingly perplexing problem raised by quantitative pressure. Staff members are increasingly difficult to recruit to match the rate of increase in student enrolment. The process of communication within the campus whereby 'deep calls to deep' hardly exists. Course content comprises lecture series in conjunction with which students are requested to read certain texts. In many examinations, the submission of answers is a note-regurgitation exercise. Thus while a prescription and a plea for educational institutions to adopt a leading role in the integrative effort needs to be made, the problems arising from a quantitative-qualitative dilemma need to be simultaneously examined.

The Innovative Role of Educational Institutions

Because the city dominates the rest of the surrounding country, it assumes the position of a Mecca of the hopes and aspirations of even those at a distance from it. There is a strong likelihood, therefore, that innovative

---

9 J. G. Millas, ibid.

action emanating from its educational institutions will gain acceptance beyond the city, provided that more than mere physical lines of communication are established with non-urban areas. There is a psychic aspect to communication which educational institutions may well recognize as theirs to accept, and to exploit it is their first function in the attempt to catalyse the development of the country as a whole.

In practical terms, this implies that there should be an educational mobility outwards from the city. Concentrated as educational institutions are in the cities and capitals of developing countries, and modelled closely after their opposite numbers in the West in respect of curricular and administrative organization, they easily lose touch with the realities of their immediate environment. Their product is therefore disappointingly prone to unrealistic aspirations and slow to respond to new situations. From primary school-leaver to university graduate, there is a characteristic loss of touch with those not of the institutions. Hence, the question should be asked as to whether organized formal education as now provided serves adequately the purpose of developing countries. Instead of gathering children of primary-school age into boarding schools in the city, because of a dearth of good teachers for the rest of the country, a plan may be considered whereby each urban educational institution of sound quality and status is asked to 'adopt' a protégée rural educational unit, based in a cluster of homes or a specific community centre for which primary education may be integrated with adult education. Educational mass media, using programmes planned by the sponsoring institution, can be used to mediate the learning; the rural unit can be visited at specific intervals by a mobile library with travelling teachers based at the urban institution.

Such a scheme will help to prevent a growing influx into towns for education since, originating as it does in urban institutions, it will be psychologically perceived as having a proper value. It will relieve the city of unemployable labour, since the curriculum based in the rural unit will help learners to occupy themselves gainfully on the land and improve their techniques in land cultivation. It will also extend education over a wider area than formal education through normal government-sponsored channels in that it is cheaper, the only extra expenses required being a team of programme planners at the base institution and a supervisor at each rural unit. No expensive boarding schools or hostels will be required.

In the city, the curriculum of schools can be viewed in two parts – in-school learning and out-of-school learning. Because of the compactness of and the facilities afforded by the city, Educational Television should be used to bring lessons to homes and to community-centres where homes cannot afford a television set. This is the out-of-school learning part of the curriculum. Instead of having all children in school every day of the week in double or treble session schooldays, children can be divided into groups which attend schools for three sessions in the week for follow-up discussions, academic exercises and extra-mural sports and other activities, which E.T.V. cannot provide profitably. This scheme relieves the teacher for more individual attention to pupils and allows closer supervision of progress. Children, normally attending morning or afternoon sessions, can come on alternate days in the mornings, releasing sports fields in the afternoon hours for the recreation of countless numbers of children in dense city areas and housing estates.

The scheme suggested may be criticized as still at a 'dreamed-up' stage, never having yet been put into practice. But city schools in developing countries cannot afford to continue in the traditional mould without a re-examination of urgent needs: a visible deterioration in standards is already evident because, as Jacobs[10] puts it, 'the unhappy alternatives have seemed to be (a) to concentrate the available resources in certain sectors, perforce slighting the rest, or (b) to dilute the effort with partial programmes in all sectors, thereby doing justice to none. By neither procedure can the established goals for national development be achieved.' Paradoxically, though faith in universal education has motivated the provision of education for all children, limited means, because of this very effort, has not improved the chances of the average receiver of education in the attainment of his personal goals.

The Catalysing Role of Urban Educational Institutions

Lerner[11] has pointed out that 'the essential elements of a democracy are the mobility and participation of its individual citizens. Mobility is essential because it liberates the individual who was bound to his inherited place in traditional society. Liberated from his native soil, he gains physical mobility by changing his position in space; liberated from his native status, he gains social mobility by changing his position in society; liberated from his native self, he gains psychic mobility by changing his personality to suit his new place and status in the world.' Thus liberated, the individual participates as a citizen by rapidly becoming 'the cash customer, the radio listener and the voter, for a citizen of a modern society can function only by participating actively in its market, its forum and its *vox populi*.'

In a sense, these three aspects of mobility form an ascending hierarchy of the freedom experience. For the developing society, however, this experience is still of the lowest order despite the industrialization process.

---

[10] R. Jacobs, 'Technology as an agent of change in development education.' *The United States and International Education*, 68th Yearbook (Chicago: N.S.S.E., 1969), p. 157.

[11] D. Lerner, 'Comparative Analysis of Processes of Modernisation', *The City in Modern Africa*, op. cit., p. 30.

Many of its people may have experienced physical mobility, some have attained a measure of social mobility, but very few have achieved psychic mobility. The co-existence in urban areas of a noticeable extent of unemployment and underemployment is one evidence of the lag behind total mobility. There is urbanization without urbanism. Thus in some of the most over-urbanized countries, like those of Latin America, for example, urbanization has as a rather deplorable concomitant, an 'inefficient and disruptive waste of lands and peoples.'[12]

Obviously, what can help to sever the status linkage with past generations and provide the way to social mobility, and more important to bring about the desired personality change in attitudes and aspirations, is education. The tasks and roles in a developing, industrializing society are complex. As the economy changes from an initially agricultural one to one dependent upon manufacturing, which in its turn leads to service industry, there is a continuous upgrading of skills from manual to mental, from the practically unschooled effort to the highly skilled. Correspondingly, the attainment of knowledge is required at increasingly high levels. Education has to supply not mere literacy, but a functional literacy with its specific association with the particular task. The more complex the task, the greater the sophistication required in knowledge.

Having placed the responsibility of bringing about change and continuing progress on education, how do schools fit into the scheme of things?

Various suggestions regarding the role of schools in a modernizing society have stressed the teaching of desirable values and reinforcing them in developing personalities, giving the correct content in terms of training and preparation for economic productivity, moulding character and fostering creative initiative so that a future generation may have more imaginative leadership and management. But is education entirely synonymous with formal educational establishments? The expectations held about what schools should and can do are, in fact, but partially supported by evidence. There are, for example, the highly examination-dominated, selective systems which produce a certain respect for goal achievement and inculcate drive and perseverance. But the same systems also produce stultified, unimaginative individuals, with rather circumscribed horizons.

Then again, change and innovation are two words enjoying popular currency in developing countries. From Latin America to Africa and Asia, team teaching, modern mathematics, the discovery approach in science and other areas are just as fervently embraced as in advanced countries. Expert advice from the West is sought. Urban schools, particularly, convert to new curricula almost overnight. The results, however, are disappointing; apart from the shibboleths that creep into the vocabulary

---

[12] D. Lerner, op. cit., p. 34.

of innovation, there are the abortive experiments which have produced unhappy teachers and bewildered children.

Thus the schools have been made to act a role for which the accepted assumptions regarding efficacy have yet to be tested. Theoretically, there is logic in the assumptions. The school is a place where teaching occurs. The various categories of knowledge to be taught are facts, values, character, attitudes, skills. But the only realm in which certainty operates is that of facts; sometimes, the more practical skills (manual or repetitive) are also competently taught. For the rest, much more thorough studies must be made to identify the indices of success in relation to the functions of the school as a catalysing agent for productive change. Or, it may be, too, that the school has already bitten off more than it can chew. Reimer[13] has stated that 'efficient production and use of the whole range of available educational materials requires radical specialization of the teaching profession and a return of many educational responsibilities to the home.' But it is precisely in the home that developing urban societies require change. What of the values of tradition can be harnessed to assist in the work of society, without hampering its progress? For example, help from the kin-group has been found to lend stability to the family life of children, especially where desertion or death has occurred.

It may be pertinent to mention an innovative practice in urban Singapore, which has seemed to carry a degree of success. Schools work closely with community leaders and parents, some of whom sit on school advisory boards. School principals and teachers reciprocate by participating as members of committees serving community centres. Thus a form of dialogue has been deliberately opened between schools and community. But more has yet to be done to evaluate and assess their efforts *vis-à-vis* the progress of the denizens of the schools. At any rate, sharing the responsibility of teaching between parents, schools and community must be accepted as important for bringing about change. Attitudes and values are better learnt informally and most often through peer groups and the home. How this can best be integrated with the efforts of the school has yet to be thoroughly and empirically investigated.

---

13 E. Reimer, 'Good Education for All', a mimeographed paper.

Section II: Introduction

Africa

Brian Holmes

In many African countries the majority of the population still lives in rural areas (South Africa is an exception (p. 79)). Characteristically growth has centred round cities which are either ports or capitals (p. 79). Of the cities referred to in this section, Lagos is the Federal Capital of Nigeria; Durban is the main port of the Republic of South Africa (p. 79); until 1876 Cape Coast was the capital of the British settlement and now serves as a residential area for senior members of the bureaucracy (p. 96). The exception is Mamelodi which is neither a port nor a capital (p. 42).

Durban and Greater Lagos have populations of over a million, Cape Coast is much smaller but people were attracted to these centres during the second half of the nineteenth and the twentieth centuries (pp. 74, 95). For the most part occupational success then depended on simple literacy and non-technical, non-specialized skills. Today Durban is 'a modern industrial city' (p. 79) and education must prepare the rising generations for life and work in an economy in which nearly 40 per cent of workers are in manufacturing occupations. Lagos, too, has become an industrial town (p. 74). Cape Coast still has no national or state industries (p. 97). As a residential area for a limited cross-section of the community its specific educational needs differ somewhat from Lagos and Durban.

The situation of Mamelodi in South Africa is different. It has not attracted political and cultural leaders and is in effect a satellite, dormitory town for a predominantly African industrial working population (p. 42). Important cross-sections of an industrial community are missing (p. 43). Other distinctive features are that it lies within an area ear-marked for white development (p. 42), and growth has been at a moderate rate.

Mamelodi apart, the populations of these cities are very heterogenous. Greater Durban in 1970 has an estimated 280,000 Whites, 310,000 Indians, 400,000 Africans and 41,000 Coloured (p. 79). Lagos has a predominantly Nigerian population but a 'large proportion of expatriates from Europe, America and the Middle East and Nigerians who are non-natives of Lagos' (p. 74). Even in 1948 some two-thirds of the population of Cape Coast were not born there (p. 96). Traditionally Europeans occupied professional and managerial positions, the Asians were mostly shopkeepers and lived together in sections of a town (p. 96) and among Africans there is often a wider range of occupations and incomes than the other sections of the population (p. 96). The similarities as well as the differences in the four situations described should be noted.

As for the people who flood into the urban areas, they are either expatriates (European and Asian) or rural Africans who have been educated in the villages (p. 96) and are in search of jobs, or youngsters in search of education (p. 96). In the past, from a heterogeneity of cultural backgrounds they were introduced to a new way of life which was dominated by a Western or Westernized élite (p. 98). Most of the early education was provided by the Christian mission countries but even so the majority of rural emigrants had been partially educated out of their traditional ways of life and inadequately prepared for life in a cosmopolitan city (p. 98). The disillusioned frequently joined the ranks of delinquents and habitual criminals.

Even in Mamelodi half the population is from rural areas, the other half having been born and bred in a town (p. 44). Culturally, Mamelodi is a polyglot community. Among it English, Dutch and American churches as well as some independent churches and animist groups have adherents (p. 43). Such is the diversity in Mamelodi that in some nine schools more than one mother tongue is used as the medium of instruction (p. 61).

Under such conditions should villagers be educated in and for rural life? To what extent should those who move to the urban areas receive an education designed to make it possible for them to live and work in a largely Westernized industrial economy? Should movements from the rural areas to the towns be controlled? Is it desirable, or possible, to rehabilitate the homelands and draw educated people back to them.?

The social problems of city life are evident – crime, unemployment, inadequate housing and so on. Educational problems include wastage through early drop-out, a shortage of qualified teachers and schools, met to some extent by double sessions. The debates and proposed solutions described in these case studies show how difficult it is to find educational solutions to the problems arising from virtually uncontrolled processes of urbanization in Africa. The schools as agents of rural reconstruction, can perhaps do little. The case study of Mamelodi is, if there is any validity in this assumption, instructive. In this township social policies are followed to control the movement of prospective immigrants. The moral basis of such action may be (and frequently is) questioned. Nevertheless, the relationships between social and educational policies where political control is possible can be studied with advantage.

4

South Africa: A Bantu Urban Residential Area*

O. F. Raum

I

Mamelodi, a Bantu residential area (or location), at one time known as Vlakfontein, is a township under the administrative control of the Pretoria City Council which has a municipal department of Bantu affairs with a director at its head. This control is exercised under the directives of the central government Department of Bantu Administration and Development which also subsidizes any approved projects, such as housing, schools and other civic facilities. The township is situated in the Pretoria magisterial district which has its own senior Bantu Affairs Commissioner and co-ordinated services. This district forms part of the province of Transvaal. The erstwhile provincial control of the education of Africans was terminated by the Bantu Education Act of 1953, when all powers vested in provincial councils concerning the financing and inspection of African education and most of the interests in African schools possessed by voluntary agencies, such as mission societies, were transferred (with compensation for land and buildings) to the Department of Bantu Education.

Mamelodi, although exclusively occupied by Africans, lies within an area ear-marked for white development. The nearest portion of a Bantu homeland, in process of being taken over by a semi-autonomous Bantu Territorial Authority, is Ga-Ranukwa, about 25 miles to the west. (A Bantu Territorial Authority has an executive councillor of ministerial rank in charge of its educational services.) Between Mamelodi and Ga-Ranukwa on the one hand, and the white city of Pretoria on the other, the suburbs of which approach the township at a distance of about five miles, lies Rosslyn, a so-called Bantu Border Industry area. The industries, including a car factory, which have been established there, have made possible the employment of Africans without the drawbacks of the migrant labour system. The workers can return to their families in the homelands, if not

---

* The argument presented in this study is based on material submitted by the Chief Superintendent, Non-European Affairs Department, City Council of Pretoria, and by Messrs P. G. Vilakazi, B.Sc., U.E.D., and J. S. Lekala, B.A., S.A.T.D. The author alone is responsible for the interpretation.

daily, at least at the weekends. Their fate has thus been approximated to that of the white managers and technicians who come to the factories from their Pretoria residences in the morning and return to them at night.

Internal Organization

The internal organization of Mamelodi provides for ethnically distinct zones reserved for the Nguni (Zulu, Swazi, Xhosa, Ndebele), the Sotho (Tswana, Pedi, Southern Sotho) and the Shangaan and Venda peoples respectively. These zones are divided into residential blocks. The various zones are represented in a Bantu Advisory Board which has more limited powers than the Bantu Urban Council that has been introduced on an experimental basis at the huge Soweto township near Johannesburg. The ethnic principle also involves representation of the chiefs of the people domiciled in the township by their agents, the provision of town houses for these chiefs, and regular visits by them to their 'subjects' in the township.

Mamelodi boasts of a number of business centres, one to every two or three blocks. Each centre has general dealers, dairies, butcheries, coal merchants, hairdressers, watch repairers, radio shops, restaurants and herbalists. The 98 businesses are owned by individuals or groups who must obtain a licence from the Bantu Advisory Board which has to be endorsed in the white location superintendent's office. In at least three business centres are mortuaries owned by undertakers. According to the policy of separate development, the business activities of Africans in townships situated within white areas have a certain ceiling. Since 'the African urban locations are white areas . . . only the small African trader (confining himself to the provision of the daily essential domestic necessities of the Bantu) is acceptable'. In other words, 'the growth of the African trade is controlled by the interests of white competitors' (with no business premises in the locations but near enough in white residential areas to be affected).

The population of Mamelodi comprises 61,083 inhabitants in Mamelodi West and 37,419 in Mamelodi East, a total of 98,502. The total number of females falls short of the number of males by 3,254, although in the family houses they exceed the males by 2,662. The difference of 5,916 represents men quartered in hostels. In Mamelodi are represented the 'classical' churches derived from European missionary efforts. The Anglican congregation numbers about 800, the Methodist 950, the Catholic and the Lutheran 900 each, the Netherlands Gereformeerde Kerk 750 and the American Methodist Episcopal Church (with African ministers exclusively) about 600. Membership in these churches is largely confined to the upper strata of the community, i.e. to teachers, clerks, nurses, businessmen and other professionals. There is a fair sprinkling of independent churches, such as the Zion Christian Church, which in membership and leadership is entirely African. Their members still have strong links with the rural areas, are often illiterate and frequently their leaders are persons with little schooling. We find also religious traditionalists, or animists, at Mamelodi and traditional views and practices crop up in the religious life of the members of the 'classical' churches, e.g. healing practices and sacrifices to the ancestors. And there is an unacknowledged proportion of atheists and religious indifferents whose views, critical or cynical, may also at times be shared by nominal church people, independents and traditionalists.

Mamelodi township differs from rural areas (from which about half the residents hail, the other half having been born and bred in town) in having certain modern facilities. The Pretoria City Council provides electricity both in the streets and in the houses. Water on tap has been installed, in older blocks in the yards, in newer blocks in the homes. The well-to-do residents, a small proportion, have hot and cold installations built in at their own expense. Houses have no bathrooms, however. The once prevailing bucket system has been replaced by a fairly efficiently working sewerage service. The main road leading into the township is tarred as well as most of the thoroughfares. The other streets are neither tarred nor macadam; they are full of potholes and become quagmires in rainy weather. The two post offices are in the charge of African postmasters. There are about 20 telephone booths and about half a dozen postboxes distributed through the township, the delivery men being Africans. Two banks maintain agencies at Mamelodi; their offices are situated near the entrance to the location. The transport of industrial workers to their place of work is subsidized by a levy raised from their employers.

There are a number of sports grounds on which amateur and professional games, such as soccer, basketball, softball and tennis, are played. There is an overall sporting association to which the various clubs are affiliated. Sporting activities, including cycling, boxing and athletics, are organized by Pretoria City Council welfare workers and the council also supervises the business activities of the association. A film theatre, owned by the council, is leased to an African. The films vary in standard and topicality, and like those shown in other South African cinemas are subject to the censorship of the country's Film Board. There are two community centres, where African music groups, such as church and school choirs, stage performances. Jazz, *mabanqa* (traditional) and classical dances are held, although the latter are not popular. There is a library run by the City Council, and the Bantu library service is recognized as efficient. Residents make full use of these facilities. There is particularly keen interest in music, dancing and sports. Events draw large crowds at weekends or in holiday time.

Occupations and Income Level

The occupational differentation of Mamelodi is roughly as follows. There is a fair concentration of professionals (doctors, lawyers, ministers of religion, teachers) and administrative personnel (clerks in municipal, provincial and central government offices). There are a number of business proprietors and garage owners and the requisite number of salesmen and saleswomen, skilled, semi-skilled and unskilled workers employed by railway, post office, health and electricity services, and by bus and taxi companies catering for Africans only. Approximately two-thirds of the residents are either domestic servants, most of whom work in the city, or industrial workers who, according to the current classification, are either unskilled or semi-skilled. There live at Mamelodi an unspecified number of unemployed, some with residential rights, but others undetected.

The income levels of the various categories of professionals, self-employed and employed workers are difficult to determine. Doctors in provincial service have a fixed salary. In private practice they can make R400 per month, and if popular are reputed to earn up to R1,000. Lawyers earn R300 per month but this too is variable. The owner of a shop is thought to make between R150–200 per month, though this is not an assured income; it fluctuates with the state of the urban economy. Women teachers, qualified to teach in the lower primary schools, earn no more than R40 per month. Teachers with a degree and married earn more than double this amount and principals up to R150 and more. Untrained clerical workers may get R30 commencing salary, rising to R60 after some years of service. Trained clerks earn up to R150 per month. The average monthly wages of industrial and domestic workers are low (R35 and R20–30 respectively). Drivers and messengers are paid R60; artisans may earn R70–80 per month. The average income of a household of five was calculated about ten years ago at R46. This figure is said to have risen to R65 today.

Income level is expressed in differential homes, furniture, dress and such modern status symbols as cars. Because of the legal status of Mamelodi as a township in a white area, houses may not be owned privately but are rented from the City Council. The average house is either three- or four-roomed (dining/sitting room, bedroom, kitchen, W.C., the fourth room being an additional bedroom). The better-off resident can hire a larger house or have his house extended by the addition of bedrooms and a garage (which may be turned into a store-room). Average homes have a table and chairs in the dining/sitting room; in better-off homes a sideboard is often found, while in poorer ones benches may be used instead of chairs. Bedrooms have a double bed or two single beds, a wardrobe (the well-to-do fancy a wardrobe each for husband and wife), as well as a dressing table and occasionally an ornamental *kist*, replaced in poorer homes by padlocked wooden boxes. The kitchen contains a stove, a fixture, one or two cupboards and possibly a dresser. In the homes of workers most items are second-hand and have been acquired by hire-purchase. In the homes of the professionals furniture is new and showy. The average home has few extras, no bookshelf or lampstand, no carpet or easy chair, items which may well be found in the homes of the better-off. Many houses have a radio set and gramophone. Only the well-to-do can afford an electronic record player. There is no television in South Africa.

The better-off, mostly salaried, residents like to display their secure financial position in visible status symbols, such as well-tailored suits or smart dresses. The car acquires a particular significance as an index of standing. Doctors and business men go in for a Barracuda or Valiant, the latest American model being preferred, or else a Mercedes-Benz. Teachers and nurses aim at the possession of a Chevrolet, a Vauxhall or an Opel, while ministers and clerks, with lower paid jobs, stick to Consuls and Austins. Not very common is the Citroën. The Volkswagen, too revealing as a poor man's choice, is not popular at all. Cars are, however, often bought second-hand, and the choice is not only determined by prestige considerations, but also by the proximity of a backyard mechanic who is able to repair, or can procure spare parts for, a particular model. At the other end of the occupational continuum the monthly outlay of a family of five has been estimated at R30 for food, R5 for clothing, R5 for rentals, and R2.40 for electricity and water, to which must be added expenses for fuel and transport, a total of almost R50, which leaves little for education, health and leisure.

In spite of general financial stringency, Africans of the more adventurous type consider the urban areas, at least at present, as having better occupational opportunities than the rural homelands. The wages paid in industrial labour are considered higher than the average cash income of a peasant; they are considered more attractive because they are fixed in amount, and office and factory work is preferred because, as distinct from farming, hours are regular, working conditions pleasant and leisure time assured. In consequence economic standards in the townships, if not the actual standard of living, are held to be higher than in the homelands (whatever the urban economist would have to say to that). The urban areas are also seen as fields of economic success where fortunes can be made in a short time by persons with intelligence and initiative. It is the category of the self-employed who are most often cited in this connexion: entertainers, owners of garages, taxi-cab owners and shopkeepers. Even the prospects of the unskilled workers are considered good. The main advantage of town over country is seen in the fact that the wide occupational spectrum in town offers a niche for a variety of abilities which would lie dormant in the homelands. In short, the planned occupational differentiation in the homelands has not yet begun to affect the evaluation of the town dweller so as to exercise a pull away from the urban areas.

II

The system of schools provided for the rising generation at Mamelodi consists of 4 crèches, 16 lower primary, 10 higher primary schools and 1 combined primary; one junior secondary (to Junior Certificate) and one senior secondary (to Matric); one senior technical school and one training hospital. There is no institution of higher education, such as training college or university, at the township. This arrangement is by no means haphazard but exemplifies the policy of separate development adopted by the South African parliament and government. The motivations and goals of this policy will appear when we analyse the reasons for providing only restricted services at Mamelodi and more advanced education somewhere else.

In the crèches the pre-school children of families in which both parents work are catered for. The Eiselen Commission (1948–9), whose recommendations for Bantu education have been implemented closely since 1954, thought that kindergartens were not necessary for the Bantu. But already in 1953 at the S.A. Institute of Race Relations conference on the Eiselen Commission report, it was suggested that this type of institution be not confined to urban areas. Presumably the Pretoria City Council, under whose aegis the crèches are run, subscribes to the Commission's views, for at Soweto, the large township with about 600,000 residents controlled by the Johannesburg City Council, 50 day nurseries are operated on the modern development technique: design prototype, and well integrated with the appropriate health services. However, the Pretoria City Council's attitude is not motivated by reactionary views: it runs a centre for the instruction of Bantu children in traffic rules at Mamelodi; in it children use toy vehicles on properly sign-posted model streets and crossings.

The lower primary schools give four years of schooling (from Sub-A to Standard II), thus providing the amount of education thought desirable for all Bantu children by the Eiselen Commission and the minimum for urban children. The higher primary schools take their pupils from Standard III to Standard VI, another stint of four years. The secondary schools offer a three-year course (Forms I, II, III) and lead up to the departmental Junior Certificate. The high school adds a two-year course (Forms IV and V). The final examination may be either the Matric, taken according to the regulations of the Joint Matriculation Board, or that qualifying for the National Senior Certificate of the Department of National Education,

Board and Department catering in their examinations for candidates of all race groups. The technical school offers an academic training which is equivalent to the Senior Certificate course and a number of crafts to qualify for the Technical Senior Certificate.

Classification of Schools

Administratively the schools may be classified according to the authority in immediate charge. The crèches and the road safety centre are, as we have seen, municipal affairs. The technical school ranks as a state school and is under the direct control, financial and administrative, of the central Department of Bantu Education. The training hospital works under the auspices of the provincial health authorities. The two types of primary school and the secondary schools form what is known as community schools. These distinctions are important as regards the distribution of schools. Quite early in the setting up of the Bantu education system the principle was adopted that government or state schools and in particular institutions of higher education and special schools, would be removed from townships in white areas and transferred to the Bantu homelands. There are no state-aided mission schools in Mamelodi, such schools having also been discontinued as a matter of policy since 1954, nor are there any unregistered schools, these being illegal.

The community school is considered one of the planks of the Bantu education system. It is so called because each one is under the care of a committee representing the local community. It was adopted as a general administrative device in the Bantu Education Act of 1953 since the mission schools allegedly placed denominational interests before community interests and alienated their pupils from them. The actual control in community schools is dual, i.e. it rests in the committees of parents and in the Bantu Education Department. The procedure followed in the appointment of members of school committees is laid down in departmental regulations. Of the nine (or more) members constituting a committee, the white Bantu Affairs Commissioner nominates two (or more) members. The white Secretary of Bantu Education nominates two (or more) persons to represent religious or other interests. In a Bantu township in a white area, like Mamelodi, the parents elect four representatives. The members of a committee serve for three years.

When comparing the membership of urban and rural committees, it is found that the urban committees comprise a higher percentage of literate members. They are thus presumed to be in a better position to fulfil their functions. (In rural committees the secretary may have to read out departmental circulars or letters from applicants to illiterate members.) But illiteracy, though it symbolizes the lack of Western education, is not equivalent to ignorance – the illiterate may have mother wit and wisdom above the average – nor does it indicate a lack of interest in schools. On the contrary, in the history of African education it was often the illiterate parent who sent his child to school to acquire there the techniques of participating in the Western world. Another charge against rural committees is that they are under the influence of either a chief, or a Bantu Authority as defined by the Bantu Authorities Act of 1951. It has the power to nominate, after consultation with the parents and the Secretary of Bantu Education, three parents and two other members to represent it; it also nominates the chairman and the vice-chairman. In fact, Kuper thinks that, 'it is the absence of the traditional authorities which distinguishes the urban from the tribal organization of education'. But neither the term 'traditional' nor the term 'tribal' is carefully chosen in this statement. A Bantu Authority is a modernized body of administration, not a traditional one. And 'tribal' organization of education might refer to the indigenous form of education, viz. initiation, whereas what Kuper has in mind is the rural system of Western schools. What constitutes the main reason for the different election procedure for urban and rural school committees is the fact that the problem of the self-government for and by the urban Bantu has not yet been satisfactorily solved.

The functions of a school committee are to institute and control school funds, to inquire into complaints regarding the school or its staff, to advise the school board concerning the welfare and efficiency of the school and to assist the board in obtaining well-qualified teachers; it may – if necessary – expel a pupil. The school board is an educational committee on a higher level. Thus the Mamelodi school board controls the activities of all the school committees in charge of particular schools. Six (or more) members of an urban school board are nominated by the Secretary of Bantu Education to represent religious or other interests; these include the chairman and vice-chairman. Four further members are elected from their ranks by parent members of the school committees. This mixed election and nomination procedure, securing a majority acceptable to the Bantu Education Department, may make for greater consensus and possibly greater efficiency, but it somewhat denigrates the principle of democratic participation of parents in the administration of schools and the right of criticism and dissent. It may, however, be a necessary transition measure before and until parents have been trained in 'the rules of the game'. Members of urban school boards have frequently been members of the professional class (doctors, lawyers – teachers in active service may not be board or committee members and their spouses may only serve as non-voting secretaries). This seems to show that the committee system, in spite of its limitations, arouses a certain measure of parental and public response.

The functions of the school board are to act as custodian of the schools under its care. It engages and dismisses teachers, maintains and controls the schools in its area subject to departmental regulations, promotes the erection and expansion of school premises, allocates and maintains school equipment and it supervises the finances of the school committees. The proper performance of these functions demands, of course, a modicum of acquaintance with the modern way of life, of informed choice in educational priorities, of budgeting according to available resources and of devising ways and means of fund-raising. Such skills have, naturally, to be learned by each generation of parents.

Three main methods of financing the schools in its charge, apart from receiving the allocations from the Bantu Education Department from resources of its budget vote, have been developed by school boards and among them that of Mamelodi. First, pupils are expected to make contributions mainly for the salaries of 'privately paid teachers', i.e. teachers whom board and committee concerned wish to employ in response to the increased demand for education but for whose post no provision has yet been made by the Department. In the primary school such a contribution is described as voluntary and may not exceed 5 cents per quarter in the lower school and 20 cents in the higher school. In the secondary school the contribution is compulsory but may not amount to more than R1 per quarter. The second method of obtaining funds is through school bazaars, sports days, school concerts and donations as well as through the sale of products of the school garden and of the arts and crafts classes. However, concerts had to be discontinued as means of fund-raising in urban areas, because being often all-night affairs they easily lent themselves to abuse. The third method of raising funds is the imposition, with the permission of the Secretary of Bantu Education, of a special levy for a particular target. Such levies have had the general support of Bantu authorities in the homelands and of the advisory boards in urban areas. In Soweto, mentioned above, the Bantu Urban Council has suggested an educational levy of 20 cents over and above the levy of 18 cents for the same purpose which all tenants are obliged to pay in recently established townships. In the older municipal townships, to which Mamelodi belongs, the community is endeavouring to obtain authority for a levy of the same amount; the levy of 18 cents does not exist there.

The principle referred to, viz. that a community should be obliged to provide for its general schools, in particular primary and secondary schools, has been applied in various ways since 1954. In that year the then Minister of Native Affairs justified the introduction of the education levy in new townships by the fact that the Bantu in town had so far been treated preferentially, since they had never contributed to the expansion of the educational system. Originally the school boards were charged with raising the money for building additional lower primary schools on the Rand-for-Rand basis. In 1956 the Bantu Education Department decided that school boards must themselves raise half the cost of building higher primary and secondary schools in their area. Later a concession was made for lower primary schools in urban areas (where the demand for such schools was much larger than the means of supply) by making it possible to include the capital costs in applications for loans from the National Housing Board. Government recently decided that this concession would be extended to the erection of schools above the lower primary level. In such instances the school boards are, of course, still saddled with the interest and redemption charges. But the question has been asked, since government has borne the full costs for a number of schools in rural areas, why should urban parents be made to shoulder a greater financial burden than rural parents? It is now expected that more money will become available to the Bantu Education Department and that former stringent rules may be replaced by an arrangement by which school boards will be asked to contribute only a third or a quarter of the costs. In fact the Secretary of Bantu Education seems to have promised that in the case of secondary schools 100 per cent of the building costs may be provided if applications from the boards are sufficiently motivated.

School committees transfer 10 per cent of their income to the school board, they maintain school buildings, sports grounds, equip laboratories and provide materials for school gardens, arts and crafts classes and pay for certain book requirements. The school boards in turn have power to establish bursaries, to organize competitions in music, sports and exhibitions of pupil work and for other educational purposes. Each secondary school is expected to have a school library and to stock it with a good selection of school and general books. The Bantu Education Department gives guidance in the form of lists of books recommended for purchase. One such list mentioned as reference works, encyclopedias, dictionaries of both official and of all Bantu languages of the Republic, Bible editions with commentary and concordance, anthologies of prose and poetry, Shakespeare in a one volume and classified editions and in a prose version, year books of various kinds, standard works on school subjects, an atlas, gazetteer, road maps, railway timetable, telephone directory, university calendars, publications of learned societies, at least two periodicals and the government gazette (which may contain lists of banned books).

Supervision and Staffing of Schools

The supervision and inspection of schools is carried out by the inspectorate of the Bantu Education Department and its field staff. For purposes of administration the Republic is divided into five regions, not counting the now self-governing Transkei, which are delimited in accordance with linguistic and ethnic considerations. Mamelodi belongs to the Southern Transvaal region which covers mainly the Bantu townships on the Rand and near the capital. Each region has a Regional Director of Bantu Education under whom serve a senior administration official and a staff of ten. For purposes of supervision and inspection a region is divided into about ten circuits each covering originally 100–150 schools, 500–600 teachers and from 25,000 to 35,000 pupils. Mamelodi is part of the Pretoria East circuit. In urban areas, such as Mamelodi, the circuit inspector is still usually a white man. He is assisted by a school administrator, assistant and relieving inspectors, supervisors and a clerk. (For specialist subjects, such as religious instruction, vocational guidance, arts and crafts, music and singing, gardening, homecraft and sewing there are special organizers who serve on a regional or nation-wide basis.) In the homelands the replacement of white inspectors by qualified Bantu personnel is proceeding gradually and surely. If such an appointment is made, care is taken that all positions to which he may have to give directives have been filled with Bantu. Teachers feel that the inspection in urban schools is stricter than in rural areas, since schools being more accessible, visits can be more regular. Moreover, the urban pupil presents more complex disciplinary problems and the urban school board is more knowledgeable.

The Mamelodi teachers number about 410 and represent just 1 per cent of the total Bantu teaching force in the Republic, excluding the Transkei. Certain general characteristics of this force are reflected at Mamelodi. For example it is estimated that the number of teachers increases by about 7 per cent per annum. Of the entire teaching force about 20 per cent were professionally unqualified in 1966, and 10 per cent taught at the post-primary level; only 3 per cent had a post-Matric teacher training and less than 1·3 per cent had a degree plus professional training. The lower primary school is almost exclusively staffed with female teachers. The majority have a standard VI academic qualification, with three additional years of professional training. Their role is, as Kuper asserts, 'that of herd girls shepherding the new generation into the Bantustan kraals'. This critic forgets the extremely difficult task of these teachers, moreover he quite omits to mention that the lower primary teacher's certificate has been on the way out for some time. The admission qualification for future primary school teachers is the Junior Certificate, that for junior secondary school teachers the Senior Certificate. Their two-year professional training is provided in 36 colleges which totalled 4,500 students in 1969.

The qualifications expected of a teacher depend on the grade of the school and not whether it lies in an urban or rural area. In the past, urban teachers often took the opportunity to improve their qualifications in night schools, of which one still exists at Mamelodi. It is now more usual for teachers to enrol as part-time external students of the University of South Africa which is well-known for its excellent correspondence courses. Teachers born and bred in the town are probably better acquainted with certain items of environmental and social studies than teachers from the country, e.g. a rail journey including the stations from home to destination, certain activities in offices, visits to museums, monuments, cinemas and abattoirs. Rural schools like to make educational tours to the city, and the Department would gladly see urban schools conduct tours in the homelands, but tours to the game parks specially reserved for Non-Europeans seem to be preferred.

Teachers are professionally organized in the Transvaal African Teachers' Association which holds meetings and conferences and publishes a magazine curiously called *The Good Shepherd*. It appears that the African Teachers' Associations went into a decline after a spell of strenuous opposition against the Bantu Education Act of 1953 and that they are slow to make up for lost ground. There exists also a Transvaal African Principals' Association. Naturally the Bantu Education Department arranges its own refresher courses and exhibitions for teachers. Thus in 1964 a course was conducted at Mamelodi and attended by hundreds of teachers. It comprised the normal measure of lectures, demonstrations, discussions and exhibitions of teaching aids and children's work.

The institution of the 'privately paid teacher' has been an important factor in meeting the unprecedented expansion of the school system after 1954. This expansion brought in its train a grave staffing problem, for government insisted on community employed teachers for recently instituted classes (perhaps to test the sincerity of the sudden zeal for education which had only lately been denounced as 'not a decent sort of education' by the Xhosa author Dr. A. C. Jordan, or as an 'education for barbarism' by ex-teacher I. B. Tabata). Even after a recent rise, the salaries of such 'privately paid teachers' are lower than those for teachers in approved posts which are paid by the Department. The fact that school boards are charged with finding the money for these salaries has rightly been called 'the most heart-rending part of Bantu school administration'. On the assumption that the proportion of enrolled children to 'privately paid teachers' is the same at Mamelodi as in some other townships, Mamelodi must have more than a hundred such teachers. If the official overall percentage of such teachers, namely 18, is taken, the number of such teachers there could hardly exceed 60.

Generally speaking, the pupil-teacher ratio favours the rural teacher. While the general ratio in 1966 is given as 1:58 (in all, including secondary schools), one informed guess gives the ratio in urban lower primary schools as 1:60 (not counting double session assignments), in the higher primary school as 1 : 50 and in the secondary schools as 1 : 35. In correspond-ing rural schools the ratios are given as 1 : 35, 1 : 30 and 1 : 20 respectively. Teachers in town recognize that their pupils, although basically of the same intelligence as rural children, have the advantage of greater alertness and better acquaintance with the conditions of modern life. This gives them the edge over rural children even in school attainments, and they are judged to be more responsive to good teaching. Rural children, handi-capped by an impoverished environment in home and school, get more easily tired of the abstract learning situation.

Examinations

The results of the Mamelodi schools are not available in detail, nor are comparisons possible with schools in other townships, such as Soweto or Kwa Mashu, nor in the townships in course of construction in the home-lands. In 1961 the Mamelodi secondary school received the Phindakhethe floating trophy for the best results in the Junior Certificate examinations. Since all Bantu secondary schools compete for this trophy and there were then over two hundred of them, the schools of the Pretoria East circuit and indeed of the Southern Transvaal region felt greatly honoured. The Regional Director attended the handing over ceremony in person and stated that the staff of the school was fairly well qualified, but that teachers in arithmetic, maths and the sciences were needed. In 1964 the Mamelodi high school entered 13 candidates for the final examination of whom 10 passed, five with Matric exemption. In 1965 the number of candidates entered for Matric was 14 but only five obtained a pass, among them only one with exemption. In 1968 a pupil of the Mamelodi technical school obtained a distinction in bookkeeping.

The disappointing results in the Matric examinations of Bantu schools after the take-over in 1954 have been the subject of much discussion, judgment being often impaired by the hasty search for a single cause. What interests us here is the question whether the difference in results between rural and urban schools is significant. In 1962 the Regional Director of the Southern Transvaal remarked that there was an improvement in the results over the previous year. In 1960 with the pass mark in the senior certificate examination at 40 per cent, only 18·9 per cent of the candidates of the region passed, while in 1961 with the mark raised to 45 per cent the percentage of passes was 25. A recent survey notes that results at boarding schools in the rural homelands have been better than those at urban day schools. 'The disparity has increased from year to year.' Thus the per-centage passes in 1962 for day schools was 25·6, for boarding schools 37·7; in 1966 it was 34·5 for day schools and 64·9 for boarding schools. In 1968 the Bantu Education Journal took the Matric results of 1967 as justification to plead for the enrolment of urban high school pupils in homeland boarding schools. Admitting that results in the training colleges which have boarding establishments and in secondary schools which have none were satisfactory, it reported that of 2,034 entries in 77 high schools 980 passed, i.e. 8 per cent fewer than in 1966. There were, the journal stated, two reasons for the decline. The Joint Matriculation Board candidates fared worse than in 1966, and almost all large urban high schools had poor results: only 120 candidates from 16 such schools passed, representing 20 per cent of their entries. The corresponding percentage for homeland high schools with hostels was 60 and in four such schools all candidates passed. In the journal's view this proved that rural homeland schools with hostels offered better conditions for work and study than urban day high schools. This does not, of course, explain the comparative success of the junior secondary schools which are day schools. It is just possible that certain other factors also play a role, e.g. overcrowding and understaffing in urban high schools, their well-known disciplinary problems and, possibly, differences in equipment or curriculum strategy.

The recommended transfer of urban high school pupils to homeland schools raises the question of costs both for the individual parents and for the school boards which are expected to provide hostel accommodation. For parents the boarding fees, ranging from R55 to R60 per annum, although low since they are subsidized, are a heavy burden to which must be added the fares, school uniforms and other boarding school requirements which have been estimated to amount to another R60. Considering the already heavy demands on their slender financial resources, the finding of these sums will be difficult for the average urban family. The other side of the coin, in how far rural school boards can be induced to provide hostel accommodation for outsiders, raises intricate administrative and financial considerations. A proposal made by a leader writer in the Bantu Education Journal to the effect that persons living near such schools should set up small private hostels taking up to ten pupils may raise more difficulties than it pretends to solve. For one thing, the intensive study effect of supervised government hostels will hardly be ensured by it.

The Technical School

The technical school at Mamelodi is not only as a state school an exception in the educational set-up. Other technical schools, such as the commercial, the administrative and the vocational, are not represented. Their field is in the homelands. The technical school at Mamelodi requires a Standard VI continuation certificate as admission qualification. Higher qualifications are taken into account. The school offers in a three-year course the ordinary academic subjects for the Junior Certificate, viz. in Form I (which is a probationary year) a Bantu language on the A Level, English B, Afrikaans A (the Transvaal is a predominantly Afrikaans-speaking province); social studies; arithmetic; religious instruction and one course in a practical subject. The choice ranges from building construction to electronics, watchmaking, woodwork, drain-laying and sheet-metal work, motor mechanics and radiotechnics. In Forms II and III extra practical work is taken in place of social studies, while workshop calculations replaces arithmetic. Candidates wishing to qualify for the Technical Senior Certificate take a five year course in one of the following subjects: building construction, woodworking or motor mechanics. The Vlakfontein technical school has no boarding establishment, so it can be attended by oppidans only. The school offers also tuition in bookkeeping and typewriting.

The training of nurses is, of course, also an educational matter, although it is not controlled by the Bantu Education Department but by the provincial health authorities who select certain public and mission hospitals for this purpose. The entrance qualification is the Junior Certificate but applicants are more likely to be admitted if they have higher academic qualifications, especially in relevant subjects. The course lasts three and a half years for the Certificate of General Nursing; to obtain the Midwifery Certificate an additional training of nine months is needed. Lectures are given by the medical staff. Sister tutors are responsible for general instruction and practical work. Generally speaking the superintendent's and leading nurses' positions (matron, ward sister, sister tutor) are still occupied by whites, even in hospitals in Bantu townships. Since applicants come from various backgrounds – hospitals do not recruit on a tribal basis – the training of African nurses takes six months longer than that of whites to make them familiar with Western medicine and hygiene and to make up for some of the cultural difference. Parents may keep their daughters longer at secondary schools than their sons because, as H. Kuper says: 'Nursing has become one of the most highly rated professions open to African women. It carries more power in the adult world, and greater personal security than teaching, which was formerly the main ambition of the educated'. Moreover, a material advantage, highly appreciated even by illiterate parents, is that a nurse in training has free board and tuition and, in fact, gets some pocket money.

School Curricula and Enrolment

The curricula of the schools of the Bantu Education Department do not differ in essentials from those of the provincial education systems catering for whites, except that they make provision for the learning of three languages (two official and a Bantu language, the mother tongue). This trilingual requirement takes away time from other subject groupings. The syllabuses of the Bantu Education Department have been generally pronounced to be meeting modern requirements. Teachers who remember the teaching programmes of the past consider the new plans to be more exacting and to require a new approach. In the subject social studies the aim is plainly to get the African pupil acquainted with the role of the Bantu in the South African complex and with that of the Republic in the world. Kuper's opinion that the subject serves as medium for conveying isolating and submissive attitudes is not justified. Some teachers still retain their antipathy to practical subjects such as handwork and gardening, since the articles produced have either no marketable value or could be better made in factories. The garden produce is sometimes stolen, and the diligent pupil has nothing to show for his trouble. Even in rural schools such topics as tree-planting and soil conservation, although of great importance in the semi-arid conditions of South African agriculture, are opposed by teachers and parents who still cling to bookish ideals of schooling. Neither the character-forming aspect of handicrafts nor the self-expressive ideal, nor the role practical subjects can play as counterweight to a heavy academic programme, are sufficiently appreciated. On the other hand, some urban teachers and parents would like a more pragmatic curriculum by the introduction of subjects like business methods.

The enrolment of children at Bantu schools is high. In 1964 it was estimated that of the total Bantu population of 11½ million, the 7–14 year age-group comprised 2⅓ million. Enrolment at primary schools then amounted to 1·7 million, a percentage of 74 per cent. Since, however, in the age-group 7–14 years from 10–15 per cent of the children can for various reasons, such as physical or mental handicaps, not be enrolled in the ordinary schools, the percentage should be adjusted to 84 per cent of the potential of schoolgoers. In townships this figure may well be surpassed. At Mamelodi 21,263 pupils are enrolled in the primary schools; 1,272 in the secondary schools, 678 in the technical school. Parents are eager to get their children off the streets and away from the temptations of gang life. They belong to a section of the African population in which Western education has become accepted, often for generations. They have acquired literary tastes and realize that modern life is continually raising educational requirements. (After a temporary slow-down the annual increase rate in the Bantu secondary schools is now calculated at 13 per cent per annum). The rapidly increasing enrolment since 1954 – the number of pupils rose above 2 million in 1969 – is an index of the fact that the schools of the Department meet a need. The attendant overcrowding of classes and overloading of teachers may be partly blamed on principals being averse to turn away children seeking admission after the official limit has been reached. Enrolment at urban schools has also increased because of the influx of Bantu into towns in an officially approved search for work in expanding industries.

The rapidly increasing enrolment has forced school boards to press for more accommodation. An overall estimate shows that there is an increase (excluding the Transkei) of at least 100,000 pupils each year. This implies an annual recruitment of 2,000 teachers and the building of 2,000 additional classrooms. The Department has used several makeshifts to meet the emergency. For instance, it introduced the double session in sub-standards, coupling it with a reduction in teaching time in these classes from four and a half to two and three-quarter hours. This means that a teacher takes two groups of children a day, the first in an early session, the second in a late session. 'Of 7,054 Bantu schools in 1964, 3,975, or more than 50 per cent, operated on the double session system.' From an administrative point of view the double session has certain advantages. It reduces pressure on accommodation without increasing the salaries bill. It is also welcomed by the parents since it takes care of their children. Teachers, and it is female teachers who are involved, feel differently about it. They still have to deal with over-size classes. There may be as many as 70 pupils in each class (the official maximum is 50), and it is hard to imagine how one teacher can give individual attention to even a moderate percentage. The second session must, in addition, receive less effective teaching than the first, since the teacher will be tired. The platoon system is a measure which overcomes the shortage of accommodation rather than that of teachers. The same building or room is used by different school populations or classes in turn. This makeshift is well-known from other rapidly expanding education systems, e.g. that of the U.S.A. It is hoped that these measures are only temporary and that they will be dispensed with when school populations have become stabilized. As long as teaching force and accommodation have not caught up with the growth in enrolment, there is no sense in introducing universal education, not even in urban areas, although this had been recommended as early as 1934/5 by the Interdepartmental (Welsh) Commission on Native Education.

Detailed attendance figures would probably show that urban children attend better than rural children, younger children better than older ones, girls better than boys. The reasons for irregular attendance may be mainly economic. Some bigger children may not attend because they may not have sufficient clothing. Adolescent boys may have the chance of a job, as newspaper vendor or caddy, which they do not want to let slip, since residence control results in the endorsing out of certain categories of unemployed persons from urban areas to the homelands. The longer school life of the girls is explained by the fact, already noted, that nursing is a highly prestigious employment avenue. Some parents are inclined to let their daughters stay longer in school since high academic qualifications raise the bride price which they can demand from suitors.

The steeply narrowing enrolment pyramid draws attention to the large number of drop-outs and the corresponding wastage of educational effort. No statistics comparing urban and rural schools as regards wastage are available, but some of the reasons explaining the phenomenon are sure to work with different stress in different residential set-ups. The comparatively high age of admission is blamed by some for the drop-outs. It is seven years, and may be postponed to 11 years in urban and 12 years in rural areas. While this gives a chance to laggards, it results in an unequal age composition in the sub-standards, and older children may well get discouraged by bright youngsters. With regard to the rural Transkei the Cingo Commission blamed the double session for the high wastage in sub-standards. With this goes the automatic promotion in the lower primary school which tempts the weak teacher to neglect slow or diffident children. A further reason lies in the strict examination rules. The internal examination at the end of the lower primary school may only be repeated once. The same rule applies for the next three years in the higher primary school. At the end of Standard VI there is an external examination, conducted by the Bantu Education Department, to determine which pupil may proceed to secondary school. In 1966 only 43 per cent obtained the continuation certificate. Some drop-outs, on the other hand, are intelligent children who, bored with humdrum lessons, get into difficulties with their teachers. Others are drawn away by the attractions of gang life and of criminal shortcuts to the good things of life which the urban environment places on show more seductively than the rural environment. A certain percentage of withdrawals of children from school reflects the poverty of their parents who, if they are blessed with many children, can no longer meet the educational expenditure for all of them on a low wage. Parents may then select those children they think the most promising for further education, or whom they can best spare in the domestic menage or whom they consider unfit for the industrial labour market. The promotion rules in secondary schools are even more rigorous than those in the primary school. In addition, certain churches demand full membership fees from the time of confirmation and boys especially may leave school to earn the money. Some of the Nguni peoples observe circumcision, when even urban boys stay away from school for the seclusion period of several weeks and then sometimes lose interest in schooling. The high failure rate in secondary schools in recent years is also discouraging. It may be a direct result of the general increase in pupils and the corresponding shortage of qualified teachers.

III

It is now possible to discuss some of the broader issues raised by the educational situation at Mamelodi. First, the so-called ethnic (or tribal) principle on which Bantu education is sometimes said to rest is in fact a principle of linguistic homogeneity. School populations are grouped together, not because they belong to the same tribe but because they speak the same or similar languages. For instance, at Mamelodi the Nguni residential zone unites Zulu, Xhosa, Ndebele and Swazi because their languages differ only slightly in vocabulary and phonetics and intercommunication is comparatively easy, and not because their tribal organization is the same; in fact they represent varied polities. In consequence the school committees which cater for Nguni schools can be linguistically homogeneous. Even this principle has to be sacrificed occasionally in order to meet special situations. It is only in the Bantu homelands and in the townships which are linguistically zoned that single-medium schools are possible. In some areas, e.g. the Orange Free State, where two numerically strong groups reside in one urban location and linguistic grouping has not yet been applied, parallel medium classes are organized. This works on the level of the lower primary school because numbers are sufficiently large. On higher levels adjustments are necessary, e.g. the combination of two standards (taught as one class) which didactically is not satisfactory. In areas where numbers do not justify either single medium or parallel medium instruction the solution is dual medium instruction, i.e. the teacher alternates in one and the same lesson between two languages and he has to be proficient in both. At Mamelodi there are still nine schools in which more than one language is used as medium. Since numbers in the secondary and high schools are too small to allow of linguistic splitting, their committees are not restricted to unilingual membership and also the school board is linguistically heterogeneous. It is sometimes assumed that mixed committees, because they are drawn from a wider linguistic spectrum, represent a greater range of administrative ability. In practice it would probably be very difficult to prove this.

The Medium of Instruction

The use of the mother tongue as medium of instruction in the primary school is justified on psychological grounds and by the research carried out in bilingual countries, such as Canada (and South Africa itself) as to the value of such education in giving children a clear conceptual framework and adequate emotional stability. Little research seems to have been undertaken to show whether these findings, obtained in countries where two European languages have to be accommodated, are equally valid when a language with quite a different cultural context is confronted with a European language. It is sometimes, however, admitted that the traditional framework of knowledge may be an intellectual hindrance. In analysing the poor showing of high school and university students in maths and physical science, for example, one investigator blamed the type of teaching available as well as the economic status of the parents, but he also blamed the traditional culture; in his opinion Zulu had no adequate scientific vocabulary nor a suitable system of numerals.

The stress on the mother tongue is also supported by reference to its didactic advantages. For instance, the Bantu Education Journal quoted the UNESCO experiment in the Philippines, where two groups, equivalent in pupil ability, home environment, economic status of parents and teacher qualifications, were compared in their attainments in arithmetic, reading and social studies, the experimental group being taught in the vernacular (Hiligaynon) and the control group in English. The experimental group proved to be superior in academic performance and emotional maturity. Similar large-scale experiments seem not to have been conducted with Bantu children in South Africa, but it is assumed that pupils, faced with the task of having to learn subject-matter through a medium which has been inadequately mastered, take to parrot-like memorization. Other factors may, of course, also be involved, e.g. the authoritarian pose of the average African teacher.

In South Africa, as elsewhere, stress on mother tongue instruction has a political goal. The pupils are expected by means of it to identify with their home groups, so that they will place the benefits of their education at the disposal of their own people. In this manner the alienation from the social background from which they emerged, so typically expressed in the conflict between illiterate parental and Western-educated filial generations in other parts of Africa, is as far as possible to be circumvented.

Undoubtedly, there exists a strong undercurrent of opposition to the use of the mother tongue in the urban milieu. For one thing, the African is of the opinion that since he knows his language no purpose is served if he is made to learn it in school. He goes to school, or sends his children to school, so that they learn the official European language. This is important not only to his intercourse with whites; it is also advantageous in communicating with fellow Africans who belong to another language family. The European language, thirdly, ensures that the African learner obtains through it access to the treasures of thought which have a wide, if not global, currency. (The two European languages in South Africa differ in their respective usefulness. While Afrikaans is indispensable in communicating with government departments, English is of greater significance in tapping currents of thought in literary and scientific publications.) A practical consideration enhances the value of the European language in contrast to African languages. Because the number of people speaking any one of the African languages is comparatively small and because they have become media of printed communication only fairly recently, the literature available in them is limited both in range and depth, and moreover must needs be expensive. This consideration gains in weight in a polyglot community like Mamelodi.

However, the view shared by so many educationists of the colonial era, viz. that African languages are not developed enough to serve as media especially of higher education, has had to be revised in view of two facts whose significance has only recently been fully realized. The first fact is that this view is based on an erroneous static conception of the nature of African languages. We now know that, especially where they are not confined by vested interests in publications and educational services, African languages can be unexpectedly dynamic. They show an amazing capacity to adjust themselves to the confrontation with the new world brought by the whites. Most African languages increase their vocabulary by borrowing from European languages. They adjust their content and forms to the demands of school and mass media. Further, new languages come to be created which overcome the spatial and numerical handicap of vernaculars. Such new languages may serve certain kinds of functionaries over a wide area as a kind of code, e.g. porters, plantation workers, soldiers, etc. Or a *lingua franca*, or inter-tribal speech, is developed which acts as a unifying means of communication for whole regions. Very frequently the locus of the invention of such a *lingua franca* is an urban centre, a meeting place of people of varied provenance. In South Africa Fanagalo has been used as a code language for functionaries, i.e. mine and industrial workers and it was once used for this purpose even on the Copperbelt in Zambia. Since then, so-called Town-Bemba has become a supra-tribal means of communication there with even some publications to its credit. Such *linguae francae* may sometimes become the symbol of urban culture and its progressive residents as happened with Swahili. All this seems to show that educationists who put their trust in the adaptive capacity and the potential of African languages cannot be far wrong.

The second fact is that there seems to be emerging an entirely new evaluation of African languages among certain African thinkers. Whereas Coleman could still write as late as 1965 that pressure from the indigenization of school curricula was restrained in former French West Africa because of the high value attached to the French school system, and the continued use of French as medium of instruction was not questioned by the new leaders, Moumouni, in a vigorous and intelligent attack, stigmatizes the retention of the French curricula and medium as symbolic of neo-colonialism. For they quite obviously prevent the rapid spread of literacy to all adults and the general *scolarisation* of the child population in the new states. Whereas the effective learning of the European language takes years and is an expensive matter, the spread of literacy in the African language, and the use of one as medium, would at once throw the door wide open for the training of the lower, middle and higher cadres which the social, economic and cultural advance of the African peoples demands. Admitting that in the ex-British territories African languages did not suffer such an eclipse as was the case in ex-French countries, Moumouni realizes that a tremendous amount of research will have to be undertaken as to the codification and development of selected African languages so that they can serve as media of rapid mass education and assist in the modernization of the new states. He feels confident, however, that African languages are capable of becoming modern media through the creation and absorption of new vocabularies and the rendering of internationally accepted scientific concepts in the phonetics of African speech. He also realizes that a selection will have to be made in each state as to which language, or languages, would serve best in the circumstances. He is certain that because of the internal kinship of many Africa languages, it will be possible for educational services to be rendered through a few of them for the benefit of all speakers of a cluster of related languages. He refers to Wolof in Senegal and Hausa in Northern Nigeria as qualifying in this respect. Moumouni does not, of course, wish to abolish the *élite's* command of French. But he seems to underestimate the difficulties his proposal involves. The selection of one among several African languages as the school medium may intensify existing tribal rivalries. Alternative political considerations, in particular those of achieving national unity and a pan-African concert, may make the retention of the European medium appear advantageous. In addition, where the admission policy to institutes of higher education favours the student trained in a European language, students trained in an African medium are handicapped and pressures for the introduction of the European medium in schools may become irresistible. Such a situation exists in East Africa.

In South Africa, in quite a different educational and political context, the recognition and development of African languages as media of instruction has been brought to a fine art. Starting from the consideration for vernaculars which is a legacy of British colonial education, the South African specialists in African education have helped to develop Bantu languages so that they have become efficient and beautiful vehicles and instruments of thought. For each major language a language committee exists on which serve white experts, African authors and educationists. Their task is to unify the orthography, to create acceptable terminologies for the various school subjects and to stimulate the publication of suitable tutorial and literary works in each language. In comparison with most of the rest of Africa, South Africa is thus in the position of being able to offer education to the masses through the inexpensive but most effective medium of the mother-tongue. Naturally this policy directly and immediately benefits the many unskilled and semi-skilled labourers in urban areas.

Changes in the Administration

The significance of mother tongue instruction is also of administrative significance in connection with the envisaged decentralization of the Bantu Education Department. For *pari passu* with the formation of a number of self-governing Bantu territorial authorities the central Bantu Education Department will be reorganized so 'as to separate existing educational services of the Bantu in the homelands from those in the white areas'. The present Bantu Education regions (five since the excision of the Transkei) will then be expanded into 11 regions, five in the white (i.e. urban) areas and six in the Bantu homelands. Each region in a homeland will be homogeneous, with people and pupils of one language though of varying tribal allegiance. The regional organization in the homelands will be converted into education departments of the particular territorial authorities. This is already the case in the Transkei and it is being implemented at present in three other newly established territorial authorities. The rump education department in Pretoria, apart from being the control organ of Bantu education in white areas, will further function as the policy-making authority, exercising professional supervision and giving guidance to the territorial education departments in consultation with the territorial authorities. (The territorial departments will presumably be allowed some latitude in interpreting the overall policy. The Transkei government, for example, modified the Bantu Education Department policy in two respects: it abolished school boards, as distinct from committees, and advanced the stage at which the European medium is to be introduced from Form I to Standard III.) The mother-tongue principle is thus many-sided in application: it is psychologically fundamental, didactically important, of nation-building significance and serves as a decentralizing motive.

The full significance of decentralization lies, of course, in the democratization of the educational system in the sense that it is made to rest on, or evokes, the participation of the entire population, or more precisely of that part of it which is directly involved, viz. the parents of school-going children. Neglect of them in the administration of schools in former French West Africa is rightly criticized by Moumouni. For in the new states the educational system still tends to be exclusively run by persons in established political or bureaucratic positions. They, naturally, wish to perpetuate a system of education which brought them recognition from their former masters and political success in a unique historical situation; with the same system they want to secure similar privileges for their children. But this system is not necessarily of great use in the present stage of development. Moumouni therefore pleads for the participation of the masses in the administration of the schools, for taking account of their pragmatic needs in devising plans for expansion and for putting the entrenched leaders under pressure from the people.

Unfortunately Moumouni leaves us in the lurch when we expect him to inform us as to the precise measures through which the masses are to participate in the formulation of aims and the implementation of the content of education. It is exactly here, that C. Arnold Anderson's advice is most helpful. Asking himself how social and economic change is best brought about, he replies that change occurs most readily in small circles which set an example, demonstrate a change in values and produce standards of speed and levels of change which can be easily accepted and imitated in the neighbourhood. It is through growth institutions of this type that 'the ecological diffusion process' is promoted. Anderson supports his argument by reference to the well-known fact that economic change occurs in patches, or foci, from which it is spread 'in gradients, i.e. demarcations between strata and localities'. Educational advance is best conceived in similar terms. Local communities are best made responsible for financing their own schools, the state aiding with a basic contribution to all areas, but assisting in particular those communities in which, because of discrete economic development, educational interest has become most intense, as has happened in most towns. Anderson accepts even differential educational norms among sub-populations as most stimulating in promoting education. For a community which is initially left behind will make the greatest effort to pull up to the level of the more advanced. General expansion of services, paid from central revenue or made possible by foreign aid, has a stifling effect on local initiative, quite apart from the fact that the one may not be possible financially, and the other may have political strings attached to it. Anderson is convinced that an economic and educational equalization policy is a luxury in developing countries which they cannot afford. He therefore welcomes the emulatory interplay of local centres as the greatest motivating force in development, even if it is not accompanied by a general raising of standards but expresses itself in a continuum of varying standards.

Much of this argument seems to bring out the rationale behind the establishment of school committees and boards in Bantu Education. They have not only given a tremendous impetus to the enrolment of thousands of children, they have also engaged about 50,000 parents in the day-to-day administration of schools. Considering that committee members serve for three years, this implies that since 1954, when the system was introduced, several hundred thousand adults have become concerned with the schools. The competition between committees and boards has been the motor which has kept the enrolment curve rising all the time.

Mamelodi, it is realized, is an urban settlement with special characteristics. Unlike some of the African cities which have been studied in detail (Accra,

Sekondi-Takoradi, Stanleyville, Kampala, Mombasa, etc.) it is neither a capital nor a port, the two most distinctive forms of urban existence in modern Africa. Neither is it a focus of uncontrolled attraction for rural people as most capitals have proved to be which have grown excessively within the last few decades and especially since independence. Mamelodi's growth has been moderate. Its existence is that of a humble satellite town near a white city, a dormitory for a predominantly industrial working population. Hence Mamelodi lacks the typical concentration of a decision-making or political *élite* which distinguishes the capitals of independent Africa. As we noted, there is a certain amount of occupational differentia-tion at Mamelodi, but the system is, as it were, incomplete at the top. It resembles a truncated pyramid, a society with political (and cultural) leadership located elsewhere. This fact is brought out even more strongly if we remember that Mamelodi exists where it is today only on sufferance. White politicians have ventilated plans of removing Bantu townships from white areas. This implies that residents of Mamelodi must include in their view of the future the chance that their township is only transitory, whatever effect this may have on their sense of security.

However, if Mamelodi seems to be a second-rate town with none of the glamour of capitals and none of the bustle of ports in other parts of Africa, it must also be stated that for this very reason it escapes some of the worst effects of urbanization without industrialization and of urbani-zation without the appropriate social processes which should accompany it. For it is a fact that 'the most conspicuous symptom (of the hurry of political leaders in the new states) is the global spread of slums . . .' Possibly, urban growth in Africa is not so excessive 'that the problem has become unmanageable', as has been asserted of another continent. In a measure Africa is still the least urbanized of the continents. It has therefore every chance of avoiding the mistakes of uncontrolled urbanization. Yet it seems that only South Africa has sufficiently anticipated the consequences of an unchecked population movement to the cities. Labour bureaux register the occupational opportunities in the industrial centres and regulate the influx into the towns in agreement with the demands of the urban labour market. This rather tight control has been criticized because it prevents the rural unemployed from selling his labour in the best market.

But who would care to reduplicate events in Latin America where, as we are told, 'a great amount of the move to town is an escape from the disastrous conditions of rural life' and is nothing but a 'transfer of un-employment from the country to the city'? In other words, there is no gain. Hence we are warned by Lerner concerning the large masses of African in-migrants: 'the point that must be stressed concerning this suffering mass of humanity displaced from rural areas to the filthy periph-eries of the great cities is that few of them experience "the transition" from agricultural to urban-industrial labour. They are neither housed, nor trained, nor employed, nor serviced. They languish on the urban periphery without entering into any productive relationship with its industrial operations.' Certainly Mamelodi prevents entry into such a social cul-de-sac and its organization forestalls such expensive transfers of urban unemployed to rural settlements as have had to be carried out in Western Nigeria, Ghana and Tanzania.

Yet the educational aspect of this situation has not yet been exhausted. Lerner, in his discussion of African cities, notes that 'the hapless condition of the displaced persons enters into the lives of their children. . . . Typically, their children do not go to school, do not find work (other than the most menial and unrewarding), do not become urbane (other than through the urbanity of delinquency). The urban poor will thus multiply well into the next century'. And he ends on a pessimistic note: 'The world's educational facilities are vastly inadequate to provide the quantity of psychic mobility required by the amount of physical mobility that is now occurring over most of the world'. What contribution do the Mamelodi schools make in providing their children with the adaptability which modern life demands? Undoubtedly, a certain measure of academic attainments is conveyed to them, some vocational guidance is given and their industrial productivity may be somewhat raised thereby. But is that all?

The answer is that if educational and occupational opportunities are limited at Mamelodi (in the interest of the whites), it is because elsewhere more advanced opportunities are created for Africans, and the school-leaver who wishes to look for better opportunities must go there. In 1964 an Interdepartmental Committee on Technical Training recommended that there should be every possible occupational and professional opportunity for the Bantu in their homelands and they should there be protected against competition from whites. It also confirmed that in Bantu townships in white areas the Bantu would have to be restricted to certain occupations to prevent competition between white and African since certain categories of white workers were privileged. If we wish to examine in how far there exists an outlet for Mamelodi in the homelands of its African residents, we have to direct our attention there.

The occupational differentiation of the population of the homelands commenced, as a result of the Native Building Workers Act 1951, with the training of teams of African builders, plumbers and electricians who were first employed in the construction of the huge Bantu satellite towns, like Soweto and Kwa Mashu, and are now engaged in the construction of housing in more than 150 townships in the homelands. The residents who are expected to settle in them will have need of many craftsmen. To provide for the full-time training of the more usual artisans 24 trade schools have been established. For the many public services which have to be set up the Department of Bantu Administration and Development has planned 'the orientation and training of Bantu in a post-school phase by means of short concentrated courses . . . for a variety of jobs in commerce, industry, public health, local and other authorities and other avenues of national development in the homelands', and in 1965 a start was made when a number of surveying assistants received theoretical training in a course at Vlakfontein, while their practical work consisted in in-service work with white surveyors. Later this course was raised in status and transferred to the University College of Fort Hare. The Department also realizes that 'trained specialist manpower will be required by the territorial authorities for all their activities – in the civil services, agriculture, commercial, industrial and transport undertakings, management of towns, health and social services'. In this respect the Department wishes to follow the natural method of growth, i.e. to supply the required manpower from the lower grades to the top positions as educational services turn out their products and job opportunities are increasingly widened and raised. In-service training for appointees will keep them abreast of developments. Thus a three-month's training course for Bantu legal personnel was recently held at Ga-Ranukwa with lectures by professors of the faculty of law of the University of South Africa.

The professional training of Africans is concentrated at the three University Colleges situated in the homelands and at the Non-European Medical School of the University of Natal at Wentworth. They are engaged in the training of 'teachers, doctors, social workers, civil servants (law), civil servants (administration), attorneys, advocates, agricultural extension officers, businessmen, commercial entrepreneurs, pharmacists, etc.' The colleges may soon be required to undertake the training of technologists as a prerequisite to the training of engineers. In the Transkei the erection of a fully equipped Technical College, equal in status to similar colleges in white communities, has been commenced. The products of these institutions of higher education are supplemented by the many Africans who acquire university education through the correspondence courses of the University of South Africa. Their number has only recently been exceeded by that of internal students.

The Department is also aware of the need of training unskilled workers from rural areas in industrial skills. The trend in vocational training is to establish training centres in connection with factories in white industrial areas (as at Kwa Ford, Port Elizabeth) or with Border Industries as at Mdantsane near East London. The Kwa Ford centre has six classrooms, five workshops, a drawing room, store room and administrative block for schooling workers in the car factory. The textile school at Mdantsane sets a pattern for joint training schemes between Department and employers of Africans. The costs are to be shared in such a way that the

Department provides the school facilities and the employer the equipment, including machinery and the raw materials. If this idea catches on, the avenues for skilled employment, so long blocked to the Bantu in deference to the interests of organized white labour, will be opened up at last in so far as Border Industries and industries in the homelands are concerned.

A special need exists, of course, for the training of political leaders. While the more outstanding ones will, as they have done in the past, go through the university colleges, the system developed in South Africa which does not dispense with the services of the traditional leaders but incorporates them into the new Bantu Authorities, duly modernized by the introduction of the elective principle, requires that careful thought be given to the training of leaders of the middle echelons. In secondary schools with a bias towards public administration – there are four – such an institution has been created for the sons of chiefs and headmen.

In short, South African planners have realized that at the present stage of the country's development and that of its African peoples 'something more than migration to towns' is needed. What is needed was, in fact, blue-printed by the Socio-Economic (Tomlinson) Commission in 1957 and can be summarized in the demand for the complete transformation of rural African society. In the past experiences of peasant communities, and we follow B. F. Hoselitz in this, illiteracy was associated with the hopelessness of farming; literacy implied the stepping out of farming and the acquisition of political power. The rural communities must be converted to the view that education is not incompatible with farming. This can be achieved if modern scientific forms of farming with better yields are introduced. This is not the place to outline the extensive measures taken by the Department of Bantu Administration and Development to carry out, with the co-operation of the local communities, the rehabilitation of African farming in the homelands. Three aspects only can be referred to. (1) Educationally, all the investment in primary education will be wasted, unless complementary investments are made in agriculture (and industry), i.e. in non-human capital, so that the low skills acquired by the people in school can be fruitfully applied in productive activity. (2) Economically, the rationalization of agriculture can be related to the growth in other economic sectors; it ensures that economic growth comes from a country's own resources and need not be primed from outside. (3) Culturally, scientific agriculture, through mechanization, soil conservation, breeding techniques, etc., will result in a modernization of life in the country and will make possible the introduction there of amenities considered hitherto exclusively 'urban'. Hoselitz admits that such a programme has Herculean proportions. A South African economist considers that 'the implementation of the government's policy in the

Bantu homelands probably presents one of the greatest rehabilitation projects ever tackled outside Soviet Russia and China'.

The educational situation at Mamelodi is thus part of a large-scale canvas of social transformation which it will take decades to complete. It cannot be understood by itself and fairness demands that the complementary situation in the homelands should be taken into consideration as well. Then it will be seen that a complete educational pyramid, leading up to full university training and out into various kinds of technical and special education, exists there or is in the course of being built up. It will also be seen that there is close co-ordination between educational development and economic advance, such close co-ordination in fact that the problem of unemployed school-leavers which has become so untractable in other parts of Africa has been kept within limits in South Africa. It will also be seen that the urban facilities which make life in Mamelodi so attractive to the African are gradually being transferred to the homelands. This is achieved in two ways: by the creation of numerous townships there and by the conversion of the old type of farming into scientific agriculture. South Africa has realized that modernization is more important than urbanization, that modern technologies, modern media of communication, modern ways of social interaction can be created and made fruitful in the homelands, whether these are rural or urban in residence pattern. Within the homelands, the schools, universities and other educational institutions will, indeed, represent foci of modern ways of life and diffuse these ways into their neighbourhoods.

Conclusion

What of the future of the South African experiment? The answer to this question will also affect the future of Mamelodi. There are admittedly certain unsolved problems and certain obscurities in the South African situation. We noted the problem of the democratic participation of the urban Africans in the administration of their townships as one such problem. There is the more momentous issue of the form which the co-operation between the several Bantu homelands and the white areas is to take. Undoubtedly, a fair amount of consultation between the political leaders of the homelands and the government in Pretoria will be necessary. The education departments of the homelands will from time to time want to have discussions with the Pretoria Bantu Education Department via their territorial authorities. All this seems to point to the fact that the political leadership in Pretoria and in the homelands is aware of the imperative need for some *modus vivendi* between the various communities which will have to be found and which by common consent will secure the co-operation of these various polities on a lasting basis. The problem is, in fact, a predominantly political one. However, it concerns the educationist in so far as he must make sure that his own work can be conducted within an acceptable social and economic framework and that his efforts in the direction of a morally justifiable harmonization of interests will be rewarded with success. In how far this is possible at Mamelodi today has been shown in some detail above. In how far it will be possible in future, only outstanding achievements in the implementation of the Herculean programme will be able to determine in a positive manner.

BIBLIOGRAPHY

C. A. Anderson, 'The Impact of the Educational System on Technological Change and Modernization' in B. F. Hoselitz and W. E. Moore (Eds.), *Industrialization and Society* (Paris: UNESCO, 1968).

S. Andreski, *Parasitism and Subversion* (London: Weidinfeld and Nicholson, 1966).

Bantu, Department of Information, Pretoria, vols. 14, 15 (1967, 1968).

Bantu Education Journal, Department of Bantu Education (Pretoria: 1962–8).

J. S. Coleman (Ed.), *Education and Political Development* (Princeton: Princeton University Press, 1965).

P. A. Duminy (Ed.), *Trends and Challenges in the Education of the South African Bantu*, with articles by the Hon. M. C. Botha, Minister of Bantu Administration and Development and of Bantu Education, J. J. Ross, J. J. de Wet, W. M. Kgware, G. J. Ackermann, R. Cingo, P. A. Duminy (Pretoria, 1967).

B. Heine, *Afrikanische Verkehrssprachen* (Cologne, 1968).

M. Horrell, *A Decade of Bantu Education*, S.A. Institute of Race Relations (Johannesburg, 1964).

B. F. Hoselitz, 'Investment in Education and its Political Impact', in J. S. Coleman, op. cit., pp. 541–65.

L. Kuper, *An African Bourgeoisie: Race, Class and Politics in South Africa*, with article by H. Kuper on 'Nurses' (New Haven: Yale University Press, 1965).

D. Lerner, 'Comparative Analysis of Processes of Modernization' in H. Miner, op. cit., pp. 21–38.

H. Miner, *The City in Modern Africa* (London: Pall Mall Press, 1967).

A. Moumouni, *L'Education en Afrique* (Paris, 1964).

J. W. Raum, *Das Bantuschulwesen in der Südafrikanischen Union*, Dissertation (Munich, 1963).

South African Institute of Race Relations Johannesburg: Conference on Bantu Education, 1969. Cyclostyled papers by F. E. Auerbach, W. M. Kgware, J. W. Macquarrie, E. G. Malherbe, F. S. M. Mncube, W. F. Nkomo, F. K. Peters, G. W. Tabor and M. Horrell.

5

Lagos*

Saburi O. Biobaku

Lagos, the Federal Capital of Nigeria and the seat of the new Lagos State, is, nevertheless, predominantly a Yoruba town. Its natural hinterland is the Western State with which it shares in common the traditional concept of Yoruba society which was based on a civic settlement. So a description of the Yoruba traditional settlement and its system of rudimentary education provides a useful background for the study of the growth of education in the city of Lagos.

In the olden days, among the Yoruba, an enterprising hunter would lead his friends and relatives to a suitable place, a clearing in the forest, and there the foundations of a new town were laid. They hunted animals for food and farmed nearby, bringing the products of their hunt and of their farms to the markets which they had established in front of the house of their chief, the hunter-leader. The products were first exchanged by barter. Later, as they made contact with the outside world, they adopted cowrie shells as currency and eventually entered the cash economy. The men hunted, farmed or fished according to the location of the town; the women assisted on the farms and traded in the markets. In their leisure they provided entertainment for themselves through their religious festivals which featured masquerades and dancing and re-enactments of historical events: their art provided the masks and carvings of ancestors which were prominent in the polytheistic religion and ancestor-worship. Their learning was essentially oral and remembered and so an elaborate tradition of oral literature was built up in praise poems, folklore, proverbs and wise sayings. The business of traditional education was how to impart all this to the young: how to ensure the continuity of the farming or fishing communities based on the small market towns.

There were no formal schools except in the groves where the young were initiated into the mysteries of traditional religion as practised in the Oro (the bull-roarer) cult, or the Egungun or Agemo[1] masquerades. Traditional education rested upon voluntary apprenticeship or clientage. The

---

* A revised and shortened version of an article which appeared in *International Review of Education*, Vol. XIII, 1967, No. 4 (Hamburg: Unesco Institute for Education).

[1] *Egungun* and *Agemo* are manifestations of the ancestor cult among the Yoruba.

little boy followed his father to the farms, to the forest while hunting, or to the lagoon or river while fishing and gradually acquired some of his skill through imitation and 'copying'. He followed his father also to the meeting of elders and learnt much of the history and tradition of the people during their discourses. The young girl went to the markets with her mother and began to learn the canons of trading by participating in the endless polite bargaining and haggling that went on. Sometimes, boy or girl was sent away from home to be apprenticed to a famous farmer, medicine man or trader and in this way additional practical education was gained. In essence, the education was aimed at fitting the individual into the community: he or she might live on the distant farm but at least annually during the festivals, the farmer returned to the town to participate in the communal town life. Neither did the advent of Islam in the Yoruba country change the situation too radically. It added learning through reading and writing in Arabic, but the Koranic Schools were conveniently arranged to hold their classes in the mornings and later in the evenings so that the middle portion of the day could be spent running errands for one's parents or going to the farms or the markets as in the indigenous societies. It was when Western education came in the wake of the Christian missionaries that the goal of education changed markedly.

Christian Missionaries and the Goals of Education

Christian missionaries came into Western Nigeria in the 1840s and were quickly followed by British traders and government officials. Starting from the Coast in the Lagos area, the frontier of British influence which they established had to be pushed into the interior and either for the propagation of the Gospel or the extension of trade and colonial rule, literate indigenous allies were essential and schools were founded for the purpose of teaching people how to read and write. Naturally, the schools began with the Christian converts and their children and in the early days the schools attempted to teach elements of agriculture and to impart technical skills. The need for clerical workers soon became paramount and the schools responded by concentrating upon the liberal arts to the extent that manual labour and practical training lost their appeal and gradually came to be despised. The effect of all this upon communities which were essentially those of farmers dwelling in small towns was traumatic. In order to gain Christian converts, schools were located in the villages which served the market towns, but in these schools the children learnt to read and write and to yearn for white-collar jobs. Some entered the church as teachers and catechists and perhaps stayed in the villages but only after they had had further training in the big towns. The majority emigrated from their villages and traditional 'home-towns' into the newly developing big towns, the seats of the missionaries and agents of the government, in search of jobs as clerks and messengers and were, in effect, educated *out* of their communities. Of agriculture, hunting, trading, and local crafts, they knew nothing and when they encountered disillusionment in their adopted cities, they joined the ranks of delinquents and habitual criminals.

Breakdown of Traditional Educational Concepts

The first and inescapable effect of urbanization is the breakdown of the traditional concept of education in Africa. Neither the old concept which ensures the integration of the young in the traditional community nor the relatively new concept which prepares him for the life of a mission or government clerical worker can cope with the problems of modernization that face Africa today. Urbanization poses new problems for education, especially since the new towns are essentially industrial rather than market towns as they were in the traditional economy. The magnitude of the problem may be illustrated by a description of the situation in Lagos, the Nigerian Federal Capital.

Lagos began as a fishing island with a few thousand people, some of whom were migrants from Benin. After the advent of the Europeans, it was effectively linked with the Nigerian mainland and a surburb rapidly developed at Ebute Metta. As Lagos grew and became the seat of government, commerce and the National Railway Administration, a satellite settlement was established at Ikoyi as a European reservation and Yaba developed as an extension of Ebute Metta (and later Apapa), to serve growing port and industrial needs. As commercial and governmental business expanded, more people came in and the surburbs further extended into the hinterland so that Mushin and Ikeja, some sixteen miles from the centre of the island, provided dormitories for Lagos workers. Lagos Airport and another suburban settlement accommodating modern residences and industrial development are also situated at Ikeja. The population of Greater Lagos is well over a million and a half and, although it is predominantly Nigerian, it contains a large proportion of expatriates from Europe, America and the Middle East, and Nigerians who are non-natives of Lagos. Such a polyglot community poses important problems to the educational administration.

Lagos tries to cope with its educational problems by the provision of a variety of schools ranging from nursery and primary schools to post-secondary technical institutions and a university. At the primary school level, education is free and universal to the extent that it is available to anyone who cares to be registered for it at the age of six years, but it is not compulsory. The number of those registering each year increases as the influx of persons from all parts of the country into the city for employment continues unabated. The demand for teachers is correspondingly high, as new schools have to be established every year in order to cater for the inevitable additional numbers of pupils. Teacher-training institutions draw their trainees from the products of the secondary schools who are recruited from those passing out of the elementary schools. From the secondary schools, boys and girls go to the Trade Centre or the College of Technology at Yaba and the best qualified among them enter the University of Lagos which, of course, draws its students from the whole country as befits a federal institution. Through concerted action by the government, voluntary agencies (the missions and religious groups which are becoming increasingly Nigerian) and private enterprise, the school provision is expanded year by year in order to meet the growing needs. The real problem, however, is whether the system is designed to cope successfully with the problems of urban life.

Coming to Terms with Urbanization

The basic question is 'How can you get them back to the farm after they have seen Lagos?' In a country which is predominantly agricultural, can you educate the young men and women in the cities and ensure that they return to the farms? This is clearly impossible in Lagos and any of the booming cities of West Africa, partly because educationists have not faced up to the problem of devising an educational system that will integrate the young persons into their own communities as well as promote the development of the African economy. There have been experiments at sending 'graduates' of secondary schools, which are located in the towns, to farm settlements and farm institutes in their own home areas with conscious efforts to reproduce there some of the attractions of the cities such as electricity and water supplies, good living quarters and even cinemas, only to discover that the urge to return to the cities could not be overcome in this way. This chapter is, however, concerned with education and urban growth and so the fascinating problem of resettlement on the land must not detain us too long, although the two are inter-related in Nigeria. The challenge to education in Africa today is that it must come to terms with urbanization.

Urbanization in Lagos at present means living in an over-crowded city, struggling with insufficient funds to begin and to consolidate the process of urban renewal, providing modern sewage disposal for all and coping with the problems of unemployment, juvenile delinquency and increasing incidence of crimes of violence. The newcomer to Lagos often arrives with inadequate education, insufficient briefing as to the hazards of unemployment and is cut off completely from his traditional moorings of tribal customs and parental control. There is little that the conventional educational system can do for him. If he is lucky and he secures a job, he can continue to improve his educational attainments by entering evening classes at the government adult education centres or at the College of

Technology or the semi-professional commercial and typing classes. In all probability, however, he will remain unemployed and dependent upon the charity of his friends and relatives and thus become an easy prey to the press-gangs of petty criminals. Even those at school, at evening classes or in regular employment, unless they are lucky enough to come under good influences, are liable to join the ranks of juvenile delinquents until they become accustomed to the wiles and blandishments of insidious boon-companions. Thus another important effect of urbanization on education is to throw a heavy burden on the educational system as far as preparing the young persons to withstand the temptations of urban life is concerned.

In urban life, informal education plays an essential and important role. Reference has already been made to adult education centres where the imperfectly educated newcomer to the cities can continue to broaden his horizon or acquire more knowledge in an informal manner. There are also the voluntary organizations such as the Young Men's Christian Association, the Young Women's Christian Association, the Scout Movement, boys' and girls' clubs which can play a vital role in rescuing the newcomers from falling into bad ways and focusing their attention and energies upon constructive actions. The temptations before the young worker, far away from home in a large city, are naturally great and the situation is aggravated by loneliness so that organizations which provide meaningful companionship for him are performing important educational roles, albeit in an informal and indirect manner.

The University and the Emerging Nation

It is, perhaps, natural to think that a university situated in an urban area has a special mission in meeting the challenge of urbanization to educational planning and development. It cannot be too strongly emphasized that education is a lifelong process and for those who are fortunate enough to be capable of receiving higher education, the opportunity to combat some of the effects of urbanization is golden. Perhaps a brief exposé of the philosophy of the University of Lagos, which is *par excellence* an urban university, will illustrate one way of tackling this problem. The University of Lagos was founded in 1962 and by 1966 it had six fairly well-established Faculties of Arts, Business and Social Studies, Education, Engineering, Law and Science, as well as a Medical School. It provides regular undergraduate courses in these Faculties and in two of them – those of Business and Social Studies and of Law – there are evening classes for part-time students who work during the day and are expected to take two years longer than the full-time students in order to graduate. There are plans for post-graduate studies and research is an important element in the commitment of the University. Yet, the University feels strongly that it must extend its activities outside its normal walls and so there is a Continuing

Education Centre which began as an arm of the Faculty of Business and Social Studies but is now designed to serve all the Faculties as the extension organization. This is a particularly fruitful approach in a growing city such as Lagos because the need for continuing the education of the adult is obvious and clamant.

This aspect of the work of a university in an urban setting can serve the dual purpose of enabling the students to widen their educational horizon and broaden their culture as well as improve upon their skills and competence in their day-to-day activities. It can, in effect, assist the urban dweller to fit himself more firmly into his cosmopolitan environment much as the traditional educational pattern served admirably to integrate the young into the more static traditional society. The continuing education apparatus can provide instruction in music and the arts, traditional history and culture no less than in science and technology, economic planning and jurisprudence. It can also mount seminars and conferences designed to acquaint the busy medical practitioners and the peripatetic engineers and architects with the latest knowledge and discoveries in their professional world. It can bring the citizens to the university and give them a glimpse of the necessities of the academic community just as it affords the academics the opportunity of keeping in touch with the real lives of the urban communities.

The University also, through its urban studies programme, seeks to shed light on the problems of urbanization. It is this kind of involvement which is a vital proof of the virility of modern universities and it is particularly essential that universities in developing countries must not shirk their responsibilities in this field. Urban studies can take different forms but, in essence, they are motivated by the burning desire to come to grips with one's environment. In Lagos, which is a port as well as a commercial centre and the metropolitan city of the most populous country in Africa, the need for bringing the disciplines of sociology, town planning, environmental design and health engineering to bear upon the problems of the growth and development of the city is obvious, and, with a properly co-ordinated programme, much can be achieved in a short time towards the amelioration of the adverse effects of urbanization.

The appalling traffic congestion and consequent waste of time in moving from one part of the town to another; the difficulties of integrating newcomers into existing communities which are far from stable themselves in certain sections and the avoidance of consequent miseries and loneliness; the lack of facilities for modern public health engineering and the attendant danger of endemic diseases – all these can be studied and useful light shed upon them for the benefit of the city authorities and to the enormous advantage of the city dwellers. The universities, then, have a vital mission in developing countries; they must take in hand the problems posed by urbanization and give powerful leadership to other educational sectors in solving them.

Conclusions

Urbanization is both a disruptive and a modernizing force in Africa. Its effects on education are essentially those of a challenging phenomenon which calls for a re-thinking of the purpose and process of education in developing societies. Formal education provided in schools and colleges needs to be oriented in such a way as to serve the requirements not only of agricultural communities but of the rising population of city dwellers who have migrated from rural areas into cosmopolitan communities. The flotsam and jetsam of urbanization pose the most difficult and the most pressing problems for the educationist, and only by employing the informal as well as the formal approaches can they be successfully fitted into the stable urban communities. In tackling all these problems, the universities cannot stand aloof and ensconce themselves in their ivory towers; the universities must become involved and through extension activities and deliberate studies in urbanization, they can and must play their parts in the integrated educational approach that is indicated if the new African industrial towns are not to be 'whited sepulchres' harbouring semi-literates, chronic delinquents and unmitigated slum-dwellers. In Lagos, efforts are being made to tackle the educational problems of urban growth at all levels.

6

Durban*

H. L. Watts

Recent Urbanization in South Africa

A century and more ago, South Africa consisted mainly of rural peoples with diverse cultural backgrounds and a subsistence-level economy. The discovery of diamonds and gold during the latter half of the last century injected large-scale industry into the economy and accelerated urban growth.[1] Today, South Africa is increasingly being transformed into an urban industrial economy, with a major portion of the population being concentrated in urban areas.[2] Table 1 indicates the percentage of the population living in urban areas at various censuses, and Table 2 the corresponding absolute numbers.

Durban is Chosen for Analysis

These data show that this century there have been major population shifts from rural to urban areas in South Africa. Metropolitan areas have developed. One of the main ones – chosen for study here – is Durban. Now probably second in size only to Johannesburg, it is situated on the eastern seaboard of South Africa. Founded in 1824 as a trading site, it is the main port of the Republic of South Africa, and one of the key ports of Africa as a whole.[3] More than any other South African city it represents the meeting-place of different cultures and languages, having Whites and Indians and Africans in relatively large numbers in its population. It also has a small Coloured population, made up of White-African and, to a

---

* I wish gratefully to acknowledge the kind way in which the Natal Education Department, and the Departments of Coloured Affairs, Indian Affairs, and Bantu Education went to considerable trouble to compile for me, where possible, raw statistics for Greater Durban. Without their assistance this paper would not have been possible.

[1] C. W. de Kiewiet (1941), *A History of South Africa, Social and Economic* (London: Oxford University Press), p. 89.

[2] It must be remembered that as a plural economy, South Africa also exhibits the subsistence rural economy of Africans in the 'Bantu Homelands'. This economy shows all the problems typical of under-developed economies throughout the world.

[3] In 1963/64 the Durban port handled 54 per cent of the total harbour tons shipped, landed, and trans-shipped by the eight ports in South Africa and South-West Africa. See *Ports of South Africa: Harbour Reference Book* (1964) (Johannesburg: Sealing Publishing Co.).

TABLE 1

THE PERCENTAGE OF EACH RACIAL GROUP IN SOUTH AFRICA LIVING IN THE URBAN
AREAS, AT VARIOUS CENSUSES, 1904–60, AND ESTIMATED FOR 1967[4]

Race	Percentage of each race residing in the urban areas at various dates							
	1904	1911	1921	1936	1946	1951	1960	1967
Whites	53·6	53·0	59·7	68·2	75·6	79·1	83·6	86·1
Coloureds	49·2	50·4	52·4	58·0	62·5	66·2	68·3	70·2
Asiatics	36·5	52·8	60·4	69·5	72·8	77·6	83·2	85·8
Africans	10·4	13·0	14·0	19·0	24·3	27·9	31·8	34·8
All non-Whites	15·4	18·5	19·3	24·4	29·7	34·0	37·9	41·0
Total population	23·6	25·9	28·2	33·6	39·3	43·4	46·7	49·8

TABLE 2

THE SIZE OF THE URBAN POPULATION OF SOUTH AFRICA, BY RACE, 1904–67[5]

Race	Population, in millions, living in urban areas at various dates							
	1904	1911	1921	1936	1946	1951	1960	1967
Whites	0·60	0·68	0·91	1·37	1·79	2·09	2·58	3·13
Coloureds	0·22	0·27	0·29	0·45	0·58	0·73	1·03	1·28
Asiatics	0·04	0·08	0·10	0·15	0·21	0·29	0·40	0·49
Africans	0·36	0·52	0·66	1·25	1·90	2·39	3·47	4·41
All non-Whites	0·62	0·87	1·04	1·85	2·69	3·41	4·90	6·18
Total population	1·22	1·55	1·95	3·22	4·48	5·49	7·47	9·32

[4] The sources for the above figures are:

The years 1904–60, Republic of South Africa, Bureau of Statistics (1966), *1966 Statistical Yearbook* (Government Printer, Pretoria), p. A24; the non-White percentages were calculated from p. A22.

The 1967 percentages were calculated from figures in Pienaar and Associates (1967), *Statistics, 1967 Population, the Republic of South Africa, Report No. 1*, Johannesburg: Pienaar and Associates (Pty) Ltd, pp. VII and VIII.

The figures are in terms of the classification of the urban areas made as at the 1960 census, which is as follows:

... a population of 500 (all races) [in a town is] the dividing line between urban and rural, with the following exceptions—

(a) all sub-urban areas are classified as urban, as by definition, they are urban in character;

(b) well established small towns with a population of below 500 have been classified as urban if the towns have a reasonably high proportion of Whites, and a number of the usual urban amenities, such as shops, garages, churches, schools, and main streets, etc.;

(c) areas with a population of more than 500 have been classified as rural if they are pre-dominantly non-White with few, if any, of the usual urban amenities.

See Republic of South Africa, Bureau of Statistics (1963), *Population Census 6th September, 1960, Volume I, Geographical Distribution of the Population* (Pretoria: Government Printer), R.P. 62/1963, p. vi.

[5] Footnote at bottom of p. 82.

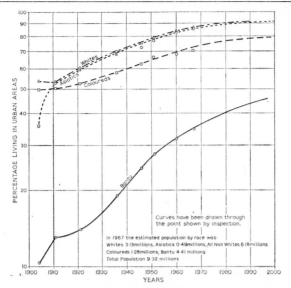

Diagram 1. Growth in the percentage of each race in the Republic of South Africa living in urban areas, 1904–67. Note that the urbanization of the Bantu is faster than for any other racial group. (Data plotted on a semi-log scale, showing the rate of growth – not the absolute growth.)

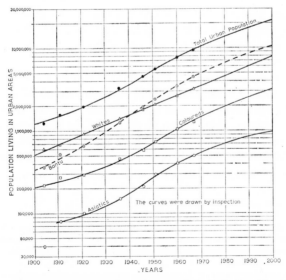

Diagram 2. The growth of the urban population in the Republic of South Africa, 1904–67, with graphical extrapolations of future growth.
(Data plotted on a semi-log scale, showing the rate of growth – not the absolute growth.)

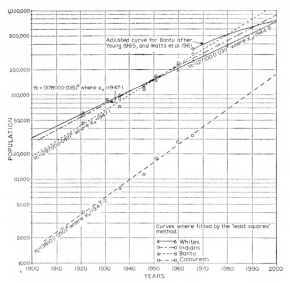

Diagram 3. Past population growth, and estimated future growth of Metropolitan Durban.
(Data plotted on a semi-log scale, showing the rate of growth – not the absolute growth.)

lesser extent, White-Indian crosses. In 1970 Greater Durban (i.e., Durban as a socio-geographical entity), will have an estimated 280,000 Whites, 310,000 Indians, 400,000 Africans, and 41,000 Coloureds – a total of 1,031,000 persons.[6]

Durban is growing rapidly. It is estimated that by the year A.D. 2000 the population in Greater Durban will be about 720,000 Whites, 180,000 Coloureds, 880,000 Indians, and some 800,000 Africans – totalling over $2\frac{1}{2}$ million persons. Thus, within three decades the population could increase $2\frac{1}{2}$-fold. The Coloureds will have the highest increase of about 4·4-fold; Whites will probably increase 2·6 times; Indians 2·8-fold; while the Africans will probably have the smallest increase at about 2·0-fold.[7]

[5] These figures are derived from the following sources:
The 1904–60 figures are based on Republic of South Africa, Bureau of Statistics (1966), op. cit., p. A22; the 1967 figures are based on Pienaar *et al.* (1967), op. cit., pp. VII–VIII. (The figures for each racial group, the non-White total, and the total population, were rounded separately from the original sources. This explains why some of the figures do not add up exactly to the totals shown.)

[6] For a description of Durban, see for instance L. Kuper, H. L. Watts, and R. J. Davies (1957): *Durban: A Study in Racial Ecology* (London: Jonathan Cape), also Department of Economics (1969): *The Port of Durban*, Natal Regional Survey, Vol. 15 (Durban: University of Natal).

[7] For reasoning underlying these estimates see H. L. Watts, R. J. Davies and G. H. Waters, (1967), *The Spatial Distribution of the Present and Future Residential Population of Metropolitan Durban*, Institute for Social Research (Durban: University of Natal), pp. 31, ff.

TABLE 3

ESTIMATED INDUSTRIAL DISTRIBUTION OF THE GAINFULLY-OCCUPIED POPULATION OF METROPOLITAN DURBAN, 1966[8]

Industry	Estimated number of workers					Per cent of all workers
	Whites	Coloureds	Indians	Africans	Total	
Agriculture	305	90	1,099	3,995	5,489	1·2
Mining/Quarrying	168	27	136	1,218	1,549	0·3
Manufacture	30,849	7,423	39,744	84,781	162,797	36·6
Construction	6,633	1,095	3,156	26,695	37,579	8·4
Power	1,404	3	827	3,422	5,656	1·3
Commerce/Finance	27,990	937	21,808	25,196	75,931	17·0
Transport	12,980	426	2,919	13,784	30,109	6·8
Services	26,495	1,470	19,490	32,161	79,616	17·9
Domestic service	—	—	135	46,537	46,672	10·5
Miscellaneous	40	10	1	9	60	0·0
TOTAL	106,864	11,481	89,315	237,798	445,458	100·0

TABLE 4

ESTIMATED FUTURE INDUSTRIAL DISTRIBUTION OF THE GAINFULLY-OCCUPIED POPULATION OF METROPOLITAN DURBAN IN THE YEAR 1990[9]

Industry	Estimated number of workers to nearest 100					Per cent of all workers
	Whites	Coloureds	Indians	Africans	Total	
Agriculture	100	100	100	600	900	0·1
Mining/Quarrying	300	100	500	1,500	2,400	0·3
Manufacture	78,900	26,700	131,700	200,400	437,700	46·5
Construction	10,600	2,300	5,500	37,500	55,900	6·0
Power	2,000	100	1,900	5,200	9,200	1·0
Commerce/Finance	50,100	5,000	35,200	50,700	141,000	15·0
Transport	21,600	1,300	5,400	27,900	56,200	6·0
Services	47,500	4,900	40,900	63,500	156,800	16·7
Domestic service	—	—	—	78,400	78,400	8·4
TOTAL	211,100	40,500	221,200	465,700	938,500	100·0

Durban can be classed as a modern industrial city. This can be seen from Tables 3 and 4 which provide estimates for the industrial distribution of the gainfully-occupied population in 1966, and the probable position in 1990.

[8] Source: L. Schlemmer, (1968): *The Spatial Distribution of the Present and Future Working Population of Metropolitan Durban*: An applied research report of the Institute for Social Research (Durban: University of Natal), p. 292.

[9] Schlemmer (1968): ibid.

Education in Durban must prepare the rising generations for living and working in this urban industrial economy.

Education involves Diverse Cultures and their Problems

In Durban, Eastern and Western cultures, and the remnants of African tribal cultures, meet. These cultural variations present the educationist with a formidable array of social differences. About half of the total Indian population of the Republic is in Durban. Both Hindu (76 per cent) and Moslem (15 per cent) are represented in the Indian population;[10] and the language groups in order of size are Tamil (35 per cent), Hindi (25 per cent), English (15 per cent), Telegu (10 per cent), Urdu (9 per cent), and Gujerati (6 per cent).[11] Amongst the Whites it is mainly English (81 per cent) and to a lesser extent Afrikaans (15 per cent) which is spoken.[12] Amongst the Africans, Zulu (88 per cent) and Xhosa (8 per cent) are the main languages used.[13] The Coloureds, who are culturally closer to the Whites than any of the other racial groups, mainly speak English (86 per cent).[14]

These peoples with diverse backgrounds and value-systems are catered for by educational systems under different authorities.[15] Despite this, the educational systems, as throughout the Western world, are essentially based on Western middle-class values – on middle-class time-perspectives and goal-perspectives – and depend on the deferment by the child of present pleasures and gratification for future rewards. Bernstein, and also Halsey and Gardner, have shown in Britain how sub-cultural differences in value-systems, time-perspectives and goal-perspectives, and methods of self-expression on the part of the child, give rise to educational problems.[16] In Durban, where we are dealing not only with important sub-cultural

[10] These and the following percentages refer to the total population of the racial group concerned. The source is: Republic of South Africa, Bureau of Statistics (1966): *Population Census 6th September, 1960, Volume II, No. 5, Report on the Metropolitan Area of Durban* (Pretoria Government Printer), see p. 110.

[11] ibid., pp. 107–8. Those speaking languages other than the ones listed amounted to less than $\frac{1}{2}$ per cent.

[12] ibid., pp. 18–19.

[13] ibid., pp. 135–6.

[14] ibid., p. 83. In other parts of South Africa most Coloureds speak Afrikaans.

[15] White schools are under the Natal Provincial Education Department; Coloured and Indian schools are under the Department of Coloured Affairs and the Department of Indian Affairs respectively; while African schools are under a Bantu Education Department. The latter three departments are all under the central Government of South Africa. There is no local education authority for cities in South Africa, and the school curricula is stereotyped for the whole province or country, as the case may be. This places a greater burden on the imagination and skill of the teacher to make the schoolwork relevant for the life of the city child, particularly among Africans where the high dropout rate gives an even shorter period of time to prepare the children for adult life.

[16] B. Bernstein (1958): 'Some Sociological Determinants of Perception: An Enquiry into Sub-Cultural Differences', *British Journal of Sociology*, **9**, 160 ff.

A. H. Halsey and L. Gardner (1953): 'Selection for Secondary School Education and Achievement in Four Grammar Schools', *British Journal of Sociology*, **4**, 60–75.

TABLE 5

The Percentage Distribution of the School-going Population in Metropolitan Durban, by Standards, 1968/9

School standards		Percentage distribution				Cumulated percentages			
Whites, Indians, Coloureds	Africans	Whites	Coloureds	Indians	Africans	Whites	Coloureds	Indians	Africans
Class I	Sub A	9·9	13·3	10·3	21·1	9·9	13·3	10·3	21·1
Class II	Sub B	10·0	12·8	9·1	15·5	19·9	26·1	19·4	36·6
Std. 1	Std. 1	9·5	11·0	12·6	13·9	29·4	37·1	32·0	50·5
Std. 2	Std. 2	9·1	10·2	12·9	11·0	38·5	47·3	44·9	61·5
Std. 3	Std. 3	9·2	10·9	13·8	10·4	47·7	58·2	58·7	71·9
Std. 4	Std. 4	9·1	10·7	10·3	8·0	56·8	68·9	69·0	79·9
Std. 5	Std. 5	8·6	10·2	9·2	6·9	65·4	79·1	78·2	86·8
Std. 6	Std. 6	9·5	9·4	7·5	7·2	74·9	88·5	85·7	94·0
Std. 7	Form I	8·3	5·8	6·5	2·5	83·2	94·3	92·2	96·5
Std. 8	Form II	7·3	3·5	4·0	1·7	90·5	97·8	96·2	98·2
Std. 9	Form III	5·3	1·2	2·2	1·2	95·8	99·0	98·4	99·4
Std. 10	Form IV	4·2	1·0	1·6	0·4	100·0	100·0	100·0	99·8
	Form V				0·2				100·0
TOTAL:		100·0	100·0	100·0	100·0				
No. of scholars to nearest thousand		46,000	11,000	83,000	70,000				
Author's estimate of percentage of children aged 6–16 years at school		100	100	92	?★				

Notes: ★ The figure is probably lower than that for Indians, but appears to be masked by possibly several thousand children with homes outside Greater Durban going to school in Durban. The White figures omit the few private schools in the area.

The Africans take 2 years instead of 1 over matriculation—hence Form IV and Form V, giving 13 years minimum schooling for a child who does not drop out, in contrast to 12 years for the other races.

Secondary schooling may be said to commence at Form I for Africans, and Standard 6 for the other races.

differences, but with different cultures as well, the problems are multiplied. Studies have yet to be made in Durban along the lines of the work of Bernstein, and Halsey and Gardner. The findings would reveal important problems, of which many teachers working in the situation are at best only partly conscious. The problem of aiding children who do not have the Western middle-class perspectives and modes of self-expression needed to enable them to adapt rapidly to the school with its long-term goals and

TABLE 6

THE PUPIL/TEACHER RATIO IN SCHOOLS IN METROPOLITAN DURBAN, 1968/9

Type of school	Pupil/Teacher ratio			
	Whites	Coloureds	Indians	Africans
Infant schools	29	35	—	57
Primary schools	21	32	30	55
Secondary/High schools	17	21	23	24
All schools	20	29	28	51
Percentage teaching posts reported vacant	1·2	2·7	3·6	0

Note: The White figures exclude the few private schools in Durban. Many primary schools include infant classes.

TABLE 7

THE INCREASE IN THE NUMBER OF TEACHERS REQUIRED IMMEDIATELY IN NON-WHITE SCHOOLS, TO ATTAIN THE AVERAGE PUPIL/TEACHER RATIO PREVAILING IN WHITE SCHOOLS, BY TYPE OF EXISTING SCHOOL, METROPOLITAN DURBAN, 1969

Type of school	Number of extra teachers which would be required			Percentage increase needed in number of teachers		
	Coloureds	Indians	Africans	Coloureds	Indians	Africans
Infant schools	13	—	27	121	—	200
Primary schools	94	665	1,809	149	130	254
Secondary schools	31	269	74	126	137	143
TOTAL	138	934	1,910	137	132	139

emphasis on verbal expression is one on which applied research should be undertaken.

One of the prominent problems facing educationists in South Africa in the first three decades of this century was the education of the poor Whites.[17] In the towns, the problem of coping with rural migrants who had been driven off the land by economic forces, and who were unfitted for urban existence and for any work except that of the simplest order, was often acute. In a paper in 1929, Malherbe – the doyen of South African educationists – foresaw that 'the poor Black problem' would in turn be-

[17] E. G. Malherbe (1929): 'Education and the Poor White', *South African Journal of Science*, **26**, 888–903.

come serious.[18] He has been proved correct. Today we have the task of educating poor illiterate or semi-literate African rural migrants and their children – as was the case with Whites – for jobs in an urban economy above the unskilled or semi-skilled level. The large scale of the problem is shown by my estimate, based on unpublished material, that in 1969, 6 out of 10 African households in Durban were below the secondary poverty datum line. This agrees with a published finding for 1964.[19] A complicating factor in the situation is that urbanization in South Africa means some degree of Westernization as well.[20] The Africans in Durban vary from the highly Westernized, who are urban-oriented through various gradations, to those still heavily oriented towards the rural areas and tribal culture.[21] Evidence suggests there are also those who at present have no reference group in either Western or tribal culture. The same school system has to cope with children of all these different types.

There is also a problem of poverty amongst some of the Indians in Durban, many of whom originally had a rural background. While the full extent of the poverty is unknown, indirect evidence suggests that amongst the Tamil and Telegu-speaking Indians, the depth and extent of poverty may be as great or slightly greater than amongst the Africans. The problem is aggravated by the small number of working females in the Indian population – the women are not yet fully emancipated.[22] Amongst Coloureds the problem of poverty and ignorance is much less serious, whilst amongst the Whites in Durban it is relatively absent.[23]

It is against the general background sketched above, and particularly in terms of the problem of the 'culture of poverty' (with its vicious circle of lack of education; lack of training; lowly skilled jobs and low incomes;

---

[18] ibid., p. 892.

[19] H. L. Watts and N. K. Lamond (1966): *A Study of the Social Circumstances and Characteristics of the Bantu in the Durban Region, Report No. 2, Social Circumstances of the Bantu*, Institute for Social Research (Durban: University of Natal), p. 13. See the report for details of the depth of some of the poverty. For a description of the poverty datum line itself, see H. L. Watts (1967), *The Poverty Datum Line in Three Cities and Four Towns in the Republic of South Africa*, Fact Paper No. 1, Institute for Social Research, University of Natal, Durban.

[20] Watts and Lamond (1966), op. cit., pp. 274–7.

[21] For an indication of some of the variations which occur, see the study made of the neighbouring port city of East London by P. Mayer (1961), *Townsmen or Tribesmen: Conservatism and the Process of Urbanization in a South African City* (Cape Town: Oxford University Press).

[22] Kuper *et al.* (1957), op. cit., pp. 66, 90.

[23] The extent of Coloured poverty in Durban is unknown, but it is almost certainly less than it was in the towns of the Western Cape at the end of the 1950s, when about half of the Coloureds were below the poverty datum line. Likewise, the White position is not known, but in 1955 only $\frac{1}{2}$ per cent of urban White households in South Africa as a whole were in poverty. See H. L. Watts (1962), *Survey of the Housing Requirements of Coloureds in Towns of the Western Cape Province*; and by the same author in 1959, *An Analysis of Some of the Housing Requirements of the Urban White Population of the Union of South Africa*. Both reports are from the National Institute for Personnel Research, South African Council for Scientific and Industrial Research, Johannesburg. See p. 11 and p. 16 respectively of the two reports.

TABLE 8

THE ESTIMATED POPULATION OF SCHOOL-GOING AGE IN 2000 A.D., WITH ESTIMATES OF
THE NUMBER OF TEACHERS REQUIRED TO MAINTAIN EXISTING PUPIL/TEACHER RATIOS
FOR EACH RACE, IN GREATER DURBAN

Race	Estimated No. aged 6–16 yrs. in 2000 A.D.	Number of teachers needed to maintain existing pupil/teacher ratios			Total percentage increase in teachers required, 1968/9–2000 A.D.
		Infant and Primary	Secondary	Total	
Whites	137,000	3,823	2,951	6,774	297
Coloureds	65,000	1,533	709	2,242	606
Indians	273,000	7,372	2,377	9,749	329
Africans	190,000	3,267	469	3,736	272
TOTAL	665,000	15,995	6,506	22,501	322

Note: 1968/9 drop-out rates and pupil/teacher ratios for each race have been assumed
for 2000 A.D.

TABLE 9

THE ESTIMATED NUMBER OF TEACHERS REQUIRED BY 2000 A.D., TO REACH IN ALL
SCHOOLS THE PUPIL/TEACHER RATIOS PREVAILING IN WHITE SCHOOLS IN 1968/9, AND
ALSO ASSUMING THE 1968/9 WHITE DROP-OUT RATES WILL APPLY TO ALL RACES, IN
GREATER DURBAN

Race	Estimated number of teachers required				Total percentage increase in teachers required 1968/9–2000 A.D.
	Infant	Primary	Secondary	Total	
Whites	728	3,095	2,951	6,774	297
Coloureds	345	1,468	1,400	3,213	868
Indians	1,450	6,168	5,880	13,498	455
Africans	1,009	4,292	4,092	9,393	692
TOTAL	3,532	15,023	14,323	32,878	472

and general ignorance including lack of knowledge of matters such as
nutrition and budgeting) that the education in Durban of Africans, and to
a lesser extent of Indians, and some Coloureds, must be seen. The heritage
from the past of social, economic, and cultural differences is reflected in
educational differences, and problems for future solution. Because of space
limitations, education will be discussed only in terms of schooling in
Durban.

TABLE 10

The Number of Existing Schools, together with the Estimated Number Required in Greater Durban by 2000 A.D.

Number of schools

Type of school	Whites			Coloureds			Indians			Africans		
	1968/9	Year 2000		1968/9	Year 2000		1968/9	Year 2000		1968/9	Year 2000	
		(a)	(b)		(a)	(b)		(a)	(b)		(a)	(b)
Infant and Primary	77	233	233	14	85	110	121	398	464	176	480	323
Secondary and High	28	83	83	4	24	39	24	79	166	14	38	115
TOTAL	105	316	316	18	109	149	145	477	630	190	518	438
Percentage increase in total number of schools, 1968/9–2000	—	301	301	—	606	828	—	329	434	—	273	232

Notes: (*a*) These columns represent an extension to the existing size of schools, and the existing distribution of scholars by type of schools, for each race.

(*b*) These columns set as target the 1968/9 White figures for the average size of school, and for scholar distribution (i.e. 36 per cent of scholars in secondary/high schools).

Existing Educational Levels and Schooling, by Ethnic Group

Existing differences in the standard of education of the peoples in Durban are not known precisely. At the 1960 census 83 per cent of the Africans of school-going age or older in Durban had less than Standard 6 education.[24] The figure for Indians was 71 per cent, for Coloureds 53 per cent, and for Whites 35 per cent.[25] Figures for illiteracy are available only for Africans – in 1960 in Durban 36 per cent aged fifteen years or older could neither read nor write.[26]

Schooling is compulsory for White and Coloured children in Durban from the age of seven years until sixteen years, or until Standard 8 or its equivalent has been passed. Plans are in hand to make it compulsory in the near future for Indians. It is not known at what stage African schooling will become compulsory. The present position for schooling in Durban is shown in Table 5.

The table shows differences between the racial groups in the extent to which schooling is being obtained by the present population of school-going age. In the absence of precise drop-out rates, they illustrate the variations in school dropout, by race.[27] These differences reveal the extent of the challenge facing educationists. If urban development and economic expansion in the Republic is not to be slowed down by shortages of educated and trained manpower, then increasingly the non-Whites must shoulder part of the responsibility for supplying the skill and ability needed.[28] First of all, the schools must play their part.

The pupil/teacher ratio for schools in Durban in 1968/9 is shown in Table 6, which groups all types of schools very broadly into infant, primary, and secondary schools.

The differences in Table 6 reflect both bigger classes and less teaching specialization amongst teachers in non-White than in White schools. The position is worst in the African schools.

---

[24] In the South African school system there are sub-classes I and II (also called Sub A and Sub B), and then Standard 1 to 10, representing 12 years' schooling for a child who goes all the way without failing. Africans have an extra year schooling in secondary school – they take two years over matriculation.

[25] Republic of South Africa, Bureau of Statistics (1966), *1960 Census, Vol. II, No. 5*, op. cit., pp. 67–72, 101–2, 125–7, and 161–2.

[26] ibid., pp. 133–4.

[27] Dropout rates for Durban are not available—only national or regional figures are obtainable.

[28] See for instance, the 1961 Educational Panel (1963), *Education for South Africa;* also (1966), *Education and the South African Economy,* both by Witwatersrand University Press, Johannesburg. Also see E. G. Malherbe (1969), 'Bantu Manpower and Education', Paper to Bantu Education Conference of the South African Institute of Race Relations, January 1969, Johannesburg.

Need for Expansion of Non-White Schooling Facilities

If, for argument's sake, the White pupil/teacher ratio is taken as the target to be reached by non-White schools in Durban, then the increase in teachers needed immediately is shown in Table 7. The existing school drop-out rate amongst non-Whites has been assumed by the calculations.

Even with the limited goal of not altering the drop-out rate amongst non-Whites, but providing pupil/teacher ratios on the scale at present applying to Whites in Durban, the number of additional teachers required is considerable. South Africa is experiencing a serious shortage of teachers amongst all racial groups, and it would take years to obtain the extra teachers. However, population growth will make the position more serious, by inexorably adding more and more children to the schools. Table 8 estimates the number of teachers which would be required by the year A.D. 2000 merely to maintain the 1968/9 pupil/teacher ratios and drop-out rates for each race.

Given only three decades to go, large-scale expansion is required to maintain an educational *status quo* in the face of Durban's rapid growth. However, if poverty is to be wiped out and the non-Whites are to contribute their share to the strained manpower resources of the country, the present drop-out rates amongst non-White school children, especially at the secondary level, must be lowered. Table 9 shows the expansion in the number of teachers which would be required by A.D. 2000 if the 1968/9 White position in regard to both the pupil/teacher ratios, and also the distribution of scholars into infant, primary, and secondary schools, is set as the target.

Unless government policies in regard to the allocation of resources to education are altered considerably, this scale of development required for Durban in the space of only thirty years cannot be achieved. It seems most unlikely that such expansion can be achieved for a further reason – there is always a good few years' lag between change in educational policy, and its first fruits.

The estimated number of schools which would be required in Durban in A.D. 2000 in terms of projecting the *status quo* for each race, or achieving the 1968/9 White position in regard to school size and the proportion of pupils in different types of schools, is shown in Table 10.

Existing school shortages aggravate the position shown in the table. At least 22 Indian schools must be replaced because of population shifts under the Group Areas Act. There is also a classroom shortage, which for years has been dealt with by the 'platoon' system, whereby children come to one of two sessions a day, and use the same facilities, but have different teachers. About 15½ thousand Indian children (or almost 1 in 5) operate under the platoon system at present. Some African schools also use double sessions, but with the same teachers, so that in fact the shortage of teachers is greater than the previous figures suggested. The number of African children involved is not known, but is probably larger than the Indian figures. The platoon system does not apply to any White children, and a negligible number of Coloured children are involved.

Shortages of equipment in the non-White schools (particularly in African schools) are also a factor to be reckoned with. Details were not available.

A problem which will affect future attempts to improve educational levels in Durban is the economic cost of education to parents. It takes two forms – the direct cost of schooling, and the loss of a child's income while he/she is at school. Given the present poverty of many non-Whites in Durban, it is the second factor which contributes to the high dropout rates. White and Coloured school education is free (only 'school levies' must be paid). Amongst Indians it is free up to Standard 6. Thereafter the parents must buy stationery and set-work books, but textbooks are loaned. African parents have to pay the full costs of schooling, which are estimated to range from R 0–50 per annum in Sub A to R 25–50 in Form V, (R 85–50 per annum if boarding is required).[29] In all racial groups, school uniforms and other incidentals must be paid for by the parents. Taking together both direct and indirect costs of schooling there are many African parents, some Indian and fewer Coloured parents who cannot afford these costs. The present set-up handicaps the African child most of all. Until the position is altered, it will put a brake on attempts to improve educational levels in Durban. No figures were available for education budgets in Durban alone, but estimating from national per capita averages, in 1968 educational authorities were able to spend roughly R $8\frac{1}{2}$ million on White scholars, R 1 million on Coloured scholars, R 5 million on Indian scholars, and over R 1 million on African scholars.

The Challenge of Ethnic Disparities in Schooling

Wide differences in existing educational levels and facilities associated with cultural variations in Durban, have emerged from the analysis. These disparities present a challenge to the educationist. The rapid future growth of Durban will considerably accentuate the problems. Educational opportunites and facilities must be improved, particularly for non-Whites. The non-White drop-out rates must be reduced. Such steps will help in the solution of the serious problems of poverty and 'the culture of poverty' in Durban, and will speed up the adjustment of the city's varied peoples to an increasingly urban industrial society. Such developments are also needed to provide the city and the country with the educated manpower

[29] *Information Sheet No. 1/1968*, Natal Region, South African Institute of Race Relations, Durban.

which will be increasingly required. Nonetheless, given a rapidly growing city, it is concluded that the problems and educational disparities are too large to wipe out by the turn of the century. The position should have improved by A.D. 2000, but the problems will only have been partly solved, given existing methods, resources, and policies regarding the allocation of these resources.

Perhaps educationists in Durban will be forced by the scale of the problems to explore ways and means of harnessing technological developments for the cheaper and more effective education of the masses – to look for methods which are cheaper in terms of manpower and per head capital costs. Further research into the problems, together with the scientific study of possible short- and long-term solutions, are needed.

BIBLIOGRAPHY

B. Bernstein (1958), 'Some Sociological Determinants of Perception: An Enquiry into Sub-Cultural Differences', *British Journal of Sociology*, **9**, 160 ff.

C. W. de Kiewiet (1941), *A History of South Africa, Social and Economic* (London: Oxford University Press).

Department of Economics (1969), *The Port of Durban*, Natal Regional Survey, Vol. 15, (Durban: University of Natal).

A. H. Halsey and L. Gardner (1953), 'Selection for Secondary School Education and Achievement in Four Grammar Schools', *British Journal of Sociology*, **4**, 60–75.

M. Horrell (1968), *Bantu Education to 1968*, South African Institute of Race Relations, Johannesburg.

L. Kuper, H. L. Watts, and R. J. Davies (1957), *Durban: A Study in Racial Ecology* (London: Jonathan Cape).

E. G. Malherbe (1929), 'Education and the Poor White', *South African Journal of Science*, **26**, 888–903.

E. G. Malherbe (1969), 'Bantu Manpower and Education', Bantu Education Conference, January 1969, South African Institute of Race Relations, Johannesburg.

P. Mayer (1961), *Townsmen or Tribesmen: Conservatism and the Process of Urbanization in a South African City* (Cape Town: Oxford University Press).

Pienaar and Associates (1967), *Stats: 1967 Population, the Republic of South Africa* Report No. 1, (Johannesburg: Pienaar and Associates (Pty) Ltd.).

Republic of South Africa, Bureau of Statistics (1963), *Population Census 6th September, 1960, Vol. I: Geographical Distribution of the Population*: R.P. 62/1963, (Pretoria: Government Printer).

Republic of South Africa, Bureau of Statistics (1966), *Population Census 6th September, 1960, Vol. II No. 5, Report on the Metropolitan Area of Durban* (Pretoria: Government Printer).

Republic of South Africa, Bureau of Statistics (1966), *1966 Statistical Yearbook*, (Pretoria: Government Printer).

L. Schlemmer (1968), *The Spatial Distribution of the Present and Future Working Population of Metropolitan Durban,* Institute for Social Research (Durban: University of Natal).

Sealing Publishing Company (1964), *Ports of South Africa: Harbour Reference Book, 1964,* (Johannesburg: Sealing Publishing Company).

South African Institute of Race Relations (1968), *Information Sheet No. 1/1968,* Natal Region (Durban: South African Institute of Race Relations).

The 1961 Educational Panel (1963), *Education for South Africa* (Johannesburg: Witwatersrand University Press).

The 1961 Educational Panel (1966), *Education and the South African Economy,* (Johannesburg: Witwatersrand University Press).

H. L. Watts (1959), *An Analysis of Some of the Housing Requirements of the Urban White Population of the Union of South Africa,* National Institute for Personnel Research, Council for Scientific and Industrial Research, Johannesburg.

H. L. Watts (1962), *Survey of the Housing Requirements of Coloureds in Towns of the Western Cape Province,* National Institute for Personnel Research, Council for Scientific and Industrial Research, Johannesburg.

H. L. Watts and N. K. Lamond (1966), *A Study of the Social Circumstances and Characteristics of the Bantu in the Durban Region, Report No. 2: The Social Circumstances of the Bantu,* Institute for Social Research (Durban: University of Natal).

H. L. Watts, R. J. Davies, and G. H. Waters (1967), *The Spatial Distribution of the Present and Future Residential Population of Metropolitan Durban,* Institute for Social Research (Durban: University of Natal).

H. L. Watts (1967), *The Poverty Datum Line in Three Cities and Four Towns in the Republic of South Africa,* Fact Paper No. 1, Institute for Social Research (Durban: University of Natal).

M. A. Young (1965), *A Study of the Social Circumstances and Characteristics of the Bantu in the Durban Region, Report No. 1: Characteristics and Future Growth of the Population,* Institute for Social Research (Durban: University of Natal).

7

Cape Coast

E. E. Ekuban

Cape Coast is a town of great antiquity. Covering an area of 3,922 square miles, it lies mid-way between Accra, the capital of Ghana, and Sekondi-Takoradi, once a busy seaport, along the coastal zone of the Gulf of Guinea. It is surrounded by little hills which are separated by narrow streets and lanes. On one of these hills stands the residency of the Administrator for the Central Region, a symbol of modern Ghana; on two other hills are Fort William and Fort Victoria, which were built to ward off enemy attack and to protect trade and lives; these are symbols of old Cape Coast. There is a further chain of hills which served as the residential areas for the officials of British bureaucracy and European commercial enterprises, and now serve as the official residence of the senior members of Ghana civil service. Yet another chain of hills bears the structures of secondary schools and the new University College of Cape Coast established in 1962.

Like many other urban areas in tropical West Africa, particularly parts of the Guinea coast and West Sudan, there was a relatively large settlement of people in Cape Coast before the beginning of the period of effective colonial administration. It may be described as a sporadic urban area, having developed in a predominantly farming and fishing community and served for a long time as one of the chief points of contact between the Africans in the country and the European merchants and officials. The Portuguese first settled there at the beginning of the seventeenth century. The Cape Coast Castle was built later by the Swedes. It changed hands rapidly; it was first held by the Dutch and then by the English, who held it from 1664. Until 1876 Cape Coast was the capital of the British settlements, but in 1877 the seat of government was removed to Accra, which is now the capital.

The period between the middle of the nineteenth century and the first half of the twentieth century was marked by a combination of increased size and density of population, and heterogeneity. Within ten years the population in Cape Coast had more than doubled. It increased from 11,614 in 1891 to 28,948 in 1901, whereas in Accra, the population had decreased from 16,280 to 14,842 during the same period. By 1901 Cape Coast contained more than the combined populations of Accra (14,842) and Kumasi

(6,280), the capital city of Ashanti. This growth in numbers was in a large measure the result of the growth of bureaucracy, trade and commerce, and the accompanying demand for services in an expanding exchange economy.

What is more, the urban element in Cape Coast during this period was often transitory, and contained an unusually high proportion of young adults. By 1931 the population had decreased from 28,948 (1901) to 22,482. During the same period the number of boys was 5,079 as compared with 3,969 girls. The young population was mostly school children from the neighbouring rural communities in search of education, or school leavers from other localities in search of clerical or commercial employment, and unskilled labourers. The town was overcrowded with the exception of the highest class of residential quarters for Europeans and Western-educated Africans.

Another feature of the urban population of Cape Coast was its heterogeneity. In 1948 out of a population of 23,346 whose birthplaces were recorded, 15,019 were not born in Cape Coast. The population was made up of Africans, Asians and Europeans. Europeans living in the town during the last quarter of the nineteenth century were mostly of professional, managerial and executive status; there were also the Christian missionaries and educationists. Their social contacts with Africans were largely restricted to those few with a reasonably high income or an education finishing at Standard VII, secondary or university level. As late as 1948, the educated percentage of Africans in Cape Coast with Standards III to VI education was 2·6 and those with Standard VII or higher education was 1·9 of the total population. The Asians were mostly shopkeepers, and tended to live together in sections of the town, maintaining as much as possible their traditional ways of life. A large section of the population was made up of persons of African descent, mostly from another locality in the same region, but some from the other regions of Ghana as well. Among the Africans, there was a wider range of occupations and income than the other sections of the population. The Africans included fishermen and farmers, skilled and unskilled workmen; drivers and artisans, teachers, clerks and lawyers.

This influx of young adults from the neighbouring villages into Cape Coast was to some extent selective in terms of age and education, and in terms of sex. Education played a significant role in this movement into urban environment. Since Christian missions, as well as the government, had established a number of schools in Cape Coast, and mission schools had spread beyond Cape Coast into the urban areas along the coastal zone, schooling had transformed some farmers' and fishermen's children into young people who could obtain 'white-collar jobs'. Cape Coast seemed to offer the opportunities for the attainment of their aspirations.

As the town supported European-sponsored economic development, it meant that most Africans, on coming to the town for the first time, were introduced to a largely new Western way of life. The most striking features of Cape Coast were its economic life and its cultural activities. The dense population had settled there because of the opportunities afforded for employment. There was no longer a local self-sufficiency characteristic of the African rural community. The town had become part of a world-wide economic system as raw materials from the interior were traded for Manchester goods. It was in Cape Coast that Africans and people from other lands came into the closest contact one with another. It was from the town that new ideas spread to the rural communities. While emphasizing the cultural importance of Cape Coast in the Gold Coast Legislative Council, G. E. Moore remarked, 'Cape Coast – the state that first came into contact with British influence, diplomacy, and civilization, and played not a little part in the introduction of these into other states of this country' (Kimble, 1963, p. 669). This view was confirmed by a later observation made in *Urbanization and the Position of Women* (Baker and Bird, 1959, pp. 99-122). They argued that 'The process called urbanization spreads through a whole society affecting even those who do not live in towns . . . These new towns act as catalysts. They are the core of the modern changes'. In the urban life of Cape Coast the Christian mission schools and government schools became the instruments of these 'modern changes'.

The newcomer to Cape Coast usually maintained contact with his place of origin or lineage community which bound him permanently to the community where the lineage was localized. In consequence the urban element in Cape Coast did not neglect kinship obligations entirely, and old tribal loyalties persisted in the new situation of urban life. This factor may account partly for the transitory nature of the urban element, and the wide fluctuations in population growth as evidenced by the censuses of 1901 (population 28,948) and 1911 (population 11,269).

Cape Coast has not taken part in the post-war accelerating rate of urban growth which has characterized some of the urban areas in Ghana, particularly Accra and Kumasi. It has lost some of its old commercial and political significance as a result of the removal of the seat of government to Accra, the re-routing of the main line of communication between Accra and Sekondi-Takoradi and the almost total absence of national or state industries in the town. However, it has retained its prestige as a secondary schooling centre and the seat of the new University College of Cape Coast.

In determining the effects of urbanization on education in Cape Coast the period of rapid growth in population provides significant evidence for analysis, and it is with this period between the middle of the nineteenth century and the first half of the twentieth century that this study will be primarily concerned.

Education and Western Culture

The British headquarters in Cape Coast was the source of one main stream in Ghana's educational history. The Rev. Thomas Thompson, a missionary of the Society for the Propagation of the Gospels, started a school in Cape Coast Castle soon after his arrival in 1751. After a precarious existence, it continued to flourish under Philip Quaque, the first African to be ordained a Church of England minister, who was appointed by the Society as its 'Missionary, Catechist and Schoolmaster to the Negroes on the Gold Coast'. It was renamed the 'Colonial School' under the British Government and later became Government School, Cape Coast. It became a tradition in the school for pupils to prepare for baptism and for work as clerks in the colonial administration and commercial enterprises, and as teachers for the mission schools, by taking lessons in the Church catechism and by learning to read and write. K. A. Busia has observed that 'It is against the historical background of . . . two centuries of Christianity and European education and a century of British rule that the present situation of *élites* in [Ghana] should be studied.' The introduction of schooling into a non-literate society creates a new *élite*. Africans who became literate were able to share European civilization. Busia explained that they learnt to speak a European language, copy his manners, and his dress, and also aspire to his occupations and manner of living in every way. The 'Colonial School' at Cape Coast provided literary education which enabled Africans to undertake employment in a European-controlled economy and enjoy its accompanying power and prestige.

A girls' school was added to the 'Colonial School' which had moved from the Castle to a rented building in the town in order to bring Christian teaching from the Castle to the people and make the school 'the nursery of the Church'. In the town the school continued to provide only the rudiments of education in addition to spelling, geography and grammar. English was the medium of instruction. Western education appeared to enjoy prestige for its overwhelmingly vocational nature. A night school was opened in Cape Coast for adults between the ages of twenty and forty-five to teach the rudiments of education. Thus the 'Colonial School' produced in Cape Coast the first generation of Western-educated Africans, which although small in number wielded an influence on the country as a whole quite out of proportion to its size.

The type of education produced in the school, according to Cruikshank, 'enabled young men to keep memoranda . . . and accounts, to superintend the discharging of cargo from vessels, oversee out-of-doors work, . . . several acquired a sufficient knowledge of book-keeping to become, at first, factors and clerks to the merchants, and finally, to carry out business on their own' (Cruikshank, 1853, Vol. II, p. 60). Some African parents considered it desirable to send their children to schools geared to the vocational aspirations of the limited opportunities open to Africans in trade, merchant offices, as clerks in the bank and the bureaucracy, and school-teaching in mission schools.

A pupil at the 'Colonial School' was a leader of a group whose request for Bibles reached the Wesleyan Missionary Society in England. After the first missionary sent by the Wesleyan Mission, Joseph Dunwell, had succumbed to the climate, the Rev. Thomas B. Freeman volunteered and arrived at Cape Coast in 1838. Thus continued an eventful history of the Wesleyan Missionary Society's activities which were confined predominantly to Cape Coast and other urban trading stations along the coastal zone; a pattern that was to persist. Freeman's first schools were opened in British settlements, starting from Cape Coast. In the Wesleyan school at Cape Coast, the Society concentrated on work in reading, writing and arithmetic, with occasional addition of history and geography. English, of a sort, was spoken in Cape Coast at that time, and the Wesleyan missionaries did not, as a rule, think it necessary to learn the vernacular which is Fanti. English was not only the language of instruction in Wesleyan schools, but also the language in which both European and African ministers preached their sermons; hymns and lessons were all in that tongue. The vernacular had its turn in the evening church service. In-service teaching-training facilities were provided which served as a model for the other mission schools. F. L. Bartels has observed that the 'roots of formal education in Cape Coast were in the Castle, but the beginning of a co-ordinated educational system is in the Wesleyan (Methodist) experiment at this time'.

The predominantly urban activities of the Wesleyan Mission during the middle of the nineteenth century, where a large child population could facilitate the education and ultimate evangelization of a large number of people, had enabled them to develop a system of day schools utilizing English as the language of instruction. As far as the Wesleyan Church was concerned formal schooling was another form of preaching (Bartels, 1965).

The Wesleyan Church became aware of a two-fold education operating in Cape Coast in particular, and in the other urban areas where it had exerted its influence. One kind of education went on in the real-life situations of the home; it was carried on in the vernacular but without the support of vernacular literature. The other was carried on in the schools, using English as the medium for conveying foreign ideas to a few Africans. This division went through every aspect of the life of the urban population, and will be more apparent as this study progresses.

The African Methodist Episcopal Zion Church (A.M.E. Zion Church) and the Roman Catholic Church followed in the wake of the Wesleyan

Mission and established schools in Cape Coast. By 1926 the Weseleyan Mission and the Roman Catholic Church had each established six assisted primary schools, while the government and the A.M.E. Zion Church had two schools each (Gold Coast Education Department Report, 1926, p. 13).

The Christian missions followed broadly similar curricula in the primary schools: reading and writing with occasional addition of arithmetic and a core of biblical instruction. These schools may be compared with the English 'charity schools' in the provision of education of a rudimentary nature for the 'deserving poor'.

Efforts made by the Wesleyan Mission to establish a technical boarding school in Cape Coast and an agricultural training centre at Beulah, near Cape Coast, where work on the land was to be closely related to instruction in the classroom, were short-lived. In spite of the enthusiastic beginning, within ten years these experiments had failed through lack of public support. So far as the Africans living in the urban environment of Cape Coast were concerned, agricultural and technical schools were not a satisfactory alternative to the usual academic instruction given in Wesleyan institutions. It is worth mentioning that the demand for technical workers came very late in the colonial period. However, the nature of European-controlled commercial enterprises and the bureaucracy made it necessary for employment needs to be oriented towards clerical workers to fill the lower levels of administration. Access to such remunerative employment was more guaranteed by academic than technical or agricultural forms of education.

The growth of urban population in Cape Coast had been the result of economic and social change. Economic change had created more town jobs; and social change had created the need for people with the requisite educational qualifications and training capable of filling those positions. Since Cape Coast was among the first urban areas along the coast of Ghana to be provided with schools, primary as well as secondary, the migrant from rural communities generally had better education there than those who remained in villages. In this regard, Philip Foster has observed that there is reasonable relationship between education and urbanization, indicating that in each of the six principal towns in Ghana (including Cape Coast) educational levels are far higher than for the country as a whole.

In Cape Coast, the demand for education other than primary became so great during the last quarter of the nineteenth century and the beginning of the twentieth century that the Wesleyan Mission at a Synod of 1870 recommended that a 'higher class school', open to boarders as well as day scholars and completely self-supporting, should be established as soon as possible. In the same year the Colonial Governor drew up a scheme which included the establishment, under the auspices of the government, of an Academy in Cape Coast for the more advanced pupils. The curriculum of the 'higher school' was to include, besides grammar and geography, the rudiments of Latin and Greek, Euclid's geometry, and music. Nothing came out of the government proposals, but the scheme indicated a response to African demand for an academic type of education which was relevant to the employment opportunities available in Cape Coast.

Unlike the colonial government, the Wesleyan Mission extended its educational activities beyond the primary level. In 1876 the Society opened its first secondary school for boys in Cape Coast. The Wesleyan Collegiate School, as it was then known, managed to survive, despite a lack of teachers and money, until 1905. In that year the Collegiate School amalgamated with the Fanti Public School established by the African Nationalists in Cape Coast, under the name of Mfantsipim.

Members of the Anglican Church, many of whom had attended the 'Colonial School' established by the S.P.G. in Cape Coast, wanted their children to grow up in the church of their adoption. They pressed for a secondary school, and S.P.G. Grammar School was opened to produce teachers, catechists and priests for the English Church Mission. The school later became known as Adisadel College.

Out of a group of 117 boys who graduated from Mfantsipim School in 1929, 56 entered the government service, 24 took up commercial posts, and the remainder entered various employments including teaching. A similar picture is obtained by looking at the estimates made by the Principal of S.P.G. Grammar School of percentages of graduates of his school for various careers at the same period. He forecast that 26 per cent would enter government service, 31 per cent commerce, 19 per cent would become bank and law clerks and the remainder would enter various employments including teaching and the ministry.

In addition to these schools run by Christian missions, the pressure for higher education of the academic variety came largely from educated Africans. It is significant that all the secondary schools established by Christian missions and private educated Africans were staffed by Africans and largely supported by them at this period, except for short periods when Europeans taught in Wesleyan Collegiate School. A group of African Nationalists, mostly lawyers resident in Cape Coast, established the 'Fanti' Public Schools Company and 'National Education Fund' for the founding of secondary schools in Cape Coast and in every large town in Ghana. Some years later a 'Fanti' National Education Scheme proposed by J. Mensah Sarbah, a Cape Coast lawyer, made reference to the need of establishing secondary or higher-grade schools and scholarships for pupils in aid of a liberal and professional education. These schools, from the social point of view, were fee-paying, highly selective institutions; from the curricular point of view humanistic and literary. A high proportion of pupils attending these schools were the sons of coastal traders, wealthy merchants and lawyers of Cape Coast and the other urban areas, supplemented by children of clerks in government employment and teachers. The future of these pupils was closely associated with the exchange economy and the continued expansion of European commercial enterprise and colonial bureaucracy.

Africans in Cape Coast were involved with the European *élite* in admittedly unequal competition for the highest ranks of the occupational ladder, and access to these posts was determined by the ability to hold equivalent qualifications and to demonstrate their equality with the *élite*. This was achieved to a great degree through education of the academic type. Thus the first African nationalists' attempt at providing Western education in Cape Coast did little to 'Africanize' the content of secondary school course, in spite of their stated intentions. The fact was that they wanted European academic and professional qualifications for their children, and this involved satisfying the demands of examining bodies in England. Besides, formal education through its increasingly close association with the process of occupational recruitment operated as an increasingly significant variable in emergent conceptions of social status. The basis of initial demand for Western education was economic and was a response to new opportunities provided in the urban areas of Ghana by European contact.

The rate of urbanization in Cape Coast was certainly accelerated by the spread of Western education. Westernization, the extension of schooling, Christianity and the growth of the town had all been inter-related. In Cape Coast, the individual's earning power was becoming increasingly related to the level of his education. In this respect, the schools seemed to reflect the bias of the occupational structure in the urban area; and the Africans' demand for academic secondary schools reflected their perception of the differential rewards accorded to persons within this occupational structure.

Teacher-Training Institutions

Schools in Cape Coast had sprung up faster than trained teachers could be provided. Boys were crammed for the College of Preceptors and other English examinations; there were coaches and professional crammers for these examinations. The Wesleyan and Anglican institutions suffered because of a lack of qualified teachers, and so did schools established by private enterprise. The Wesleyan Mission employed the 'British and foreign system of monitorial instruction' in the Cape Coast School. A training institution was attached to the Wesleyan Collegiate school and the English Church Mission established St. Nicholas Training College in Cape Coast. Later St. Augustine's College, managed by the Roman Catholic Church, combined secondary education with a teacher-training department. However, these training institutions could not survive the keen competition offered by the academic secondary schools and were transferred to other towns in Ghana. Up till now there is only one training college, as compared with seven secondary schools, in Cape Coast, while as yet no government-assisted technical school has been established there.

Girls' Education

The process of African adaptation to urban life in Cape Coast involved the growth in importance of the immediate family, as a counter-balance to the decreased importance of the traditional tribal society, an improvement in the status of women and participation with persons of similar cultural or occupational interests to perform functions traditionally the responsibility of kinship organization.

Girls' education has been the concern of the colonial government and the Christian missions. Sir Gordon Guggisberg had remarked in a speech given in 1927 that the men should 'mount the [educational] ladder' with the women. In spite of this expression of intention, the Elliot Commission (1945) observed that the ratio of the number of girls to the total number of pupils in assisted secondary schools was one to eight. However, there were schools in Cape Coast, including a government girls' school, which provided primary education for girls. Besides, there were three girls' schools in Ghana which purported to provide education other than elementary. Two of these schools were in Cape Coast: the Roman Catholic Holy Child School and the Wesleyan Girls' High School. The Wesleyan Girls' High School aimed at inculcating 'the domestic arts and virtues' as well as pursuing courses leading to public examinations. The curriculum of the school included domestic science, laundry, needlework, handwork and elementary school subjects which led to the Cambridge Local Examinations (Preliminary and Junior). In the 1930s there were limited occupations available for literate and educated girls in Cape Coast. The curriculum of the girls' schools reflected the future roles of many of these girls as mothers, as evidenced in the Inspector's report for the year 1930 which stated that the 'present work in Domestic Science is solid . . . the girls are receiving a training that is in line with their needs.'

The direction of change of family life in Cape Coast was towards convergence with the Western family. Monogamy as the Christian way of life occurred more frequently as Western educational standards improved in the urban areas, and it was noticeable among the professional men, senior civil servants, teachers in mission schools and Christian ministers.

Voluntary Associations

A number of voluntary associations sprang up in Cape Coast from mid-nineteenth century to the 1930s. The interests around which they centred may be classified as intellectual and cultural, social and political. Western-educated Africans, in particular, felt the need for integration with those who shared their command of English which made possible the association with Africans belonging to ethnic groups other than their own. Great importance was attached to building up all kinds of clubs and societies to foster social contacts and common interests. At first these associations were modelled on European pattern with local variations. The associations in Cape Coast included the Philanthropic Society, the Rifle Club, the Masonic Club and the Grand Ancient Order of Foresters (Kimble, 1963, p. 147). Literary and Debating Societies also flourished, and reading rooms were opened. English clothing and English names 'became the postulates of Christian life.' According to Edwin A. Smith 'Everyday life in Cape Coast took on the colour of the Victorian era.' (Smith, 1929, p. 43.)

An 'old boys' association of graduates of the secondary schools in Cape Coast was one of the popular associations. Generally, these clubs and associations were short-lived. However, they served not only as a social gathering of Africans with a certain level of formal education, but also helped to maintain the morale and further education of that section of the population upon which the colonial government relied in large part to keep the economy and the administration in the town functioning. These groups also provided the migrant to the town with his first introduction to a new life in urban environment. Voluntary associations have also functioned as a mechanism by which the society effectively and inexpensively taught large numbers of migrants the norms and values they needed to operate in an urban environment. These associations were also places where Africans eventually learned the organizational skills and acquired the ideas that enabled the nationalist movements to recruit the necessary cadres to agitate for independence. Political activity was often conducted under the guise of voluntary associations. Generally, the leadership of these groups overlapped heavily. It was in these associations that the major conflict had occurred between the colonial government and the nationalist movements before independence in 1957.

Education and Christianity

Most educated Africans in Cape Coast were products of mission schools, and accepted their religious teaching as a guide to their Western way of life, and background political thinking. It was in the religious associations, too, that the churches fulfilled educational functions by teaching singing in the choir, reading at Sunday Schools and sewing at Women's Fellowship meetings. They also fulfilled social functions by encouraging and sponsoring service to the sick and needy. The various church associations brought together people of different ethnic groups in the town who shared the same faith.

The social changes brought about by Christianity through its educational institutions went deeper than the formation of church societies. The Christian missionaries were among the earliest bearers of Western culture to Cape Coast. Children in mission schools were trained to be citizens of a minority Western-educated Christian community rather than of the community as a whole. It was through these institutions that Western cultural and social influence was asserted. A reaction set in against this excessive Anglicization. As Nana Anno Adjaye remarked, 'Is God a European? I am a Christian myself, but I do not believe in a Christianity that spells denationalization' (Kimble, 1963, p. 160). Dr Aggrey was making a similar protest when he remarked 'We want to be "civilized" and not "Westernized".'

Furthermore, the training of Africans not only for Church leadership but also for democratic organization, was the basis of Wesleyan mission work in Cape Coast. In the growth of self-governing institutions the churches were usually ahead of government, and promised some African leaders a forum and freedom of expression, both in the pulpit and the press. The Wesleyan Mission was responsible for some of the earliest Gold Coast newspapers printed in Cape Coast which had a reasonably large population. The 'Christian Messenger' was produced in Cape Coast by the Rev. T. B. Freeman as early as 1859. The *Gold Coast Methodist Times*, founded in 1894, was originally intended to follow a strictly religious policy; but later became the outlet for major political grievances. *The Western Echo* was for a number of years 'a source of inspiration to the rising youth in matters relating to the political enfranchisement of the Gold Coast'.

In Cape Coast, newspapers had become increasingly a source of communication before the beginning of the twentieth century, and as education became widespread, had helped to channel latent nationalism into an organized political movement, and to publicize self-improvement organizations and advocate more and better education.

Nationalist Movements

The growth of urban life in Cape Coast allowed nationalist movements to develop. It was in this town in the nineteenth century that there emerged a group of Western-educated African lawyers and merchants who had both the wealth and the leisure to enable them to take part in nationalist politics. In 1889 the 'Mfantsi Amanbuhu Fekuw' (Fanti National Political Society) was founded in Cape Coast. As Mensah Sarbah, one of its members, put it, 'dissatisfied with the demoralizing effect of certain European influence', the society was 'determined to stop further encroachments into their nationality'. It was at the suggestion of this society that Sarbah produced the *Fanti Customary Laws*. Cape Coast was the headquarters of the Gold Coast Aborigines' Rights Protection Society which

existed for the 'avowed purpose of opposing and blocking any action by
the government or by any person which may in the opinion of the members be subversive to their interests, or likely to be prejudicial to their
native customs and canons of land tenure'. Participation in nationalist
politics was effectively limited to those with some command of English.
They alone were able to negotiate with the British governing *élite* and to
read the nationalist press. The rate and direction of social change in Ghana
had in no small way been affected by the urban *élite*, not merely because
some of them held decision-making positions, but also because they
formed the main channel through which external influences acted upon
the community as a whole.

Conclusion

Karl Mannheim suggests that historically, *élites* have always been selected
on the basis of blood, property and achievement. In Cape Coast, the
traditional *élite* was based on blood or lineage. It was the traditional *élite*
who benefited from the process of land alienation, and to some extent
from farming and fishing. As formal education became widespread the
dignity and prestige of the chief suffered greatly. In fact, it was in inverse
proportion to the spread of Western education. Western education then
introduced the principle of achievement, and with it, occupational and
social mobility. Christianity offered the utilitarian advantage of education
which led to wider economic opportunities, as well as contradictory
patterns of behaviour due to the persistence of old beliefs and practices
side by side with the new teaching and practice of Christianity.

As money incomes of educated Africans increased, wealth tended to
accumulate in the hands of younger men, who were more adaptable and
more susceptible to outside influences. Mensah Sarbah in his book *Fanti
Customary Laws* has characterized the structure of an urban society like
Cape Coast. He indicates that in addition to the illiterate masses there were
three groups, differentiated on the basis of educational and occupational
criteria. First, there were those who could barely scrawl their names and
who were restricted to a narrow range of menial occupations. Second,
there were the 'petty clerks' who despised the dignity of labour and were
too idle to improve their status in life by further education. Third, Sarbah
describes the class that was 'known and respected of all men', the professional group. This minority was regarded as exemplifying the benefits
of 'higher education', and was differentiated from the rest of the community by specific cultural characteristics, by the extent to which they
had assimilated European patterns of behaviour and, above all, by their
ability to employ the language of the colonial *élite* which further differentiated them from most traditional rulers. Sarbah's views indicate the
degree to which the Western-educated minority had abandoned tradi-

tional concepts of status and how occupational, economic and educational criteria were replacing traditional evaluation based on blood, lineage and age. In a society like Cape Coast, in which respect and high standing had been accorded to age, this reversal of status brought about a widening dichotomy between the generations. The significance of these changes for the individual might be regarded as a movement toward achieved, as opposed to ascribed, status.

These changes were gradual and partial, rather than sudden and total. Even though the European officials and the Christian missionaries never became an integral part of the Cape Coast community, they introduced economic requirements, political prohibitions, religious attitudes and patterns of behaviour through an alien institution – the schools; and all these have profoundly modified social norms and orientation in Cape Coast down to the present day. The past is not lost.

SELECTED BIBLIOGRAPHY

Tanya Baker and Mary Bird, 'Urbanization and the Position of Women', *Sociological Review,* New Series, Vol. VII, 1959.

F. L. Bartels, *The Roots of Ghana Methodism* (Cambridge: The University Press, 1965).

K. A. Busia, 'The Present Situation and Aspirations of Elites in the Gold Coast' in *Unesco International Social Science Bulletin,* Vol. VIII, No. 3, 1956.

K. A. Busia, *The Position of the Chief in the Modern Political System of Ashanti* (London: International African Institute, Oxford University Press, 1951).

John C. Caldwell, *Population Growth and Family Change in Africa* (London: C. Hurst & Co., 1968).

Brodie Cruikshank, *Eighteen Years on the Gold Coast* (2 vols.) (London: Hurst & Blackett, 1853).

Philip Foster, *Education and Social Change in Ghana* (London: Routledge & Kegan Paul, 1965).

Gold Coast, Census of Population, 1901, 1911, 1921, 1948.

Gold Coast, Census of Population, 1931, Urban Population (Censussed on Form B), pp. 6, 9, 13.

Gold Coast, Report of the Education Department, 1925–26.

Gold Coast, Report of the Education Department, 1926–27, 1927–28, 1929–30, 1930–31.

David Kimble, *A Political History of Ghana, 1850–1928* (Oxford: The Clarendon Press, 1963).

H. O. A. McWilliam, *The Development of Education in Ghana* (London: Longmans, Green, 1959).

J. M. Sarbah, *Fanti Customary Laws* (2nd edition) (London: William Clowes & Sons Ltd., 1904).

Edwin W. Smith, *Aggrey of Africa* (London: Students Christian Movement, 1929).

Section III: Introduction

The Americas

Brian Holmes

The educational systems of North and South America are different but both derive from Europe. Neither system can cope, apparently, with problems arising from the growth of cities.

The case studies show similarities and differences. Chicago increased tenfold from 386,000 in 1900 to about 3,700,000 in 1970 (p. 150). Over 50 per cent live in the metropolitan area outside the central city (p. 150). After 1940 economic and ethnic polarization took place, the centre decayed, people moved out to the suburban areas and, in the fifties, unskilled people looking for jobs moved in (p. 152). As Catholics moved out, Negroes moved in and not more than 6 per cent of the latter are Catholic (p. 157). In New York City the out-migration of whites coincides with the in-migration of Negroes and Puerto-Ricans (p. 124). In Buffalo continued migration from the rural south has increased the socio-economic gap between the blacks and whites. In short the most urgent problems facing city schools in the U.S.A. are exacerbated by the fact that the growth due to in-migration results from the movement not only of people with different attitudes, inferior economic skills and so on, but are black.

Greater Buenos Aires has grown to about eight millions out of a total national population of twenty-three millions (p. 194). The Argentine has a high proportion of culturally backward immigrants (p. 195). Caracas, with a population of two millions, has grown quickly since 1930 and increases at some 3·6 per cent per year (p. 199). Many foreign groups come to the central city but the flow of poorer rural people to the urban area during the period 1945–8 and since 1958 has been tremendous (p. 200). Rio de Janeiro has grown too, as rural people pour into it. Thus one feature of urban educational problems in Latin American cities, as in the U.S.A., is basically that rural people with very traditional peasant attitudes swell the population. Ethnic differences in Latin America are less significant and certainly no one ethnic group dominates the movement. Moreover the pattern or urbanization is different. In the cities described shanty towns are created on the periphery. In Buenos Aires there is a huge belt of *villas-miserias* (p. 195). The slums or *favelas* of Rio house nearly half a million people or about 11 per cent of the population (p. 134). The *barrios* on the hillsides around Caracas house some 600,000, about one-third of the population (p. 200).

Conditions in the decaying central ghettos of North America may from a material viewpoint be very different from the shanty towns of Latin America but they bear a close socio-psychological resemblance (p. 132). They are the source of cheap labour (p. 133) and unemployment is high (p. 131); high crime rates (p. 111), extensive mental illness (p. 115), racial discrimination (p. 111) and poverty are some of the shared characteristics. In the North American cities air and water pollution and housing shortages prevail (p. 111); the shanty towns of Latin America replicate many features of the rural background from which their inhabitants come (p. 196). The attraction of the town grows, but many adults may not be satisfied by higher city wages. The strife-torn cities of the U.S.A. suggest that resentments lie near the surface.

There is agreement among the contributors that education has failed. In Latin America among the many difficulties a very high drop-out rate (p. 197), in Venezuela hardly 30 per cent of rural children finish school (p. 197), highly selective systems based on academic achievement (p. 201) are quoted as serious. In the U.S.A. there is also a widely expressed feeling that the city schools have failed. They are, as far as quality is concerned, in 'a steadily worsening spiral of decline' and the clients of the public schools complain of failure (p. 139). Previously enjoying a higher reputation and having better facilities, the big city schools used to compare very favourably with those of the suburbs (p. 158). No longer. Some of the reasons are evident. Over-crowding, young, less well qualified teachers (p. 163) and a smaller per capita financial base (p. 159) are among the disadvantages now experienced in big city schools.

The main reasons for failure given by the contributors in this section are, however, two. The first is that without the support of other community agencies the schools can do little (pp. 163, 164). The second cause of failure is that faced with groups of people unused to city life, educationists do 'know very little about how to prepare children for life in the city' (p. 110). Most of the cherished values of Western civilization are denied in the cities of the U.S.A. and no more so than in the black ghettos. Yet most of the teachers are white and middle class (p. 124). They continue to preach values which either are irrelevant or seem to be. Educationists have not lost faith in traditional solutions. The community must participate (p. 168) and educationists should be the agents of reconstruction. Now, however, emphasis is on the schools of education and the part they can play. It is proposed that they should not only conduct worthwhile research and train teachers but should become, as in some cases they have (p. 169), actively engaged in the cities. Other proposals include the establishment of educational sub-units within the big city systems and the creation of educational plazas (p. 164).

8

The U.S.A.: Cities and Conurbations

Francis A. J. Ianni

Quite soon now, someone will very likely produce a film entitled 'The Urban Crisis' dramatizing the plight of our sick cities. There will be scenes showing rampant crime in the streets and creeping congestion and pollution everywhere. And somewhere in the film will be a long soliloquy in which Urban Man laments that his technology has made it possible for him to send men to the moon but has yet to produce a learning system which can teach all of his children to read. For, after years of ominous previews, 'the city' has finally emerged as a distinctive way of life and 'the urban crisis' as its own very special disease. There are no case histories, no repository of experience, and no tested cures or antidotes, but 'the disease' is likely to become endemic, for, by the year 1980, nine out of ten Americans will be urban dwellers and the rest of the world is moving in the same direction. Everyone is looking to education as the primary means of preparing man to live a physically, emotionally and socially healthy life in the city and how we are to educate for urban living must become a critical – if not the most crucial – social concern of our day.

Despite the urgency, we really know very little about how to prepare children for life in the city. Our educational system continues to be animated by essentially agrarian values and, despite massive effort, we do little more than try to adapt the traditional educational system to urban needs – or at least what we think are urban needs. If urban man is a different breed from his rural forebears and if the modern metropolis is a distinctly different ecological system for living, then we must develop a new education which grows out of this environment and is responsive to it. Unfortunately, we have yet to take the time to look at what the city is as an environment for learning and so continue to mould children to a confused set of standards. Before urban education can work, we must set the objectives for education for urban living. Before we can even hope to set such objectives we have to recognize that the modern metropolis is not the city of the past.

The City and How it Grew

Up until this century 'the city' has been identified as a concentration of multiple human activities; one recognized a city by the increased intensity of economic, social, and cultural life within geographical boundaries. The city had been a focus for the most sophisticated, civilized aspirations of modern man. A person chose urban living to facilitate and maximize communication, financial stability and cultural exposure. How many heroes relinquished the comfort of small-town life for the unpredictable competitive spirit of the city?

The literary love affair with Metropolis, however, has waned since Horatio Alger. When describing Oakland, California, Gertrude Stein remarked, 'There is no there, there.' She, like countless others, bemoaned the draining of the urban core and the concomitant chaos which seems to have replaced it. As urbania sprouts haphazardly, the exhilaration of a dynamic, visible whole is relegated to nostalgia. We call it 'sprawl', 'scatterization', 'spread-city'; a creeping phenomenon which threatens to deprive us of those qualities which originally defined an urban area. The city has become so unwieldy that we wonder how the psyche can survive in its clutches. The housewife in the city is as earnest as Lewis Mumford: 'What have we done and what can we do?'

What we've done, in the past fifty years, is ooze. Through an acceleration of population and technological development, the urban and suburban complexion has eroded before our eyes. The urban crisis is frequently described as the discrepancy between that acceleration and our capacity to deal with it. The city's amorphous growth cannot contain the demands of contemporary realities; we have thousands of automobiles and inadequate highways, more and more people and decaying housing facilities, debilitating pollution and diminishing retreats, ad infinitum. In Victor Gruen's words, 'We have carelessly strewn around the trash of our civilization and horrified by our own sloppiness, have moved out into the suburbs.'

The symptoms of the urban crisis are overwhelmingly apparent; loss of popular unity due to unmanageable size, conflicts of interest, congestion, air and water pollution, housing shortage, destruction of natural resources, unaesthetic architecture, poverty, racial discrimination, staggering crime rate. It is almost universally acknowledged that the city is crippled, and that it is crippling us. The suburban exodus accelerates each year. Between 1950–9, there was a 1·5 per cent population increase in American cities, as compared with a 44 per cent increase in the suburbs. But as becomes increasingly apparent, suburbia is only a temporary phenomenon. If the prophecies are fulfilled, we shall have run out of suburban space before too long.

In the era of the urban plague, panaceas are offered constantly. Much of metropolitan planning is based on the premise that the city contradicts all those values which Western civilization cherishes and so let's change the city back toward those values. If we need peace and quiet, then let's get rid of the traffic. If we need solitude, then construct self-contained habitats. People need recreational facilities, so let's build more parks. No human being should be assaulted by the billboards, gas stations, dilapidated shacks of 'sub-cityscape'; it contradicts and offends all the aesthetic expectations of western man. In short, urban diagnosis and prescription and, consequently, the educational programmes we design for urban areas, are directed toward the preservation of classical tradition. Human nature is being opposed and threatened in the 'anti-city' and we have to resolve the conflict.

Perhaps the 'urban crisis' can be more easily handled and understood as the 'human crisis'. Our cities, after all, did not move in on us like malevolent monsters in search of our souls. The city, and its outskirts, is no more than a reflection of specific human behaviours. We cannot cure the disease without examining the germ, and man is the ultimate source of infection in his society. It is tempting to sever the city from its people, but the result is merely confusing and self-deluding. We, whether haphazardly or purposefully, have created this urban environment. Somehow we have to learn to live with it. And that becomes the gargantuan task of education.

The city is an extreme expression of man's social, economic, and political evolution. As the process advances, and the mechanisms are further complicated, what begins as an expression becomes an exaggeration. Sounds, sights, institutions, compete with each other for attention, and one finds oneself in an environmental hall of mirrors. The closer an individual clings to his self-image, the more distorted the reflection seems. Looking for the pastoral life in Metropolis is an odyssey of futility, and subsequent frustration. Perhaps it is time we stopped and learned to live with as well as in cities.

Antiquated Values in an Urban World

The city as it exists today, contains blatant contradictions to Western man's self-image, an image which is patent in our traditional educational programmes. The traditional concepts of tranquillity, communion with nature, solitude, pleasure in harmony, knowledge as an intrinsic good and happiness through personal relationships are not functional in the modern world of urbanization. The dangers of this may seem remotely academic but, 'It is an accepted fact that neuroses develop when an environment makes it impossible for a person to achieve the ambitions and goals that he has been taught in youth to believe within his grasp, if only he sincerely strives . . . there is also the cheerful school of thought which believes that most urban miseries exist only in the minds of those who are possessed of an incurable rural nostalgia'.[1]

---

[1] Edward Higbee, *The Squeeze: Cities Without Space* (New York: Apollo Editions, 1960) p. 10.

Urban man must find much of what is in traditional education confusing as he makes his way in life. Most of what we emphasize in our values still harks back to the Western philosophical and literary tradition which gives high positive marks to beauty and tranquillity of the communion with nature. It is rather difficult, however, to 'wander lonely as a cloud' in the midst of the bustling city. The first and most obvious obstacle is the noise . . . the screeching of automobiles, taxis, and buses, the occasional assault of a siren, not to mention the constant chatter of passing crowds, hinder and are likely to prevent a single man's concentration. If he needs or thinks he needs quiet, he is doomed, for there is no escape from the din. A city dweller has no idea of silence; at best the sounds of the city are sufficiently muffled for him to think, to relax, or to sleep. For his survival, his natural sense of hearing must be blocked out, and only extraordinary noises provide auditory stimuli. He no longer expects quiet; on the contrary, he is unduly worried if a street is quiet.

The common cry of the commuter, as he hustles off to his suburban retreat, is the need for quiet. But, even in his potentially quiet home, the mass media invade. Television and radio are as prevalent as bread-boxes and the noises of the news, of war, of simulated violence, bombard his living room with the ferocity of the city. The sole remnant of his noiseless haven is a quiet sleep.

The effects on those deprived of silence are already apparent. Inherent in 'rock' music is the value of volume. The shrill scream of an electric guitar, the persistence of drums, have satisfied a generation of music lovers – a generation which is frequently indifferent to the ease of the romantic ballads of our youth. They are moved, elated, and in a sense, calmed by a sound which conquers all others. Outdoor lectures are interrupted by airplanes, legitimate plays often vie with the noises of the street, but a 'rock' concert obliterates the technological clamour.

The age of the jet has further affected many suburban areas. 'Noise-abatement' movements have sprung up in the territory surrounding the airport. Sitting in the backyard on a Sunday afternoon is a lesson in stamina, and talking on the telephone is a series of pauses when flights are heavily scheduled. A few years ago, the Federal Bureau of Investigation confiscated anti-aircraft weapons in the attic of a desperate American suburbanite. With the arrival of the super-sonic jet and the sonic boom, more attics may need investigation.

The Western philosophical and literary tradition has also consistently emphasized man's need for fresh air, open spaces, fields, and forests. The so-called simple life of working with the soil has characterized the beginnings of all nations, but some of us have outgrown it – either through destruction of natural resources during urban development, or disinterest after city living. The sounds of the farm are romantic, antiquated notions for much of the urban population. For many city children, a pig is the funny-looking animal in the zoo. But they do have their own familiar sights as well as sounds through which to learn about their world.

In addition to substituting sidewalks for dirt, pocket parks for country-side, and skyscrapers for sky, those natural sights which persist have been polluted in the process. The rivers which attracted urban growth origin-ally are now lined with dismal factories and contaminated almost beyond recognition. The air itself is clouded by the particles of technology. We have obstructed the view, and surrendered the reason for looking anyway.

So, to get back a patch of green, urbanites swarm to the outskirts of the blemished city. But the suburb is the limbo between rural and urban life. Trees are cut down to make room for housing developments, playing fields are filled with shopping centres, and the airports expand into wilder-ness. We have to travel further and further to escape citified suburbia, only to find billboards promising the eventual development of untouched locations. In Victor Gruen's appropriate analogy, we behave like sloppy picnickers. We look around for a suitable site, and once we've settled in with all the luncheon paraphernalia, the spot has ceased to be attractive. We blame it on our choice (never on our debris) and move on to a new place. The process repeats itself until all we can see is a succession of sloppy picnic grounds.

Now that we and nature have parted ways, another relationship is offering its bid. The urban kaleidoscope, the barrage of sensory stimuli, affords an entirely different ecological framework. Whereas man once found solace in natural proportions, took pleasure in the ordinary, he now requires the gigantic dimensions of his self-made environment. The head-lines, the cinema, the urgency of every news broadcast, exhaust his capacity for drama. He is distracted by the outlandish, the preposterous, and has been forced into anaesthesia by the unrelenting pitch of urban emergency. His survival has hinged on apathy. 'Focused on the exciting and extreme, man is becoming indifferent to average dimensions, though these are the dimensions of mankind. The charm of the small has been transformed into the cult of the cute; indifference has become contempt. Moreover, for the man in the street, not involved in chemistry or nuclear physics, the minute has but partial interest. Only the supercolossal, such as a manned vehicle sent to the moon, or the shocking, such as a ghastly mur-der committed around the corner, really hold him.'[2]

It has been disclosed, for example, that American children have not been impervious to their nation's recent history of assassination. In several cases, when told of illness or deaths in the family, youngsters asked if their adult relatives had been assassinated. According to the psychologists involved,

[2] Serge Chermayelf and Christopher Alexander, *Community and Privacy: Toward a New Architecture of Humanism* (New York: Doubleday-Anchor, 1963).

the children inquired as a matter of course – not to arouse or display horror. With the turbulence of history tuned in with the frequency of a family member, the children of today will surely surpass their parents in conditioned awareness of violence, war, and the brutality of contemporary society.

The increasing complexity of stimuli has evoked comparable responses. In a recent psychopathological study of Yorkville, a middle-class section of New York City, the following findings were reported: Of the 1,660 residents of Yorkville; 18·5 per cent were mentally well, 36·3 per cent mildly disturbed, 21·8 per cent moderately disturbed, 23·4 per cent impaired.[3] Urban men have not been unscathed by their funhouse.

The Reaction of the Young

This loss of simplicity in modern man is often painful, and sometimes unbearable, particularly to young people. The 'hippie' movement in the United States originated as a reaction against technological complexity, and its accompanying pressures. The first hippies were actually clinging to the values of eighteenth-century America, and found them incompatible with the contemporary United States. The openness, the enthusiasm, and the warmth of a nation in infancy have been extinguished by that country's development. Many young people concluded that it was an unworthy battle of survival, and 'dropped out', first from the school which they found absurd, and then from society which they found intolerant.

Before the hippies became profitable for the mass media they were comprised of a few sincere, young adults, many of whom had the ability, but not the inclination, to 'make it' in the world that had been created for them. They attempted to delete all those characteristics which threaten to separate us from each other, and from ourselves. They substituted the flower for the dollar, reconstructed innocence in a land of scepticism, and followed barefoot in the steps of pointed-toed, high-heeled shoes. What seemed so shocking was their lack of a 'programme'; they knew society was wrong, but had both the innocence and the honesty to admit that they had no alternative as yet.

The resentment which bombards the hippies is ironic. The common complaints deal with their economic backgrounds; people are somehow offended that the children of the middle class dare to threaten those tenets which have, after all, been under close scrutiny for a long time. That most Western religions are drenched in the values of community, brotherhood, sharing, scorn for material goods, allows a certain sense of martyrdom to the hippie movement, and seems irrelevant or insignificant to the infuriated public.

---

[3] Edward Higbee, op. cit., pp. 9–10.

That the movement began apolitically and functioned as a 'leave us alone' fringe has not minimized the resentment. At a recent convention of psychiatrists in New York, selected hippies were invited to discuss the 'generation gap' with participating doctors. The young people were received warmly, and at the end, rather approvingly. One psychiatrist maintained that the anger which often victimizes the hippies is, more accurately, jealousy. Many people, the doctor claimed, would gladly relinquish the pressures of modern society, if they had the courage and/or stamina.

Liquor has always been a sufficient means of escape in social situations. Following the recent death of a Columbia student, it was disclosed that his death was caused by an overdose of opium, and that 85 per cent of the undergraduate population had tried marijuana at least once (*New York Times*). The statistics on drug traffic in America are staggering, and cannot be exclusively blamed on organized crime. The growing use of marijuana and LSD among offspring of the middle class, and heroin more specifically among the poor, is symptomatic of the inadequacy of our old means of relaxation. We require more powerful stimuli and depressants to accomodate the frenetic atmosphere of 1970. Since the atmosphere is unlikely to slow down, the use of drugs may well increase with the societal pace.

'Psychedelia' has so invaded our culture that Madison Avenue can hardly adapt quickly enough. There are entertainment spots in New York, like 'The Electric Circus', where liquor is *verboten*. One either comes in 'high on pot', or concentrates his energies on the myriad of lights. Pop-pot culture, pepsi-cola vases, beach-ball chairs, love beads in the kitchen, the realm of 'camp' are indications of the texture, sounds, and sights which reach our sensibilities. Stanley Kubrick still marvels at the youthful audience he attracted with *2001: A Space Odyssey*, though he claims to have been oblivious to the McLuhan generation in devising the special effects.

In so far as a work of art reflects the society of the artist, the effects of our technological and urban development can be found in the theatre, painting, literature, etc. Dadaism responded to a world gone mad during World War I, in the same way that pop art has scorned a mechanized, de-individualized atmosphere. The hamburger and the Campbell soup can are still life for today's youngsters. The Theatre of the Absurd, more fashionable in the 1950s and early 1960s than now, has served as a desperate scream against automation and social conformity. Much of contemporary literature is a battle against classical forms; if the world has no continuity, no beginning, middle, or end, why should a story? The Living Theatre, Julian Beck and Judith Malina's *enfant terrible*, came back from a European exile to an extraodinary welcome. We have grown accustomed to formless aesthetic experiences, and the critics greeted their chaos with a new-found respect. The Aristotelian structure has been replaced by an arena for confrontation; the barrier between art and audience is giving way to a frantic fusion and confusion. The pervasive mediocrity of modern architecture is the nemesis for many urban critics. They claim that the 'look' of our cities, the distasteful pile of garbage which we have to live with, assaults our sensibilities, and inevitably deadens our awareness. In short, we have gone blind from sore eyes, and are impervious to beauty. Architecture, much more than the other arts, has function to consider, but the disorganized, incomplete quality of our buildings and structures contradicts our classical precepts, in much the same way as $8\frac{1}{2}$ is not *Gone With the Wind*. We look for the Acropolis, and find the skyscraper. Our error, perhaps, is in looking for Doric columns when we'll find telephone poles in their place. The possibility of deriving pleasure from harmony is non-existent in a sea of clutter. When symmetry is the consideration of land developers, we come up with the sort of uniformity which carries monotony to a new high. Frequently, financial and political limitations produce uninspired architecture, and we feel doomed to faceless buildings.

In every aspect of its life, in its sounds, its sights, and its functioning, the city differs from the social and physical world enshrined in our value system. Yet, while our young people and children see the lack of it between the picture painted by our values and the real world, our schools do not because we have, after thousands of years of civilization, succeeded in defying our value system. They expect peace and find violence, look for a river and instead discover liquid muck, demand justice and get expediency. And then, when our children are shocked by the fallibility of those inherited 'truths', we wonder why growing up involves such an upheaval. White men are appalled by the demands of black men, yet, the principle of those demands has been swallowed *a priori*. It is the cliché discrepancy between preaching honesty and being less than honest in paying one's income tax. The so-called 'urban crisis' is just another way of saying that we have never changed our 'idea' of ourselves in the course of our development. We cling to a self-image which may have been erroneous from the outset, but is now so removed from the reality of twentieth-century life, that we may be subsumed by the environment we have created.

Having established the blatant contradictions of urban living, how is the educational system reconciling them? First of all, what is education supposed to accomplish? The universal view of the learning process includes: (1) preparing a child to succeed in his environment; (2) acquiring skills to achieve that success; (3) instilling moral values in the learner which will allow him to contribute to society and his immediate community; (4) dispensing information which will develop his sense of history, the arts, the sciences; (5) developing his critical and analytical abilities (teach him how to 'think').

Educating Urbanites

Judging from the dominance of the city in the western hemisphere, one would assume that our children are being trained to function in it. For the most part, the school succeeds in providing the tools of language, a general competence for approaching the various disciplines, and a degree of exposure to cultural activities. In the mechanical sense, then, the school does provide a general basis for learning; its teachers pass along the alphabet, train children in multiplication tables, and keep plants on the window sill. Even in this preliminary area, however, some secondary-school students still read on a third-grade level, and many educated thirty-year-olds have trouble computing percentages. Our competence in this first, most obvious level of education is not entirely foolproof. There is a thriving business in remedial reading centres, private tutoring in subject areas, and functionally illiterate high school drop-outs, indicating that the schools are not equipping every child maximally. What we eventually do is blame the student (bad grades, punitive measures) for the inability of the school to train him in basic, mechanical areas.

One premise of educational philosophy is that knowledge is intrinsically good: that the learning experience is a pleasurable one, and the 'best' children are those who enjoy their homework. In an urban society, knowledge is *not* a luxury, but a necessity, and education in America is not voluntary, but compulsory. What was once considered esoteric is commonplace for the masses of the United States. For the nineteenth-century farmer, the acquisition of knowledge was a diversion, something he earned after a hard day of work. With technological progress, informed opinions are a necessity, an integral part of the working day. Now that we have machines to do menial jobs, men are forced to have more-than-menial concerns.

Children are told they study history so that civilization can learn from its mistakes. They are also taught the ancient activities of men as if there were a logical continuity, a network of reason superimposed on the world. Nothing is more apparent to the average person than man's persistence in repeating his mistakes; the first world war did not prevent the second, John Kennedy's assassination did not prevent Robert Kennedy's, one summer of riots was not followed by a quiet one, *ad infinitum*. And, the so-called network of reason which pervades history books belongs to the author, because he requires order for expression. A school need not prepare prophets of futility, but often that is *exactly* what they do. If one is deluded into believing in a unified humanity, if he expects to grow up to a rational, purposive universe, he is bound to be disillusioned. Why must his intellectual energies exhaust themselves in that recognition? By giving our youngsters a view of history *we* do not believe, we simply waste their time, and obstruct their ability as adults. Inadvertently, we render our children impotent.

In our socio-political traditions, democracy is the only form of government, and anyone opposed to it must necessarily be a villain. Democracy, it is learned, is a synonym for freedom, and the United States is a country of participatory democracy, a living monument to 'the general will', a place where anyone can do what he wants. But, if you are caught smoking in the bathroom, you will be suspended. 'Show me your late pass!' 'What do you mean you have to go to the lavatory, the class has just begun.' 'Your skirt is too short'. 'Your hair is too long'. And five minutes after the harangue, those same children reiterate 'with liberty and justice for all'. The phenomenon of this paradox is that we somehow expect youngsters to swallow it, absorb it, and live by it. And we have been convinced of its validity.

Until now, the uprising of students all over the world has not been an impulsive accident, nor the direct result of a communist conspiracy to overthrow our institutional equilibrium. Millions of parental hands have been thrown up in despair: 'What have we done?' Well, just about everything. No one likes being duped, and students everywhere have been the victims of their ancestors' self-deceit; in 1970, the extent of deceit has never been more blatant. The gap between what we are taught in the classroom and what exists, is now an abyss. The ever-popular 'generation gap' is no more than our societal schizophrenia. It is not so much a question of age as of non-functional absolute values failing in a chaotic unreasonable world.

This notion of democracy is not the only discrepancy in the classroom. Nearly all American children have been nurtured by George Washington's proverbial honesty in admitting to chopping down the cherry tree. Moral of story: it is *always* better to tell the truth than to lie. An hour later in the faculty lounge, a concerned teacher protects one of his students by blaming himself. Any adult who maintains that truth is consistently preferable to fiction risks being institutionalized. And honesty is not always attractive in a student. If a teacher notices a child yawning, and asks him why he is tired, he could lie: 'I stayed up all night', or tell the truth, 'Because you're boring me'. It would take an inordinately self-confident teacher to control his anger.

The alternative method to this fallacious preaching need not extol lying. The first question to answer is: How do men behave in regard to truth-telling and lying? Perverse lying, after all, is not admirable. Truth is preferable to fiction when the circumstance allows it. But, the circumstance does not always allow it. Arbitrarily blurting out exactly how one feels is not a constant virtue, nor a constant vice. Learning the difference is an infinitely more arduous prospect, and there can never be a definite conclusion to live by. Even a partial discussion of the problem, however, is better than delusion.

Again, emphasizing the relative nature of political systems does not imply that we suddenly preach communism in our schools. This has undoubtedly been the fear of the defenders of educational absolutism. It seems that straightforwardness in the classroom is a threatening prospect for some; it eases the academic controls. There will always be a parent somewhere accusing his child's teacher of 'pink' tendencies, or weak moral fibre. Intimidated by the thought of that parent, we have persisted in our pedagogical ignorance. The consequences of our 'expediency' cannot be blamed so much on Mark Rudd and Cohn-Bendit, as on the intellectual hypocrisy which provokes their anger.

The American high school offers 'academic', or college preparatory, and 'technical/vocational' programmes; the objective is to supply some students with a liberal arts foundation, and others with sound technical training. The academic adjustment of college freshmen – the changeover from secondary school to university life – can be attributed to several considerations. Many eighteen-year-old youngsters in the United States are academically coddled ('Here are the questions on your exam tomorrow; I want this class to do well.'), deprived of the tools of scholarship by teachers too lazy to grade term papers, and exposed to behavioural choices for the first time. After years of doctor's excuses, faked colds, understanding mothers on lovely spring days, a professor tells him he doesn't have to come to class if he doesn't feel like it. He goes crazy. He's delirious. He cuts the class for the pure pleasure of not having to go. He stays up all night because no one is around to make him go to sleep. Many college students spend their freshmen year in a state of exhiliration, then exhaustion, and final exam hysteria. That he doesn't experience this kind of self-experimentation until he is eighteen years old is a horrifying reflection on his previous experience – at home and in school.

In college, a student is required to submit cogent papers, analyse a topic in depth, and participate in class discussion. A good part of his English studies course in high school is wasted on literary classics for 'young adults', like *Junior Miss*, *A Date With Judy*, *ad infinitum*. Shakespeare is thrown in occasionally, the Mark Antony speech is memorized, and, for the most part, a clever high school student can survive on classic comics. What a pleasure it is in college, to get rid of those enormous, unattractive textbooks, and substitute paperback editions of Herman Melville, Henry Commager, Charles Darwin.

A strong foundation of the humanities is built on familiarity with the Greeks and the Bible. How much of art and literature requires a knowledge of Greek mythology; this subject is just coming into the classroom on a junior high school level. As for the Bible, the Old and New Testaments, we have circumvented it by separation of church and state. Yet, the Western World is immeasurably influenced by the Bible. It is often said that all of philosophy is a footnote to Plato, but he is omitted from most high school curricula. The 'classics', the girders of the liberal arts tradition, are not considerations in the American high school, and its graduates are deprived of a general framework for concentration in the humanities.

For the non-college-bound students, technical facilities depend upon the school's area. But, they too suffer enormously from the ineffective educational system. Their teachers in major subject areas – i.e., English, Social Studies – ought to be better than those in the college preparatory programme. Their need, after all, is greater. That so many American youngsters achieve any proficiency of thought and action is a tribute to them; they are learning *in spite* of the schools. But the unmotivated children, the prospective drop-outs, require first-rate people who can communicate the necessity of fluency, and proceed to ensure it for them.

The Urban Cure

'The Urban Crisis' is a euphemism. We can continue blaming our cities for the diseases of humanity, but this will only alleviate, not cure, the essential difficulty. Yes, less traffic, cleaner air, more parks, and so on are necessary to prevent technological strangulation. But technological strangulation is one aspect, one symptom of the enormity of man's self-delusion, and merely accelerates the urgency.

If there is a crisis in urban living it centres very distinctly on our failure to prepare our children for life in the city. And this failure grows out of our own lack of ability to comprehend this new way of life and use it as the basis for planning educational programmes. We are still involved in the grand search for new models for urban education. What we find ranges from a return to the primitive system of learning by doing and observing in nature, which some of the social critics of education romanticize, to the electronic take-over of the schools by the computer. In each case, however, the problem remains one of trying to adopt and adapt 'revolutionary' new methods for an educational system which marches to a different drummer than the one beating cadence for the real world. If we are to educate for urban living then we must develop a comprehensive set of educational objectives which are consonant with life in the city and *then* develop the techniques and approaches which are the means to these ends. For here, the questions are not 'Where do we look for new models for education' or 'What will the urban school of the future look like?' or even 'What kind of structure shall we build to house the process of urban education?' The ultimate question becomes 'What is the code of rules that make for healthy living in the city and how do we prepare people to play this game?' By observing, recording, and analysing these rules, we can define the optimal educational objectives for educating urban youngsters and then try to attain them.

Robert Redfield (1897–1958), a great American anthropologist, used to tell a fable about a hen who was giving a survival lecture to her chicks, precariously balanced on the roof of a chicken coop, while they were being swept downstream by a flash flood. One of the lesson units in her hurried curriculum concerned future sources of food supply, but as she looked at the trees of the forest along the banks of the river, she realized that she remembered very little about forests because she had been away from them so long, and that she wasn't doing too well in telling the chicks about food sources in the forest. So she called out to a wise old owl that she saw in the trees interviewing other wild birds about their reaction to this stress-provoking flood. 'Professor Owl,' she said, 'won't you be my consultant and help me teach my chicks about life in the wood, for you stay there and study it and are indeed a wise old owl.' But the owl had overheard what the hen had been telling the chicks, and he was astonished and appalled at her scientifically inaccurate and superficial information. Besides, he was anxious to proceed with his interviewing and hurry back to his study to speculate on how individuals react when placed suddenly in a new and frightening situation, for he was working on a paper on this subject. So he pretended not to hear the hen and went on with his interviewing. Left to her own devices, struggling to maintain order among her chicks, and occasionally having to grasp at one as it fell off the coop into the water, she went on as best she could and described what she thought food sources in the forest would be like. The chicks, as resilient and eager as chicks everywhere, took rather well to it, and later, when the coop finally came to rest far, far downstream, the chicks bade farewell to their mother hen and set off bravely to begin their adult lives – in a treeless meadow.

Three problems for chickens, owls, and humans emerge from the adventures of mother hen and her chicks: First, how do we go about making sure that the owls and the chickens talk to each other before the flood? Secondly, how do we take into account in educational planning the fact that the chicks we are preparing for life in the forest may have to face life in a desert? Thirdly, how do we get owls, who know a great deal about forests but not much about chicks, to work with hens, who know all about chicks but can't see the forest for the trees?

9

The Americas: The University, the Ghetto and the Favela

The universities must turn toward the problems of the urban society and provide service to the cities, the lower classes and the poor.

Clark Kerr, *Chairman, Carnegie Commission on the Future of Higher Education*

Unless the university involves itself in service, eventually it will be ignored.

Charles Abrams, *Chairman, Department of City Planning Columbia University*

Gordon Edwards

America's foremost educators and urbanologists are 'up tight' about the future of democracy and the American education system. Many fear that 'America is moving towards two societies, one black and one white – separate and unequal.'[1] The rapidly expanding black ghetto has had a profound impact on cities and educational systems. Washington, D.C., Gary, Indiana, and Newark, New Jersey, are already over 50 per cent Negro. In ten years, ten more American cities will become predominantly black. If recent trends continue, ten more cities will have a black majority by 1984.[2]

The cutting edge of communications between the black community and the white community is the riot or demonstration or disturbance. The whites read the message of the riots to mean that blacks wanted a bigger slice of the good life – the American dream – that blacks wanted more and better jobs, education and housing. Black Panther leader Eldridge Cleaver said it like it is: 'We cannot accept anything less than that black people, like white people, have the best lives technology is able to offer at the present time. Black people know what's going on. They're aware of this country's productivity and they want in on the good life.'[3]

This reading was correct but the method of correcting the injustices of the past is equally important. The blacks were not only demanding a larger share of the nation's resources; they wanted a larger voice in determining how these resources were to be used. They wanted self-determination, they wanted to create black institutions and black businesses and they wanted

---

[1] Report of the National Advisory Commission on Civil Disorders, (Washington, D.C.: United States Government Printing Office, March 1, 1968), p. 1.

[2] ibid., New Orleans (1971), Richmond (1971), Baltimore (1972), Jacksonville (1972), Cleveland (1975), St. Louis (1978), Detroit (1979), Philadelphia (1981), Oakland (1983), Chicago (1984), p. 216.

[3] *Playboy*, December 1968. Interview with Eldridge Cleaver and *Playboy* magazine. Vol. 15, no. 12, p. 90.

to own and operate them. There was a deeper concern about 'getting ourselves together.' Nowhere was this more evident than in education.

The shift in urban population from white to black has had a dramatic impact on the control of educational policy, teacher hiring practices and curriculum. In the fall of 1968 the New York City school system was paralyzed by teacher strikes. The cause of the turmoil was black power, black self-determination and the breakdown of a traditional school system which was not relevant or responsive to black needs or demands.

In 1954, 29 per cent of the elementary school population of New York City was made up of Negro and of Puerto Rican children; a decade later the figure was 50·5 per cent, and today it is even larger. This rapid change in the racial composition of the schools is the product of city in-migration by Negroes and Puerto Ricans and of out-migration by whites: net white emigration between 1955 and 1960 was 365,000, an average of 200 every day. The vast majority of city teachers are white. This increase in the number of deprived black children occurred in a city beset with budgetary problems of crisis proportions; a city which was inflexible and incapable of responding to the challenge. Even before the public schools went black, many middle-class New Yorkers took their children out of the public schools, and put them in private schools.

As the number of black children increased, the school system did not change to meet their needs. Tensions grew. In an effort to reform the system from above, the city decided to make demonstration models of certain school districts including the Ocean Hill-Brownsville section of Bedford-Stuyvesant in Brooklyn. Here authority was granted to community school boards, partly chosen by the mayor and a central education agency. The Ocean Hill-Brownsville demonstration failed when the governing board tried to oust white teachers which it felt were not sympathetic to the community or black control. The teacher's union resisted such firings and closed down the city's school system. The moribund bureaucratic system was too slow to change and the agonizing adjustment to the new realities could come only through the confrontation of the white-dominated United Federation of Teachers and the New York City School System. A confrontation by black people demanding control of their schools and relevant education for their children followed.

After the riots in Watts (Los Angeles), the children were reluctant to return to school. They said, 'Why should we go back to school and interrupt our education?' As Marshal McLuhan has observed,

Our 19th Century school and college systems, based on fragmented subjects and classified data which derive from the old hardware environment, cannot relate to the new integral electric environments of information.

Unfortunately, as Stephen Carr and Kevin Lynch have observed,

Schools are conservative institutions normally closed to the world around them and obsessed with the training of 'skills.' Formal education looks to the filling of career slots, certifying performance by a succession of numbers, grades, and diplomas. For the poor, and especially for the black poor, schools fail to do even this much. For many, as Peter Drucker points out, schooling has become a way of filling time, sometimes a way of staying alive, more often a way of postponing entry into work. In a more reasonable society, time has other uses.[4]

In the city of Buffalo, New York, the State University of New York at Buffalo developed a storefront education experiment as an attempt to provide an alternative educational opportunity to the formalized school system. The storefronts were designed to overcome some of the problems of the traditional education systems.

The Buffalo Storefront Education Experiment

There were riots in Buffalo's ghetto in July of 1967 and again in April of 1968 after the assassination of Dr. Martin Luther King. Many stores were fire-bombed along Jefferson Avenue, the main street of Buffalo's ghetto. One storefront operation was not burned. It was the Woodlawn Education Information Center, sponsored by the State University of New York at Buffalo together with seven other colleges in the area.[5] The concept was simple: to 'hustle' or sell education in the same way as the old storefront churches hustled religion, right on the street where the action is. Ghetto residents had learned that the small Jefferson Avenue store was a place where they could obtain accurate, honest information about education, jobs and a variety of other problems. It was one place where hostile blacks and bewildered whites talked to each other freely.

The Center was headquarters for people who wanted to 'cool it', to find an alternative to violence. It was for people more concerned with building the future than burning the past. The blacks respected the Center because it was theirs. It was the only educational institution in the ghetto operated by blacks for blacks. President Martin Meyerson expressed the university perspective as: 'The storefronts were designed to provide a two-way channel for communication and information between the institutions and the communities in which the centres are located. They provided a meeting ground for the development of communication and understanding of the problems of ghetto life.' Early in 1967, two other storefronts had opened – one in the grim First Ward of Lackawanna and another in the Buffalo ghetto. In mid-1968 a fourth, in the Niagara Falls black community, was opened.

---

4 *Daedalus*, Fall, 1968, Vol. 97, No. 4, pp. 1277–1278.
5 The consortium included Canisius College, D'Youville College, Erie County Technical Institute, Niagara County Community College, Niagara University, Rosary Hill College, State University College at Buffalo and State University of New York at Buffalo.

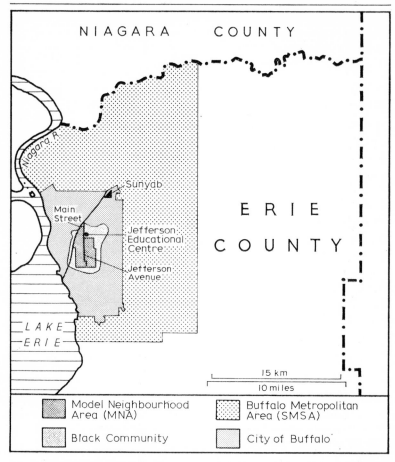

NIAGARA COUNTY

Niagara R.

Sunyab

Main Street

Jefferson Educational Centre

Jefferson Avenue

ERIE COUNTY

LAKE ERIE

15 km

10 miles

Model Neighbourhood Area (MNA)

Buffalo Metropolitan Area (SMSA)

Black Community

City of Buffalo

The Buffalo Metropolitan Area

The Storefront Education Centers developed in response to demands for education and service programmes. Essentially they were an innovative experimental programme and facility-designed to demonstrate how the resources of the universities and colleges in the region can help people in the ghetto to help themselves. They were financed by a series of federal grants under Title I of the Higher Education Act of 1965. The following are examples of education services offered.

High School Equivalency Instruction In response to requests for an informal type of high school equivalency programme, small classes were organized. This programme was instituted only after efforts toward placing those desiring it in the school system's regular equivalency classes had failed. Those regular classes are, of necessity, more structured; the storefronts' classes were informal and allowed the students to work at their own pace.

While this was an indirect criticism of the school system's existing programme, that of the storefronts was organized merely to serve those who could not, or would not, take advantage of the other programme. Even more important, the school system initiated its own storefront education system some two years later.

Remedial Reading With the co-operation of the Community Aid Corps, a student group on the campus of the State University of New York at Buffalo, plus volunteers from most of the other member institutions of the Co-operative Urban Extension Center, remedial reading instruction was offered to many ghetto youngsters who had fallen behind their grade level. The 120 student volunteers worked under the supervision of a professional remedial reading instructor.

Tutoring Some 130 student volunteers, from the co-operating institutions, provided individual tutoring for ghetto men, women and children.

Computer education This programme trained some 35 ghetto residents in the basics of computer programming. This preliminary training has permitted a number of them to go on to more advanced programmes at Erie County Technical Institute, or to on-the-job training.

The first project director was bright, energetic and committed but unfortunately he was a white Ph.D. from the State University of New York at Buffalo's School of Education. At the outset of the project on January 1st, 1967, Dr Frank P. Besag said:

It is not the place of the university and colleges to tell the community what is needed but rather that the university and colleges find, through interaction with the community, what contribution can be made and then seek, in conjunction with the community, to fulfill the needs.

Dr Besag's rejection of worn-out paternalism was not just fashionable rhetoric, as was the case with many federal poverty programmes which call for 'maximum feasible citizen participation'. He made it work. It was the old American philosophy of pragmatism. What is impressive is that the storefront project adhered to the policy in practice. The device for achieving citizen participation was the steering committee. The steering committee grew out of the active involvement and interaction of neighbourhood residents.

The steering committee was essential to the success of the project. Mainly through the mechanism of the democratically-constituted steering committee, the director and his staff scrupulously maintained a posture of meeting needs expressed by the community. The steering committee was, in the opinion of its members (who were residents of the neighbourhoods surrounding the centres), a body which makes policy decisions subject only to the limitations of the budget, which was the responsibility of its parent organization, the Co-operative Urban Extension Center, which represented the colleges and university. As one member put it: 'The steering committee really runs the programme. That's what makes it good, not like other agencies somewhere else. When outside people run things you're a flunky or a fool.' Another remarked: 'Sometimes we don't agree with the director and when we don't we can put him down.' On balance, however, some members felt that there was 'too much red tape; the policy goes through too many hands'. But significantly, there was no feeling that decisions made by the steering committee were frustrated or distorted elsewhere, only that the committee would welcome a greater ability to implement its decisions autonomously, including those of a financial sort. In time, this objective was partially achieved and the administrative network was rationalized to give the steering committee, later reconstituted as the Board of Directors, even greater decision-making powers.

In retrospect, the composition of the steering committee turned out to be the key to achieving a successful community orientation, and 'maximum feasible citizen participation'. Many programmes have floundered because of an effort to select staff members from among the hard core, urban poor or rural migrant peasants who are emotionally unprepared to make a constructive contribution; perhaps being either too hostile or too apathetic or too diffident for such participation. Or, even more important, the citizens were never given any decision-making responsibility. The citizens were never represented in the 'power structure'. They felt their views were not expressed. As Eldridge Cleaver said: 'Remember how the War on Poverty looked on paper and how it worked out? You may recall that of all the organizations around then, it was CORE that rushed in most enthusiastically to embrace that delusion; in some cities, they formed a large part of the staff. But they didn't have the decisive control, and that's where it's at'.[6]

In the Buffalo experiment, those selected were men who lived in the neighbourhoods but were upward-mobile. They owned small businesses (like a dry cleaning or a butcher shop), a skilled trade (such as barbering or crane operating), or were in a profession like the ministry or teaching. Many observers consider that these men had a combination of personal strength and optimism, and continuing involvement in the community which made it possible for them to speak as respected black leaders, not 'Uncle Toms'. There were often overtones of alienation and hostility, but generally the attitudes of these men were as individuals whose approach to American society was positive and hopeful, based on their own personal experience of 'making it'.

---

[6] Interview with Eldridge Cleaver, Vol. 15, no. 12, p. 91. *Playboy*, December 1968.

Having initiated the project and carried through its first year of operation, Dr Besag was replaced by a 'black brother' (Robert Hawkes, a professor at State University College at Buffalo), thus symbolizing the desire for black control of the project and setting the stage for the development of the Jefferson Education Center or the 'University of the Streets,' as it was called by Dr James Moss, a black sociologist from SUNY/B.

The University of the Streets Concept

Early in 1968, the steering Committee and the new project director, Robert Hawkes, decided that the project needed more elbow room and that the University and colleges should make a greater contribution and commitment by providing relevant courses and classes in the ghetto. A larger amount of federal assistance was requested and granted, largely as a result of the success of the storefront projects.

The 'University of the Streets' contained three offices, four classrooms and a small auditorium where dances and other community get-togethers were held. Classes covered both basic skills (such as Small Business Management, Accounting and Financial Analysis for Small Businesses, Beginning Shorthand and a related Charm and Grooming class, College Mathematics, Computer Programming, Laboratory Technicians, Maintenance training, Practical Salesmanship and others), and the black experience (including Philosophical Analysis of Revolution, Black History, African History, Legal Problems of Ghetto Life, Constitutional Law and Civil Rights and a series of courses in the Sociology of the Ghetto).

In September of 1968, the Jefferson Education Center or 'University of the Streets' was officially opened in a renovated old industrial plant on Jefferson Avenue. The run-down condition of the building and lack of physical amenities turned out to be irrelevant. What was important was that it was a black institution. It was perceived to be 'ours' not 'theirs', by the black Board of Directors and the community. A black organization had co-opted the white establishment, they were working together as 'equals'. This was not a 'hand-out'. This perception and perspective fit into the new black mood of 'getting ourselves together'. The courses and classes taught there were of secondary importance. The spirit of the place, as expressed through the soul music broadcast over radio station WBFO[7] to the black community was one of means; advertising the merits of education – as a means of 'getting your mind together' as well as your soul; one of helping young brother 'make it' in a tough alien white world. The message, in short, was one of helping each other 'make it' through education.

---

[7] The SUNY/B campus radio station which developed a 'satellite studio' in the Center.

The Urban Setting

The Jefferson Education Center or 'University of the Streets' is located in the heart of Buffalo's black ghetto, known officially as the Model Neighborhood Area (MNA). The MNA was designated by the city in response to the federal model cities legislation which provides assistance for creating a plan to improve the 'quality of life' in the area.

Buffalo was one of the great cities of the nineteenth century, but by the 1960s it was characterized by a declining economic base, mostly obsolete heavy industry and an out-migration of middle-class whites, an influx of poor blacks, mostly from the rural south. In 1966 the Buffalo metropolitan area had a population of 1,337,000. The city of Buffalo had a population of about 480,000 which had been declining since World War II. It also had a Negro population which had grown rapidly over that same period, from 36,645 in 1950 to well over 100,000 by 1968. This white decline and black growth pattern reflected the dominant trend in big, old, industrial American cities.

The economic base is heavily dependent upon primary metals (notably steel manufacturing) and automotive equipment manufacturing, each of which employ nearly 30,000 persons. In recent years, there has been a significant increase in research-and-development oriented economic activities. This increase is largely related to the rapid expansion of the State University of New York at Buffalo, the nation's fastest growing graduate education centre.

While the city continued to lose population, it was still the major place of employment for industrial and commercial enterprises in the metropolitan area. But the sagging tax base was reflected in the financial situation of the city administration which was rapidly deteriorating (with firemen and policemen threatening strikes).

Slum housing is located in three general areas: in the older central portion of the city, generally spreading eastward in a concentric pattern into the Masten and Ellicott Communities (MNA); within the industrial areas along the lake and the river; and south of the central business district, extending south and east through a mixed industrial area as far as the neighbouring city of Lackawanna, the home of Bethlehem Steel Company.

In 1960, of the total housing units in the city (177,224), 146,470 were considered sound, 24,363 were classified as deteriorating and 6,391 were considered dilapidated (U.S. Census figures). The MNA is the black ghetto. It is characterized by worn out housing and overcrowded conditions. Two-thirds of the city's welfare cases are located in the MNA. More than one-half of the old-age assistance load is in the MNA and the tuberculosis rate is twice that of the city as a whole; 26 per cent of persons over 25 with less than eight years of education reside in the MNA.

Most businesses are owned by whites living outside the MNA. This is one of the reasons these businesses were burned in the riots of 1967–8. It was, in effect, a redress of old grievances. Even some black-owned or 'soul-brothers' stores were burned. The unemployment rate in the MNA is twice that for the Buffalo labour market as a whole, and for young males it is three times as high. By almost any indices, the so-called MNA is the largest slum in the region. The black community is suspicious, indeed hostile, towards any changes proposed by the larger community represented by the city and county governments.

The Lessons Learned from the Education Center Experiment

The task of instituting change from the outside by traditional patronizing or 'neo-colonialist' methods is made more complex and difficult by: (1) the basic peasant attitude or image of a limited good, and (2) the new black militant 'togetherness' ideology found in the ghetto. As Professor George Foster pointed out in an intriguing article in the *American Anthropologist*:

(T)he primary task in development is not to attempt to create the need for achievement at the mother's knee but to try to change the peasants' view of his social and economic universe, away from an Image of Limited Good toward that of expanding opportunity in an open system, so that he can feel safe in displaying initiative. The brakes on change are less psychological than social. Show the peasant that initiative is profitable, and that it will not be met by negative sanctions, and he acquires it in short order.[8]

Two black psychiatrists, William Grier and Price Cobbs, have discerned the same phenomenon in the American black culture:

The bickering, the sniping, the backbiting so often said to characterize black people in their relationship with one another seems to very much to be the rivalry of siblings. Underlying it all is a feeling that 'you're no better than I.' It is an unfortunate corollary of such a feeling of 'sibship,' but it is probably a small price to pay for the comfort and the web of support provided by a brotherhood.[9]

Even more specifically in the southern context was the individual with initiative seriously handicapped:

The brother with property in the South is highly visible and is usually the target for business rivals. What would otherwise be healthy competition becomes under these circumstances a deadly game of defense in which the most he can hope for is to avoid capture. Retaliation is out of the question.[10]

---

[8] *American Anthropologist*, 67, 1965, 'Peasant Society and the Image of Limited Good', George M. Foster, University of California, Berkeley.

[9] William H. Grier and Price M. Cobbs, *Black Rage* (New York: Basic Books Inc., 1968), p. 105.

[10] op. cit, p. 107.

The Board of Directors of the 'University of the Streets' has demonstrated that initiative is profitable. Not only have they created an institution which gives them pride in themselves – for black pride is even more of a 'gut issue' than black power – but they have also shown how other well-intentioned but often fumbling white assistance programmes can succeed.

While the experiment is still in progress, at least three lessons have emerged from the project, in addition to the major lesson that the university's resources can indeed be used to help improve the quality of life in the ghetto. These three lessons are:

(1) Start small and do not make a lot of promises.

(2) Try to get maximum community participation.

(3) Do not plan ahead of the community policy-makers – let them make the key decisions about the future directions of the education programme.

From the university perspective, this last lesson means to 'plan backward'. That is, give the blacks time to talk over ideas, get them involved and follow their advice, suggestions and demands to the maximum extent possible – then design the plan.

Viewed from the perspective of the urban ghetto dweller, the university has relevant services and opportunities which are wanted and needed. If the university system is reasonably 'open', the feedback into the university can help make curriculum relevant to the critical issues of urbanization, racism and the education needs of black children.

Suggested Comparative Studies: a Non-System Alternative for Black Education

One of the questions that runs through this section of the 1970 World Year Book is: 'Is our present education system suitable for an increasingly stratified social, economic and racial grouping'? If we examine the existing systems and how they serve the ghettos of New York or the favelas of Rio, we can, in my opinion, conclude that the existing urban education system fails miserably.

The massive rural-to-urban migrations under way around the world have had an enormous impact on education. The ghettos of the United States, the favelas of Brazil, the ranchos of Venezuela, the bustees of India, the shanty-towns of Hong Kong are 'way stations' in the rural to urban migration. The rural to urban migration is a push-pull effect of people seeking the 'good life', essentially through better job opportunities in the city and the rapid decline in farm employment due to agricultural industrialization. The favela or the ghetto is a step up from the rural plantation. The problem, of course, is that more and more people are getting hung up at the 'way station'.

In the long run, the real problem is how to speed up the process of urbanization through education. That is, how can we make individual, family and communal adjustment to urban living and the good life rather than the debilitating experience of the urban slum? Based on our experience with the storefront information centres and the 'University of the Streets', the key is to provide educational opportunities and the medical, legal and job counselling assistance necessary to permit the individual to fulfil his education potential.

While the cities of Buffalo and Rio are very different in character, size, style and economic base, the ghettos of Buffalo and the favelas of Rio bear a close socio-psychological resemblance. They are a source of cheap labour for industrial and domestic employment. They are pockets of economic colonialism characterized by alienation and mistrust of the larger outside world. They are also vibrant enclaves of a dynamic population and culture and soul music – the bugaloo of the ghetto, the bossa nova of the favelas; the combos and the samba bands.

The education system which services the dominant middle class fails to provide a relevant experience for the ghetto or favela. For all too many, the 'way station' is the end of the line. They do not relate, they do not even try to 'make it' in the larger society and the ghettos and the favelas are burgeoning. Relevant education alternatives are needed. Our experiment demonstrated that the university can create an innovative education experience in urban slums.

In underdeveloped countries where resources are limited, investments in education services for the poor can have a great impact. In the United States, some hard-headed economists and sociologists have said that we don't need all these federal programmes and that the best cure for poverty is money; that what we need is a guaranteed annual income to provide a floor under poverty, through a negative income tax or some variation on the theme of outright support. This may be true, but the system also fails the human spirit. In addition to security, people need opportunity. Opportunity should have a priority at least as high, and perhaps higher, than economic security. The university, which has traditionally been a stronghold of the rich, must move into the field of community service or face the risk of becoming irrelevant.

The Buffalo Project Concept as it Relates to the Brazilian Context

Two essential elements were present in the development of the Buffalo project: (1) Community control and direction, and (2) University commitment and the concept of planning with the people. With this all important community leverage, organization for a variety of job training projects, medical assistance programmes and physical improvement programmes became possible and real. If we ask the question: How can the lessons learned from the Buffalo project be related to a favela in Rio?, we must understand the context and the failure of past efforts to rehabilitate the favelas.

The picturesque slums or favelas of Rio de Janeiro provide housing for some 500,000 people, or about 11 per cent of Rio's total population. There have been several efforts to 'improve the quality of life' in Rio's colourful favelas. Proposals, plans and suggestions by architects, planners and politicians range from total elimination and relocation in new towns to rather sensitive and sophisticated physical and social rehabilitation programmes. The plans have all, more or less, failed. The quality of life, the social, economic or physical conditions have not been improved. The problem has not been with the paper plans, which are often spectacular, but rather with community education and organization: a failure to understand what the people – the 'favelados' – wanted. For instance, the Fundação Leão XIII worked for the redevelopment of Barreira de Vasco for a number of years and some significant improvements were evident. The Fundação, in collaboration with COHAB and with United States A.I.D. financial help, started a programme to instal a water supply system, electricity, roads, walks and steps, in Vila da Penha but the work was stopped, about 50 per cent completed, when funds ran out. The project was apparently initiated without any comprehensive plan or community participation and support. After the project was well under way, BEMDOC completed a socio-economic survey of the area which served no purpose in the developments of the project.

Again, in Jacarezinho, a favela with a population of about 50,000 people, the process was repeated. Although there apparently were fairly comprehensive physical plans for roads and utilities, work was started without any community organization or input by the people who live there. The programme was discontinued in its early stages.

The past efforts of public agencies such as COHAB (Corporativas Habitacionais), BEMDOC, and A.I.D., have failed to achieve their objectives because they were imposed from the outside. They have failed to find a vehicle for on-going community education, organization and planning. They have not built an institution – rather they have tried to 'implement their plans'. We might ask, what has happened? First, a poor understanding of the people in the favelas, their problems, their needs and their lives; and second, improvement programmes were often planned and started without the knowledge, participation and support of the favelados. The improvements planned were not necessarily those wanted or needed by the community. Third, the improvement plans generally did not require community contributions of labour or money, and the work planned did not have guaranteed financing to completion. The community had no real interest and when projects were stopped, what little faith, support and participation that existed was lost. Lastly, the improvement programmes were often too limited in scope and were not aimed at the ultimate goal of providing the security of home ownership, land tenure, and the integration of the favela as a legal and permanent part of the larger community.

In our original United States A.I.D. study of the favelas, Bernard Wagner, David McVoy and I recommended that the rehabilitation of selected favelas should be built on existing social organizations and institutions. As a result of the Buffalo experience I would further recommend that the university could play a key role in community organization through education. The university, with aggressive students seeking outlets for social energies, and committed faculty seeking bridges between social theory and practical concern with his fellow man, could make this possible. Moreover, the increasingly desperate urban condition around the globe may make it imperative.

I disagree with Jacques Barzun, a leading scholar and critic of higher education, who said,

I have nothing against the university studying social problems or commenting on what is going on out of its fund of knowledge, but the university is getting to resemble the Red Cross more than a university, with direct help to whomever is suffering now.[11]

The university has become increasingly worldly and students and faculty have benefited. The university, like the church in its era, must create missions and missionaries, but must also avoid the pitfalls of paternalism. The great Catholic universities of Brazil have an opportunity to provide true community organization, where the church alone has apparently failed.

Many favelas have schools, meeting houses, churches, stores and small shops; they also have self-help constructed water and electricity distribution systems and, in some instances, sewer systems. Here and there the favelados got together and built sidewalks and steps or widened a road and paved it. Small industries are scattered throughout most favelas and are operated by individual owners or as family enterprises. Favelas have all kinds and types of structures and a good many houses are of perfectly sound construction with fairly generous space standards. Estimates made by COHAB indicate that upgrading of favelas could be achieved at an average cost of $500 per unit.

Some favelas have existed for thirty years or more. To many inhabitants, the favela is the only home and community they have ever known. During their history they have grown through natural population increase and urban in-migration and have become permanent, though technically illegal communities. Internally they have well-organized, long-standing community organizations and complex relationships of a nature and structure which is not necessarily typical of the middle-class community. In addition, there are strong economic, social and political ties with adjacent communities and the larger urban community.

The residents of the favelas are generally more intelligent, sophisticated and urbanized than might be suspected and are not, on the whole, recent migrants from the rural villages. Although poverty, unemployment and under-employment exist, at the same time a large percentage of the families are substantial wage earners. Under difficult circumstances, they have made their homes where they could and have developed a fairly high degree of social organization.

The problem in introducing social change, however, is to introduce new ideas, gain acceptance and mobilize community action. This is a difficult and complex task; a task in which the university could play a critical role as educator, technical advisor and catalyst for community organization.

The fact that the favela has an existing social organization and even community organizations does not mean that they can be effectively used for creating social change. As anthropologist George Foster points out, '... peasants must demonstrate to themselves that initiative is profitable.'[12] The people of the ghetto or favela must create their own plans. But, since their experience, training and education are limited, they often need the ideas, concepts and communication capabilities that can be provided by university students and faculty.

The Buffalo experience also shows that it is essential to build institutions within the community with residents who are upward-mobile, trusted, and essentially optimistic in their outlook. But even more important, they must be self-selective. They must organize themselves around the ideas and opportunities introduced by the university. The university may be the instigator but the 'change agents', the innovators and the planners, must be from the community organization. The suggested marriage of the intellectual élite, represented by the university, and the people of the ghetto or favela must not be a patronizing affair. Rather, it must emphasize the need for equal status. It must emphazise the concept of service rather than research on the part of the university.

A final comment on the university posture is needed at this point. It would appear evident that it the university's service programmes are to succeed, it must be willing to subordinate its goals, plans and programmes to the local community, or ghetto. The university system must be willing to relinquish control without a concommitant decrease in commitment.

---

[12] *American Anthropologist*, 67, 1965, 'Peasant Society and the Image of Limited Good', George M. Foster, University of California, Berkeley.

The university must be willing to help the community people implement their own ideas, whether it considers them to be wise or not. The university must be willing to permit the community to make mistakes, to grow, find its own way and eventually even to grow independent; to operate much like the Marshall Aid Plan did for Western Europe. The resources of the university should be regarded as a beginning – a seed planting and cultivating process – not a continuing programme. The experience gained by the university will have value and use in other poverty areas in new ways.

10

The U.S.A.: Alternatives for Urban School Reform

Mario D. Fantini

Big city school systems once regarded as exemplars of quality education, at least in the U.S.A., are caught in a steady worsening spiral of decline. Applying the standard test of quality – namely, the effect that formal education has on children – urban schools are failing. The shelves are full of thorough studies depicting their shortcomings.

Cities are paying a heavy cost for the decline, including a growing lack of confidence in public education. This is especially true in those parts of the city that need education most desperately – the low income neighbour-hoods. The city's poor, usually black and/or other minorities, have little choice but the public schools for their children's education. In urban centres black populations are increasingly becoming majorities, if not in total city population, then certainly in city school population. In Washington, D.C., for example, 93 per cent of the school population is black. In New York, Philadelphia and Chicago the figures are well over 50 per cent.

The continuous denial of quality education to urban residents leads to a cycle of frustration with quite severe consequences. The 'clients' of the urban public schools – students, parents, communities – are increasingly protesting the failure. No teacher, no parent, no citizen, no business or industry, no public official can rest easy while this erosion continues. A gradual disconnection among the parties that make up public education in our cities is taking place. Already the conditions in certain cities have reached a state of deterioration in which the disconnection has turned to open conflict between community and school.

As the crisis in urban education accelerates, so will the attempts to rectify the problem. Patterns for urban school improvement have already commenced. It will be the purpose of this statement to outline some of these patterns and to comment briefly on the assumptions, practices and promise of each. The alternatives discussed below have a common objective: To restore quality education to urban schools. Most start with the most serious problems, the education of the so-called 'disadvantaged'.

Compensatory Education

This form of intervention is currently the most prevalent and dates back to the Higher Horizons Project, the Ford Foundation sponsored Great Cities-Grey Areas Project, Title I projects under the Elementary and Secondary Education Act, More Effective Schools in New York City, etc. It is based on the assumption that you improve education by utilizing remedial measures to deal with problems such as under-achievement, lack of motivation, etc. (For example, lower class size, added reading teachers, extra counsellors, more materials, etc.) This pattern is rehabilitative. It assumes that the central problem is with the learner and not the school, that children of the slums are disadvantaged because of environmental and cultural deficits, and that through a programme of remediation the learner can be 'lifted' to profit from the standard education programme. This is an additive pattern – it attempts to 'add on' to and strengthen existing programmes. It builds layers on to the standard education process. For example, Head Start builds a new pre-school remedial layer on to the existing educative process.

The advantage of this pattern is that it is the least threatening to the present educational establishment. The evidence available from such efforts, however, indicates that this pattern is not having a significant impact on the problem. That is, the results of our Great Cities Project, Higher Horizons, and Title I, suggest little scholastic achievement gains for disadvantaged children. Consequently, this pattern is being viewed with increasing distrust by the parents who disagree with the assumption that something is wrong with *their* children. They feel that compensatory education is giving a more concentrated dose of what did not work in the first place. The U.S. Office of Education is also alarmed about this 'more of the same' orientation, but can do little to change it without giving the impression of greater government control. Title III of the Elementary and Secondary Education Act, however, is conceived of as the instrumentality that can probe for new patterns.

Desegregation

Since the 1954 Supreme Court decision, considerable effort toward integration has been based on the assumption that Negro pupils' achievement is enhanced in an integrated school environment. The Coleman Report tends to support this view, and the U.S. Civil Rights Commission is unequivocal in stating: 'Negro children suffer serious harm when their education takes place in public schools which are racially segregated, whatever the source of such segregations may be. Negro children who attend predominantly Negro schools do not achieve as well as other children, Negro and white'.[1] Achieving greater racial balance through such efforts as school buses and educational parks have had limited results.

Moreover, there is a growing shift of emphasis by minority group members themselves away from desegregation at the option of the white majority. The new focus of racial-minority parents is on power and control over the schools their children attend. The changing mood springs not only from the poor record of integration efforts, but also from a revolt against the condescension perceived by minority group members in the school desegregation efforts of the post-1954 decade. First, many resent the fact that integration is, under current power arrangement, an option of the white community. Second, they believe that the dependent status of the Negro in American society is perpetuated by the notion that the only way to help the black child is to seat him alongside white children. Beneath this mood is a quest for stronger racial identity and pride, and a desire to gain more control of their own destiny. The desire for integration was based, rather, say many Negro spokesmen, on the belief that parents in predominantly white schools exercised enough power to insure that the school offered quality education, in which Negro pupils should share. The converse is powerlessness, further destruction of identity, and increasing disconnection from the larger society.

The implication for public education is greater participation by Negroes in control over predominantly Negro schools. This is rather different from the 'separate but equal' doctrine, since some 'black power' philosophers reason that when Negroes achieve quality education under their own aegis, they will then be prepared to connect (integrate) with the white society on a ground-work of parity instead of deficiency. A good school then would be defined not by the kind of children who attend it, but by the quality of the education offered by the school. In short, they seek connexion as equals.

The goals of integration, therefore, must be broadened to restore a quality that has been sidetracked in the emphasis on the scholastic-achievement goal of desegregation. That is, we must reaffirm our commitment to connect with one another as human beings. We must recognize that viewing *diversity* and differences as *assets* rather than unfortunate barriers to homogeneity has as positive an effect on human growth and development as the teaching of academic skills. All of which is to suggest that militant Negro demands for participation in control of public education is actually a means of greater connexion to society, precisely opposite from the connotations of separatism usually associated with 'black power'. However, desegregation as a path to quality education has been legitimized as an important alternative.

---

[1] U.S. Commission on Civil Rights, *Racial Isolation in the Public Schools* (Washington: U.S. Government Printing Office, 1967), I.

Model Subsystems

The answers to the problem of improved learning are unknown and must be searched out. The Subsystem is a search unit for the total system. It assumes that a form of intervention which utilizes a 'more of the same' approach is limited and that we do not yet know what is the best approach to school improvement. It also assumes that the educational process has to be updated and that one of the key factors missing from large city school systems is a 'Research and Development' component, a component that becomes the chief instrumentality for revitalizing an outdated system. This component can introduce new perspectives, new energies and new actions to the total system, by providing new and tested approaches for change. The model subsystem approach usually attempts to tackle the problem from within 'the establishment' and to utilize outside resources such as universities, community groups, etc. It co-ordinates those outside resources which may have a role to play in educational improvement.

The assumption here is that the school and its process is perhaps as much to blame as the environmental differences of the students. In a progress report (by a panel headed by Jerrold Zacharias) to the Commissioner of Education in March 1964, the model subsystem notion for big city systems was highlighted and gave birth to the model subsystem division of the Washington, D.C. public schools. Other cities are utilizing this option, Boston for example.

An outgrowth of the subsystem is a notion of contracting out for delivery of educational services. In this pattern a school system can contract out with business and industry for the operation of sections of the city's school system. The assumption underlining this approach is that the real change cannot be changed simply by 'inside resources' alone. To increase efficiency and pay off, new energies and resources must be brought into the educational system.

Equally important, it introduces a dimension of competition for the services. That is, a Board of Education can specify what it expects from a contract, indeed, a contract with two or three different outside organizations, each one in essence competing with the other. The net effect of this competition could be to provide a new motivation to renew urban school systems.

Under this subcontract notion a Central Board of Education can ask for bids to various organizations for the operation and management of a school or groups of schools in the system. In Washington, D.C., for example, the Board of Education entered into an agreement with Antioch College to operate the Morgan school. This arrangement has since been altered. An elected community council now oversees the Morgan school.

The problem with efficiency notions of school improvement such as the subsystem approaches is that they tend to by-pass the new emerging publics – students, parents, and communities who are increasingly projecting the expectation that they must be involved in any decision concerning programme options for schools in their localities. The increasing realization of urban school systems to increase the role of the community in school affairs has prompted the establishment of subsystems which are community based or community oriented. In Washington, D.C., for example, there are two community-centred subsystems: first, is the Adams-Morgan Community School; the other is the Anacostia Demonstration District, which is a ten-school unit. Each unit has a citizen's board that effects policy for the subunit. Each has an experimental status with the Board of Education.

In New York City, three subsystems were created by the Board of Education to test the results of greater community participation in local educational affairs. These subsystems include, IS 201 in East Harlem, Ocean Hill-Brownsville in Brooklyn and Two Bridges in the Lower East Side, each with elected local governing boards to oversee the education of the school clusters (intermediate schools and the feeder schools).

In Chicago, the Woodlawn experimental district is a tri-partite arrangement in which the central board, the University of Chicago and the community are represented on the local board.

Another promising Model Subsystem development is the so-called *In Town New Town*. Somewhat related to Model Cities legislation is the option to develop a totally new educational system for a new community. In Washington, D.C. for example, the old National Training site is being planned as the Fort Lincoln-New Town. The heart of that New Town is its educational system. While it will still be a part of the D.C. public school system it has a special experimental status that will allow it to depart dramatically from the conventional conceptions of education to draft a totally new educational system.

Parallel Systems

One set of approaches to quality education is not really intervention in public education; rather, it is an escape into a parallel system. Such approaches assume that if the poor (or others) cannot reform public education, the system is meaningless to the poor and they should be afforded options to it.

A few privately managed schools have been established in urban ghettoes, and several others are in the planning stage. Precedents for such schools exist in southern Freedom Schools (notably Neil Sullivan's school for Negro pupils deprived of educational opportunity when the Prince Edward County, Virginia, public schools closed to avoid integration).

Some northern counterparts include Harlem's Street Academies and the New School and the Highland Park School in Boston's Roxbury section. The New York Urban League-sponsored Street Academies are sending more than 75 per cent of their students – hardcore rejects from the public school system – to college.

Of considerable potential significance to urban education is an act approved by the Massachusetts Legislature late in 1967 which enables the State Department of Education to assist and sponsor experimental school systems, planned, developed, and operated by private non-profit corporations. Assuming a greater role in education and urban problems, states could establish yardsticks, 'educational TVAs', in order to measure the effectiveness of different forms of educational innovation.

Project Head Start schools are also 'private,' in the sense that they exist apart from the public school system and are not subject to its rules and regulations, governing personnel, curriculum, and other matters. Some of these schools are financed under Federal tuition grants and foundation funds, and efforts are being made to obtain support for others from business and industry. A special hybrid, a publicly-financed but totally independent school system (an enclave apart from the regular New York City system), with a per capita budget received directly from the state, was proposed in 1967 by the Harlem Chapter of CORE (Congress of Racial Equality), though it failed in the New York State Constitutional Convention.

Kenneth Clark, noted Negro psychologist, has proposed a number of alternatives to urban public schools. These include:

Regional State Schools – These schools would be financed by the states and would cut across present urban-suburban boundaries.

Federal Regional Schools – These schools would be financed by the federal government out of present state-aid funds or with additional federal funds. These schools would be able to cut through state boundaries and could make provisions for residential students.

College- and University-related Open Schools – These schools would be financed by colleges and universities as part of their laboratories in education. They would be open to the public and not restricted to children of faculty and students. Obviously, public students would be selected in terms of constitutional criteria, and their percentage determined by realistic considerations.

Industrial Demonstration Schools – These schools would be financed by industrial, business, and commercial firms for their employees and selected members of the public. These would not be vocational schools but elementary and comprehensive high schools of high quality. They would be sponsored by combinations of business and industrial firms in much the same way as various churches and denominations now sponsor and support parochial or sectarian schools.

Labour Union-sponsored Schools – These schools would be financed and sponsored by labour unions largely, but not exclusively, for the children of their members.

Army Schools – The Defense Department had been quietly effective in educating some of the casualties of our present public schools. It is hereby suggested that the Department now go into the business of repairing hundreds of thousands of these human casualties with affirmation rather than apology. Schools for adolescent dropouts or educational rejects could be set up by the Defense Department adjacent to camps – though not necessarily as an integral part of the military. If it is necessary that such operations become an integral part of the military, so be it. The goal is to rescue as many of these young people as possible. They are not expendable on the altar of anti-militarist rhetoric.[2]

Non-public schools have advantages; they do not have to deal with distant and entrenched bureaucracies, with school boards unfamiliar with their particular needs, or with teachers' unions. They are free to hire teachers from a variety of personnel pools and to sidestep rigid credential-granting procedures. They may even abandon such practices as tenure and retain, promote, or discharge teachers purely on the grounds of merit and performance. If the schools are governed by boards with a substantial representation of their pupil's parents, they are likely to be more responsive to the children's needs and thereby encourage better rapport and partner-ship between the home and the school. In the most general sense, they afford the poor the choice that is open to many middle-class parents: to educate their children elsewhere if they are dissatisfied with the perform-ance of the public schools. And if enough private schools are available, the pattern ushers in an entrepreneurial system in which parents can choose, cafeteria-style, from a range of styles of education – Montessori, prep school, Summerhill, and others.

Carried to its logical conclusion, however, the parallel-school approach would reduce the scope of public education, if not dispense with it alto-gether. The establishment of private schools sufficient to handle significant numbers of poor children would require public support and, in effect, establish a private system of publicly-supported schools. Middle-income parents would demand similar privileges. For financial reasons alone, the parallel-school approach is hardly likely to become widespread in the foreseeable future; moreover, the scheme would flounder on political, if not constitutional grounds. Finally, since private schools are not subject to public control, there would be no guarantee that some private education might not be organized by special interest groups for ends inimical to a free and open society. Support of such enterprises at public expense would be difficult to justify.

These arguments are, of course, no reason to discourage programmes

---

[2] *The Schoolhouse in the City*, Alvin Toffler (Editor) (New York: Praeger Press, 1968).

that enable more low-income pupils to attend private schools. Private schools could serve a valuable yardstick function if they were run under conditions that simulated the resources and inputs of public education – particularly comparable per capita expenditures, and admission policies that would embrace a range of low-income pupils, including the 'disruptive'. But that is the limit of their usefulness as an alternative to improved public education, for they could never serve the majority of the children of the poor. They remain at present, another emerging option.

Credit for Tuition Purposes

In order to provide for a family unit with the broadest possible scale of options, some have proposed that families have a credit-voucher which could be utilized for tuition to attend various schools in an 'open' market. Under this plan, a poor family would have the option to send a child to private or public schools. Further, he can 'shop' around for certain kinds of private schools. This plan would certainly tackle the problem of equalizing opportunities. It would also serve as an incentive for school systems to become more efficient through the competition which would be engendered. This plan may or may not be threatening to public schools depending on how it is developed. This is still a relatively new option having been proposed by a handful of education analysts and critics including Milton Friedman, Christopher Jenks and Ted Sizer.

Participatory Systems

As big city schools increasingly are challenged by the demands of the clients, the students, the parents and the community for quality education, the demands to join the school reform movement take on a different dimension. The impact of massive failure of both the student and his parent has resulted in a growing alienation to the schools and those who run them. In some urban communities this takes on deep racial antagonism. There is a feeling in some minority communities that the 'establishment' is engaging in a systematic conspiracy of non-education of minorities, thereby perpetuating their inferior status.

Communities, especially black communities, are in different stages of developing their expectations for participation. Some communities would welcome an *advisory* participatory role. Others would want an *equal* voice in educational decision-making. Still others have reached the point where they would want 'total control'.

In certain large school systems the movement toward increased participation has resulted in the development of the notion of *decentralization*. The new movement toward decentralization is far more than an administrative plan; that is, it is more than a movement for a big city overcoming the deficiencies of bureaucratic management. It is rather a *political* movement in which minorities, especially blacks, can begin to assume a new trustee role, a new governmental role with the schools in their localities. In New York City, decentralization is taking the form of a 'community school system' composed of a federation of semi-autonomous school districts and the central education agency. In certain quarters of New York City, for example, decentralization does not provide sufficient community participation in educational decision-making. In these cases, the call is not for decentralization but *community control*. Under community control, communities *secede* from the big city system and assume an *independent* school district status similar to that of suburban school districts which are independent and responsible only to the state. Harlem CORE, for example, is proposing an Independent Harlem School District.

Because of the importance of the participatory movement in the United States, especially among youth, parents, and other community residents, it is imperative that there be the fullest possible understanding of this dynamic. Unless there is understanding and the goals of effective participation projected, there are chances for increased misunderstanding and retaliation.

The goals of effective participation are emerging. They begin from the position that when people have a part in their institutions, they share responsibility for them and are more likely to pay close attention to the stated mission and actual performance of the institution.

Thus participation has a positive effect on the participants as well as the system. For example, as parents in East Harlem became more engaged in the education process, 'quality education' replaced 'black power' as the slogan. Responsibility comes with the power of an effective voice. In the train of responsibility, judgement, stability, and dedication to constructive purpose are likely to follow. The classic pattern of the revolutionary is that when he takes power, he shifts from destroying institutions to building order and new institutions (of his own kind, to be sure).

Participatory democracy in education should also give parents and community a tangible respect for the intricacy and complexity of the professional problems in urban education. It is not likely that parents who have gained admission as true partners in the process will oversimplify and lay the blame for educational failures solely on the professional. As things stand now, low-income communities outside the system understandably lay the blame squarely on the assigned professionals: 'You are paid to teach, to deliver a certain product. When overwhelming numbers of our children fail to learn, you are not delivering. You are not meeting your professional obligation.' The syllogism is simplistic: it ignores the fact that professional talent can be thwarted by a system, and it does not take into account extra-school factors in teaching and learning. But it is an altogether natural response from parents to whom the system provides no access and offers but two alternatives: Total resignation and apathy; or anger, protest, and sooner or later, some form of retaliation.

Sceptics who concede the right of parents to participate in the education process nevertheless question their technical qualifications to engage in educational decisions; the question is raised particularly (though not exclusively) in relation to low-income, poorly educated parents. But the question should not be what parents know now, but what they can come to know about the technicalities of education. That they want to know is suggested by the few instances in which they have become more or less equal partners in the process. Their concerns soon broaden; they begin to ask, for example, who are the most talented reading specialists in the country, because we want them to help us. In qualifying for school board membership, too, they seek training for themselves – something rare among would-be school board members even in wealthier communities.

Admitting the public to the education process, therefore, should result in the addition of many new hands and minds to the tasks. These would be true partners, who participate in the enterprise and know it from their own experience, rather than simply taking its established goals and procedures as virtues because its professional managers say so.

The school, after all, is only one side of the *total* curriculum to which children are exposed. Considerable learning takes place at home and in all manner of community institutions including the street corner, the church, the press and other mass media, and neighbourhood organizations. As parents are admitted to participation in the schools' education process, they will become better equipped 'teachers' of the part of the 'curriculum' in which they are the prime agents – rearing in the home. Studies under Basil Bernstein of the University of London's Sociological Research Unit have illuminated a discontinuity of socialization among the home, the child's peer group, and the schools.[3] Continuity could be restored if parents participated in the formal education process.

Greater public engagement in the public education process also should add political strength to pressures for increased financial support for education; a 'parents' lobby' with unprecedented motivation and commitment might arise. Nor should the possible effects on parents in their own right be overlooked. Few people can engage in a social cause and not themselves be transformed. Relevant education in an institutional setting that is willing to experiment in the art – and the mysteries – of learning and teaching is such a cause. It could bring into the lives of men and women working at tedious jobs, or leading lives of boredom (factors by no means peculiar to low-income groups), a new spirit in an activity with immediate

---

[3] See, for example, Basil Bernstein, 'A Socio-linguistic Approach to Social Learning' in Gould (ed.), *Social Science Review* (New York: Pelican, 1965).

relevance to their own families. This is to say nothing of the possible chain-reaction that meaningful engagement in the education process could have in stimulating parents to enlarge their own education.

Thus the realignment of the participants in public education could produce rich yields for all the main participants:

– for the parents, a tangible grasp on the destiny of their children and opening to richer meaning for their own lives;

– for professionals, surcease from an increasingly negative community climate and, even more positively, new allies in their task;

– for the children, a school system responsive to their needs, resonant with their personal style, and affirmative in its expectation of them.

And finally there is the goal of participation for its own sake, an intrinsic concomitant – and test – of democracy. Education could no doubt be conducted efficiently if it were contracted out as a technical service, without the furniture of lay boards, community relations, and so on, especially if quality is defined strictly in terms of grade-level achievement. Totalitarian systems, as we know only too well, have demonstrated educational efficiency in these terms. But in an open society, the process of participation itself is a social and educational value, no matter what waste and inefficiencies it may appear to entail.

11

Chicago: Educational Development in a Metropolitan Area

Robert J. Havighurst

The typical North American big city has evolved since 1900 through a complex redistribution of human population that makes it different from what it was at the turn of the century, and so much of a problem that it *must* be radically transposed and improved before the end of this century. If we think of a big city as one with a half million population or more, there are twenty-five such cities in the United States.

Chicago is an example of what has happened. Up to 1900 the city of Chicago grew by spreading out from the original city centre at the entrance of the Chicago River to Lake Michigan, and by annexing a number of small villages that had grown up along the railway lines leading into the city centre. At this time the outward movement of the city boundaries came to a stop, because they met some stabilized boundaries of suburban cities which did not wish to be annexed by the growing city. Evanston on the north, Oak Park and Cicero on the west, blocked further growth in those directions, and the area to the south was low, swampy ground that was not attractive for residential purposes. The city continued to grow in population until 1930, by filling in the open spaces left between the nuclei of settlement in the outer areas. Population reached 3,400,000 in 1930 and was not to grow much more during the subsequent 40 years.

TABLE 1

POPULATION GROWTH OF CHICAGO METROPOLITAN AREA, 1900–1970
(in thousands)

	1900	1920	1940	1950	1960	1970(est.)
City of Chicago	1,698	2,702	3,397	3,621	3,550	3,600
Ring 1. Inner suburban	112	303	594	742	1,170	
2. Middle suburban	70	123	227	374	810	
3. Outer suburban	114	170	229	264	395	
4. Rural periphery	91	98	123	177	295	
All outside Chicago	386	693	1,173	1,557	2,670	3,700
Total SMSA	2,084	3,395	4,570	5,178	6,221	7,302

Meanwhile, the suburban communities continued to grow, as is seen in Table 1. They increased in population from 386,000 in 1900 to an estimated 3,700,000 in 1970, a ten-fold increase. Thus, in 1970, more than 50 per cent of the population in the 'Chicago Metropolitan Area' are living outside the city limits. This is true of American metropolitan areas in general as is seen in Table 2. The proportion of the population

TABLE 2

DIVISION OF METROPOLITAN AREA POPULATION BETWEEN CENTRAL
CITIES AND OUTSIDE CENTRAL CITIES: 1900–1960

	Total SMSA* population	Per cent of SMSA population within central cities	Per cent of SMSA population outside central cities
1900	31,895	62·2	37·8
1910	42,094	64·6	35·4
1920	52,631	66·0	34·0
1930	66,915	64·6	35·4
1940	72,834	62·7	37·3
1950	89,317	58·7	41·3
1960	112,895	51·4	48·6
1963	118,761	50·0	50·0

SOURCE: U.S. Bureau of the Census. *U.S. Census of Population: 1960. Selected Area Reports. Standard Metropolitan Statistical Areas.* Final Report (PC(3)-1D).
 * Standard Metropolitan Statistical Areas.

living outside the central city but within the metropolitan area reached 50 per cent in 1963. The basis for this growth pattern was the development of the automobile and motor-bus as quasi-universal means of transit, and the building of expressways that permitted a person to go from his home to his place of work in less than an hour, no matter where he lived or worked.

As a result of this pattern of population growth and distribution, it became necessary to create the concept of a *metropolitan area*, which is the area served by and serving a central city in economic and cultural relationships. The United States Census defined a 'standard metropolitan statistical area' (SMSA) as any city with a population of 50 thousand or more, together with its surrounding county, and such other counties as were tied to the central county by economic and cultural ties. The operational definition of an outlying county that is part of a standard metropolitan statistical area includes such elements as: occupations of the working force more commercial-industrial than agricultural; more than a certain proportion of the county working force employed in the central

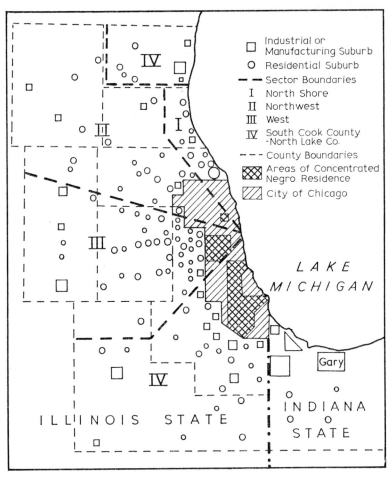

The Chicago Metropolitan Area.

county, etc. A metropolitan area is not a governmental unit; it is only a geographical unit useful for social statistics.

By 1966 there were 225 SMSAs in the United States, with 67 per cent of the nation's population and 9 per cent of the land area. The Chicago SMSA consisted of Cook County, containing the city of Chicago, and five other counties. This was the second largest SMSA in the country, only exceeded by New York.

An important and unhealthy characteristic of metropolitan growth during the period after 1940 was the economic and ethnic polarization that took place between the central city and the suburban area. As the central city dwellings and factories and business buildings decayed and grew obsolescent, their residents and owners moved out to the outer shells of the central city and to the suburban areas, leaving behind the old structures to be lived in and used by people and businesses who were less affluent. This process was hastened in the 1950–60 decade which was one of rapid economic expansion for most cities, with consequent in-migration of unskilled people looking for jobs, and out-migration of workers from the 'inner city' as the decaying sections of the central city came to be called, and out-migration of business concerns and light industry, which could easily move to low-cost land in the suburban areas, served by the new highways.

TABLE 3

POLARIZATION IN METROPOLITAN AREAS IN TERMS OF EDUCATION OF
ADULTS WITHIN CENTRAL CITY AND OUTSIDE CENTRAL CITY
(Per cent at ages 25 and over who are at least high school graduates)

SMSA	1960		1940	
	Outside CC	*Central city*	*Outside CC*	*Central city*
High Polarization				
Cleveland	55	30	45	21
Chicago	52	35	31	25
New York	52	37	33	22
Washington	65	48	43	41
Philadelphia	46	31	27	19
St. Louis	41	26	23	18
Newark	50	27	33	17
Milwaukee	53	40	29	22
Buffalo	44	30	23	20
Baltimore	41	28	21	19
Medium Polarization				
Detroit	47	34	27	26
Boston	57	45	39	32
Minneapolis – St. Paul	60	47	27	34
San Francisco – Oakland	58	49	41	37
Cincinnati	41	34	21	25
Atlanta	48	41	26	31
Kansas City	52	47	27	40
Pittsburgh	43	35	22	24
Low Polarization				
Los Angeles	54	54	42	42
Houston	46	45	27	36
Seattle	56	56	31	43
Dallas	48	49	31	40
San Diego	54	55	38	41

Some of the consequences of this polarization were: increasing proportions of people with above average education and income in the suburban areas (as seen in Table 3); growth of slum areas in the central cities into areas so large that children born in a slum seldom come into contact with other children of middle-class status; growth of segregated residential areas of Negroes and other disadvantaged minority groups, including Spanish Americans. For Chicago the situation is described in Table 4, where the socio-economic ratio (SER) is seen to differentiate more and more sharply between the central city and the suburban area.

TABLE 4

SOCIO-ECONOMIC CHARACTERISTICS OF CHICAGO AND SUBURBAN AREA
1940–1960

Population in Thousands	City of Chicago		Suburban Area	
	White	Non-White	White	Non-White
1920	2,589	113	684	9
1940	3,115	282	1,148	25
1950	3,112	509	1,512	45
1960	2,713	838	2,588	82
1965	2,579	980	2,980	113
1970 (est.)	2,427	1,173	3,525	175
1980 (est.)	2,234	1,540	4.499	347

Median grade of school completed by adults 25 and over	City of Chicago	Suburban Area
1940	8·5	8·9
1950	9·6	10·8
1960	10·0	12·1

Socio-economic Ratios*		City of Chicago			Chicago	Chicago Suburbs only
	U.S.A.	Total	White	Non-White	SMSA	
1940	0·66	0·69	0·75	0·17	0·71	0·77
1950	0·71	0·73	0·84	0·18	0·77	0·86
1960	0·82	0·69	0·82	0·25	0·92	1·28

* The socio-economic ratio (SER) is an approximate ratio of male white-collar to manual workers.

Birth-rates and School Enrolments

Since 1900, birth-rates have fluctuated in the U.S.A. to an unusual degree. This is due partly to actual changes in the numbers of children born to the average woman, and partly to fluctuations in the child-bearing population of the big city, because of in-migration and out-migration of women of child-bearing age.

The average number of children borne per woman started the century at a relatively high rate, then decreased in the late 1920s and during the 1930s to such a low point that it was not sufficient to maintain the existing population level. Then the birth-rate rose around 1940, and went up sharply in the post-war years, reaching a peak about 1953. Since 1960 there appears to have been a slight decline, but this cannot be verified until the present generation of women of child-bearing age pass through this period.

The results of these fluctuations are shown in Table 5, which gives the

TABLE 5

BIRTHS AND BIRTH-RATES IN CHICAGO

Year	Number of births	Births per 1,000 population	Population of Chicago
1900	39,000	23·0	1,699,000
1910	49,000	22·4	2,185,000
1913	56,000	24·1	—
1915	57,000	23·2	—
1920	57,000	20·9	2,702,000
1923	56,000	19·4	—
1926	60,000	19·2	—
1930	58,000	17·1	3,377,000
1931	53,000	15·5	3,400,000
1934–36	47,000	13·9	3,397,000
1938–42		15·1	3,400,000
1941	57,000	16·8	3,400,000
1942	68,000	—	—
1945	59,000	—	—
1946	74,000	—	—
1947	83,000	23·2	3,583,000
1950	79,000	21·8	3,621,000
1955	90,000	—	—
1959	98,000	—	—
1960	89,000	27·2	3,550,000
1964	82,000	22·8	—
1966	73,000	20·5	—
1967	70,000	19·4	3,600,000

SOURCE: State of Illinois, Dept. of Public Health. *Vital Statistics Report.*

numbers of children born in Chicago and the crude birth-rates (numbers of births per thousand population). This table reflects both the fluctuations in birth-rate and the fluctuations due to in- and out-migration of women of child bearing age. The first twenty years of this century saw a large in-migration of young adult Europeans, who were marrying and having children as soon as they became established in Chicago. After World War I, the flow of European immigration was reduced, and the birth-rate decreased. This decrease was sharpened by the Depression of the 1930s, with the result that the absolute numbers of births fell off from a high of 60,000 in 1926 to a low of about 50,000 in the mid-1930s. Then the birth-rate increased, and after 1946 the absolute numbers of births exceeded the earlier peak of 1926. The crude birth-rate rose to 27 per thousand in 1959, highest in the century. This dropped down to about 20 after 1965.

The consequence of this fluctuation of birth-rate was a fluctuation in the school enrolments, seen in Table 6. The high point of 1931 (530,000) was followed by a drop to about 390,000 in 1950, after which there was an increase to about 600,000 in 1968.

TABLE 6

ENROLMENT IN CHICAGO PUBLIC SCHOOLS
(in thousands)

Year	Elementary	High school	Total
1925	416	66	482
1930	422	104	526
1935	369	137	506
1940	315	143	458
1945	279	111	390
1949	293	96	389
1955	352	93	445
1960	410	103	513
1965	439	140	579

These fluctuations of school enrolment in the City of Chicago were *not* paralleled by school enrolments in the suburbs, due to the fact that the population of the suburbs increased throughout the century, and this increase was great enough to maintain an increasing school enrolment in 3 of the 5 counties outside Cook County, as seen in Table 7.

Enrolment in Private Schools

Big cities in the United States generally have a large non-public school enrolment. The principal group of non-public schools is maintained by the Roman Catholic Church, though other churches have a few schools, and there is a small number of independent schools.

TABLE 7

ENROLMENT IN PUBLIC SCHOOLS OF CHICAGO METROPOLITAN AREA,
1925–65

Total enrolment in public elementary school districts in the Northeastern Illinois
Metropolitan Area for decennial intervals by County. (Data are from the Biennial
Reports of the Superintendent of Public Instruction of the State of Illinois.)

County	1925	1935	1946(1)	1955	1964(1)
Cook					
Outside Chicago	66,710	77,762	71,578	141,801	259,192
Chicago	421,872	380,108	279,030	342,245	417,153
DuPage	9,276	13,978	14,143	33,196	65,268
Kane	13,746	14,546	13,438	23,233	41,164
Lake	12,748	14,432	15,182	31,582	54,541
McHenry	5,287	4,625	4,874	8,836	14,541
Will	13,463	13,413	11,455	17,109	30,971
Total	543,112	518,864	409,680	598,002	882,830

Total enrolment in public secondary school districts in the Northeastern Illinois
Metropolitan Area for decennial intervals, by County. (Data are from the Biennial
Reports of the Superintendent of Public Instruction of the State of Illinois.)

County	1925	1935	1946(1)	1955	1964(1)
Cook					
Outside Chicago	14,714	32,769	34,012	41,527	103,067
Chicago	89,757(2)	142,547	119,935	101,855	143,427
DuPage	2,107	5,649	6,607	9,211	23,515
Kane	4,154	6,548	6,115	6,503	13,191
Lake	2,515	5,829	6,240	9,146	21,050
McHenry	1,457	1,943	1,921	2,842	5,606
Will	2,782	5,348	4,693	5,136	10,738
Total	117,486	200,633	179,523	176,220	320,594

(1) Data are given for 1946 and 1964 because 1945 and 1965 are not available.
(2) These Chicago figures include continuation and apprentice schools.

Chicago has one of the largest Catholic populations in the world. The
system of Catholic schools is the fourth largest school system in the
country, exceeding all but the three largest public school systems. Table 8
shows how the percentage of school children attending Catholic schools
rose from 1930 to 1950 and 1960.

The immigrants to Chicago from Europe were predominantly Catholic.
At first they settled in the inner city area where rents were low. Then as
they prospered, they moved out from the inner-city slums to better
houses, first in the outer parts of the city and then in the suburbs. Con-

sequently, the Catholic school enrolments have been rising each decade since 1920, in the suburbs and the outer shell of the city.

The proportion of suburban children in Catholic schools slowly increased as Catholics moved to the suburbs. At the same time the suburbs took a growing proportion of the total Catholic school enrolments in the SMSA, as can be seen in Table 8.

TABLE 8
PROPORTIONAL ENROLMENT IN CATHOLIC SCHOOLS

	1930	1940	1950	1960	1965
Percentage of total school enrolment in Chicago Catholic schools	25	25	36	34	28
Percentage of Chicago's white children in Catholic schools	26	27	42	45	45
Percentage of suburban white children in Catholic elementary schools	16	17	20	23	28
Percentage of total metropolitan area Catholic high school enrolment in suburban schools	13	12	14	21	31
Percentage of total metropolitan area Catholic elementary school enrolment in surburban schools	14	15	19	36	41

The public schools of Chicago have been most affected in their social composition by the interplay of population movement of Catholics and Negroes. Since not more than 6 per cent of Chicago Negroes are Catholic, these two large population elements seldom reinforce each other. Generally, where one group increases, the other decreases in the central city, and the public schools as well as Catholic schools are affected by this interaction.

The areas of heaviest Catholic concentration of the central city have generally maintained themselves since 1925, and have even increased enrolment in Catholic schools. The growth of Catholic school enrolment in the outer areas of the city and in the suburbs has been due to increase of Catholic population in these areas, but not at the expense of decreased Catholic population in the inner city. Since 1960 the Catholic school enrolment in the City of Chicago has been nearly constant, with a slight tendency to decrease since 1965.

The Negro population has tended to settle in areas not heavily Catholic. The areas now occupied by Negroes had only 17 per cent of their children in Catholic schools in 1930, when these same areas were mostly white. By

1960 this proportion was still 14 per cent, even though it was then heavily Negro. A number of the children in Catholic schools in these areas are now Negro, but not more than half. The presence of Catholic schools seems to have aided the maintenance of a white minority in these areas.

The most striking fact about the Catholic population of the Chicago Metropolitan Area is its upward economic mobility. This, combined with its fecundity, has produced a 137 per cent growth of Catholic school enrolment between 1925 and 1965, while the public school enrolment increased by 86 per cent.

Central City versus Suburbs

Before 1930, while the suburbs were just beginning to grow, the central city schools generally had a better reputation than most of the suburban schools. The central city paid higher salaries to teachers, and teachers tended to move into the central city system after gaining experience in their early careers in the suburbs. School expenditures also were higher in the central cities than in all except a few high-status suburbs. This situation changed sharply after World War II, with the suburban school system generally better off in these various respects than the central city schools.

There were a few suburban school systems with national and even world-wide reputations as early as 1930, and several more emerged after 1950. The Winnetka system (in a suburb on Lake Michigan north of Chicago) became known throughout the world as a model of 'progressive' education, and its superintendent, Carleton Washburne, became a world figure in the field of education. The Winnetka system extends only to the 8th grade, and is part of the New Trier Township High School District, which became widely known as a model high school, especially after World War II. Other suburbs with school systems recognized throughout the country are Evanston, Oak Park, and Hinsdale – all mainly upper-middle-class communities.

Structure of State School System

In order to compare schools of the central city with those of the suburbs it is necessary to know certain facts about the structure of the school system in the State of Illinois. (Each state is the final authority on education, and consequently there are 50 different state school systems in the United States.)

There are three types of school district governmental units in the State of Illinois. Elementary school districts serve children from kindergarten (age 5) through the 8th grade. High school districts serve youth from the 9th through the 12th grade. An alternative is the unit school district, which provides an education programme from kindergarten through the 12th grade, and has generally been formed by combining a high school district with several elementary school districts which sent these pupils to that high school. Chicago has a unit school district. Most of the suburban communities have the dual district organization, with elementary school districts serving communities that were originally rather small, though some of them have become rather large through growth of the suburb. Generally, a high school district serves a township, which is likely to have several elementary school districts within its borders. While it has long been legally possible to combine the elementary and high school districts into unit districts, most of the suburban communities have chosen to continue the old dual district plan. This is partly due to advantages of the dual district plan in conferring taxing power and bond-issuing power on the school districts. This advantage has been reduced by legislation in the most recent years.

TABLE 9

FINANCIAL DATA ON CHICAGO CITY AND SURBURBAN SCHOOLS

	Assessed valuation per pupil	Operating expenditures per pupil	School tax rate per $100 valuation
City of Chicago (Elementary and High School combined)	$19,302	$523	$2·260
Suburban Schools			
Elementary School Districts	40,412	564	1·897
High School Districts	65,424	967	1·630

Note: Data for year 1965–66. Average figures.

The suburban schools as a whole have a significant financial advantage over the Chicago city schools, as can be seen in Table 9. The assessed valuation of real property in Chicago, when divided by the number of students, comes out at $19,302. This is to be compared with $30,412 per elementary school pupil in the suburbs, and $65,424 per high school pupil. Consequently, the operating expenditure per pupil in 1965–66 was $523 per pupil in Chicago, and substantially more in the suburbs. The Chicago school tax rate of $2·26 per $100 assessed valuation was almost at the legal limit, but less than the combined elementary and high school tax rates in the suburbs, which was $3·527. One reason that the suburban districts can have a higher school tax rate than the central city is that the central city needs relatively more tax money for other city government services, such as police and fire protection, garbage collection, street repairs, parks, etc. The schools in Chicago receive about 40 per cent of the proceeds of the property tax, whereas the suburbs schools receive about 60 per cent of these funds.

Although the real property tax provides most of the funds for operating public schools, the state legislature in recent years has supplied 'state aid' funds to supplement the money obtained through the local property tax. Thus, in 1967, Chicago received 29 per cent of its operating expenses from the state, 11 per cent from the federal government, and 60 per cent from the local property tax. The elementary school districts in the suburbs received about 70 per cent of their operating expenditures from the local property tax.

Suburban Socio-economic Structure and Education

The financial advantages of the suburban school districts over the Chicago city district are impressive, but the suburban districts are not all the same in this respect. Some of them have a much stronger financial base than others. The amount of taxable property behind each student depends essentially on three factors: the average number of school children per family, the average value of the homes in the district, and the value of the commercial and industrial property in the district.

The elementary districts are highly variable in terms of the assessed valuation per pupil. The wealthiest district is located in an industrial area with very few homes, few pupils, and high industrial property values. The assessed valuation per pupil in this district was $239,000 in 1965–66, compared with a median value of $26,100 among elementary school districts, and a low value of about $10,000 per pupil.

A district with high assessed valuation per pupil is likely to be one with relatively small numbers of school age children per family, together with generally expensive homes and/or substantial commercial and industrial property.

There are two broad principles which seem to govern the nature of the communities and therefore of the school systems in the suburban area. First, people of a similar occupational status, style of life, and income level tend to come together in a suburban community. Second, suburban communities of a given type tend to cluster together, and therefore to divide the suburbs into areas of high, middle, and low status.

To the north on the shore of Lake Michigan are a chain of quasi-exclusive residential suburbs. To the west of the city stretch another set of middle-class residential towns only slightly less sumptuous than the North Shore group. To the south and southeast are industrial towns with residential communities for factory workers. To the northwest, past the airport, is an array of middle-class towns that have grown up since World War II, serving the light industry and the regional offices of insurance and other business concerns that have been built on the former farm lands of that area. In the counties outside Cook and DuPage is a set of old towns that once were independent of Chicago, but have been drawn into its ever-widening orbit, and are now growing rapidly. And there still are a few sleepy rural villages.

Thus, there are four sub-areas, or sectors – the North Shore, the North-west, the West, and the South. The socio-economic data for these sectors are given in Table 10. The order of wealth and school expenditure is: North Shore, Northwest, West, and South Cook-North Lake. (The industrialized area in Lake County north of the North Shore suburbs is combined with the industrialized area of South Cook County.) It will be noted that the mean level of assessed valuation per pupil in the South Cook-North Lake sector was $11,000 below the mean of all suburban districts, while the North Shore districts averaged $9,000 above.

TABLE 10

DIFFERENCES BETWEEN ELEMENTARY SCHOOL DISTRICTS, BY GEOGRAPHIC REGIONS IN THE CHICAGO SUBURBAN AREA

School district characteristics	North Shore	North west	West	South Cook North Lake	All districts
Mean Median Family Income	$15,044	$9,682	$8,520	$7,587	$8,932
Mean of Median Years of Ed.	13·8	12·5	11·7	11·0	11·8
Mean Assessed Val. per Pupil	$39,034	$33,731	$37,284	$19,428	$30,412
% Large Family/ Young Population	16	52	33	73	50
Mean Op. Exp. Per Pupil from Local Revenue	$638	$461	$465	$254	$404
Mean Total Op. Exp. per Pupil	$744	$612	$584	$480	$564
Mean Aid per Pupil. State & Fed.	$106	$151	$119	$226	$160
Mean Tax Rate	$2·043	$1·990	$1·773	$1·953	$1·897
No. of Districts	12	25	56	52	145
Total ADA	28,000	73,000	106,000	101,000	308,000
Mean ADA	2,349	2,927	1,866	1,933	2,112

Note: School District data for 1965–66; Population data from 1960 Census.

This systematic difference of sectors is due considerably to the family size differences, that is, the wealthier sectors have relatively fewer school age children per family, while the poorer sectors have more children of school age per family. This is shown in Tables 10 and 11. The small family districts tend to have high assessed valuations per pupil, and

TABLE 11

MEAN PER PUPIL OPERATING EXPENDITURES IN ELEMENTARY DISTRICTS OF
DIFFERENT FAMILY SIZE: LARGE FAMILY/YOUNG POPULATION,
SMALL FAMILY/OLD POPULATION

SES	Large Family/Young Population		Small Family/Old Population	
	Assessed Valuation Per Pupil			
	Low	High	Low	High
High	$535 (10)	$630 (9)	$575 (4)	$712 (25)
Medium	$491 (25)	$563 (5)	$497 (3)	$618 (16)
Low	$463 (23)	$464 (1)	$498 (8)	$589 (16)

Median Per Pupil Expenditure = $543 for all 145 suburban districts in 1965–66.

high operating expenditures per pupil. In contrast, the large family districts tend to have low operating expenditures per pupil.[1]

It will be noted that the South Cook-North Lake sector of suburbs has a level of operating expenditures per pupil rather similar to that of the City of Chicago. This area has the lowest average socio-economic level in the suburbs, as well as the lowest assessed value per pupil. In these and other ways this area is rather similar to the City of Chicago. Its problems tend to be similar to those of the central city.

Inner-city School Problems

Returning to the central city, we may note some of the major problems confronting the school system, taking Chicago as an example. The central city of a large metropolitan area may be divided roughly into three sub-areas. The slum or low-income area is generally called the 'inner city' because the slums tend to lie close in to the central business district, consisting of old-style obsolescent or obsolete housing. An area of relative affluence is located on the outskirts of the city, and is rather similar to a suburban upper-middle-class community. This kind of area has a favoured location near a lake, or on the high land above a river, or near a country club. It is marked by expensive homes and high-status institutions of various kinds. An area of intermediate status is found between the 'inner city' and the high status areas, or on the edges of the city where large

---

[1] The association between assessed valuation and operating expenditures per pupil is very high, with a Q value of 0·95 as computed from a simple two by two cross-classification table. The association between operating expenditures and a measure of socio-economic status of the residents of the school district is somewhat lower – Q ≅ 0·66. The section of this paper on Suburban Socio-Economic Structure and Education draws heavily from an unpublished Ph.D. Dissertation by David O'Shea, entitled 'The Influence of Community Characteristics upon the Level of Operating Expenditure in Suburban Elementary School Districts', Department of Education, University of Chicago, 1969.

numbers of small homes have been built in recent decades for lower-middle-class and upper-working-class people.

Every city of a half-million or more has this kind of ecological structure, which is reflected in the nature of the schools in the various areas. The survey of the public schools of Chicago made by the writer in 1964[2] delineates these areas and describes the schools in them. The most desirable schools, from the points of view of most teachers and parents, are those in the high status areas. Teachers use their seniority rights to transfer to such schools, and parents who can afford to live in a high-status area choose between it and a high-status suburb. At the other extreme, in the inner city or slum areas, the youngest and most inexperienced teachers are working, including many who do not possess full licenses based on training and examinations, but are employed when fully licensed teachers are not available.

There are some exceptions to this rule. A few inner-city schools are directed by dedicated and experienced school principals who believe they are doing a most important and valuable work, and draw to them teachers with similar ideals of service. Also, many experienced teachers prefer the intermediate status schools because the parents are not so critical and demanding of the teachers, and because they themselves live in such areas and were reared in families of intermediate social status.

The situation of the inner-city schools has improved very much in the past decade, partly because many obsolete buildings have been replaced by the newest and most modern buildings, but more because extra funds have been devoted to improving the conditions of teaching and learning in these schools. In 1965 the federal government passed the Elementary and Secondary Education Act which allocated substantial funds to schools in areas of poverty – urban and rural. Roughly $100 per impoverished pupil was supplied to school districts on the basis of a count of low-income families. This money has been used in various ways, mainly to reduce class size, employ non-professional teacher aides, add remedial classes after school hours, support summer classes, and purchase books and other teaching materials.

Nevertheless, not much progress has been made on the basic problem of segregation of pupils by race and by income level. It is widely agreed in the United States that socially disadvantaged children learn more successfully if they are grouped with more successful children, which means, in practice, if they are grouped in classes with children of the dominant Caucasian group and with children of middle-class families.

Another major problem of the big city is that of securing enough well-prepared teachers and assigning them equitably to the various types of

[2] Robert J. Havighurst, *The Public Schools of Chicago – A Survey Report* (Chicago: Board of Education, 1964.)

schools. Some progress is being made on this problem through special programmes for selecting and preparing teachers for inner-city schools, developed by the universities and teacher-training institutions closest to the big cities. Young people with a service motive and with realistic preparation for teaching in inner-city schools are collecting in greater numbers in such schools. Furthermore, the teacher shortage of the 1950s and early 1960s is being relieved by the increasing numbers of university graduates who were born in the high birth-rate cohorts of the years from 1947 to 1957.

An interesting set of ideas for improvement of central city schools has emerged since 1960, around the concept of the 'educational park' or 'educational plaza'. This term has collected a variety of practical meanings, but essentially it is a site with school facilities for large numbers of children, drawn from a variety of racial and economic groups. In its simplest form, it might consist of a set of buildings for pupils from kindergarten through 12th or 14th grade, located on a spacious site, with ample library, theatre, food-preparation, and recreational facilities. The number of pupils might be on the order of 16 to 20 thousand, serving a population area of 80 to 100 thousand. This kind of educational unit might serve to reduce racial and economic segregation, if skillfully used for that purpose. It also might provide better educational facilities at a lower cost than the present dispersed facilities.

The educational park concept is still pretty much in the 'mental image' and 'paper design' stage, and has many practical and theoretical drawbacks, but it will be developed and adapted in various ways in the big cities and in a few mixed socio-economic suburbs in the coming decade.

Summary and Conclusions

The general problem of providing a good and efficient educational system for a democratic society in the metropolitan areas of the United States is one of reversing the following disadvantages:

(1) Large areas of racially and economically segregated residence in the central city.

(2) Large numbers of small school districts in the suburban areas, with unequal and inequitable financial resources.

(3) Unequal and inequitable distribution of financial resources between the central city and the more affluent of the suburban areas.

It is clear that the school systems alone cannot solve this problem. The problem stems from a socially unhealthy distribution of people in the big metropolitan area, and a socially unhealthy system of local governments and tax structures. Therefore the solution must be a broad one, involving all the major social systems of the metropolitan area – government, business and industry, churches, civic associations, as well as the school system.

Taking Chicago as an example, the following proposals have been made by responsible organizations, and some of them are being put into action.

(1) Compensatory education for disadvantaged children and youth, beginning at the pre-school level and extending to the age of 18 or 20.

(2) Building of 'magnet schools' in areas of racial and economically integrated residence, the schools being of such excellence that they hold and draw students from families that want to live in such areas of the central city.

(3) Increased financial support of the schools from state and federal government, so as to reduce the inequities of support from the real property tax in small local districts.

(4) Formation of regional school districts in the suburban areas, to serve a number of local school districts and to equalize financial support and to provide school programmes which small districts cannot provide (special classes for the physically handicapped, special programmes in the arts, vocational traning, and television).

(5) The most general and far-reaching proposal is that of providing a new 'master plan' for the entire metropolitan area, that can be implemented over a period of several decades and will produce a redistribution of population, of business, industry, recreational areas, and educational and other cultural institutions which will make all parts of the metropolitan area attractive and accessible to people of various income levels. This is becoming a conscious goal of citizens in the great cities of the country.

12

Urban Change and Schools of Education

S. M. Miller and Pamela A. Roby

In the 1960s the United States became enormously concerned with social mobility, with the ability of low-income and discriminated groups to move ahead economically, socially, and politically. At the same time, education emerged as the predominant route for upward social and economic mobility.[1] Consequently, everyone has a stake in education; groups formerly unconcerned about it now place it high on their agenda.

How do these changes affect schools of education? In the first part of this article we shall look more closely at the social and educational changes in the United States. In the second part we shall explore the implications of these changes for schools of education seeking to construct a new role in urban areas.

Educational Changes
The relationship between educational institutions and society has changed in four ways: (1) schools are charged with meeting the needs of formerly neglected groups; (2) there has been growing awareness that much education takes place outside of the school; (3) discontent with the traditional processes of education is growing; and (4) power shifts mark educational institutions. In the following sections we shall examine each of these changes.

New Groups and New Expectations – During the last decade increasing social concern has developed for groups formerly neglected by educational institutions. Schools and universities throughout the United States have given more attention to the disadvantaged. This is a significant step forward. Ten years ago in a study of a suburban school system, one of us tried to find out how many pupils had discontinued high school without a diploma. None of the school's staff could provide an answer. In other school systems throughout the United States there was similar disregard of children who were not 'making it'. This has changed enormously. We are now concerned with the 'disadvantaged', a euphemism for today's young black children.[2]

---

[1] See S. M. Miller and Frank Riessman, *Social Class and Social Policy*, Chapter 5, 'The Credentials Trap' (New York: Basic Books, 1968).

[2] A note on terminology: Formerly Negroes were defined as 'non-white'. Now in the

Educators and social policy makers are now also concerned with another neglected group, the 'non-young', the adult with limited education. Educators' responsibility extends not only to children but to those who have left the school system and are floundering economically. New ways are being sought to help adults with limited education.

The social interest in formerly neglected groups has led to new expectations about teachers and schools. Increasingly, the responsibility for a student's failure is said to belong to the school rather than the individual. Educators and administrators cannot easily define problems away by saying that there is something wrong with the students. Indeed, schools have been charged with the responsibility of improving their students' prospects for social mobility. Schools are expected to assist everyone in reaching a decent level of income by overcoming initial family handicaps.

Out-of-School Education – There is a dawning recognition that education does not only take place in organizations called schools or by people called teachers. For example, there has been much recent discussion about the role of the family in the education of youth. Many believe that the Coleman and Pettigrew studies[3] indicate the significance of family backgrounds and of peer groups in the education of children. People concerned with black power, which manifests itself in such cries as 'I'm Black and proud' and 'Black is beautiful', believe that the way a person views himself in terms of a collective ideal affects his ability to learn in school as well as the way the school responds to him. Similarly, jobs are coming to be viewed as part of the educational process rather than as unconnected with the educational world. New ways of learning on the job are extensively discussed, and training is often given after the job is obtained rather than before. Thus, we are increasingly recognizing the variety of influences on education and the limited, though not minor, role of the schools.

Paralleling the recognition of the educational significance of non-educational institutions is the growing awareness that many people other than teachers are educators. Currently there is much discussion concerning 'community participation' in educational decision-making, and the role of parents in relation to schools is hotly debated. There has also been both experimentation and discussion concerning the use of sub-professionals such as teachers' aides in the schools.[4] Thus, we are beginning to recognize

---

U.S. Office of Education report by James S. Coleman, Negroes, Puerto Ricans, Mexican-Americans, and Indians are listed separately; there is a separate category of 'others' who are the continental whites. This represents an enormous reversal of thinking from classifying blacks as a residual category of 'non-whites'!

[3] James S. Coleman, *Equality of Educational Opportunity* (Washington, D.C.: Department of Health, Education and Welfare, 1966); U.S. Commission on Civil Rights, *Racial Isolation in the Public Schools*, Vols. 1 and 2 (Washington, D.C.: Government Printing Office, 1967).

[4] cf. Pamela A. Roby, 'Educational Aides in Inner City Schools', *Integrated Education*, Vol. 6, No. 6, November 1968; Arthur Pearl and Frank Riessman, *New Careers for the Poor* (New

the importance of involving people other than teachers in the school system in an effort to improve educational opportunities substantially.

Sometimes educators use this awareness of multiple educational influences as a 'cop-out' by claiming that institutions other than schools bear the responsibility for educational failures. In another perspective, this proliferation of educational activities has meant that no one had responsibility for all elements of the educational process. For example, no one takes responsibility for assuring that there is a connexion between the family and the school. To some extent new federally-supported educational institutions, such as Head Start (under the Office of Economic Opportunity) and vocational training (under the Manpower Development and Training Act Programs) have expanded and are competitive with local public schools.[5] These various educational units are not effectively connected.

At its best, the recognition that other activities must be developed to support education is very positive. But fragmentation characterizes the total educational experience. In a sense there is no educational system. We are dealing with a number of separate activities only loosely connected at various points rather than systematically linked together.

Changing Educational Processes – Professionals tend to assume that they know more than they do about educational practices and effectiveness. Magical solutions are sought that might solve all problems of all children with one swift method or one sure approach. Consequently, we lose the sense of individuality, the sense of change in children, the sense of the specialness of the individual teacher, and the sense of trying to relate to specific circumstances. The educational professionals do not know what is effective. We do not know how children differ in vital respects nor what is appropriate for each child at a particular stage in his life.

The most glaring example of our lack of knowledge, we believe, is found in the teaching of reading, which falls far short of qualifying as a professional discipline. The competing claims of different schools of reading appear ritualistic. There is little discussion of the different needs of children and the variations in these needs during their lives. Too much attention is directed towards fostering a technique rather than towards responding to a child. We must come to recognize the inconclusiveness of what we know.

Education is in a revolution of discontent rather than in a revolution of new purpose. Increasing public recognition that something is wrong with pedagogy is forcing educators to rethink traditional notions. Currently, professional barriers and perspectives are limiting the re-evaluation of educational issues. As professionals and educators, we seem to lack the

York: The Free Press, 1965), and Garda W. Bowman and Gordon J. Klopf, *New Careers and Roles in the American School* (New York: Bank Street School of Education, 1968).

[5] S. M. Miller and Pamela A. Roby, 'Educational Strategies', stencil, 1969.

humility that will enable us to undergo and learn from new experiences. Professionalism is certainly important, but it sometimes becomes a way of avoiding issues rather than a way of obtaining standards of excellence. We must recognize that we really do not know as much as we think we know about what is effective in the classroom. We need much more candour about our ignorance and much more willingness to explore rather than to conform to poorly working practices.

The Transfer of Power – A transfer of power is taking place within the educational setting in three ways. First, teachers are pushing for more power. One is not obliged to give many illustrations after the 1968 siege of teacher strikes in the United States. There is a big change taking place in the traditional notion of the teacher as one who is frightened, unassertive, emasculated, and unwilling to fight. The second move is that new community groups are fighting for power in the schools. Decentralization in New York City is symbolic of new community groups' fighting for power. Third, national groups, including the Federal Government and an increasing number of Foundations, are involved in education today.

Anyone concerned with education must therefore develop ways of relating to these new, frequently crosscutting, currents of power. The old liberal rhetoric is no longer satisfactory to teachers, community groups, and federal officials. We must think about educational problems in fresh ways. When we do think about educational problems, it is important to recognize that no one solution can be a permanent, complete answer to these problems. For example, decentralization is one way of breaking through the encrustations of time and a way of beginning to develop new movement, but decentralization does not guarantee great improvement in children's educational achievement. Certain activities are done best when there is centralization; others are accomplished more effectively when there is decentralization. When we look at the administration of schools from a long-term perspective, we find that neither centralization nor decentralization by itself is *the* solution. There must be a continuing, evolving process of change. Currently decentralization is on the rise, and schools of education must learn how to relate to this fact and play a more effective role than previously. Doing so will require great sensitivity to the problems of power in the school system.

Against this background of educational change, what are the roles for a school of education? Rather than offering one answer, in the next section of the paper we offer a variety of possibilities.

Schools of Education: Some New Possibilities

In the coming years schools of education can perform six functions. They can serve as training centres for teachers and administrators; as research and demonstration centres; as operators of a school district; as junior partners and facilitators in school districts; as a connecting link between various institutions; and as policy critics and advocates.

1. *Training Teachers* – What role can schools serve in the development of teachers? Organizations frequently change because new people move into them rather than because new policies have been formally adopted. An organization such as a school of education changes because different kinds of students and new faculty arrive. In urban areas both sets of new faces are needed.

University efforts to obtain more students and faculty from the so-called minority groups or to recruit students and faculty with particularly interesting experiences or potential are extremely important. It is difficult, however, to achieve a rapid alteration in the nature of students or faculty if universities insist on traditional recruiting practices and credentials. For example, it will be difficult to hire new faculty members from Harlem if the procurement of a Ph.D. is the basic requirement for full faculty status. We are reminded of a white person who is a most interesting speaker. He publishes seldom but has fascinating ideas about youth and education in this country. He has been unsuccessfully recommended for several university positions. Despite his outstanding experience it is very doubtful that he will obtain a university position worthy of his talents. He lacks a Ph.D. His unusual abilities are lost to universities because of the insistence on credentials. Professionals are so unsure of their capability of judging people that we insist on a person having a Ph.D. and assume that without this degree a person is unqualified. We do this even though we ourselves engage in extensive criticism of the fact that the Ph.D. experience is largely a degrading ceremonial.

Schools of education should take some risks with faculty and students. They should recruit different types of students, including those who have not obtained high scores on Graduate Record Examinations. Merely to enrol different kinds of students, however, is not significant. We must make it possible for them to succeed in school.[6] We should plan more effectively to help students, especially when they come from backgrounds that are not traditional to the school. A different kind of relationship between student and faculty is needed, one in which feelings of collegiality and responsibility for one another exist on all sides. If new kinds of students are sought, new professors will be needed.

2. *Research and Demonstration Centres* – Research is today's immediate solution to problems, just as in earlier periods education was the facile

---

[6] In 1968 the Southern Education Foundation reported that of the 159 United States institutions of higher education sampled, only eight made any systematic effort with preparatory guidance or tutoring programmes or allowances in the curriculum to work students who were unquestionably 'high risks'. John Egerton, *Higher Education for 'High Risk' Students* (Atlanta, Georgia: Southern Education Foundation, 1968).

solution. In the 1950s, people with sex problems were sent to a sex education course; accident-prone types took courses in driver education. Today, we are somewhat more sophisticated; we no longer encourage people to take courses, we do research on their problems. We do not believe, however, that the question is whether research should or should not be done: rather, the issues are which research, in what ways, and with what yields?

We became acutely aware that 'research' is not necessarily an effective answer when some seven years ago we studied the literature on school dropouts. It was a disheartening experience because most of the material was unbelievably bad – stupid and/or irrelevant. In some instances, the data was gathered rigorously but without relevance to the subject; however, in most cases the material was obtained in a slipshod manner and lacked relevance as well.

It is important to do research, but we must think about research in new ways. We believe that the research model employed in contemporary educational research is too limited. The statistical-experimental model leads to a detachment from what is taking place on the scene. It lacks the quality of a clinical orientation and of learning from practice. An example of sterility is a study of what makes a good teacher. The design was fairly typical: on the basis of students' test performances, teachers with good students were to be separated from those with poor students. Then, both groups of teachers were to be tested to see what differentiated teachers with good learners from those with poor learners. An alternative design was suggested once good teachers were identified: they would be studied in their classrooms to see what made them more effective, other teachers would be interviewed about the effective teachers, and the effective teachers would also be interviewed to find out what it was they saw themselves doing. The general strategy was to see how effective teachers worked instead of relying solely on testing, which could only provide some general characteristics rather than specifics about actual classroom behaviour. The alternative approach is not always the preferred way to design a study, but the interesting fact here is that the suggestion for a more clinical orientation was flatly rejected without examination. It did not meet conventional standards of the process of 'rigorous' research.

Perhaps we overgeneralize, but it seems to us that there is a need for humility and courage among researchers today. New methods of dealing with existing problems are required partly because different problems are emerging and partly because old methods have been largely unsuccessful. There should be more concern with action, with the clinical approach, rather than an almost exclusive reliance on testing or experimental models. In the clinical model, researchers are involved in the action they are investigating, and they both learn from the action and contribute to it. This differs from research that is unconnected with action.

We are not attacking the statistical-experimental model as such, but the excessive emphasis on it as *the* 'scientific' approach. The stress on the traditional model has led to a dearth of clinically oriented research regarding the classroom. There is need for researchers who understand action, who can do research relevant to action, and who know how to communicate their findings so that something happens as a result of them.

3. *School System Operators* – The third possibility for a school of education is to operate a school system. The old economic concept of the market is being resurrected in discussions about public institutions, including schools.[7] The trouble with public institutions, some contend, is that they are monopolies and lack competition. This situation differs from the private market where the individual consumer has a choice among competing goods. This thinking leads to the demand that competition be introduced into the educational system.

This analysis leads to different policy conclusions. One recommendation is the supplying of educational vouchers to families so that they can purchase education in any place they wish. Another is that institutions other than the traditional school board should run the school system, perhaps IBM, a school of education, or the Urban League plus Boston College could operate a school system effectively.

4. *Junior Partners* – A school of education may also serve as a junior partner and facilitator in a school district. Certainly there is an urgent need for schools of education to assist some of the decentralized school districts. A school of education could help recruit teachers, facilitate the operation of the schools, and provide the resources to assist the districts in whatever way necessary. The school of education might provide many different resources for one or two decentralized school districts. These new school districts need content for their programmes; they need help. The world is very complicated; just getting around in it is difficult. A school of education could take the responsibility of working with a school district in an effort to achieve worthwhile change. It would be rewarded by changes in the education of the youth and by the vitality and relevance that its teaching would gain from the experience.

5. *Co-ordinators* – The fifth possibility for schools of education is the role of linking the various educating institutions. As noted above, no institution, agency, or individual is responsible for making education an effective system. A school of education might have a special role in trying

---

[7] Christopher Jencks, 'Private Management for Public Schools', Memorandum No. 4 (Washington, D.C.; Institute for Policy Studies, October 1965); James S. Coleman, 'Towards Open Schools', *The Public Interest*, No. 9, Fall 1967, pp. 20–27.

to connect the family, the rapidly increasing job-training institutions, and the community to the school. We suspect that the greatest current increase in educational expenditures is for job-training activities rather than for direct aid to schools. No one is connecting these educational spheres or working out the appropriate inter-relationships among them. In the school system, those concerned with the Board of Education's Head Start programme have little contact with people involved in other community programmes. People involved in job training outside the school have little contact with those people who are responsible for the strictly vocational educational programmes in the schools. A school of education could have an important role since it has people involved in many educational areas. One problem is that even within a school of education itself people do not effectively communicate with one another.

If a school began to make new types of connexions internally, then it might be possible to play a role outside the school in forging connexions among the many groups carrying out educational functions.

6. *Policy Critics and Advocates* – The sixth role of the school of education is that of a policy critic and advocate. This is a difficult and complicated role, but one that many like to play. It is striking that the most important critiques of education in the last dozen years have been pursued by non-'educators', and certainly not by members of the faculties of schools of education. Schools of education need to play a broader role of critic and advocate than in the recent past.

Obviously there is a need for careful and thoughtful critical analysis of changes taking place in the schools. In a sense, education faculties need to act as the loyal oppositions to the schools rather than serve as courtiers to the schools. Some of the faculty should have the perspective of the outsider, trying to examine independently what is taking place.

Undoubtedly what is most needed is a good theory about education and a good theory about our society. We have had an exhaustion of ideas; the exhaustion not only of Marxist ideology, which Daniel Bell and others described as the 'end of ideology', but more disturbingly, the end of liberal ideology as well.[8] Conventional wisdom and unexamined assumptions about democracy are severely under attack. For example, integration and separation have been critically debated. These issues are extremely difficult to debate since people are frequently not discussing the same things. A common perspective is lacking. Similarly, youth's concern with freedom and authenticity does not fit in easily with the egalitarian concerns that were focal to New Deal liberal ideology. We are lost because we do not know where we are and where we wish to go.

Perhaps the goal of understanding our current plight and the possibilities

---

[8] Daniel Bell, *The End of Ideology* (New York: The Free Press, 1962).

of new values and directions might be an essential occupation for a school of education. This would entail not only the immediate examination of concrete policies but also a broader interest in what is taking place in society and the reverberations of these changes on educational direction and practice.

Conclusions

Most importantly, urban schools of education need a link – rich, profound, and feeling – with the action that is taking place outside. This connexion must be more than just a mechanical and perfunctory link; it must be a connexion that will change the schools rather than confirm their position.

Educators face great challenges during the next decade. In facing these challenges they may be buoyed by the gains made during the last decade. The very fact that educators throughout the country are concerned with children who have been excluded from the educational mainstream, with children who are troubled and in difficulty, with children who have been forgotten as society has become more affluent, is a very encouraging step. A few short years ago we were not concerned about these children.

There is also a widespread acceptance of the notion of full employment for black people in this country; twenty years ago, a full-employment bill, largely for white people, failed in Congress. Despite racial tensions, current polls indicate that the majority of Americans accept the concept of full employment for black people.

It is our belief that there is a hidden liberal feeling that is searching for a purpose and seeking a way of surfacing and having impact. The situation is not as desperate nor as difficult as it appears on the surface. Many people are searching for answers, but we do not know how to relate to one another. We have difficulty – black and white – in talking to one another, but these difficulties are not irreversible.

We stress some of the positive trends in order to overcome the apathy that comes with the feeling that nothing can be changed. If we look at events in terms of weeks, months, or even a few years, change is difficult to perceive. A longer view is needed. The changes occurring are largely humanitarian and positive, even though we have experienced backlash effects. Generally, people today are concerned about the neglected, the discriminated, and the ignored in our midst; this is a significant step forward.

In this age schools of education have a chance, if they cultivate purpose and commitment, to move into significant roles in the struggle towards making this a just and humane society.

13

Montreal

Reginald Edwards

Montreal is often thought of as the world's second largest French-speaking city, the seventh city in size in North America, second only to Rotterdam as an inland port. It stands at the entrance to the St Lawrence Seaway, that billion dollar waterway which opens the Great Lakes to ocean-going ships. But Montreal is more. It is at once a municipality, an international city, a mountain, an island, a metropolitan region and a way of life. As a municipality and a walled city it existed before municipalities were legally created in Canada, being founded in 1642 as a Christian outpost, supported by French philanthropy, later becoming part of the feudal property of the Gentlemen of St Sulpice and remaining so until the forms of the seigneurial system ended in 1940. As a walled city it resisted neither the English in 1760 nor the Americans during the Revolutionary Wars. The Parliament of the United Canadas met here until an English mob set fire to the building in 1849.

Within the present city of Montreal lies the mountain rising from the St Lawrence to a height of some 760 feet. The city has spread out from its foothold near the river and circled the mountain, but enough of its open space still remains to provide ski slopes in winter, an open air concert hall in summer, a 500-acre park and the 100-foot-high illuminated Cross, a glowing reminder of Maisonneuve, founder of Montreal. The city itself is international and polyglot, with daily newspapers in French, English and Italian, and with additional languages such as Greek and German heard on the radio. It provides the headquarters of more Canadian firms than any other city, as well as the International Civil Aviation Organization, and the International Air Transport Association. Its architectural skill in arranging the space from the mountain to the waterfront in a series of terraces, with skyscraper office blocks, highrise apartments and its forty acres of underground shopping plazas, give the central city a high population density per superficial square foot but provides space and ease of access to all services. Truly it is the metropolis geared to twentieth century living. Its parks, its more than 4,000 restaurants, its variety of languages, its garish night life, its largely English cinema, its almost entirely French theatre, its music, its fourteen feet of winter snowfall, its daily crime figures (more than two bank hold-ups per day), its recourse to bombings in time of industrial strife, its legacy of Old Montreal, its new Metro (subway) and its Exposition Universelle, have contrived to make Montreal a way of life.

Historical Development

Historically the very development of Canada has been seen in a metropolitan context. Trade and market facilities, industrial production, newspapers, banking and commercial facilities are of first importance to the economist in defining a metropolis, but to the historian the actual location and the communication network are more important still. Lines of communication aid in the distribution of people, their customs and their ideas as well as their goods. The St Lawrence river valley was an excellent communication network. On it the French founded Quebec, Three Rivers and Montreal. The English conquest transformed the river into a portion of the English communication net emanating from metropolitan London. The Quebec Act confirmed the French seigneurs in their property rights, and gave to all the French who remained the rights to language and religion, the latter as the guarantee of the former, provided that it was not reinforced by clerics from outside New France. Quebec City became the governmental part of the network, Montreal its dynamic commercial extension. Merchants came first from Boston and Albany, and later from London. Railway and canal building extended the network still further. Within this dynamism the seigneurs remained content, and farmers were able to sell their wheat on the London market. But a new professional middle class arose in Quebec City and Montreal, an *élite* which lacked economic vested interests and was originally without political power. It was this group which was responsible for the development of French language newspapers, which was the spearhead of the struggle against the London-based metropolitan interests of Montreal and became the focus for French survival against the assimilative tendencies advocated by Lord Durham. Because of them the United Canadas led not to the existence of one English area but to the imperfect recognition of English rights and French rights, the struggle for clarification of which is being continued in the Constitutional Conferences of the 1960s.

Confederation in 1867 strengthened the metropolitan position of Montreal, in spite of a satellite development in Toronto linked by the Erie canals and railways to New York and year-round access to the Atlantic. There was some early development of small industry under French control, but the peasant attributes of thrift in 'money stockings' rather than banks denied any possibility of the emergence of large-scale risk capital. Two factors in the last decade of the nineteenth century contributed to the growth of Quebec and even more to the growth of Montreal. The first was English investment emanating from London, and the second was the rapid growth of the eastern United States. The latter created the demand for materials and the former supplied the large financial backing which local resources were unable to sustain. Industrial development also created a demand for skilled labour which did not exist. Canada in its past history has relied heavily on the immigration of skilled technicians to meet the needs for industrial expansion; its present immigration policy is still directed towards the increase of such skills. At the end of the nineteenth century the results of a growing industrialism in Quebec were to impoverish still further the rural French population who became the lower paid workers in English and foreign owned enterprises. It also stimulated a movement from rural to urban areas. Concern about the situation led to demands for state intervention on the one hand and for movements towards self-help on the other. The latter gave rise to the setting up of many co-operatives, and to small-scale banking through the *Caisses Populaires*; the former presumed that only the whole monetary resources of a Provincial government could compete with foreign enterprise. This has led to electricity generation and supply being brought under state control with the formation of Hydro-Quebec, which in turn has proceeded to construct the world's largest hydro-electric project on the Outardes and Manicouagan rivers in Northern Quebec. Quebec has set up a nationalized steel complex, purchased from private enterprise. It has also established nuclear power stations. Politically it has led to the policy of *Maître Chez Nous* and to ideas of complete political and financial separation from the rest of Canada.

Political Organization

Politically Quebec has been the only Canadian province to have an upper and lower house of Parliament, though in December 1968 the upper house was abolished. Quebec's parliament, now known as the National Assembly, has been under the control of Conservative or National Union control for the greater part of the last hundred years, although federally Quebec has generally been represented by Liberal members. On the Provincial scene the balance of power resides with the rural areas, which have the smallest vote per member. This produces distorted electoral results, so much so that the present National Union government was elected by a 40 per cent vote compared with a Liberal vote of 47 per cent. But this is much less distorted than the 1952 election which gave 89 per cent of the seats to the National Union party for 51 per cent of the votes cast. There have been two periods of Liberal rule during the past thirty years. In the first from 1939–44 they established Hydro-Quebec, enfranchised women and legislated for compulsory education to age 14, with exemptions at age 12 and upwards. In their second period from 1960 to 1966, they extended the operation of Hydro-Quebec, laid plans for a state controlled steel industry, reduced the electoral age to 18, raised the school leaving age to 16 without exemptions, and instituted a complete reform of education. The great voting strength of the Liberal party resides on the island of Montreal where it controls all seats save two.

Demographic Development

This island of Montreal, some thirty miles long and approximately four miles wide, contains two-and-a-half million people, 46 per cent of the population of the Province and one-eighth of the total population of Canada. During this century the population of the Province has increased less than four times, that of the island by more than six-fold, from the 1901 census. In the same period the rural population has declined from 60 per cent to 25 per cent, with the remaining 29 per cent living in other urban regions. The natural increase of population now accounts for only 83 per cent of total growth, and some 325,000 immigrants have arrived in the last ten years, most of them settling in the metropolitan region. Birth rates for the Province have declined in each of the past eleven years, there being a high of 30·4 in 1946–50, to a current figure of 18·0 per thousand. In each year the metropolitan figure has been lower, the 1968 figure being of the order of 14 per thousand. Family size is also lower, being 3·6 per family against a high of 5·8 for many rural areas.

Immigration now averages 30,000 per year, most of whom settle in Montreal. The largest single group, 6,000, come from Italy, 4,000 each from France and the U.K. and about 2,000 each from Greece and the United States. Rather more than half are workers, of whom probably 1,000 could be described as higher professional, 4,000 as lower professional (including teachers) and more than 2,500 as in clerical occupations, of whom nearly 1,000 are stenographers. It can be seen that many of these will affiliate with the English speaking groups – the Anglophones, since English is the predominant language of business and commerce. For the Province of Quebec as a whole, 82 per cent have French as the mother tongue, but on the island of Montreal only 64 per cent do so. Since the two official languages of Canada are French and English the continued growth of Montreal appears to predicate an eventual majority of Anglophones, a hypothesis extremely disturbing to those who seek to defend and extend French influence and French culture.

Montreal may be said to have developed an agglomerate economy. In the city there are some 5,000 firms employing a total of a quarter of a million employees of whom 55,000 are employed by the clothing industry, 30,000 by the food and drink industries, 60,000 by machinery, metal products and electrical goods industry. Tobacco and textiles account for a further 40,000 and printing about 16,000. Within the city also are the large numbers employed in such commercial undertakings as banking, finance, insurance, to say nothing of those in communications and service trades employment. Outside the city limits will be found the large petrochemical industry at the north end of the island, a largely capital intensive industry with an investment/employment ratio of $20,000 per employee. There are also some engineering and sugar refining plants. For those industries located within the city the food and drink industries have sales of over one billion dollars annually, with the clothing trades producing $650,000,000, and machinery, metal products and electrical goods realizing another billion between them.

In the field of government, the major divisions of power were laid down in the British North America Act of 1867. Provinces were given the right to direct taxation, this being the more onerous, whilst the Federal government took indirect taxation as its source of revenue. The provinces were given power to license shops, saloons, taverns and auctioneers for the purpose of raising money for provincial, local or municipal purposes. The emergence of metropolitan, or even large municipal areas could scarcely have been foreseen. Montreal in 1867 possessed the right to levy a property tax, a water tax and a business tax. Its incomes derive from the same sources today. For a brief period it had an income tax, when the Province did not, and from 1949 it had the right to impose a sales tax of 1 per cent on the majority of non-food items, later raised to 2 per cent, which was to be given to the local School Commissions in the city. It also imposed a 2 per cent sales tax for its own municipal purposes. In 1961 the Provincial government instituted a Province-wide sales tax of 6 per cent (now 8 per cent) and withdrew from Montreal its taxing rights. In return Montreal receives an annual grant of $33 million, somewhat less than the revenue it gave up. The city therefore relies for its finances upon the property tax. It collects by this means, on behalf of the Schools Commissions, over whom it has little or no control, a sum of $125 million, 30 per cent of the total budget of the city. In order to balance its budget it has been compelled recently to increase the tax rate by 23 per cent.

The reasons for these demands stem from the metropolitan nature of the area, and Montreal, as the largest of the twenty-six municipalities on the island (the others range in size from 3,000 to 80,000), must bear the largest proportion of the cost. At the turn of the century it had a population of 360,000 and a budget of $4 million. By 1935 its population was one million and its budget $48·3 million; by 1968 the figures were one and a half million and a budget of $410 million.

In the field of transportation the City of Montreal is the effective agent through the Montreal Transportation Commission for providing public transport for those twenty municipalities which lie within or adjacent to the city boundaries. It does so through the joint operation of a bus system and a subway system completed in 1966. The former came from the purchase of an obsolete, privately owned tramways system, which required some $83 million for purchase and conversion, the latter through a direct borrowing of $225 million for construction. Debt charges for this cost the city $10 million annually and the other eighteen municipalities $2 million. The cost of street improvement and maintenance for the city is equivalent to an annual subsidy of $123 for every automobile registered in the city.

Problems of Language and National Origins

Apart from the historical imperatives of the ethnic differences, differences recently accentuated by a newly found pride in French-Canadian nationalism and answering overtones from the *grandeur* of Metropolitan France, the problems of Montreal are those of any metropolitan area, given the responsibilities of a 'city state' without the corresponding financial powers, and subject to the centralizing tendencies of higher levels of government. But in educational matters, the complexity engendered by a confessional school system subject to the strains of an increasingly urban, industrial society, and responsive to the pressures of the technocrats on the one hand, and restrained by the entrenched interests of many power groups on the other, produces a highly emotionally-charged situation for metropolitan Montreal.

It will be remembered that the Quebec Act recognized the rights of the French to language and religion. This latter right they safeguarded by the establishment of confessional schools, rejecting a system of public schools divided by religion and language. On the other hand in 1841, the Parliament of the United Canadas recognized the right to set up dissentient schools, controlled by elected trustees. In 1846 School Commissions were appointed for Catholics and Protestants in Quebec City and Montreal, and these provisions were confirmed by the British North America Act. For a few years the Province had a Minister of Education, but in 1875 the position was abolished, and a Superintendent of Education was appointed, who reported to Parliament through the Provincial Secretary. At the same time the Roman Catholic Bishops became members of the Catholic Committee of the Council of Education, whilst dissentient ministers had representation on the Protestant Committee. Each Roman Catholic parish could have its School Board, and even today, in spite of some amalgamations there are nearly 2,000 such Catholic School Boards. Of these, 49 have less than 47 students each; another 1,000 have less than 500 students. Over the years the dissentient schools have been grouped in progressively larger units, and for a number of years nine Central School Boards were sufficient. Within the city of Montreal the forty separate Catholic schools boards were reduced to a single Catholic School Commission. From 1925 the Protestants were encouraged to form a Central School Board grouping of the city of Montreal and nine neighbouring municipalities under a single tax scheme.

Even before compulsory schooling was started in 1943 difficulties arose when large numbers of immigrants arrived who spoke neither French nor English. Even earlier there had been difficulty in accommodating a non-French Catholic population of Irishmen. But the real problem came with the arrival of large numbers of Jews from Eastern Europe. The earlier Sephardic Jews had paid taxes to the majority group but educated their children privately. The new immigrants were unable to afford such luxuries. Eventually they were perceived as non-Catholic, and were affiliated to the Protestant Schools. In Montreal a special agreement was made in 1930, and modified in 1931, which created a Jewish School Commission which could make agreements with certain Protestant School Boards for the education of Jewish children.

A large influx of Italians came after 1924 when the United States drastically changed its immigration laws, and many who came saw Canada only as a temporary home whilst seeking admission to the U.S. Over 93 per cent who stayed in Quebec settled in Montreal, mainly in two French speaking areas. As Catholics they sought a Catholic education, as workers on a North American continent they desired some major part of their education in English. From 1925, like the Irish before them, they were given bilingual elementary schools where the lessons were in French in the morning and English in the afternoon. In order to get a secondary education in English many parents had to abjure their religion, so that eventually the archbishop encouraged them to go to *les écoles Irlandais*. This move, coinciding with an English Catholic desire to create Catholic High Schools, rather than *Collèges Classiques* on the French pattern, has set the pattern of Italian education within the city. Of the more than 34,000 children in the English Catholic Schools of the Montreal Catholic School Commission, more than 12,000 are of Italian descent, 7,000 are Scots or English, less than 3,000 are Irish and more than 4,000 are French.

School finances come from two sources, taxes on property and government grants, school fees having been abolished in 1961. The major School Commissions, the Protestant School Board of Greater Montreal which deals with 65,000 out of the island's 78,000 Protestant children, and the Catholic School Commission which is responsible for some 225,000 out of the 285,000 Catholic children, are both appointed boards. They can demand that the City of Montreal collect the property tax which the School Boards impose. There is one rate of tax for Protestant and Jewish property owners set by the Protestant School Board, and a different, lower one for Catholic property owners set by the Catholic School Commission.

These charges are passed on to tenants without regard to their religion. Business and industry forms a separate tax portion, known as the Neutral Panel. The two school authorities jointly fix the tax rate for the Neutral Panel, higher than the general property tax rate, and the proceeds are divided between the two groups in proportion to the numbers of children of the two faiths between the ages of six and sixteen. Recently because Jewish property owners paid more in taxes than would cover the cost of education of Jewish children (reckoned on a per capita basis) the Protestant Board was required to transfer the balance to the Catholic Commission.

In other areas elections are held for the position of School Commissioner and School Trustee. The elections are on a confessional basis, restricted to Canadian citizens. Formerly they were also restricted to property owners, but voting has now been extended to parents. In most areas Jews are neither eligible for membership of Protestant Boards nor are they allowed to vote, although amending legislation is now promised. Jewish rights have been guaranteed by allowing the Canadian Jewish Congress to name five appointees to the Montreal Protestant School Board. In one particular area, St Leonard, which has an elementary school Commission, many of the residents of Italian origin were declared ineligible to vote in a recent School Board election, as they were not Canadian citizens, though they were property owners and parents. A group which sought to have a unilingual Quebec, and saw education as the means for this achievement, *Le Mouvement pour l'Integration Scolaire*, ran candidates for three vacancies on the Commission. With their success they were able, quite legally, to decide that the language of instruction in the St Leonard Catholic elementary schools would be French. Since the general practice until now has been to give *de facto* language recognition, and *de jure* religious recognition, counter-pressures have mounted, leading to marches on Quebec, and the Parliament in Ottawa. The preamble to the Education Department Act of Quebec of 1964 states that every child is entitled to the advantage of a system of education conducive to the full development of his personality, and parents have the right to choose the institutions, which according to their convictions, ensure the greatest respect for the rights of their children. The question remains whether convictions extend only to religion and not to language. The Provincial Premier promised a Parliamentary Bill to guarantee language rights to parents, but under pressure from French nationalists and others it was remitted to a Committee for study. This committee is now hearing briefs on this matter. In the meantime the English-speaking Catholic children of St Leonard are being educated, privately, in makeshift premises, organized by a committee of parents.

The 'Quiet Revolution' of the present decade has been powered by a new metropolitan *élite*, a new technocracy, which like an earlier *élite* was without vested economic interests and final political power. Some of the new *élite* see the future of French Canada resolved by the 'Magna Carta of Education', a series of laws which followed the Royal Commission of Enquiry into Education (1961–66) and which have radically changed the educational structures. Others see its future through the emergence of a French state, separate from the rest of Canada. The efforts of the first group produced a euphoria among many of the English community, and a French ambience which was attractive. There was a rush to learn to speak French and to accommodate to French cultural advance, a rush cooled somewhat by the demagoguery of the advocates of the latter.

Education has changed radically. There is an active Ministry of Education which extended the limits of education, provided grants for students, grants for research, gave substantial annual sums to universities for the first time and sought for a regionalization and secularization of educational control. The Provincial budget for education has increased from $170 million in 1960 to $792 million for the current year, 30 per cent of total provincial revenue. Of this almost $400 goes in new statutory grants to school boards, which themselves raise $428 million in property taxes. Education has become a billion dollar enterprise in the Province of Quebec.

It has had its setbacks, too. It is true that secondary education is now under the control of fifty-five Catholic and nine Protestant regional boards, but the rural and clerical influence retained several thousand school boards to control elementary education. It sought a secondary education which would be 'polyvalent', offering opportunities for choice to students, a system of 'electives' rather than the constraints of a single, required group of courses. It sought to end the *Collèges Classiques*, whose eight-year course had existed for three hundred years. It offered them the choice of becoming either part of the secondary school system, or an initial part of higher education, and had some measure of success. It created a new level of education above the secondary but not part of higher education – the *College d'Enseignement General et Professionel* – or C.E.G.E.P. which would constitute the twelfth, thirteenth and, for some, the fourteenth year of education. They would be free, non-confessional, provided by the state and organized on language lines. The products of C.E.G.E.P.s would be either those going on to universities, or members of a skilled technician class. The future economic well-being of a Quebec society would rest heavily on the 'polyvalent' secondary schools and the C.E.G.E.P.s. Whilst this is still true, reaction has set in, and the new, more conservative National Union government has slowed down the pace of change, bowed to the demands of groups supporting the old *status quo*, and by a great deal of support for private education ($300 per student, at least) has enabled many a *Collège Classique* to survive, and many a Jewish

Parochial School to thrive. Many members of the English community have resisted the establishment of English language C.E.G.E.P.s, wrongly visualizing them as part of higher education, and as a threat to an English (Protestant) system which, to them, seemed so superior.

Because of the establishment of C.E.G.E.P.s., higher education is to undergo change. Admission will be after at least thirteen years, instead of eleven, as at present, and the minimum course will last for three years instead of four. The *Baccalaureat* of the *Collèges Classiques* will disappear, and the English system of bachelor's, master's and doctoral degrees will be adopted. A new university, the State University of Quebec, is being established, with the first portion being built in the city of Montreal. This will add to Montreal's existing universities, McGill, Montreal and Sir George Williams University, and the two English institutions of Loyola and Marianapolis College whose future status within higher education is not yet determined. Officially they are English language Classical Colleges affiliated to the French language University of Montreal but awarding English style B.A.s after a four-year course. Under the new laws, teacher training will cease to be confessionally provided, will come under the control of universities, whilst the State University will take into associate status the French normal schools, whose numbers are to be drastically reduced.

There is one other area of controversy, to which reference should be made, the control and operation of the school systems on the island of Montreal. Here metropolitanism, and technical development, would visualize a unified structure, possibly divided on language lines. The *status quo*, and forces seeking to maintain it, would see confessionality and local control as more important. The planning operation for the re-organization of secondary education produced two regional Protestant boards, one of which operates schools in the French as well as in the English language, and regional Catholic boards, several of which operate schools in English as well as French. Modern conditions would demand that a school should be provided for children of those parents no longer interested in preserving confessionality. The most recent Council for the Restructuring of Education on the Island of Montreal has recommended a three-tier system. At the upper level there will be a single Schools Council for the Island of Montreal, the thirteen members of which would be drawn from the next lower level, the thirteen School Commissions, of which nine would be French and four English, the whole island being divided into four for the English Commissions and into nine for the French School Commissions. The Commissions would be required to provide sufficient schools for the language-based population of their region, the English groups being required to produce Protestant Schools, Catholic Schools, and Neutral Schools, whilst the French would operate only Catholic and Neutral Schools. To ensure democratization as well as regionalization, each individual school would have an elected School Committee, electoral status being available to parents and others without regard to Canadian citizenship. The School Committees would be able to elect less than half of the Regional School Commissioners, the other Commissioners being elected by general ballot, but one reserved to Canadian citizens. In the past, the Provincial government has extolled participation, democratization and regionalization. This plan for metropolitan Montreal's educational service meets all three requirements. However, it should be noted that no single recommendation by the Committee was unanimously supported. Perhaps this is typical. Entrenched interests and modern technocracy do not go hand in hand.

In the years ahead, as in the past, new *élites* will arise, and their thrust, their tolerance on the one hand, and partisanship on the other, will no doubt continue to make Montreal the metropolis *par excellence* of North America, and a city which repays with delight those who study its complexities and nuances.

14

Newfoundland: Problems of Urbanization on a Small Scale

G. A. Cooper

In the mid-Atlantic, almost halfway between New York and Ireland, lies the island of Newfoundland with a population of less than half a million in an area of over 40,000 square miles. Its Labrador territory is even more sparsely occupied. Its population is almost entirely of English and Irish extraction and has been, traditionally, more oriented towards Europe than to North America, of which it is a geographical part and, since 1949 when it became a Canadian province, a political part. Twice previously in 1869 and 1895 her people had decided against such a Union, thus tangibly showing her British orientation, expressed forcibly in the nineteenth century political jingle:

> With her face turned to Britain, her back to the Gulf[1]
> Come near at your peril, Canadian wolf.

For almost a century Newfoundland enjoyed self-governing status, but agreed during the Great Depression, when in financial straits, to an administrative arrangement whereby appointees of the Dominions Office of H.M. Government of the United Kingdom assumed the duties of government. The paternalistic rule of 'colonial' experts lasted until 1949 when, after two referenda, and by the slimmest of majorities, Newfoundlanders voted to become part of Canada. The two decades which have since elapsed have seen great changes in standard of living, in wealth, in development, in orientation. They have seen also the creation of new problems and the aggravation of old ones which occur in times of rapid change, especially where the courses of action and the organizational pattern have not the advantages of consensus.

The tardiness with which Great Britain developed a national educational system was reflected in British North America, for whom the 'Mother Country' was the model of the ruling *élite*, in varying degrees closely related to distance. Thus, the nearer the territory to Britain, the more haphazard the development; the further removed, the more American and indigenous influences were felt. Thus, in British Columbia,

---

[1] The Gulf of St Lawrence separates Newfoundland from the mainland of Canada.

the province of Canada farthest west, an educational system evolved with complete separation of church and state. All are taxed to support the public schools and private or denominational schools must operate without state financial assistance. In Newfoundland, the nearest to Britain, the tax-supported voluntary school, a logical development from British nineteenth-century custom, has been embedded in the constitution and can only be changed by the opting-out of the churches which operate the schools, the province paying approximately 90 per cent of all costs.

In countries like the United Kingdom and the Netherlands, where tax support to church (voluntary) schools is accepted practice, there are alternative publicly-supported common schools, which usually provide a standard to which the voluntary schools must conform to qualify for assistance. In Newfoundland this presence is missing, since smaller sects, such as the Pentecostal Assemblies and the Salvation Army, operate schools on the same basis as the Roman Catholic and Anglican Churches. Since almost all Newfoundlanders profess a church affiliation, children attend either a school of their church or one operated by another church where their own denomination is not well represented. When compulsory school attendance laws were enacted (1943), children were excused attendance where the denomination to which they belong did not operate a school within two miles of their homes. A sizeable proportion of children of school age are, therefore, not required to attend school, but the fact that very few children of this age-range fail to do so suggests either that compulsory school laws may no longer be necessary to ensure attendance or that many are in ignorance of their legislative 'rights'.

The Trend to Urbanization

Until World War II, Newfoundland was a rural, tradition-bound, closed society. There was virtually no immigration, and emigration, largely to the eastern United States and central Canada, was on a no-return basis. At the beginning of the war, however, there was an exodus of its males to war service overseas and a large influx of Canadian and American servicemen, the Americans establishing three large bases on the island on leased territory. The impact of a new way of life with new patterns of relationships was not lessened as the war ended and when the Newfoundland servicemen returned, they themselves were much changed by their wider experiences.

The following are some of the factors which have made for reorientation in recent years:

(1) World War II drew many from the smallest settlements to the services, or to urban areas to work on military installations. After years away from their tiny home settlements, influenced by travel and widened horizons, most were loathe to resettle in their former homes. This ac-

celerated the trend to larger settlements where job alternatives and more varied life patterns existed.

(2) With the entry of Newfoundland into Confederation in 1949, trends toward Canadian (North American) norms were accentuated. The old subsistence economy, often dealing in kind, gave way to a cash (or credit) economy, and the expectancy of social services obtaining elsewhere.

(3) Because the cost of providing these social services with a population so dispersed would have been prohibitive, the government became interested in shortening its lines and concentrating services where they could be provided within the competency of the economy.

(4) The wish of some people to live in urban settings offering more diverse life patterns plus the government's stake in centralizing population where the desired social services could be obtained, changed the demographic pattern from rural to urban (urbanism is here a relative term and does not connote the 'metropolis').

(5) The ever-growing influence of electronic media has changed the values and expectations of the people, standardizing speech patterns, introducing common entertainment forms and facilitating the adoption of the social norms of the wider community.

(6) The increased mobility brought about with increased urbanism has broken up the old settlement patterns on which the organization of educational services along denominational lines was rationalized. The forms remain but their rationale is gone.

The problems connected with urban growth are discussed widely in current literature. A growing number of social scientists are investigating and describing them in the hope of producing at least partial solutions. Historians have taken to theorizing as to the meanings of trends and deriving therefrom grand theories (à la Spengler or Toynbee). Others point to analogies in the past, selecting comparative data which suggest that the problems of today are similar to those of other eras, especially in that man, a gregarious animal, tends to move from what is conceived as a restricting environment to one which allows mobility – physical, social and spiritual. In doing this he takes on different attributes as he moves into larger and more complex groupings. Yet, not all men are so motivated: there are those whose roots are in the 'natural' environment and who resist social, political, or other pressures to change their values for supposed benefits in a different mode of living. When the structure and the value system of a society encourage the trend to urbanization and where urban values are dominant in the society, issues may be determined on a 'rational-legal' basis. When the value system is rural-oriented but the impetus to change derives from envy of or attraction to cultural characteristics exposed in neighbouring areas, there appear conflicting currents which threaten the stability of the society, drawing resistance from the sectors whose value-system and way of life are threatened and who dread the anonymity and impersonalization they tend to see in urban life.

The best known and most influential formulation of these contrasting types of society is provided by Ferdinand Tönnies in *Fundamental Concepts of Society*. Variations on the same general theme, e.g. Maine's[2] concept of the development of human society from determination by 'status' to that by 'contract', have become commonplace. Whilst these suggest a changing relationship of man to man over a long period of historical development, the whole process can be seen in compressed form in the problems of modern urban society, especially where it is fed by populations uprooted from rural areas no longer economically viable or by former rural dwellers more oriented to urban ways but unprepared by previous experience to fit into them. There is, however, no evidence that with appropriately framed and controlled experiences, i.e. *education of a certain kind*, the problems of value change and/or social adjustment cannot be overcome. There is now available enough knowledge about human engineering to obviate many of the difficulties and to by-pass many of the problems inherent in the transition. One of the drawbacks is that human engineering is suspect and unpopular, and the question of who should be entrusted with its directions and directing is unresolved. It might be that large numbers could be persuaded to be guinea-pigs, but abortive efforts such as the attempted assimilation of the population of Tristan da Cunha Island into British life carries warnings of some of the pitfalls of attempting human engineering experiments without sufficiently sophisticated theory or with inappropriate techniques.

If it is not feasible, for one reason or another, to test hypothetical solutions on human beings, it is appropriate to observe the development of such problems, chart their course and assess their effects. This can, perhaps, be more readily done in the microcosm than in the large urban centre where sheer size and proliferation of problems make it impossible to isolate or to clearly analyse any one. If it be found that the problems are different in kind as well as in degree, at least 'a' problem of urbanization in another area will be bared and examined. Although the bulk of literature on urbanization refers to the metropolis, urbanization may be defined as any movement from *Gemeinschaft* to *Gesellschaft*, any trend from rural organization and values to social organization based on a rational contractual character of activity. Harvey Cox has suggested:

> We must ask more precisely about the other key term we have used in describing the ethos of our time, 'urbanization' . . . In trying to define urbanization, however, we are confronted with the fact that social scientists themselves are not entirely agreed about what it means. It is clear that urbanization is not just a

---

[2] Henry Sumner Maine, *Ancient Law* (Oxford U.P., 1931).

quantitative term. It does not refer to population size or density, to geographic extent or to a particular form of government. Admittedly some of the character of modern urban life would not be possible without giant populations concentrated on enormous contiguous land masses. But urbanization is not something that refers only to the city ... Urbanization means a structure of common life in which the diversity and the disintegration of tradition are paramount. It means an impersonality in which functional relationships multiply. It means that a degree of tolerance and anonymity replace traditional moral sanctions and long-term acquaintanceships. The urban centre is the place of human control, of rational planning, of bureaucratic organization ...[3]

Blueprint for Educational Change

A look at a society in which urban development has not taken on the dimensions found in the great cities of the world is thus justified. It may exemplify problems, perhaps the same problems, on an earlier or smaller segment of the developmental plane. With the changes in post-war Newfoundland, the Union with Canada, the increased movement of population, the tendency to urban patterns of settlement and the change towards urban patterns of thought and action, it was evident that schools would have to be the focal point of change agents. The levels of schooling and the acquisition of skills required for the rural life of fishing, logging and subsistence farming did not allow for transfer to new industries or life forms. The general level of education was low, as shown in the following table extracted from the Census of Canada, 1951:[4]

	Canada Pop. 5 years and over in thousands	Newfoundland Pop. 5 years and over in thousands
Attending school	2,469	77
Not attending school	9,818	226
No schooling	654	34
1–4 years schooling	700	44

Accepting the criterion of less than five years of schooling as functional illiteracy it will be seen that of the population over five years of age not in school in 1951, 34·5 per cent of Newfoundlanders could be so designated compared with 13·8 per cent of Canada as a whole. Using other criteria the level of educational output appeared equally disturbing. It was apparent that an onslaught on illiteracy was called for and the annual rate of government spending on education from 1950 to 1968 increased more than

[3] Harvey Cox, *The Secular City* (New York: The Macmillan Co., 1965), Revised ed., pp. 3–4.

[4] *The Census of Canada*, 1951 (Ottawa: Dominion Bureau of Statistics, 1953), from Tables 51 and 52.

elevenfold, from less than $4½ million to approximately $50½ million (this does not include post-secondary education on which large sums are spent and which is even more a reflection of a changing ethos).

When the government decided in 1964 to appoint a Royal Commission on Education and Youth, it could reasonably have been expected that the adverse situations were well on the road to solution. There was a sense of shock when, after two years of investigation, the Commission's report pointed to inequities, inequalities and backwardness which belied the sums spent and the attention given to education. The *Report of the Royal Commission on Education and Youth* (1967)[5] was highly critical of the structure of education, especially the policy of leaving crucial decision-making to agreement between participating religious sects.

The Report is essentially a conservative document which does not come to grips with the changing ethos resulting from an increasing secularization of life. It notes the demands of a changing economy and a shrinking world and how these demand a complete 'new look' in education, but goes on to suggest that the churches should still run the schools, even though the parochial orientation and divided and divisive organization of the churches are obviously antithetical to the emerging society. In 1966 the Commission found no less than 270 school boards in the province operating schools of which only 22 served 1,000 pupils or more. A decade before, the number of boards was greater for fewer pupils. Obviously consolidation of school districts and boards was a necessity if the education system was to be rationalized. With increased mobility and urbanization, almost all regions were denominationally heterogeneous; the obvious need was to organize districts across denominational lines, for then at least a legal responsibility for organizing and operating schools could be fixed. However, either forces of secularization and the urban ethos had not caught up with the Commission or they were striving for a politically expedient solution, for their recommendation ran thus:

> The denominational system presents the thorniest obstacle to any attempt to change the boundaries of present districts. Without the consent of the denominational authorities in education, consolidation of school districts across denominational lines would be construed as an infringement of the rights guaranteed under the Terms of Union . . .
>
> Our first suggestion is that whenever possible, without detracting from the quality of education, the consolidated districts should be denominational in character . . .
>
> Secondly, in areas of relatively dense population, districts of sufficient size might be organized within the denominational framework . . .[6]

---

[5] *Report of the Royal Commission on Education and Youth* (St John's, Newfoundland: The Queen's Printer, 1967).

[6] op.cit., pp. 82–83.

It would seem the only criterion was a viable *size* of administrative unit. The operating principle was to be: establish districts based on minimal size but without transportation of children to schools exceeding a pre-established time. Only when districts of a denominational character could not be established with sufficiently strong administration and the special services required, would school districts be established across denominational lines. Furthermore, no school districts would be exclusive geographically; thus, no group could be held responsible for providing school services for an area, although there would be an understanding that each church would be in some way responsible for the schooling of its adherents.

The most controversial recommendation of the Report was that the Department of Education should be reorganized along functional rather than denominational lines. This meant that church representatives, who constituted the governing Council of Education, would be replaced by the usual bureaucratic central structure. The churches would act in an advisory capacity, with greatly reduced powers, from outside the Civil Service. Agreement on implementing this recommendation became contingent on offering the churches subsidized offices outside the department from which to run the schools. These offices would name the members of school boards, and in addition they would share between them, on a *per capita* basis with respect to the preceding census figures, such funds as would be allocated by the legislature for capital expenditures in education. Thus, with control of both boards and moneys, the churches emerged with more rather than less power and influence. In effect, the lines of authority are no longer clear as the schools are answerable to the official Department of Education and to what could be another 'department of education', the Denominational Education Committee responsible for running them.

Unresolved Problems

The school is the institution which, above all others, must respond to, if not lead, the rapidly changing society, for there the value system is either reinforced or weakened and each generation is prepared to feed into and to renew the constituent parts of the society. A tradition-based education, inculcating values and patterns inimical to the changes occurring or desired will vitiate the efforts and performance of the society at large.

If the educational institution should ignore the traditional values and norms and concentrate on adjusting the way of life of the province, Newfoundland, to that of the country, Canada, to which she has tied her political life, the question arises whether the people can, or should, be manipulated to this extent. Furthermore, the losses might be greater than the gain. Some observers have been struck by a richness of culture in the traditional life; others dismiss such observations as rural mysticism and have pointed to the material poverty as more than offsetting any advantages. This lack of consensus, whether in outside observers or in the province's authority structure, makes for vacillating and half-hearted efforts, now tending one way, now the other, which can be noted in most developing countries. The possible exceptions are where strong, totalitarian governments deem the likely gains to outweigh the disruption and ruthlessness necessary to effect the changes. In such cases, the loss in social product is impossible to assess, as whole ways of life have disappeared to be replaced by borrowed and artificial forms not always suited to the people on whom they are imposed.

It is evident, however, that any society must have an institution at the centre, capable of and charged with the co-ordination of societal functions. This political function has sometimes been assumed by, or dominated by, the military, or the ecclesiastical, or some other institution. The argument here is not which of the various institutions should be the dominant or core institution of a society. It is, rather, that the institution which dominates, co-ordinates or organizes the primary socialization function, the school system, should derive from, and answer to, the society at large, and should incorporate and foster the values and norms deemed desirable within that society. This should obtain, whether the desired mode is diversity or standardization – this ultimate philosophical question being decided at the general societal and political levels, not in the school. The school should not be a pivotal point of opposition to the society of which it is a dependent and a feeder.

The experience of the next decade in Newfoundland should therefore resolve some fundamental questions:

(1) whether a society should be restricted by constitutional guarantees made in a different context and whether such restrictions can be reconciled with democratic principles;

(2) whether an essentially conservative institution (the church) is more likely to increase rather than lessen the cultural lag between Newfoundland and a rapidly changing North American culture by its control of the schools;

(3) whether efforts in the economic field can be effective without a closer tie-in with the schools, necessitating co-ordinated control; and

(4) whether the educational institution can properly serve the society at large without a large degree of autonomy from all but the central co-ordinating authority, the state.

These and other questions await resolution and will be crucial in determining the emergence or otherwise of Newfoundland within the general framework of North American society.

15

Latin American Cities: their Growth and their Educational Problems*

Julio Larrea

Buenos Aires, the largest of the Latin American cities, furnishes ample evidence of the complexity and gravity of urban problems which have manifold and far-reaching implications in the field of education. Yet Buenos Aires is relatively new among Latin American cities; during the colonial period it occupied a very secondary position, the vice-royalty of the River Plate ranking fourth in importance after Mexico, New Granada and Peru. One of today's serious problems is the distribution of population between the capital and the rest of the country. Whereas Mexico City has only six million inhabitants out of a total population of over forty millions, the corresponding figure for Greater Buenos Aires is disproportionately greater – about eight millions out of a total of twenty-three millions. Modern Buenos Aires, with its immigrants and its intense commercial and political activity absorbing a very large part of the budget, is a problem-city. And when educational activities are considered in conjunction with those of a commercial character, the problem is seen to be a nation-wide one. In the first place, the importance of education is underestimated and thus one may find servants earning more than a schoolmistress and even more than a first-year university teacher. Secondly, the public authorities' underestimation of the role of education can be largely attributed to the teaching profession's lack of social and political influence in the life of the nation. In this respect the Argentine situation is in marked contrast with that which obtains in such countries as Chile, Ecuador, Costa Rica, Mexico, Brazil, Panama and Venezuela. Thirdly, the features of a theocratic state still find expression in the Argentine's political constitution, which affirms the Catholic religion to be the state religion. At the other extreme are all those national states of a strictly secular character, like Ecuador, which do not subsidize Catholic educational establishments and which provide full guarantees for a life of religious tolerance. Lastly, the financial resources of the secular countries are not diverted to the defence and police forces to such an extent as to preclude any appreciable growth in educational institutions at all levels

---

* A shortened version of a much longer article (Editors).

in both urban and rural areas. Costa Rica and Panama are other countries, like Ecuador, which spend nearly a third of their national budgets on education; but Ecuador has no generals.

Not surprisingly, there is a huge belt of *villas-miserias* on the outskirts of Greater Buenos Aires, with the physical characteristics of similar shanty towns elsewhere. Really satisfactory schools are lacking in such surroundings, but modern schools are also lacking in more affluent districts, for teaching methods are in a deplorably backward state. Eminent Argentine educators, like Victor Mercante, have been misunderstood and badly treated as a result of their systematic researches in the educational field. There is instead a tendency to create a plethora of muddled statutes, most of which are not put into effect. At the present time, professors and teachers throughout the republic are strongly criticizing the so-called preliminary plan for organic educational reform (*Ante-Proyecto de Ley Orgánica de Educación*). The most serious comment made by educators is that the *Ante-Proyecto* would mean a return to the colonial state of affairs in which the education of the common people was neglected and teaching was limited to only a few student grades. They justify their assertion by reference to Article 37 which enables parents to avoid sending their children to school and allows the state to escape responsibility for compulsory primary education.

No Latin American country has such a high proportion of culturally backward immigrants as the Argentine, yet no provision is made for their cultural assimilation by means of gradual or adult education. By law these immigrants are allowed entry to work in agriculture, but instead they nearly all manage to remain in Buenos Aires with a view to getting rich within a few years. The Spanish, for example, are prominent in the running of hotels, restaurants and food distribution generally, among other commercial activities. Since they reject a secular education or university study for their children, their contribution to the progress of education at any level is nugatory. Spanish and Italian immigrants in Venezuela send their sons to study in their respective mother countries. And well over half the population of Caracas, some 800,000, are Spanish, Italian and Portuguese immigrants in roughly equal proportions. It must be remembered that the immigrants are found in the most productive countries offering the greatest opportunities for profit-making in industry and commerce. From this general attitude largely stems the total indifference of immigrants and their children, and even of their grandchildren, to the Latin American problems of poverty, ill health and insufficient education, both in quality and quantity. The *nativos* (inhabitants of early American origin) become confined increasingly to the outer suburbs of the cities and to the oldest and poorest parts of the colonial towns. These marginal areas everywhere reveal the contrast between two opposing economic forces which sometimes gives rise to social tension: the encroachment of the modern buildings of an affluent society upon what were formerly the rural suburbs of a distant urban centre. Thus one is able to see in the same suburbs old scholastic buildings, often of a poor and primitive character, together with examples of modern architecture. Generally speaking, the 'university cities' are to be found in the suburbs, e.g., in Panama, Costa Rica, Mexico and Ecuador.

Socio-Economic Differences

Latin American cities in many ways reveal the painfully marked economic and social differences between classes in each country. Although it is usual for governments to be run by the middle classes, the class structures are such as to preserve the old and deeply rooted privileges of a dominant class of the colonial type. Rags and riches are visible at one and the same time in the city streets, and the rags may be seen on the backs of many poor whites as well as on Indians, *mestizos*, mulattos and negroes. The middle classes in general hardly make any contribution towards the fusion of these large social groups, whose differences are rooted in racial discrimination which tends to limit the potential of each race for individual and social development. Where such opportunities do exist, as in Mexico, we find talented and distinguished Indians filling very responsible posts in public administration and working in complete harmony with the *mestizo* and the white populations. That great Indian Benito Juárez, who as President of his country preserved its unity in facing and defeating the French invaders, remains an outstanding historical figure exemplifying the high intelligence of the Mexican Indian. Eugenio Espejo was yet another illustrious Indian; pioneer of independence in Ecuador and neighbouring countries, he also acquired doctorates in medicine and in the humanities. It seems inconceivable therefore that, in the Andean countries and in Mexico, there should be so-called *indigenista* institutes which through bureaucratic inefficiency and lack of resolution are doing nothing really effective towards integrating the Indian into the national culture by political means, in accordance with the Universal Declaration of Human Rights. The same might be said about the situation of the negroes in the coastal cities of Brazil, in Venezuela, Colombia and Panama. At all events, the racial discrimination which appears in the streets of Latin American cities is not carried into the schools, and in Brazil black and white pupils study together. Discrimination takes, rather, the form of limited opportunities for active participation in national life, more especially for the rural poor, since there has never been an active dialogue between town and country. The towns, particularly the larger urban centres, are expanding as a result of the exodus from the countryside of men unable to find remunerative work and, partly also, of the younger generation whose fathers are determined to procure for them the best education available.

One very notable exception can be found to the evolution of a political city through the economic support of powerful old family groups, namely, Brasília. Unlike Buenos Aires, Brasília is a capital which has been newly created in the hinterland in order to dominate, so far as possible, the immensely vast interior of Brazil; the Atlantic seaboard constitutes only the periphery of what is one of the largest countries in the world. This project may of itself be considered a mighty enterprise in demographic, political and administrative planning. All that is needed are complementary resources and communication lines reaching out across the country, to give lasting life to the concept of a new capital which will overcome the centuries-old mistakes of a routine administration. Without doubt, Brazil appears to be the country which evinces the greatest knowledge of its own national realities; but the Brazilian tradition of investigation goes right back to the days of those early explorers, the *bandeirantes*.

As yet no equilibrium has been reached between urban growth and the protection of the land and its potentials for development in the rural areas of the continent. Thus, in a country like Venezuela hardly 30 per cent of children in the rural districts finish school and, indeed, everywhere there is a deplorable amount of absenteeism. Semi-literacy takes on as serious a character as illiteracy, since many of those who learn to read and write return to a state of illiteracy through disuse of the written language. According to the Argentine Ministry of Education, more than half of the adult population of Buenos Aires neither reads nor writes nor has adequate knowledge of the Spanish language. The fact that the majority of people in the most southerly countries of Latin America appear to be quite well dressed – for climatic reasons – may therefore be somewhat misleading. They spend much less proportionately on books and libraries than do the inhabitants of the northerly countries. These latter countries, unlike the Argentine, for example, are seeking solutions to their economic problems by way of agrarian reform for which purpose special laws have been enacted.

In regard to general educational planning, it may be said that plans are only superficially different. Solutions are being sought along standardized lines without the encouragement of initiative and without pedagogic inquiry and experiment. There is no conscientious study of the individual circumstances of pupils and little attempt to introduce more flexibility into courses to modernize examinations or to use evaluation tests. This kind of situation gives rise increasingly to discontent, unrest and instability leading sometimes to open protest by adolescent students and especially by university students. These educational and socio-psychological problems tend to be dealt with, misguidedly, by forceful confrontation. Apart from the police, there are large cliques of over-politically-minded teachers who also resort to the discipline of force when it suits them, using staff members to incite students and create intimidating situations.

16

Caracas: Educating the Urban Invaders*

Michael Bamberger

Caracas is one of Latin America's richest and most modern cities. With a population approaching two millions, its growth and style is largely attributable to the discovery and exploitation of oil in the decades following 1930. This sudden and unexpected wealth changed Caracas in a few years from a small, quiet city modelled on Paris of the 1870s, and the capital of an agricultural country, to a modern, bustling American-style metropolis, the capital of a suddenly rich country which no longer felt the need to depend on its agriculture.

The newly rich rulers sought to centralize the economy and government, both to wrest power from the local agricultural barons, and to provide the base for industrial expansion. The centralization was accompanied by a vast public works programme, which, by offering wages three or four times higher than what could be earned in the countryside, attracted *campesinos* in their thousands to the cities. The rural exodus still continues, and whereas in 1935 some 70 per cent of the population were living in the countryside or in small towns, by 1965 the proportion had dropped to 30 per cent.

Although wages were high for those who could find work, the fact that Caracas has relatively little heavy industry, that companies prefer to become capital intensive rather than expand their labour force, and that the population growth rate at 3·6 per cent is the highest in the continent, has meant that unemployment rates have constantly been very high. In addition to the lack of jobs, Caracas is situated in a narrow valley, which means that the supply of building land is limited and expensive; as a result the poorer groups have been forced to invade the hillsides and form huge squatter settlements known as *barrios*. Most of the *barrios* were founded either in the first three years of Venezuelan democratic government in 1945–8, or

---

* Centre for Research and Training in Urban Community Action. The Centre is sponsored by Accion International, the Neuman Foundation and Accion en Venezuela to conduct research into the problems caused by the rapid urban growth of Latin America. On the basis of this research, training programmes are developed to show how community development methods can be used to overcome this problem.

The Centre is working actively with community development organizations in Venezuela, Brazil and Peru.

in the years following the overthrow of the Dictator Perez Jimenez in 1958. Despite their recent origin, the *barrios* now house some 600,000 people, which is approximately one third of the total Caracas population. Caracas, according to the leading Venezuelan anthropologist Rudolfo Quintero, is an artificial city imposed upon a rural economy by the pressure of foreign groups brought to Venezuela by the wealth from the petroleum industry.[1] Physically, economically and culturally the city has grown faster than its ability to adjust to its changing circumstances. This lack of adjustment can be seen in the archaic administrative system which divides the city into two separate administrative and political entities, in the road system which becomes completely strangled by the rush-hour traffic, by the economic structure which allows the labour supply to increase about three times as fast as the creation of new jobs, and in the cultural system which faces hundreds of thousands of people born and educated in the countryside with the need to work in a modern industrial economy, but which gives them very little guidance on how to make the adjustment.

Effectiveness of the Educational System

It is within this context of rapid economic and social change, and with a population growth of 3·6 per cent per annum, that one must interpret the effectiveness of the Venezuelan educational system. In addition to the rapid population growth, the system also has to make up for the deficit accumulated during the years 1948–58 when the educational system was largely neglected. Taking into account the very rapid growth of the school-age population, the educational system as a whole has made remarkable progress during the past decade. During this period the number of students in primary education increased by 48 per cent,[2] the number in secondary education by 185 per cent and the number of university students by 160 per cent. During the same period public investment in education increased by 82 per cent and the share of national expenditure devoted to education increased from 12·75 per cent to 18·19 per cent. At the same time progress has been made in overcoming the very high drop-out rate. In 1954, only 27 per cent of students starting primary education graduated six years later; in the six years ending in 1968 the figure increased to 38 per cent. The system has also diversified to place more emphasis on technical education and the needs of the more modern Venezuelan economy.

Despite the great strides which have been made, the educational system, as one would expect from its sudden and extensive growth, still suffers

---

[1] Rudolfo Quintero, *Antropologia de las Cuidades Latino-Americanos* (Editorial Universidad Central de Venezuela).

[2] All educational statistics, unless otherwise stated, are taken from the *Memoria y Cuenta* of the Ministry of Education, 1968.

from a number of very serious problems. Within the system itself the biggest problem is still the very high drop-out rate. Of students starting first grade of primary school, only 38 per cent complete sixth grade without either having to repeat a year or dropping out completely. At the secondary level, 56 per cent of those who commence never complete the course. In addition the system is burdened with a large number of students who are repeating a year. In all grades of primary education an average of 11 per cent of the students are repeating the year.

An even more serious problem arises when we consider the relationship between the educational system and the needs of Venezuela's urban economy. Leading Venezuelan educator Felix Adam observes: '. . . actually the present education is the enemy of the development of the country because it is programmed toward university studies, thus creating a false hope which ends in being a frustration for the majority of Venezeulan youth.'[3] He goes on to point out that less than one per cent of Venezuelan students ever get to university. Other writers have criticized the very academic orientation of the system and the great emphasis placed upon memory.[4] In addition to its role in preparing people for a career, an educational system is one of the most important social institutions for acculturating the young into the social roles they must play in later life. This is even more important in a country such as Venezuela where the social change has been so rapid that the adults are not able to guide the young as well as they could in a more stable society.

The urban area where this acculturation is most urgently needed is in the *barrios*, the hillside settlements where the recently arrived urban squatters live. The rest of this article will try to evaluate the effectiveness of the educational system in satisfying the needs of this one third of the urban population. The fact that in every major Latin American city at least 10 per cent of the population live in shanty towns, suggests that this case study will throw some light on perhaps the most difficult problem currently being faced by Latin American educators.

Education is of particular importance in the *barrios* as an extremely high proportion of the population is young. The figures in Table 1, taken from a typical *barrio*, shows that over half the population are under the age of 19.

These 350,000 youths who have not yet reached adulthood are the children of parents born in the countryside. The rural background can be seen in the forms of housing, in the customs, and in the general attitudes to

[3] Gilberto Alcala 'Reforma Integral de la Educacion por Considerar su Funcionamiento Enemigo del Desarrollo del Pais', *El Nacional*, Caracas, April 4, 1966.

[4] Hugo Manzanilla, 'La Condicion Actual del Hombre Venezolano en Relacion Directa Con Su Aptitud para el Trabajo' in *La Responsabilidad Empresarial en el Progreso Social de Venezuela*, International Seminar for Executives, Maracay, Venezuela, 1963.

TABLE 1

THE AGE OF DISTRIBUTION IN A TYPICAL CARACAS BARRIO

Age group	Per cent of the population
0–7 years	23
8–10	8
11–13	7
14–16	8
17–19	10
20–25	10
26–30	8
over 30	24

SOURCE: A study conducted by Accion en Venezuela in Barrio Isaias Medina Angarita, 1968.

life. The majority of adults seem to be more or less satisfied with their life in the *barrios,* because, in comparison with the village where they were brought up, conditions are undoubtedly better in the city. To take just one example, the average monthly family income in the *barrios* is in the region of 100–150 U.S. dollars a month. This is at least twice as high as a *campesino* could expect to earn.

In common with most *campesino* groups, the adult *barrio* dwellers obtained very little education in their youth. Although less than 20 per cent are illiterate, the following figures, taken from another survey, show that less than 40 per cent of the adults have finished primary education.

TABLE 2

EDUCATIONAL LEVEL OF THE ADULTS IN A TYPICAL CARACAS BARRIO

Grade	Per cent of the population
Illiterate	14
Primary education	
1st grade	3·2
2nd and 3rd grade	21·2
4th and 5th grade	25·6
6th grade	25·2
Secondary education	
1st year	7·5
More than one year but not completed	3·0
Secondary completed	0·3

SOURCE: Studies completed by Accion en Venezuela in barrios of Catia and Petare.

It is this generation which still thinks and to some extent lives, like *campesinos,* and which has had very little formal educational experience, which must guide and motivate the maturing youth, and show them how to live in the city. As in all societies one finds that the youth rebel against the values of their parents, but in Caracas the generation gap is accentuated by the fact that very often the young people do in fact know the city and its ways better than their parents, so that this contributes to an even further reduction of parental authority.

The lack of parental control and guidance means that young people must look to formal institutions such as the Church and the school for their orientation towards life. It is against this context of the crucial need for education, that we shall show, firstly that *barrio* youth have very limited access to the educational system, and secondly that the type of education they receive is often not very useful to them. In terms of access to the educational system, it has been calculated that approximately 64 per cent of the students in the *barrios* who start first grade of primary education never complete sixth grade, and that only about 25 per cent complete sixth grade without having to repeat at least one year. Calculations for a typical cohort are given in the following figure:

TABLE 3

THE EDUCATIONAL LEVEL ACHIEVED BY A TYPICAL GROUP OF BARRIO YOUTH
STARTING THE FIRST GRADE OF PRIMARY SCHOOL

Grade	Per cent who start the year★	Per cent desserting end of the year	Per cent repeating the year★★
1st	100	21	17·8
2nd	64	13	9·4
3rd	49·5	21	10·8
4th	34·8	9	10·7
5th	28·2	0	7·9
6th	26·3	—	3·7

Percentage approving final examination 25·6 per cent.

★ The figures are calculated by the procedure of taking a cohort (in this case all students starting the first grade) and following them through all six grades.

★★ Figures for repetion were not available so the standard national figures were taken from the Annual Report of the Ministry of Education 1968. Source: Report submitted to the National Congressional Committee on the barrios by Accion en Venezuela.

Failures in School Attendance

A number of reasons have been put forward by Venezuelan educationists as to why educational attendance should be so low. The following are the main reasons usually given. Firstly, we have already noted that parental discipline is weakened by the fact that the parents grew up in the countryside and their knowledge of the city is limited. Discipline is further weakened by the very high percentage of broken homes, or homes where there is no regular father figure.

Secondly, schools are often inaccessible. A recent study by Revenga and Fernandez[5] showed that in the most populous *barrio* zone the educational deficit was 71·69 per cent (i.e. lack of school places), which is more than twice the deficit for the city as a whole. *Barrio* schools, where they exist, tend to be small and overcrowded. Most government schools do not have a free bus service, so many children do not go to school either because there is no place, or because they are unable to get to the school. If a mother has several small children, she may not be able to take the child herself, and because of the danger of main roads, and the occasional cases of kidnapping, she will not let the child go alone. A third reason is purely economic. Although public schools are free, children are usually required to wear uniforms and to buy their own books.[6] In addition fares will often have to be paid. Another factor is the loss of income which the child could be earning if he were not studying. All these contribute to force many families to select which of their children can continue studying and which must go out to work or stop at home.

A further motivational factor which is very important in understanding Venezuela, is that the sudden wealth from petroleum has lead to the philosophy (not only among the poor), that there is no need to work hard, because if one has friends a living can be made without too much effort. This means that the importance of education as a way of improving oneself is lessened.

A fundamental factor which must be taken into account is that the combination of the continued migration to the cities from the countryside and the population increase of 3·6 per cent a year, produces an annual increase in the *barrio* population of 9 per cent. Any educational system in the world would be hardpressed to provide schooling for all who need it for an increase of this magnitude.

A final factor to be mentioned is the very low standard of health of the average *barrio* dwellers. Childers[7] quotes a number of sources to show that very large numbers of children suffer from debilitating diseases caused by malnutrition and unsanitary conditions. There is not sufficient space here to enter into details, but he presents extensive evidence to show that the

[5] Edmundo Fernandez h. and José Rafael Revenga, 'Analisis de la Educacion Primaria y Secundaria en el Area Metropolitana de Caracas', in *El Farol* November–December 1967, Caracas.

[6] Legislation was passed in 1966 to provide textbooks and writing materials free in primary education. Already 3 million textbooks, and 36 million exercise books have been distributed so it is hoped that soon this particular problem will be solved.

[7] Victor Childers, 'Unemployment in Venezuela', Ph.D. thesis, Indiana University Graduate School of Business, 1967.

intelligence of large numbers of children is permanently retarded by brain damage caused by dietary deficiencies in the early years, and that the general health level is sufficiently low to be likely to interfere with the studying capacity of large numbers of children.

The Education System Evaluated

Having shown that access to formal education is severely restricted for *barrio* children, it remains to evaluate the quality of the education which is offered. We have already mentioned that the educational programme is excessively formal, and related to an academic rather than a practical career. The educational methods are particularly difficult for a child who has been brought up in a background where it is difficult to study (many teachers do not set homework in *barrio* schools, because they know that most children do not have the facilities in their home to be able to study in the evening). Little attempt is made to offer anything like the American Head Start programmes, except in a few private or experimental schools. Although no formal study results are available, informal conversations with employers and educationists, as well as with teenagers, suggest that many young people in the *barrios* have a potential far above their educational achievement, which suggests that educational methods are lacking in flexibility to adapt to the *barrio* environment.

In addition to the poor methods and syllabus and the often inadequate schools, a further disincentive is often the attitude of the teacher. Many if not most *barrio* school teachers look upon their work as a job and not a vocation, so that very few extra-curricular activities are developed, there are very few parent-teacher associations, and the rapport between teachers and students is not developed.

Some of the same criticisms can be levelled at the technical training programmes which the government offers to unemployed *barrio* youth. In the first place the teaching methods are too formal and theoretical and do not make allowance for the lack of formal education experience of the student. The selection methods are also more appropriate for young people from a different social environment. Use is made of a battery of psychological tests which places emphasis on verbal skills (an area in which the *barrio* youth are often weak), and secondly create an atmosphere in which the student is likely to be nervous and not perform well.

The value system of the instructors is often similar to that of the primary school teachers. It is felt that the boy is fortunate to have the chance to learn and that he should be grateful.

Basic Criticism

A more basic criticism is that the courses implicitly assume that the student is aware of the nature of different types of job and that therefore no orientation or vocational guidance is needed. Many boys take a course assuming either that they will automatically achieve a job when they finish, or have a completely false idea of what the job they do obtain will be like. Many of students have no idea what is involved in working in a factory because they do not come from an industrial background, so it is essential that an effective technical training programme must include vocational guidance and job orientation. These are both almost non-existent at present.

The courses themselves are criticized by industrialists as being too short and too general. This is probably true, and one would expect it is an almost inevitable consequence of the desire of the government to train very large numbers of people in as short a time as possible. Once the students leave the course they are given almost no help in finding a job. As a consequence many of them simply return to what they were doing before the course, and technical training is considered by them as being a waste of time.

To a large extent one could say that programmes designed to integrate the unemployed *barrio* youth into the industrial economy have so far failed. A study of the occupational patterns of *barrio* youth would show that the majority work in commerce and in small companies near where they live. Most are either afraid to venture into one of the large companies, or their attitude is so hostile that they assume the company would automatically exploit them. Nearly all of them find a job through a friend (i.e. continue to work in the same type of job as others from the *barrio*), and will change very frequently from one job to another. These boys are drifting towards the margins of the modern economy, with neither the training, the motivation, nor the cultural background to have much hope of becoming part of modern Caracas.

Conclusion

In conclusion, the picture we draw is far from optimistic. Venezuela is a rich country which is trying very hard to improve its educational system, and which by most standards could be said to be making very commendable progress. Even so, the enormity of the problem continues to overwhelm all efforts. The access of *barrio* youth to the educational system is very limited, with less than 40 per cent completing primary education, and with only perhaps 10 per cent (or less) completing secondary education. Virtually nothing is being done in the educational programme to help these young people bridge the huge cultural gap between the rural background from which they come, and the needs of the modern sophisticated city in which they find themselves. Although technical training courses are available (for those who have finished primary education), the evidence so far has not been very encouraging as to their value. It would seem that the youth of the *barrio* are gradually drifting towards the margins of modern society and that no programme has yet been found which can integrate them into the mainstream of modern city life.

Although many people in Venezuela would suggest the problem could be solved by a revolution and a new social system, it would seem that it is deeper than the relative merits of different political systems. The essence of the problem is that the *barrio* population continues to grow at about 9 per cent per year, whilst jobs increase at less than 4 per cent and the gross national product increases at perhaps 6 per cent a year. It is difficult to see how any political system could effectively absorb such a rapidly increasing population into its cultural and economic system. It is clear from this that the blame cannot be placed upon the educational system which is fighting against almost impossible odds. If, however, the diagnosis of the future of education in the *barrios* of oil-rich Caracas is so pessimistic, then the picture must surely be gloomy for the poorer cities of Latin America which face the same problem but with far less resources at their disposal.

17

Rio de Janeiro

Josildeth Gomes Consorte

The city of São Sebastião de Rio de Janeiro, capital of the State of Guanabara, was founded on 20th January, 1565, and is located on the west bank of Guanabara Bay, in the eastern part of Brazil. On 1st July, 1969, its population was estimated at 4,261,000, including the rural zones. The city and its rural zones occupy a total area of 1,171 square kilometres, giving a density of 3,639 inhabitants per square kilometre. Rio de Janeiro is unique amongst world capitals, in that speaking of the city is tantamount to speaking of the State of Guanabara.

Capital of the country since 1763, Rio de Janeiro lost this position in 1961, to become the capital of the State of Guanabara. However, it lost only part of its administrative importance, remaining the leading political, cultural and recreational centre of Brazil, and being second as a centre of industrial, commercial and port activities. Its beauty and other attractions, amongst which the Carnival is a unique event, have made it an increasingly important tourist centre.

The State of Guanabara is divided into 23 regions, each responsible to an administrator directly subordinated to the State Governor. The activities in the field of elementary education, however, are exercised through 40 educational districts. In general each administrative region embraces one to five educational districts. In two cases, two administrative zones cover only one educational district.

As slums exist all over the city and within every educational district, slum children are found in practically every public school, although educational statistics usually do not show separate counts of slum children and non-slum pupils. Nevertheless 1963 statistics indicate the distribution of slum children in the school system in that year. Of the 383 establishments in the school system, slum children attended 261 schools in the following proportion:

Slum Children Enrolled	Schools
1 to 25 per cent	139
25 to 50 per cent	55
50 to 70 per cent	19
70 to 100 per cent	48
	261

Demography and the Growth of Slums

An analysis of the Guanabara population from the point of view of age, shows a high proportion of young people and an unusual number of people of optimum working age, as shown by the following table:

Age	Per cent
0– 4	11·8
5– 9	10·8
10–14	9·1
15–19	8·4
20–29	18·9
30–39	16·1
40–49	10·9
Over 50	13·8
Age unknown	0·2

Growth: Natural and through Immigration

According to IBGE[1] data, the population of the present State of Guanabara increased as follows:

Date of Census	Absolute Numbers
1.8.1872	274,972
31.7.1890	522,651
20.9.1906	811,443
1.9.1920	1,157,873
1.9.1940	1,764,141
1.7.1950	2,377,451
1.9.1960	3,281,908

Migratory movements account for the greatest part of this increase. Of the rise of 606,000 inhabitants between 1920 and 1940, about 220,000, i.e. 36 per cent, can be attributed to the surplus of births over deaths, while the remaining 386,000, or 64 per cent, are the surplus of in-migration over out-migration. Of the increase of 613,000 between September 1st, 1940 and July 1950, about 178,000, or 29 per cent, are attributable to the greater number of births, while 435,000, or 71 per cent, represent the surplus of immigration over emigration. An analysis of the growth between July 1st, 1950 and September 1st, 1960, shows that at least 642,264 of the increase of 904,457 was due to migration. Statistics further

---

[1] IBGE – Brazilian Institute of Geography and Statistics.

indicate that migration was predominantly of native Brazilians from other States in the Federation.

The 1960 census defines a slum as an agglomerate of people located in a non-urbanized area, with rustic or temporary habitations without public utilities, built on land belonging to third parties (Government, private or undefined ownership). However, in view of the different definitions existing in connexion with slums, census figures vary widely, not only regarding the number of slums, but also the number of people living there.

The 1920 census refers to only one slum on the Gamboa Hill, in the centre of the city. Twenty-eight years later the statistics prepared by the Department of Geography and Statistics of the then Federal District, classified 105 slums scattered over the centre, north and south zones, in the suburbs and on the Island of the Governor, with a slum population of 138,837. The 1950 census, while acknowledging only 58 slums in the entire city, counted a population of 169,305, indicating that in the two year interval between the two counts the slum population grew by 30,468, or a yearly average increase of 15·23 per cent. From that date the information available on the slum population is so contradictory that any calculation of its growth would be guesswork.

Origins of the Slum Population

According to the 1948 census, foreigners represented only 1·75 per cent of the slum population. Among native Brazilians, those originating from Guanabara represented 38·82 per cent. The States that contributed most to slum growth were Rio de Janeiro, Minas Gerais and Espírito Santo, and to a lesser extent, the eastern and north-eastern States. Migration from other States was negligible.

In 1960, foreigners, compared to Brazilians of a non-specified origin, constituted 0·12 per cent of the total population. Of the native Brazilians 47·94 per cent originated from Guanabara. The situation did not alter much in respect to the contribution from other States, although Espírito Santo gave way to Paraíba, and the contribution from the eastern and north-eastern States increased slightly. The rest remained without alteration. Although the census does not specify the rural-urban origin of these migrants, data obtained from a sample research into the parentage of slum school children show the following:

Place of Birth	Father	Mother
Guanabara	19·5	16·9
Cities of over 20,000 inhabitants	22·4	18·5
Cities of less than 20,000 inhabitants	58·1	64·0
Foreigners	—	0·6

School-Age Population: Changes in Growth and Characteristics
Figures from IBGE show the following population growth in the State
of Guanabara between 1920 and 1960, in the 5 to 14 age group:

Census	Total Growth	Average Yearly Increase
1920–40	109,928	5·49
1940–50	62,025	6·20
1950–60	237,240	23·72

According to the 1964, 1965 and 1966 school census, the same age bracket
had the following development:

Census	Total Growth
1964–65	34,725
1965–66	99,403

It should be noted that the increase in 1964–5 was greater than the
registered growth between 1950 and 1960. Again although the 1920
census mentioned one slum in the Gamboa district, it did not supply
population figures in the age bracket under consideration. The count
made in 1948 by the Federal District Department of Geography and
Statistics adopts a different division of age groups, making it impossible
to compare the figures, so that we can only use the results of the 1950
census for comparative purposes:

Census	Population	Urban Districts	Per cent	Slums	Per cent	Rural	Per cent
1950	415,241	363,413	87·52	34,095	8·21	17,733	4·27
1960	652,481	248,837	84·18	82,158	12·59	31,486	3·23

The school census of 1964, 1965 and 1966 considered only two main
divisions – urban and slum zones – and presented the following results:

Census	Population 5–14	Urban	Per cent	Slums	Per cent
1964	676,473	592,446	87·58	84,027	12·42
1965	711,198	602,762	84·76	108,436	15·24
1966	611,795	541,387	88·56	70,408	11·44

Both the general census and the school census, except the one made in 1966, make the same point clear: an ever greater increase in the slum population of the age group under review.

Administrative, Financial and Transportation Problems Created by the Increased Demand for Schooling

The first problem that arose as a consequence of the increase in the demand for education was, of course, the need to widen the capacity of the school system. The solutions found, many of which are still being applied, reflect all the difficulties (financial and of personnel) that had to be faced.

From 1940 to 1960, according to figures supplied by IBGE, the public school network grew by 127 units; the number of public school teachers on the other hand increased from 3,100 to 6,904 in the same period. Nevertheless, this increase was not sufficient to maintain the school service up to the standard existing prior to the population explosion, and a number of hitherto untried steps had to be taken to implement it. Disregarding the order in which they were enforced it is possible to summarize these steps as:

(1) an increase in the number of pupils per teacher,

(2) an increase of shifts and reduction in the number of school hours,

(3) the introduction of a system of priority for enrolment of sons of military staff, circus artists, teachers and other staff of the Board of Education, and of brothers and sisters of children already enrolled,

(4) the distribution of pupils from teacherless classes to other classes within the school,

(5) double sessions, i.e. classes operating in the intermediary period were attended by two teachers (one for the morning shift and one for the afternoon), who each took charge for one and a half hours,

(6) the elimination of the teachers' collective weekly free day and the introduction of a rota of rest days,

(7) a reduction in the number of kindergarten classes, to permit their use by others,

(8) the promotion of a private school system, financed by the State, in order to deal with the extra number of school children. This became such a profitable business that the private system increased from 771 schools in 1940 to 853 in 1957,

(9) an increase in the number of teacher training schools with the opening of the new 'normal' courses; this step caused an increase in demand for normal courses and consequently in the number of teachers available, the numbers rising in the public schools from 6,904 in 1960 to 8,197 in 1962 (data from IBGE).

Although these were general measures to benefit all the population, a number of problems contributed not only to make it difficult for the slum population to enrol in the existing schools, but also placed them in the unfavourable position of not being able to attend classes after enrolment. Attendance by slum children at existing schools was also restricted by some schools claiming that there were no vacancies. Their attendance was even more uncertain because the majority were frequenting three-shift schools and were placed in the intermediary shift, and also because their schools were the most under-equipped and served by teachers who were constantly absent.

Even though the problem of supernumerary pupils is no longer acute and private schools no longer benefit from it, the priority for enrolment is limited to two categories, the number of available teachers is larger than the number of classes, and the distribution of pupils to classrooms with teachers occurs only rarely with a tendency towards eliminating the three-shift system. A large number of schools still work to a tight schedule where the ratio of pupils per teachers is still high.

The location of slums near urban districts and close to the existing school system, means that the problem of transporting slum children to school has never arisen.

Problems Arising from Changes in the Socio-Cultural Composition of the School Population

Rural migration to Guanabara, and the consequent appearance of slums, brought to the elementary public schools a new type of pupil practically unknown until then. Previously elementary public schools were accustomed to accommodate children of normal primary school age, possessing good standards of health, average bio-psychological development, a common pattern of language, values, ambitions and behaviour in conformity with those of the school, and with expectations geared to the aims of the school.

With the growth of the slums, schools had to contend with groups of children above the normal age limit, who were under-fed and under-developed, had bad teeth, poor sight and hearing deficiencies, infected tonsils, verminosis, were poorly co-ordinated, unstable, and who faced problems of language (poor and inadequate vocabulary), and possessed values, aims and behaviour patterns different from those of the school, with badly or even undefined ideas of what to expect from the school.

Slum children brought two types of problem to the school: pedagogical and social. The first arose from the incapacity of slum children to respond to the teachers' expectations; the second was a result of the social and cultural gap between these children and their contemporaries and teachers. The high incidence of failure and school evasion among slum children indicated what difficulties the public schools had to face and for which they were totally unprepared.

Besides the general social assistance already being given, such as medical and odontological care, school funds, and the introduction of a special snack meal, which for the slum children amounted to a main meal, a number of pedagogic measures were taken by the schools to meet the new situation. From a strictly educational point of view, the great difficulty came right at the start, in the teaching of reading and writing. Once this problem was overcome, the other stages became easier. The measure taken to solve the problem after seven was introduced in 1953 as the age to enter school, was the formation of a 'Preliminary' grade. As a large proportion of the slum children showed that they were not sufficiently mature to learn to read and write when submitted to the Lourenço Filho ABC test, on entering school at this age or even older, the creation of this class was intended to solve the problem and prepare them for the normal elementary school. The poor attention that children received in these classes, however, as well as the persistence of the conditions of which they were victims nullified the expected effects of this 'Preliminary' grade.

Why the poor attention? Firstly, due to the lack of continuity in the teachers' work. Through a system of class distribution adopted unofficially by the schools, by which the older and more experienced teachers had priority of choice, the classes with children of higher potential remained with these teachers, while the other classes were assigned to provisional teachers, to those about to go on leave or who were often absent, or to those who were generally not interested in their work or were incompetent. Secondly, through the inability of such teachers to deal with the slum children and to prepare an adequate programme for their intellectual development. Thirdly, due to the lack of time to carry out their work in schools operating in three shifts, aggravated by the large number of pupils in class. What has been said of the 'Preliminary' grade, could be repeated about the first grade, always considered as a very difficult class and of dubious success.

After two years in the 'Preliminary' grade or in the first grade, without reaching the necessary level to be promoted to the next grade, the child was submitted to the Gille intelligence test and if his or her IQ was below normal, he would be put into a special class and as such complete elementary school. As a special pupil, or AE (*aluno especial*) he was transformed into an educational outcast: nothing was expected or demanded of him.

As maturity may be delayed but will in time be reached, the situation of the preliminary grade pupil was not so serious. However, the situation of the first grade pupil who was unable to learn to read and write in one year was grave. As the difficulties of acquiring the skills of reading and writing increase with age, the number of pupils repeating the first grade and still unable to learn exceeded the number of newcomers. As the Gille test, compiled on a different cultural basis, takes for granted certain knowledge that Brazilian children, or at least Brazilian slum children, have no means of acquiring, the treatment to which these children were submitted could not have been more inadequate and damaging.

The situation today does not greatly differ from what we have described, except for a few details. Although the age of entry to schools has been lowered to six, and preliminary classes, aimed at the immature children of six years old, have taken the place of the preliminary grade, and while the percentages of pupil promotions no longer affect teachers' careers, the preliminary classes have a poor record of progress, and the percentage of level 1 students (formerly first grade), who learn to read and write is still low (47·49 per cent in 1968).

If, on the one hand, the features of the education of slum children are unchanged, the preliminary classes are today considered as a reward for the teacher who is tired and wants an easy job for a while, and those of level 1 are entrusted to the newer and less experienced teachers, since in the yearly choice of classes the senior teachers continue to prefer the higher levels.

On the basis of interviews carried out among educationists in Guanabara, the conclusion was reached that the main obstacle to the teaching of reading and writing to slum children is the method or methods used. It seems that the introduction in Guanabara of the global method for teaching reading and writing, coincided with the appearance of slum children in school. However, it daily becomes more obvious that the global method gives excellent results with children who have plenty of experience and who learn by any method, but it does not seem to be the most appropriate method for slum children, unless they are properly prepared for it. For these children, methods immediately revealing the mechanism of reading would have better results. Recent school experiments provide proof of this statement.

A great number of slum children begin school later than the statutory age of seven, and soon feel old compared with the other pupils; the early demand from the majority of the families that they take on part of the domestic responsibilities or even contribute towards the family income leaves them with very few years in which to attend school – barely sufficient for the acquisition of the fundamental techniques for reading, writing and calculating. A considerable proportion of school drop-outs is due to these factors, and the low rate of learning is only an additional reason.

Problems Caused by the Inadequacy of Teacher Training
for the Needs of the New Population

Until the Carmela Dutra School was set up in 1946, the only institution for training teachers for public schools in Guanabara was the Institute of Education. After 1950 six other schools were created, bringing the total to eight official normal schools, where all the teachers for state schools are trained. Guanabara is the only State in the Federation in which only teachers trained at the normal schools or the Institutes of Education may teach in public elementary schools. For this reason it is the only State with a staff trained according to the highest standards and has no unqualified members in its schools.

In spite of this, the training given to future teachers does not enable them to handle the many types of children taken in by the public schools, and particularly the slum children. They have had no contact with this type of child, but only with children of nearby kindergartens and elementary schools, who generally come from the middle or slightly lower classes. Although still living in city districts, they regard their profession in a very romantic and not quite professional way. Research carried out in 1957 with a group of students from the Institute of Education and the Carmela Dutra Normal Course, showed that one of the advantages frequently claimed by future teachers was that their profession would allow them to be wives and mothers. Most of these girls come from a middle class background and share all the values and stereotyped ideas of that class towards the slums, which gives a clear picture of their attitude to slum children in the classroom. Although many teachers live or work in neighbourhoods close to the slums, they usually only know them from a distance, or through what is said or written in the newspapers, and their knowledge of the slum population is limited to their contact with the children in school and in the street-markets where they work, or with the adults who work as house servants.

If the teachers' training to deal with slum children is deficient when they leave normal school or the Institute of Education, it is hardly improved when they actually begin to teach. In spite of countless circulars issued by the State Board of Education and texts prepared for their guidance, the manner in which these instructions are transmitted from the Department of Norms and Programmes to the Coordinators of the Regional Head Offices, and from the latter to the Coordinators of the School Grade, and from these finally, through meetings, to the teachers, makes them ineffective. The practical training tried out in a pilot project, which gave excellent results, has not yet been introduced in the school system.

Special Problems: Resistance to Change. The Pilot Project and its Application

The Pilot Project for educating children living in slums was an experiment carried out between August 1962 and December 1965 in five elementary public schools in Guanabara. Its objects were research and the carrying out of a programme of compensatory education for children from poorer areas, which would fulfil their specific needs and permit them to develop their potential capacity to the greatest extent, while taking into account their personal interests and those of the community.

The Pilot Project involved a group of 300 children who began school in March 1962. They were hand picked from amongst the most deprived. The results obtained clearly demonstrated that with proper care, the slum child makes much more progress than when given only standard attention within the public school system, although in this special group the percentage of potentially able children was much lower than the average in the normal school population.

The experiment provided the selected children with remedies for everything that was considered responsible for their slow progress – poor health and nutrition, lack of experience and vocabulary, need for sensorial development, religious guidance and proper pedagogic treatment.

To make this possible, the selected schools were separated from the main system, suitably equipped and provided with specialized staff; the children spent eight hours a day in school during which they received 2,000 calories of food, dental and medical treatment, health education, recreation facilities, religious education, and carried out their studies under the guidance of teachers who had been trained by a team of special pedagogic and educational advisors. The schools remained open during the holidays so as not to interrupt the programme which aimed at the development of creative abilities and social habits, as well as maintaining the supply of food, medical and dental assistance and recreation. For example all the children were carefully examined by the Medical Department of the Project at the beginning of the experiment, were given necessary treatment and underwent similar tests at the end for control purposes.

The children were also tested psychologically by the relevant department, and their families visited and interviewed by social researchers in charge of the general appraisal of the experiment, and by the social service in charge of the family-school links.

In 1964 the project was expanded to include four additional points:

(1) the training of teachers and the reformulation of the school structure, and the organization of seven new schools located in areas with the same type of child population;

(2) the creation of the Observation and Adjustment Centre for Speech Therapy, aimed at diagnosing and treating language disturbances;

(3) the creation of a Section of Adjustment Classes connected with the Guidance and Control Service of the Official Elementary School System, in order to give expert attention to the children who after three years of school were unable to read and write;

(4) vocabulary research, handed over to the Institute of Clinical Psychology of the Catholic University of São Paulo.

At the end of 1965, the Pilot Project had become a Training Centre for teachers working with children from the poorer classes. The conclusion of the project experiment and the consequent creation of the training centre coincided, however, with the end of the Administration during which the project had been planned and developed. Due to the change in government the Director of the Training Centre, the former Pilot Project, had to leave her post – a great loss. The Ford Foundation had made it a condition of its grant of one billion old cruzeiros that one of the members of the Group of Supervisors of the Pilot Project would be permanently on the Board of Directors, and the new government in an attempt to circumvent this, placed on the Board of the Centre a member of the team of advisors from one of the schools, but this was not considered satisfactory by the Foundation which finally withdrew its co-operation.

Deprived of resources, the Training Centre has been unable to develop its work although attempts to restore it are now being considered. The Centre for Speech Therapy still functions but the Vocabulary Research was stopped and the Adjustment Classes ceased to exist.

It is obvious that such an expensive experiment as the Pilot Project could not be extended to the entire State. However, it could benefit the Guanabara slum population in at least two ways: through the practical training of teachers working with slum children, and through the adjustment classes, the results of which had been very promising.

Present Methods and Future Plans to solve Educational Problems
Steps adopted from 1960 onwards to solve the educational problems and promote new ideas, will be examined from the quantitative and qualitative points of view.

Steps of a Quantitative Nature
The law of compulsory school attendance introduced with the Law of National Educational Bases and Guidance, obliged the State to create vacancies for all children of school age living in Guanabara. As the number was unknown the first step was a school census, carried out for the first time in Guanabara and in the country as a whole in 1964 and

repeated every two years. As from 1967 estimates of the school population were made annually by calculating the rates of natural and migratory growth.

The next action taken was the construction of extra classrooms in the existing school buildings, the construction of new schools, the installation of elementary public schools in buildings donated by private or official entities (the so-called co-operation classes), the adoption of the three-shift system in schools, the elimination of the collective weekly day off and adoption of the teachers' rest day in turn, which permitted that five rooms could accommodate six classes (one without a fixed classroom), earlier period of enrolment, notices through the newspapers for enrolment of children of school age, and finally the training and recruiting of more teachers.

At present the capacity of the elementary public school system in three-shift turns, is greater than the demand. The number of teachers available is also larger than the number of classes in operation, although the ratio of pupils per teacher is still high. Double groups have disappeared, the squeezing of classes is exceptional, and only two of the enrolment privileges remain.

For the future, it is planned that all schools will work on two shifts of four and a half hours. This system is already enforced, as can be seen since 1966 from the decrease in the number of schools and classes working in one and three shifts, and an increase in the number of those working in two shifts.

Number of Schools Working in

Year	1 shift	2 shifts	3 shifts	Total
1966	32	223	325	580
1967	33	280	285	598
1968	24	277	306	607
1969	21	336	258	615

Number of Classrooms in

Year	1 shift	2 shifts	3 shifts	Total
1966	173	1,947	2,693	4,813
1967	231	2,362	2,456	5,049
1968	140	2,310	2,684	5,134
1969	128	2,831	2,277	5,236

Steps of a Qualitative Nature

Although a great number of measures have been taken to improve the quality of schooling, the problems in this field are still largely unresolved, as is shown by the low percentage of promotion from the preliminary classes and level 1, and the high percentage of drop-outs that still occurs.

Aggravated by the problems of a quantitative nature, the qualitative problems are indeed more difficult to solve, as they involve changes in areas where great resistance is always encountered through long-existing habits and attitudes.

Among the measures taken to improve the quality, there are preventive measures and those of a purely pedagogic nature, although the former have predominance over the latter. We mention the following, disregarding the order in which they occurred:

(1) entry to elementary school at an earlier age, i.e. at 6 years of age;

(2) the creation of preliminary classes to help immature children aged six and over;

(3) an increased number of kindergartens, preferably in slum areas;

(4) the creation of a department for guidance of special classes;

(5) the inclusion of a doctor's opinion in the assessment of a child recommended for the Gille Test; and

(6) an attempt to adapt the Gille Test to local conditions, at present being undertaken at the Research Institute.

Pedagogic instructions, however, are still transmitted to the teacher over a chain which greatly diminishes their impact. The practical training of teachers for slum area children is at present only an ideal. Preliminary classes, on the other hand, are not producing the expected results, for the reasons already outlined. On the initiative of the INEP,[2] research is being carried out in experimental schools to find a quicker method of teaching reading and writing, and in the same schools attempts are being made to teach mature and immature children together, as it is suspected that once a teacher is aware that a child is immature, she tends to deal with it as if it were incapable of normal progress.

---

[2] INEP – National Institute for Pedagogical Studies.

Section IV: Introduction

Europe

Brian Holmes

In this section the problems of planning education are described in a variety of situations. First there are the old cities – Rome (p. 308), Prague (p. 277), Sofia (p. 315), Ankara (p. 326), Rotterdam (p. 299). Then there are the new communities in England – Milton Keynes (p. 285) and Chelmsley Wood (p. 240). Again the largely rural and small community situation in Denmark (p. 267) may be compared with conditions in the megalopolis of the Ruhr-Rhein complex (p. 251). The characteristics of urbanization in the latter 'brought about by the arrival of heavy industry' (p. 252) may be contrasted with the problems in Denmark where until the 1950s 'it was taken for granted that agriculture must be considered the principal industry of the country' (p. 267). The shanty towns (*gecekondu*) around Ankara (p. 326) seem more characteristic of Latin America and Asia than of the suburban sprawl which is a feature of much European urban decay (Nottingham, p. 289).

Another point of comparison in this section is between educational policy in countries committed to social welfare policies such as Great Britain (p. 224) and Denmark (p. 267) and countries such as the U.S.S.R. (p. 229), Czechoslovakia (p. 278) and Bulgaria (p. 320).

One issue in the old cities is how to preserve the old and yet accommodate the new. It causes particularly acute problems in Rome (p. 308). In other cities such as Rotterdam, the towns of the Ruhr and Sofia, World War II damage made possible a measure of city planning difficult to achieve in centres virtually untouched by war. In Rome there is little room in which to expand the schools and build new ones (p. 310). Yet in some of the new communities education may receive such high priority that some of them may become cities of learning (p. 285).

Conditions in the cities of Europe vary greatly. In Denmark slums are said to be virtually non-existent (p. 267). In Britain over one million dwellings were, in 1965, identified as slums and in Nottingham a few minor ghetto areas have developed (p. 292). A recent survey in Rotterdam shows what a high proportion of the accommodation in an old district of the town is substandard (p. 300). Some of the personal difficulties resulting from urbanization are mentioned in the U.S.S.R. case study (p. 236).

Most of the cities are administrative centres or capital cities or centres of an international communication network – Prague, Sofia, Ankara, Moscow. Many are also the centre of the cultural activities of the country in which they are situated. Nottingham, as an industrial town and the Ruhr complex are exceptions. Many of the cities, as might be expected, are cosmopolitan. In some cases more than one language is spoken and account has to be taken of this in the formulation of educational policy (p. 229). All the cities attract immigrants. To Ankara (p. 327) and Sofia (p. 316) come many rural people. Rome's economic development seems to lag behind the in-flow of people; it is purely an administrative and tourist centre (p. 308). Ankara feels the impact of rural mobility (p. 328). In Rotterdam the lack of education among parents makes it difficult for them to help their children acquire the skills of modern citizenship (p. 302). Only in the case of Nottingham are the ethnic characteristics of the immigrants mentioned. Immigration from the West Indies, India or Pakistan (p. 292) has been high. Poverty and decay are to be found in some of those sections of the city to which these minority culture groups have moved.

Generally speaking, however, while signs of the forces which have created crisis situations in North America and elsewhere are found in European cities and while problems admittedly exist, they seem to be less severe. Certainly the differences between the immigrants and the older city inhabitants are not very profound. Minority groups are still very much in a minority. Paradoxically war time destruction helped rehabilitation. And in an important sense the authors stress the value placed on the traditions of the old city. Europeans are anxious to preserve these although the cost is sometimes high.

Another general feature of the European situation is that governments in collaboration with local authorities are anxious to plan their cities. The welfare statism of Great Britain is seen in the new towns, and in developments in Denmark. The participation of social agencies is encouraged: in Denmark from a traditional family base. But many aspects of society are subject to planning and many formalized agencies are involved. So, too, in communist countries. In these, at least in theory, 'the present day school is the product of urban culture' (p. 230). Polytechnical theory in communist countries is designed to meet the educational problems of an industrial age. Yet in these case studies, apart from interesting experiments, it is evident that no major transformation of education has occurred. The new cities may need such a transformation if they are to avoid some of the worst consequences of urban growth.

18

City Planning for the Future:
A Comparative Study

Peter G. Hall

Participation in planning has recently become a vogue word in planning journals on both sides of the Atlantic. It is generally thought to demand a new look at education for planning. The difficulty is that there is considerable misunderstanding about what participation is, and what it is supposed to achieve. This arises principally from the very different contexts of planning in Europe (particularly Great Britain) and in North America (particularly the United States). Before one attempts to discuss the future evolution of planning education, it seems imperative to look more closely at this context, and at how it may change in the near future in the two continents.

The call for participation in the American context is associated with a shift in the emphasis of the planning profession. It is argued there that city planning has failed to identify the important urban problems, because it has been too much obsessed with an idea that urban problems must be amenable to a physical or spatial solution. The argument is that physical arrangements in themselves have a very limited effect on life styles, or the quality of life, in cities. This movement against what has been called 'architectural determinism' is having profound consequences for planning education in North America. It amounts to nothing less than a total re-orientation of the subject, away from the physical aspects and towards the fundamental examination of the social system, its varied malaises and the possible danger of its breakdown.

The reasons for this new emphasis need no elaboration; they are a product of contemporary American urban, social and political history. The call for participation, of course, is a necessary by-product. What was wrong about the old planning was that it was dominated by middle-class professions, who pursued their own intellectual interests, rather as a gentlemanly diversion. Because of the type of education they had received in the architecture and planning schools, these interests were spatial or physical. The planners had no training which might have allowed them to recognize the true urban problems that faced them. Indeed, their whole education had provided a way of allowing them to ignore the most obvious facts about the urban environment. Participation in this view was needed so that those who did understand the problems, from the ground up, could tell the professionals about priorities as they saw them.

The situation in Britain, and by extension in most western European countries, is quite different. Here, to administer the 'Welfare State' as the idea evolved in Europe, there grew up, parallel to the town and country planning profession, a whole set of professionals concerned with what Americans now call 'social planning': child care officers, social case-workers, social security workers, housing officers. The result was that there were two professional structures, which interacted, not always effectively, in certain areas such as housing. Training for 'social planning' was provided not by University departments of 'Planning', but by Departments of Social Administration. Professors of Social Administration, notably at the London School of Economics, became the intellectual guardians of the Welfare State. Yet the London School of Economics has never had a planning school, and began to teach regional planning (not, notice, city planning) only in 1967.

It can well be argued that these professionals paid all too little regard to the need for participation. After all, the British Welfare State was created largely by upper middle-class figures like the Webbs, who put the social services in a strictly paternalist mould, in which the professional always knew best. Only recently, in a bout of self-criticism among the social administrators in Britain, has this attitude come in for fundamental questioning. The point is that there was a separate professional structure to deal with the non-spatial, non-physical urban problems.

The impact of the American debate has been therefore a double one. Physical planners have taken notice of it because some of them read the American journals, and listen to distinguished American lecturers. But because they rarely find echoes of the American concerns in their professional lives, they tend to reinterpret it in a British mould. Many of the more dedicated professional planners in Britain live and work in the counties; their chief work consists in controlling suburban growth and in balancing its needs against the requirement to conserve nature and the countryside. When they hear the word participation, they automatically think of a middle-class civic association in a village, not a militant black power group in a ghetto. The intellectual and emotional gulf between the two sets of planners could not be greater.

The social workers, on the other hand, have been able to interpret the American debate much more directly from their own experience. They have developed an awakened interest in concepts like an integrated social planning service, which received official expression in the report of the Seebohm Committee on the Organization of the Social Services (1968). In the cities, this does create a potential conflict of interest between the social worker and the physical planner, as to who should direct these operations. Already, one sociologist turned planner, Francis Amos of Liverpool, has stated his view that the physical planner should have this rôle. But he is almost certainly an unusual planner; for very few British physical planners received their first training in sociology, and the subject makes notoriously little serious contribution to most planning courses in Britain up to the present time.

These fundamental distinctions have many interesting implications. For there is all the difference in the world between giving the right of participation to middle-class groups, with a strong sense of cohesion, clear ideas of purpose, organizational skill and the ability to present their case in writing and in open inquiry; and giving the same power to historically disadvantaged groups, with next to no sense of cohesion, unclear understanding of final aims, and little ability to organize or to present their case coherently. The second, if it can be achieved, represents a redressing of the balance against the professional. The first can only guarantee a sort of gladiatorial contest between two groups of professionals: one of which pursues planning as a full-time vocation, the other of which pursues it as a spare-time avocation. In any event, the contest can hardly strengthen the voice of the weaker groups of society; rather, if anything, it is likely actually to weaken it.

How, if at all, are social changes in the next thirty years likely to affect this analysis? Some urban sociologists seem to see a permanently disadvantaged group remaining at the bottom of all possible ladders to higher positions in the urban housing market. They will remain in marginal housing near the city centre, and if and when this is redeveloped they will merely find another area of low-grade housing at an earlier stage in the redevelopment cycle. These are likely to be people unable to cope adequately with the problems of a technologically and socially complex society. They might include unmarried mothers, broken families or unstable families, families affected by physical or mental illness of the chief economic support or a mother, or families with members of sub-normal intelligence. Areas containing these groups, which are likely to have a high rate of turnover of population and a limited amount of social cohesion, should be sharply distinguished from the traditional 'urban village' inhabited by stable working-class groups, which may tend increasingly to break up under the influence of suburbanization.

It is here, if anywhere, that close parallels with the American ghetto and its problems might be found. For it would be true here in the future, as it is true now of the ghetto, that the gulf between the disadvantaged and the mass high-consumption society tends to grow, in relative and still more absolute terms. This has been abundantly demonstrated by American investigations of the living standards of black groups; it seems to be true too of the poorest groups in British society, as is apparent from the studies of Titmuss and his colleagues.

If this analysis proves to contain any truth, it demands that planners think of participation in quite a different light than physical planners in Britain now think of it, and far more as social planners in America tend to think of it. This is the relevant framework to judge the Skeffington Report on Participation in Planning, which appeared in July 1969.

The main effect of the Skeffington Report, as is perhaps inevitable, is to formalize the opportunities for public participation in planning. True, there are many proposals in the Report for opening up informal avenues of participation. But the main effect would be to compel all councils to take formal steps to consult public opinion, before and during plan preparation. They would have to announce their intention to prepare the plan, and simultaneously announce the timetable for participation. They would be required to pause after their initial survey, when choices for action could be discussed; and again after publication of their recommendations.

If adopted, this formal procedure would in itself be wholly desirable. It would compel all authorities to do what the best now do. The critical question, however, is who would fill the statutory slots thus created. In the case of middle-class issues and middle-class areas, this is presumably no problem. (Symptomatically, perhaps, the Report is illustrated by light-hearted pictures of participation in practice; they identify obviously middle-class individuals and groups fighting middle-class battles, notably for preservation of old buildings.) The question remains, how to awaken what the Report calls the non-joiner, especially in those situations – often the most problematic – where almost everyone, from suspicion or despair or plain apathy, may be a non-joiner.

Here the Report borrows, and adapts, two suggestions which have been canvassed and used in other contexts, especially in North America. One is that the local authority should take the initiative in setting up a Community Forum in the area where a plan is being prepared, composed of interested individuals and groups. This might at least act as a focus for the people, and the bodies, willing to involve themselves. But for the real non-joiners, the other proposal is perhaps more important: it is for a Community Development Officer, appointed by the local authority or by some independent body, who would provide a sort of catalyst for the unspoken, even unthought, views of the community, and who would work in ways appropriate to the area, the time and the problem.

The Community Development Officer already exists in some areas in Britain, usually where there are particularly acute social problems like racial integration or resettlement in a new town. Often employed by the local authority but setting himself up as the people's friend – against the authority that pays him, if need be – the Officer has a difficult, ambiguous life liable to permanent misunderstanding and suspicion. Furthermore, as the Skeffington Report admits, it may be totally impossible in many cases to distinguish the 'planning' aspect of his work from other aspects concerned with personal welfare of one kind or another – housing, allowances, education, delinquency.

The Community Development Officer, the report says, should be a full-time worker, suitably qualified. But the question must be, how qualified.

In truth, in a slum area waiting redevelopment he would have to be a master of most trades; he would have to combine these with rare personal qualities. These seems to be an indication here of the need for a quite new kind of voluntary service, equivalent perhaps to a Domestic Peace Corps, and financed not by local authorities but by sources independent of them, though perhaps indirectly relying on central government support. (If the Maud proposals for local government reform are accepted, this might be a provincial responsibility.) It would ideally employ young professionals during, or immediately after, their training, for periods of one or two years, and it would bring them up against grass roots problems, in situations where they would be compelled to practise advocacy planning *vis à vis* the professionals whose ranks they were soon proposing to join. This would not only harness young idealism and freshly acquired professionalism, it would also provide a highly effective and respected foil to the professional planner; and most important of all, some of this early experience would surely carry through into the subsequent career of the planner, with immeasurable benefit to the profession.

BIBLIOGRAPHY

F. Amos, 'Approach to Planning – a planning officer's view of the next ten years', *Journal of the Town Planning Institute,* 55 (1969), 141–6.

P. Hall, 'The Urban Culture and the Suburban Culture', in R. Eels and C. Walton (ed.) *Man in the City of the Future* (New York: Collier Macmillan, 1969).

People and Planning: Report of the Committee on Participation in Planning (the Skeffington Report) (London: Stationery Office, 1969).

Report of the Committee on the organization of the Social Services (the Seebohm Report) (London: Stationery Office, 1968).

M. M. Webber, *Beyond the Industrial Age* and *Permissive Planning.* Two lectures. (London: Centre for Environmental Studies, 1968) (mimeo).

19

Functions of Urban Educational Establishments: the U.S.S.R.

A. A. Migunov

Recent years have witnessed the growth of big cities (from 100,000 to 500,000 inhabitants) and super-cities (above half a million inhabitants) in the U.S.S.R.

Only ten years ago the urban dwellers comprised the lesser part of the country's population – 48 per cent (100 out of 208·8 million). By the beginning of 1968 the figure grew to 55 per cent, the absolute growth of the urban population being 30–1 million. During this period 800 new towns have appeared with a total population of some five million people (at the beginning of 1968). That means that the major share of the population growth has fallen to the old towns: 25–6 million people. Moreover, the bigger the city, the greater the absolute population growth. In absolute population growth, Moscow ranks first with more than half a million new inhabitants within the last ten years, followed by Leningrad (431,000), Tashkent (397,000), and Kiev (372,000). In the population growth rate first place is held by cities whose population in 1959 amounted to 400 to 600 thousand people, such as Lvov, Krasnoyarsk, Zaporozhye, Alma-Ata, Yerevan, Riga, Ufa, and Minsk – fourteen cities in all. Each of them has grown by approximately one-third, on an average. A total of 54 per cent of the urban population lives today in big cities and super-cities; in 1959 the respective figure was 47–9 per cent.

Growth of Cities and Super-Cities

The growth of big cities and super-cities is accompanied by still greater development of agglomerations, which is a characteristic feature of the habitation pattern in the twentieth century. It should be noted that the outskirts of the agglomeration, that is the peripheral areas, are growing, as a rule, much more quickly than the centres. Take for instance the Moscow agglomeration. As was mentioned before, Moscow, the centre of this agglomeration, has grown by a mere half million people, which is a low increment compared with the growth of other big cities of the Soviet Union. But while the Moscow population growth is rather small, the growth rate of the towns surrounding Moscow is extraordinary high. Thus, rather small towns located within the radius of 50 kilometres from Moscow, such as Reutovo (24,300 people in 1959), Khimki (47,800 people), Mytishchy (98,600 people), Krasnogorsk (35,200 people) and others have grown over the same period by 38–9 per cent; at the same time other small towns of the Moscow Region, outside the agglomeration limits, have grown only by 19 per cent.

The appearance of new towns and the growth of old ones, as well as the expansion of agglomerations, are caused first and foremost by the tempestuous economic development, building of new industrial enterprises, development of new industries, retooling of old factories and plants.

The recruitment of workers, employees, technicians and engineers for enterprises in big cities is largely carried out in the Soviet Union in an organized way. It is carried out, as a rule, not so much within individual towns or settlements, but throughout the *whole territory* of the multinational Soviet Union. This is accomplished in several ways: by the distribution of the graduates from higher and secondary specialized educational establishments in accordance with the requests of the planning bodies of Union Republics; by means of organized recruitment (*orgnabor*) of workers through commissions specially formed for this purpose under local Executive Committees of the Soviets of Working People's Deputies; through the republican personnel departments.

Thus many towns and settlements of the country have multi-national populations. For instance, in such towns as Bugulma, Almetyevsk (industrial centres of the Tatar Autonomous Soviet Socialist Republic), Sibai and Ishimbai (industrial centres of the Bashkir Autonomous Soviet Socialist Republic), among the workers, employees, technicians and engineers, there are many Russians, Ukrainians, Chuvashes, Mordovians, etc., in addition to the Tatars and Bashkirs who comprise approximately half of the population. In Alma-Ata, Tashkent, Nalchik, Tbilisi, Yerevan and all other big cities and workers' settlements of all the U.S.S.R. Union Republics, as well as in some towns and settlements of the Russian Federation, the population is also multi-national. This explains why in schools and pre-school establishments of the majority of towns children are taught in various languages. In each of these towns there are schools teaching in Russian and in the language of the indigenous population. If as a result of organized recruitment of workforce for a developing local industry children speaking a different language appear in a town, special forms are organized in schools or a special school may be opened. Mixed schools are fairly common in the towns of Union Republics, with several (2–3) parallel forms where teaching is in two, three or even more tongues.

Soviet law gives all people an opportunity to receive secondary education in their own language. The mixed schools mentioned before ensure the *realization* of this law for every citizen of the Soviet Union who can choose for himself and for his children the language in which to be taught.

It should be noted that in the Georgian S.S.R. and some other national republics, lectures in universities and other higher educational institutions are delivered in two languages: Russian and national.

Thus the growth of urban population in the conditions of a multinational state affects first of all the *structure* of school from its primary to highest stage. In rural areas the school is not subjected to such influences; only in some large villages with multi-national population are there mixed schools. In general in rural schools the pupil body is homogeneous, so teaching is done in one language.

The urbanization process also affects the content of the secondary education. The progress of science and engineering requires not only thorough general training, but also versatile technical knowledge, labour skills and labour discipline.

Soviet general education (see Table 1) from its very start combined labour and polytechnical training, especially in urban schools. At present urban secondary schools not only give pupils sufficient education to enter any institute of higher learning, but also some knowledge of the elementary laws of modern industrial production, as well as psychological and practical training for work in the spheres of both material and non-material production. From this point of view the present-day school is the product of urban culture. In turn, it has had a favourable effect on rural schools, which are also influenced by the industrial development of agricultural machinery and chemicalization of agriculture; as a result, more stress is laid on technical subjects in the curriculum of the rural school.

The Decree of the C.P.S.U. Central Committee and U.S.S.R. Council of Ministers 'On Measures of Further Improving the Work of Secondary Schools' (November 1966), put the task of improving the polytechnical training of pupils, of preparing them for socially useful labour, side by side with the main task of the secondary general school – to give pupils a thorough knowledge of the fundamentals of science. With this purpose in view, schools are helped to organize labour training of pupils, and to provide the necessary educational facilities. Specialists are sent to work at schools and the pupils are acquainted with various branches of national economy so as to be better oriented when choosing a career. In senior forms (9–10), the pupils are given a special practical programme at industrial works and the urban and rural Soviets of Working People's Deputies decide the necessary number of vacancies and instructors to be allotted. The most skilled workers, technicians and foremen at industrial establishments act as instructors. Some establishments have entire shops catering for vocational training. In Moscow, Leningrad, Kiev, Kazan, and other cities, these shops are controlled jointly by the industrial establishment and the school. It should be stressed that conditions in big cities especially favour the functioning of general secondary schools.

TABLE 1

GENERAL SCHOOLS
(at beginning of school year; in thousands)

	1940/1		
	Schools	*Pupils*	*Teachers*
General schools of all types including:	199·0	35,552	1,238
primary, incomplete secondary (eight-year) and secondary (ten-year) day-time schools	191·5	34,784	1,216[1]
schools for working youth, rural youth and schools for adults	—[2]	768[4]	—[2]

	1958/9		
	Schools	*Pupils*	*Teachers*
General schools of all types including:	215·0	31,483	1,900
primary, incomplete secondary (eight-year) and secondary (ten-year) day-time schools	199·7	29,600	1,813[1]
schools for working youth, rural youth and schools for adults	15·5[3]	1,916[4]	—[2]

	1967/8		
	Schools	*Pupils*	*Teachers*
General schools of all types including:	206·0	48,902	2,563
primary, incomplete secondary (eight-year) and secondary (ten-year) day-time schools	186·3	44,451	2,437[1]
schools for working youth, rural youth and schools for adults	19·9	4,451[4]	—[2]

[1] Including teachers holding several employments.

[2] No data available.

[3] Including primary, seven-year, eight-year and secondary schools to which classes for working and rural youth were attached, and independent correspondence schools.

[4] Including those studying by correspondence.

As a result of the development of secondary education in the country (see Table 1), there are almost no primary or eight-year schools in big towns and workers' settlements, but predominantly secondary schools with two, three or more parallel forms. Thanks to this a teacher in an urban secondary school has a full-time job in his special subject. As the teachers

TABLE 2

ENROLMENT AT URBAN AND RURAL PRIMARY, INCOMPLETE SECONDARY AND
SECONDARY DAY-TIME SCHOOLS
(at beginning of school year; in millions)

	1940/1	1950/1	1958/9	1960/1	1967/8
Total enrolment including: in towns and urban-type	34·8	33·3	29·6	33·4	44·5
settlements	10·8	11·8	13·7	16·1	22·4
in rural areas	24·0	21·5	15·9	17·3	22·1

are materially well off and interested in their work, the body of teachers in schools is stable. Over 90 per cent of teachers have qualifications corresponding to their occupations, that is, secondary or higher teachers' training. Two-thirds have a long working record. In short, urban schools have skilled and experienced teachers.

Schools are housed in standard buildings, with all the necessary study and subsidiary rooms. The majority of schools have the required number of studies, labs and workshops, equipped in accordance with the standards set by the Ministry, as well as sporting facilities and experimental plots of land. All schools have their own libraries, assembly halls with film projectors, radio and TV sets, electricity, water supply, gas, etc.

All schools are closely linked with industrial establishments, where senior children have their practice. Skilled workers, foremen, technicians and engineers from these establishments help schools with technical training. Thanks to this the training of children in urban schools (see Table 2) is better organized and more effective than in rural schools.

Secondary School Network

Soviet big cities have a broad network of secondary schools training specialists of medium qualification for all branches of the national economy. As of January 1st, 1968, there were 4,000 schools (see Table 3), of which more than three-quarters are located in towns and workers' settlements. The number of specialized secondary educational establishments in each town is related to the number of industrial undertakings in the town.

In 1963 compulsory eight-year schooling was introduced throughout the Soviet Union. Now complete secondary education is being introduced. As a result, specialized secondary schools now have an additional function: to provide their pupils not only with a special training but with a general education within the scope of a general secondary school. Such extension of the functions of a specialized secondary school fully corresponds to the

TABLE 3

TOTAL ENROLMENT IN ALL TYPES OF SCHOOLS
(at beginning of school year; in thousands)

	1914/5	1940/1	1950/1	1958/9	1960/8
Total enrolment	10,588	47,547	48,770	46,057	76,025
including:					
general schools of all types	9,656	35,552	34,752	31,483	48,902
vocational schools and industrial schools	106	717	882	904	2,129
specialized secondary schools	54	975	1,298	1,876	4,167
schools of higher learning	127	812	1,247	2,179	4,311
those learning new trades or perfecting their skill at work or at courses, as well as those studying by other methods	645	9,491	10,591	9,615	16,516

country's economic development. The general educational background of a technician, apart from his special training, as our investigations have shown, makes his work more productive and helps him to continue his studies and to perfect his skill. This extension of the functions of the specialized secondary school is also of a great benefit to students as anyone who graduates from any specialized school with top marks can enter *any* institution of higher learning immediately after his graduation. As a result, the number of boys and girls seeking admission to specialized secondary schools has grown, necessitating further extension of the network of these schools. (See Table 3.)

Industrial Development

The rapid industrial development and improvement of technology and technical facilities have caused an extension of vocational schools training highly-skilled workers. Like specialized secondary schools, vocational schools are usually located in towns and workers' settlements (approximately 80 per cent of them). Each vocational school trains workers of definite specialities. Some of these schools admit students with complete secondary education and teach them a worker's trade for a year but a somewhat greater number of schools are based on the eight-year education, and in the course of three years give students a secondary education as well as a worker's trade. The majority of vocational schools today admit boys and girls who failed to finish eight-year school. These three-year vocational schools train highly-skilled workers and give them some additional general education.

A significant part of young workers who failed to obtain secondary education continue their studies in evening schools without leaving their jobs. Urban evening schools first appeared in 1943, followed in 1944 by rural evening schools. Their purpose is to help young people to get secondary education without leaving their jobs. These schools have special curricula and are adapted to the student's working shifts. Evening schools for young workers successfully cope with their tasks, opening up for millions of Soviet boys and girls a road to secondary and higher education. At present (1968/9 academic year) there are 22,000 schools for young workers in the Soviet Union with an enrolment of 4,600,000 pupils. The majority of these schools are urban.

As is known, various social strata of the urban population – employees, trade workers, workers in industrial undertakings, transport and service establishments – have various conditions of labour and rest and different amounts of leisure time which depend on working shifts at factories and offices, as well as different family status. To satisfy the requirements of all people, the educational system should be flexible. That is why besides general, specialized secondary and vocational schools (functioning in the day time) there are other educational establishments, either attached to these schools or working independently – evening, correspondence or shift schools (adapted to working shifts), schools combining day-time and correspondence studies and external-studies departments.

Thus, a modern city has a ramified network of educational establishments. In a socialist society all secondary educational establishments are closely bound together. They all give their pupils sufficient knowledge either to enter institutes of higher learning or to go to work immediately after school. Their curricula on general subjects are so drawn up that if a pupil changes schools (for instance, if he enters a vocational or a secondary specialized school after studying in a general secondary school), he has a full opportunity to continue and complete his general education. Even those young people who enter three-year vocational schools without finishing their eight-year schooling, add to their general education. The graduates from the vocational school are assigned jobs and in an *organized manner* are enrolled at the nearest school for working youth, where they complete their secondary education.

All this variety of educational forms and types of establishments, providing for both general secondary education and labour training, is to a certain extent the product of the urbanization process brought about by the rapid industrial development. The existing system of educational establishments, though in the main satisfying society's requirements for education and facilitating the general cultural development of the people, still needs improvement.

The share of the vocational schools in this system is not as yet big enough. Today only two million people are studying in vocational schools. Moreover, the vocational schools providing both secondary education and speciality are not sufficient in number, while the numbers of young people seeking admission are growing day by day. Young people of today are mostly technically-minded and are eager to become independent as soon as possible, to earn their own living. So the network of vocational schools should be greatly expanded by increasing the number of such vocational schools which give their students both secondary education and vocational training.

The further improvement of general and vocational education requires theoretical elaboration of the didactics of labour and technical education, of individual methods for teaching adults who combine their studies with work, and methods of teaching young workers who are simultaneously studying at a secondary school and are receiving speciality training as apprentices either individually or in a team.

The curricula for adults receiving secondary education must be revised just in the same way as has been done by a special commission of two academies – the Academy of Sciences of the U.S.S.R. and the Academy of Pedagogical Sciences of the U.S.S.R. – for secondary schools for children.

One thing is certain – new curricula both for adults and children should keep pace with the achievements of modern science. But they should differ in the content and volume of subjects taught with due consideration given to the wealth of working and life experience of adults. However, the schools for adults, evening schools for young workers, both urban and rural, and vocational schools, when teaching general subjects, still use programmes, textbooks and teaching aids designed for children's schools.

Schools for Expert Workers

In the past ten years a new type of school for adults has developed in Soviet cities – schools for expert workers. They are supervised by the industrial establishments and local (regional, district, city) bodies of public education. These schools are intended to teach those experienced highly skilled workers, team leaders, assistant foremen and foremen, who have no secondary education, and sometimes even no eight-year education. The course takes two or two-and-a-half years, and classes are held three times a week for six hours (18 hours a week). The students of these schools go through an accelerated programme for the secondary or eight-year school – depending on their educational level – and also study some special subjects on engineering and technology for their type of production. Approximately the same number of hours are allotted to general and specialized subjects. The latter are taught by works engineers and scientists, and general subjects by teachers from the local school.

Curricula and programmes for schools for expert workers are worked out by specialists from the industrial establishment responsible for the technical education of workers, in collaboration with teachers of the general secondary school, and the plans and programmes are approved by the administration of the establishment and the public education department. These schools enjoy wide popularity in many Soviet cities, but as experience has proved, the plans and programmes should be improved, and more stress laid on the fundamentals of technical sciences. Special teaching aids and textbooks on general subjects should also be devised with due consideration of the fact that the average age of pupils in these schools is 30–5.

Social Aspects

Of the social phenomena, one stemming from the attempts to regulate the growth of big cities is noteworthy.

During the past ten years attempts have been made to limit the growth of the biggest Soviet cities. But the developing industry of these cities requires still more manpower which is acquired from the towns and settlements within its agglomeration. This has resulted in the growth of the population of these towns. The crowds of commuters going every day to the big city to work and back are growing with every year (so-called pendulum-like migration).

Among these commuters are many students attending specialized secondary schools and vocational schools situated in big cities. These students spend daily some three, four, or even five hours in getting to and from the city, not counting the time taken to reach their school after arrival in the city. Obviously, this greatly impedes their studies and reduces the quality of training. The problem can be solved only by eliminating the pendulum-like migration of workers, as these two types of migration are closely linked. Partially, the problem of students' migration can be solved by providing small hostels for students living in towns within the agglomeration limits.

Sociological investigations recently conducted in such big cities as Moscow, Leningrad, Kiev, Tashkent, Alma-Ata, etc., revealed the keen interest displayed by all strata of our society in the arts, theatre, music, sports, natural sciences and engineering. This yearning for culture calls for all-round extension and improvement of the dissemination of scientific and political knowledge. This problem is solved through the creation of 'People's Universities' attached to workers' clubs, of lectures, organization of people's theatres and artists', actors' and singers' groups, sports societies, etc. These cultural organizations supplement, to a great extent, the work of educational establishments. The general cultural and educational level of workers and other population strata is noticeably rising.

Problems of Organization

The control over the complex and diversified activity of cultural and educational establishments in conditions of a big city is a matter of great difficulty. It requires great effort and a wealth of knowledge and experience, not to mention time. That is why the state bodies at the head of public education, national economy and culture are assisted by voluntary public organizations. In the field of education they are teacher's councils and parents' committees in schools; public education councils attached to departments of public education; commissions for assistance to schools at enterprises; standing school commissions attached to local Soviets of Working People's Deputies.

Actively participating in these organizations are teachers, parents, workers, employees. They help schools to bring up and teach children.

Parents' committees (for an individual form or for an entire school) organize parents who help teachers in their work. Some parents help pupils who lag behind, assist teachers in organizing school parties, celebration meetings, vacations; they also guide the work of pupils' clubs or societies. These clubs are very popular in urban schools and cover not only academic subjects (mathematics, literature, history, geography, physics, chemistry, etc.), which are widely spread in rural localities as well, but also arts (singing, drama, dancing, musical instruments), technology, designing and many other aspects. The work of those circles is directed by poets, writers, actors, engineers, designers and scientists from among the parents. Parents' committees also organize meetings at which mothers and fathers from the most successful families take the floor and speak of their experience in bringing up children. Parents also help to control the behaviour of children in the street, in public places, during collective theatre visits, mass games, etc.

Public education councils attached to the departments of public education are mass public organizations uniting experienced teachers, directors of schools, physicians, active parents, managers of city enterprises, well-known engineers, technicians, skilled workers, scientists, actors, and Party and trade union leaders.

These councils help the bodies dealing with public education to establish links between businesses and educational establishments, organize the Soviet public for work with children and young people in their neighbourhood, direct the activity of clubs, theatres, cinemas, etc., so that they meet the cultural requirements of both adolescents and young children; they also see that the law on compulsory eight-year education is enforced.

Commissions for assistance to factory schools comprise workers and representatives of public organizations at the factory. They help general schools and schools for young workers: check the attendance of school by workers, see that the administration of the shops and the enterprise as a whole provides for adequate conditions of work and studies, check whether students enjoy all the privileges granted them by the state, e.g. shortened working day or working week, additional leaves during the examination periods, payment for shortened working day or week in accordance with the mean quota, etc. These commissions have standing ties with schools and check on the successes of their workers, helping them in their studies if need be.

Standing school commissions attached to local Soviets of Working People's Deputies consist of deputies to these Soviets. They control the implementation of the law on universal compulsory eight-year schooling within the territory of their Soviet. They also help schools to organize practical studies of senior pupils at industrial premises.

Art Councils and General Cultural Activities

Workers' clubs also have standing art councils which help the administration of schools and local Soviet to direct the artistic amateur activity of workers and employees, to organize parties and concerts; they also help schools to carry on club work with children. Their clubs have special children's sections which carry on mass work with children in the arts, sports, etc.

The All-Union Society *Znaniye* also conducts active and fruitful work among the population. It has its affiliated organizations in all the big cities of the Soviet Union, as well as almost all large workers' settlements. The society organizes numerous lectures on the latest achievements in science, the arts and literature and on political events in the country and abroad. With the administration it carries out consultations at factories, on problems of engineering, thus promoting the work of inventors and rationalizers from among the workers. For children and young people it organizes series of lectures on literature and concerts (Soviet and foreign, classical and modern), the arts, painting, music, history, etc., in clubs, cinemas and concert halls.

As a rule, urban general secondary schools have a large body of pupils – 38–9 in each form, the limits being 40 pupils in each of the first eight forms, and 35 in the ninth to tenth forms. Usually a school has some 1,400 to 1,600 pupils. Naturally the teachers' team of 50 or 60 has a lot of difficulty in controlling the out-of-school activity of their pupils. To help them, special premises in big apartment houses are given to children where they can gather in the evenings and any other time they are free from school. These premises are specially equipped. Some of them have libraries, facilities for various games, rooms for dancing, with a stage, film projectors, TV sets. The work is organized by the inhabitants of this building, often pensioners, under the control of teachers from neighbouring schools. Some of these children's rooms, as they are called, are attended regularly by 150 and more schoolchildren, and some older children also use them.

One can hardly overestimate the significance of all the school activities mentioned above. One fact is proof enough: the general development level of an urban schoolboy or schoolgirl is much higher and the volume of concrete and abstract knowledge is greater than those of a rural pupil.

A big city calls forth powerful educational forces which cannot appear in places with insignificant concentration of population. True, the process or urbanization gives rise to unfavourable phenomena such as increased nervous tension among young people, anaemia, headaches. It also increases the danger of the negative effect of the street. But in a socialist society such negative phenomena are gradually being eliminated. With this purpose in view, the Soviet public, and the educational bodies supported by trade unions organize holiday tourist and pioneer camps for young people, summer camps attached to schools, excursions and trips along short and long-distance routes, send children and young people to holiday homes, sanatoria, forest schools, etc.

The system of public organizations which has been outlined above, and the character of their activity testify to the fact that they are in the main advisors and assistants of state bodies (Ministries of Education and their local departments, Ministries of Culture, Ministries of Higher and Secondary Specialized Education, the State Committee on Vocational Education). These public organizations never supplant the state bodies and have no administrative functions. In this respect a special place is held by standing school commissions attached to local Soviets of Working People's Deputies, which work on a voluntary basis, but act on behalf of the local authorities.

The work of all the educational establishments throughout the country is controlled by the central state bodies – union and republican Ministries of Education and Ministries of Higher and Specialized Secondary Education. They are responsible for the elaboration of curricula, teaching programmes, textbooks and teaching aids; they train teachers, build schools and other educational establishments, supervise the production of teaching aids and equipment for schools, control the work of all the offices concerned with public education. Their control is direct through special inspectors and local departments of public education. Such organization of control over public education corresponds to the basic principles of the Soviet school system.

20

England and Wales : Planning Schools for New Communities*

Randall Smith

Introduction

Why are new communities needed in Britain? The answer can be found by considering the relationship between the population of the country and its housing stock. First, the number of people living in Britain has increased steadily in recent years and is predicted to go on increasing, though there is room for conjecture about the rate of increase. Currently, the annual rate of natural increase is about seven per thousand population. The migration pattern shows typically a small net loss in population, but not so big as to offset the natural increase. Thus the changes in population size and structure in the future can be estimated though the estimates are liable to error.

Secondly, the population numbers or forecasts have to be converted into numbers of households of different sizes. The conventional way of doing this is to divide the total population up by age, sex and marital status, and work out what proportion of each subgroup forms separate households. This proportion is called the 'headship rate'.[1] Some groups have higher headship rates than others, and if these groups form an increasing proportion of the total population, then the pressures for forming separate households are so much the greater. In Britain the proportions of older people and of married people are increasing and these groups do have relatively high headship rates.

Thirdly, once the size and structure of the country's population in the future is known and a forecast of headship rates is made, this has to be converted into a figure representing the number of dwellings needed on the assumption that each household should have its own dwelling. The current number of dwellings may be known but calculation of the number needed can be complicated by a variety of factors such as use of two dwellings (which is increasing), the different kinds of shared dwelling (luxury hotel in a seaside retirement resort or multi-occupied Victorian

---

* ©Randall Smith, 1970.

[1] See J. B. Cullingworth, 'Housing Analysis' in J. B. Cullingworth and S. C. Orr (eds.), *Regional and Urban Studies*, Allen and Unwin, 1969, pp. 177–82 for further consideration of headship rates.

artisan terrace dwelling in a city's twilight area), the numbers of empty dwellings and the earlier age of marriage and consequent earlier household formation.

Fourthly, once the shortfall between the number of dwellings needed and the existing dwellings stock is calculated, it is still necessary to compute the number of dwellings which need to be replaced (mainly through slum clearance schemes) or which will be demolished in the near future because of new road programmes or other planned change in land use.

In 1965, the British Government published a White Paper[2] and assessed dwelling needs as follows:

(i) a million dwellings to replace unfit dwellings identified as slums;

(ii) up to two million dwellings to replace obsolescent housing;

(iii) 700,000 dwellings to overcome shortages and provide a margin for mobility;

(iv) 30,000 dwellings *annually* to replace dwellings demolished because of area redevelopment;

(v) 150,000 dwellings *annually* to cater for formation of new households.

Some rethinking has taken place since 1965, particularly in relation to the improvement rather than replacement of older dwellings, but there is still a substantial shortfall between the current number of dwellings and the demand for dwellings. It has been officially forecast that by 1973 there will be a million more dwellings than households requiring them, providing a substantial five per cent margin for mobility.

Even if this forecast were accurate – and it has been challenged – the picture it presents is a national one, and there are likely to be great variations between different regions and localities. The rate of increase of population may vary in different parts of the country as may headship rates; internal migration patterns may indicate areas with greater job opportunities; the proportion of obsolescent housing may vary from one region to another; the availability of manpower in the building industry and the availability of building land may affect the rate of new building. A multiplicity of interacting factors thus creates a demand for new dwellings and new communities.

New Communities

In Britain, four main types of large-scale new development can be identified:

(i) new towns under the New Towns Acts, which set up special administrative machinery to carry out the development;

(ii) town expansion schemes under the Town Development Act, which

² Ministry of Housing and Local Government, *The Housing Programme 1965–70*, Cmnd. 2838, H.M.S.O., 1965.

facilitates co-operation between different units of local government in exporting and receiving both population and employment;

(iii) peripheral housing developments whether through private enterprise or through municipal enterprise under the Housing Acts;

(iv) central or inner area redevelopment, also under Housing Act powers.

Not only do new communities serve to increase the total housing stock or to decongest city areas where building land is in short supply, but they may also help to rejuvenate the area in which they are located by the importation of employment opportunities in growth industries together with population from an overcrowded conurbation. The designation, for example, of Dawley (now Telford) new town in Shropshire, 30 miles west of Birmingham, was not only to aid the city by receiving 'overspill' population but also to revive a declining area which had been a seat of the Industrial Revolution in Britain.

All four types of new community are represented in the West Midlands region of England which is centred on the city of Birmingham. There are two new towns (Redditch and Telford), a number of town expansion schemes (including Droitwich and Tamworth), large peripheral housing estates, and central redevelopment areas, particularly in Birmingham, which, with a population of over a million, is the largest all-purpose local authority in the conurbation.

The Centre for Urban and Regional Studies in the University of Birmingham is currently studying examples in the West Midlands region of three of the four types of new community: Redditch new town – 14 miles south of Birmingham; Tamworth town expansion scheme – 14 miles north-east of Birmingham; and Chelmsley Wood, a large peripheral (mainly municipal) housing development located just over the eastern boundary of the city of Birmingham in the administrative county of Warwickshire. All these developments have as their main purpose the decongestion of the city of Birmingham or other parts of the West Midlands conurbation, an area which is desperately short of land for housing the numbers forecast to be living and working in the region in the next 10–15 years.[3]

All three new communities involve more than one local authority under the current British local government system. Birmingham, the main exporting authority is, like the other authorities in the conurbation, an all-purpose county borough, responsible for all local services though at times acting jointly with neighbouring authorities. Birmingham and the other conurbation authorities are surrounded by three administrative

---

[3] Estimates of regional housing need can be found in two recent official publications: Department of Economic Affairs, *The West Midlands: A Regional Study*, H.M.S.O., 1965 and West Midlands Economic Planning Council, *The West Midlands: Patterns of Growth*, H.M.S.O., 1967.

counties, Staffordshire, Warwickshire and Worcestershire, which are upper-tier local authorities responsible for a wide range of local services, one of the most costly of which is education. Within each of these upper-tier authorities there are district or lower-tier authorities, such as Tamworth Municipal Borough in Staffordshire, Redditch Urban District Council in Worcestershire and Meriden Rural District Council in Warwickshire. (The housing estate of Chelmsley Wood lies within the boundaries of Meriden Rural District Council.) These lower-tier authorities are responsible for a limited range of services, of which house building and management are the most relevant in this analysis. Because these lower-tier authorities are often small and not very wealthy, special arrangements are made for the development of planned new communities. This is true of the three developments being studied. As required under the New Town Acts, a special development corporation appointed by the Minister of Housing and Local Government has been established to take charge of the development at Redditch. At Tamworth, a joint development committee was created, composed of representatives from both the upper-tier authority (the county of Stafford) and the lower-tier authority (the borough of Tamworth). Birmingham is also offering technical assistance. For Chelmsley Wood, the city of Birmingham is acting in the capacity of an estate developer, just like a private building firm, and is providing engineering services, roads, dwellings as well as acting as agent for Meriden Rural District Council on such matters as landscaping and open space provision. The city proposed to sell appropriate quantities of land to the county of Warwick so that the latter could provide the services for which it was responsible, including education, health, welfare, police and fire brigade. Land is also being sold to Meriden Rural District Council where required for its various services, including housing.

Thus, the formal setting at the local level for examining the planning of school provision for a new community (except in a redevelopment area) is that (1) a conurbation authority exports its 'excess' or 'overspill' population; (2) an upper-tier receiving authority is responsible for providing schools (and some other services); and (3) a lower-tier receiving authority is responsible for other local services, including housing of the migrant population, if special arrangements have not been made to perform this service on behalf of the receiving authority.

Planning School Provision

Local education authorities in England and Wales have to submit a forward building programme for schools and other education buildings to the central department of government concerned with education matters, the Department of Education and Science. The Department asks for the programme to be set out in priority order of projects and to be accompanied by a written justification of the reasonableness of the programme submitted, including an analysis of places available in existing schools and a trend analysis of the numbers of pupils produced by comparing younger and older cohorts of the school population. If, in addition, a case is put forward for establishing schools to serve a new community, information should be provided on the ultimate size of the new development, progress so far by numbers of dwellings completed, expected progress in each of the following few years, the number of pupils who will have to be catered for each year once the new development has settled down, and the place of origin of the population moving to the new development. Obtaining reliable data on these matters presents some problems, yet the allocation of building approvals by civil servants in the Department of Education and Science is essentially based on these written justifications supplemented by local knowledge of the area provided by district inspectors and by discussion with officers of the local education authority.

The exporting authority keeps a register of tenants in municipal housing and of those on the waiting list for housing, who have said they are willing to move to overspill areas.[4] Therefore, it can be argued that information is, in principle, available on potential migrants, including such data as number, sex, and age of children. It could also be argued that knowledge of the characteristics of the population willing to move could help in taking decisions about the number of dwellings of different sizes and types to provide in the new community. This information about population characteristics and derived information about dwelling size could be made available to the upper-tier authority responsible for the education service (as well as other relevant authorities). This, however, is not enough. Even if a picture of the eventual overall development is available, it is still necessary to obtain from the appropriate planning and/or building authority the rate of development of the new community, because the education building programme is required to be sensitive to the speed at which a new and increasing child population must be provided with school premises.

Other sources of useful information, apart from the exporting authority and planning authority, for an education authority planning school provision for a new community could be: past experience of earlier new developments within the boundaries of the local education authority (for an instance of this, see below); experience of other local education authorities in planning schools for new communities, passed on at meetings and conferences of local education authority officers; published articles, which seem to be few in number.[5]

---

[4] For details, see Sheila A. Ruddy, *Industrial Selection Schemes*, Occasional Paper No. 5, Centre for Urban and Regional Studies, University of Birmingham, 1969.

[5] For instance, T. H. Forsyth, *Forecasting Demand for School Places in Developing Urban Areas*,

The Case of Chelmsley Wood

What happens in practice? The rest of this paper follows through the earliest stages of planning school provision for a large housing estate situated beyond the boundaries of the city it is serving.[6] ChelmsleyWood is situated in Meriden Rural District in Warwickshire on the eastern edge of Birmingham. In January 1964 the city of Birmingham applied to Warwickshire County Council (as local planning authority) for permission to develop 1,540 acres by building 15,590 dwellings for 59,240 people, together with the necessary ancillary services. This was to be a commuter development with no employment except of the service kind generated by shops, schools, health services etc. The county of Warwickshire objected to the proposal – the site was in the proposed Green Belt area of the West Midlands intended to restrain the further outward development of the conurbation – and a public inquiry was held in May/June 1964. In December 1964 the Minister of Housing and Local Government granted Birmingham's application.

In January 1965 the city appointed a consultant planner who promised to produce a master plan within nine months. In February 1965 the first formal meeting of officers from the city and the county took place, and it was made quite clear that the county, as local education authority, was responsible for calculating the school provision required. This had to be done rapidly and had to be translated into terms of acreage required (by using the Standards for School Premises Regulations produced by the Department of Education and Science) for inclusion on the proposed master plan for the designated area. The county realized that the city was desperately short of land for building houses and would want to use every available acre in Chelmsley Wood. Therefore, the county had to produce well-reasoned arguments on land requirements for all the services for which

Local Government Operational Research Unit, 1967; C. L. Myers, *New Methods of Forecasting Child Populations*, Local Government Operational Research Unit, 1966; H. B. Rodgers and D. T. Herbert, *Overspill in Winsford*, Winsford Urban District Council, 1964, Chapter VI; R. E. W. Saunders, *Education in a New Town*, Royal Society of Health Paper (Alcester meeting, November 24th, 1967); Ministry of Housing and Local Government, *The Needs of New Communities*, H.M.S.O., 1967, pp. 36–7; and rather older, A. Tropp, 'Population Trends and Education Planning', *Education*, March-April 1956 (four short articles). Other publications have concentrated on demographic analysis, including child population, e.g. R. L. Cooke, 'An Analysis of the Age Structures of Immigrants to New and Expanding Towns', *Journal of the Town Planning Institute*, Vol. 54, No. 9, November 1968; A. J. Kellaway, 'Migration to Eight New Towns in 1966', *Journal of the Town Planning Institute*, Vol. 55, No. 5, May 1969; J. A. Moss, 'New and Expanded Towns – Demographic Characteristics of New-comers', *Town Planning Review*, Vol. 39, No. 2, July 1968.

[6] This summary of a complicated series of events may mask at times the considerable co-operative efforts of officers of the local authorities concerned to overcome difficulties. This description is an attempt to show how complicated it can be to plan school provision for a new community, not to judge whether particular authorities appreciated or failed to understand this complexity.

they were responsible. Education was by far the most important service in this respect. At the end of March 1965, the county told Birmingham that it had calculated that there was need for 45 classes of 40 primary school pupils for each cohort or age group and therefore 60 classes of 30 secondary school pupils for each cohort or age group (otherwise referred to as form entries or F.E.s).

How did Warwickshire reach these figures of 45 F.E.s at primary level and 60 at secondary level? We shall follow the argument for primary school provision. A decade earlier, Birmingham had obtained permission to develop a much smaller housing estate in Warwickshire, called Kingshurst. The first houses there were occupied in 1956 and the development was completed in 1964–5 by which time there was a total of 2,080 dwellings. Between 1956 and 1963, 1,558 dwelling units had produced 981 additional children between the ages of six and ten, or 196 per age group. Warwickshire therefore argued that as the proposed Chelmsley Wood development was to be ten times as big as Kingshurst, it would produce 1,960 primary school pupils per age group (40), or 49 F.E.s. It was felt that this figure represented some kind of peak, and an apparently arbitrary reduction by one-quarter (490 primary pupils per age group) to 1,470 per age group, or 37 F.E.s, was suggested. At this stage, the county recalled that during the course of building Kingshurst, the city had increased densities by providing a higher proportion of family housing than had been originally expected. To allow for this possibility at Chelmsley Wood, the county felt that a compromise between 37 and 50 F.E.s would be appropriate viz. 45 F.E.s, an equivalent of 1,800 primary pupils per age group. The county added that if this did prove generous, then the opportunity could be taken of lowering the size of the primary school classes as recommended in the Plowden Report on primary schools.[7]

Birmingham found it difficult to accept these figures of 45 F.E.s at primary level and 60 at secondary level. The basic land use implication was that the education service would require nearly 300 acres, nearly a fifth of the total designated area. Therefore, the county offered to present to the city the basis of its calculations.

In April 1965, the city architect's department asked the city housing management and education departments to look at the county's calculations and to produce their own estimates of the likely school population of Chelmsley Wood. The housing management department told the education department, that broadly, there would be 24 per cent one-

---

[7] A separate calculation was also made using figures for Kingshurst primary school pupils on roll at September 1st, 1964. There were 1,763 primary school pupils from the 2,080 municipal dwellings, giving an average of 0·85 of a primary school child per municipal housing unit or 0·12 per age group per municipal housing unit. If this figure is applied to the proposed 15,590 dwellings for Chelmsley Wood, a figure of 1,870 primary pupils per age group is obtained, or 47 F.E.s.

bedroom dwellings, 31 per cent two-bedroom dwellings, 40 per cent three-bedroom dwellings and 5 per cent four-bedroom dwellings.[8]

In May 1965 the city education department stated that if information about school children from dwellings of different size on a recent city estate located within the city boundary was applied to Chelmsley Wood, the number of primary school children per age group would be something over a thousand, so 27 F.E.s (1,080 children) at primary level and 36 at secondary level would be sufficient. The education department also pointed out that the average birth rate for the city was about 20 per thousand population. Therefore, a population of 60,000 – the target population of Chelmsley Wood in round figures – would produce 1,200 children per age group or 30 F.E.s at primary level and 40 at secondary level. The education department recommended the adoption of this second estimate based on the city birth rate in order to reflect long-term needs rather than rely on figures from a particular housing estate at a particular stage in its development. The land use requirements of 30 F.E.s at primary level and 40 at secondary level were calculated to be not much over 200 acres, a figure very much nearer to the estimate made by the city in its original planning application.

An urgent meeting between the city and the county was held in mid-June 1965 to discuss the matter of school provision, as the development of the master plan was being held up. It was at this meeting that the county education department were told of the breakdown of the 15,590 dwellings by number of bedrooms, information that the city education department had used in May, some weeks earlier.

With this fresh information, the county were able to undertake a slightly more refined calculation. The basic dwelling information used is contained in the following table.

Size of Dwelling	Kingshurst			Chelmsley Wood		
	Numbers	(%)	Bedrooms	Numbers	(%)	Bedrooms
1 Bedroom	218	(10)	218	3,742	(24)	3,742
2 Bedroom	289	(14)	578	4,833	(31)	9,666
3 Bedroom (4 person)	671	(32)	2,013	} 6,236	(40)	18,708
3 Bedroom (5 person)	816	(39)	2,448			
4 Bedroom	84	(4)	336	779	(5)	3,116
5 Bedroom	2	*	10	—	—	—
TOTAL	2,080	(100)	5,603	15,590	(100)	35,232

[8] The county did not have this information when it did its calculations, based on the Kingshurst figures.

With complete information for Kingshurst, the county noted that the total number of bedrooms was 5,603. Excluding the 2,080 bedrooms (one in each dwelling) used by parents, 3,523 (5,603 minus 2,080) bedrooms were available for other members of the family and produced a total of 1,679 primary school pupils or 240 per age group on average, or 14·7 produced one child per age group. Translating this last ratio to Chelmsley Wood, the county found that there were 19,642 bedrooms apart from parents' bedrooms (35,232 minus 15,590) so that 1,336 pupils per age group on average could be expected from the 19,642 bedrooms (in other words, 19,642 divided by 14·7). This total of 1,336 pupils per age group is about 33/34 F.E.s at primary level and 44/45 at secondary level, quite close to the city's estimate of 30 F.E.s at primary and 40 F.E.s at secondary level. For planning purposes, the county accepted the city's calculations, though they received details of the calculations after the mid-June meeting. The county education department emphasized that school needs could change if building densities changed, and that planning approval of particular phases of the development should be granted only if the proposals were in accord with the overall plan. If changes were proposed, then there might have to be changes in education provision as well.

Even at this stage it was not possible to put forward a convincing education building programme to the Department of Education and Science, because the expected rate of development of the estate was not known in enough detail. The number of dwellings expected to be completed in each year of the development was made known in April/May 1965 but there was no breakdown by area or by dwelling size. An area breakdown of anticipated dwellings completions was first produced in August 1965. In addition, the county assumed that the proportion of dwellings of different size to be built in each phase of the development would reflect the overall dwelling size proportions. This assumption was confirmed by the city architect's department at the end of June 1965.[9]

Comment

The study of the planning and development of selected new communities in the West Midlands is still continuing at the Centre for Urban and Regional Studies in the University of Birmingham. The foregoing can be seen as an interim report on just one aspect of planning services for new developments.

---

[9] It must be emphasized that this study covered only the very earliest stages of the planning of Chelmsley Wood, and that the process of estimating the amount of school provision required has been refined as the development has proceeded by incorporating the results of monitoring the actual development into a model for forecasting child population levels in later stages of the development.

The essential feature of this brief description of the earliest stages of planning school provision for a new community is that the authority (Warwickshire) responsible for undertaking the planning, appeared not to have relevant information that did exist (from the city of Birmingham). This is not to suggest that it was deliberately withheld, but the question may be put: what is and what should be the responsibility of the exporting authority? Should it have an obligation to provide certain kinds of information to the receiving authority? Would available information flow more easily if the planning of education provision were a regional function? How important are the administrative barriers? Are the information demands of the Department of Education and Science (DES) realistic? What should be the role of the central department?

The planning of school provision is a difficult job in the most straightforward circumstances, and maximum flow of available information is needed to make such planning a useful exercise. In the case of Chelmsley Wood, the local education authority had to deal with a number of very significant subsequent influences on the education planning process. These influences are being examined at present and include:

(1) the political and administrative problems of comprehensivization after the publication of DES Circular 10/65 in July 1965 on the reorganization of secondary education;

(2) the severe economic retrenchment in Britain in the second half of the 1960s, which included postponement of raising the school leaving age from 15 to 16 in January 1968 and a £70 million cut in the national major school building programme in the financial year 1968–69;

(3) the publication of the Plowden Report in 1967 recommending the reorganization of primary school education;

(4) the existence of a considerable number of currently spare places in primary schools in the east of Birmingham within two or three miles of Chelmsley Wood (the Department of Education and Science insist that the basic priority for approving school projects is that the children would have no other school to attend; this condition did not apply for Chelmsley Wood children, and the places in east Birmingham schools were seen as available on a semi-permanent basis rather than as a reserve to cater for unexpected 'surges' in the school population at Chelmsley Wood);

(5) the change in submission procedure of school building programmes announced in DES Circular 13/68 published in July 1968.

The problems of planning school provision are many and varied – we have not touched upon the problem of teacher supply or the intricacies of schedules of accommodation, for example – and means of avoiding or alleviating those problems should be grasped. There is a case for increasing the duties of exporting authorities in aiding the development of satellite new communities. Demographic and socio-economic information of the kind that could be extracted from reliable housing management records would be of value to the planners of other social services quite apart from education. The recent Seebohm Report on personal social services[10] has suggested the extension of the activities of housing departments of local authorities. One way they might extend is by providing this kind of service to new communities and the receiving authorities responsible for developing them.

---

[10] *Report of the Committee on Local Authority and Allied Personal Social Services* (Seebohm Report), Cmnd. 3703, H.M.S.O., July 1968.

21

A Megalopolis: the Ruhr/Rhein Complex

G. Hausmann

Introduction

The area of industrial concentration, thirty kilometres wide and seventy kilometres long, that extends from Duisburg in the west to Dortmund in the east, and from Recklinghausen in the north to Hattingen in the south, can be regarded as the first megalopolis of tomorrow's Europe. Already its towns spill into one another, and there is an urgent need for a cohesive infrastructure to be planned and developed for the whole of the area. Socio-cultural considerations dictate that a high degree of priority be given within this structure to the needs of educational systems.

A hundred years ago, the countryside lying between the Rhine, the Ruhr and the Lippe rivers was devoted almost entirely to agriculture. After the opening up of its rich coal deposits it became a vital centre for the inflow of ore for smelting and the outflow of sheet metal. From 1840 it quickly developed into one of the greatest industrial areas in the world. With industrialization came an influx of mineworkers, and the resulting urbanization gave rise to problems that could not be solved by the application of old administrative systems. Regional councils were set up, with responsibility for water supplies, sewage facilities, and the interests of the workers in general. These were early examples of district planning in a fast-expanding mining and industrial community

Even now, the administrative integration of the industrial Ruhr has not been achieved by the province of Nordrhein-Westfalen, newly set up after the Second World War. As long as this thickly populated and economically extremely complex area continues to be governed from outlying administrative centres (Düsseldorf, Münster and Arnsberg), it offers an excellent example of the problems that surround the processes of urbanization and education.

The Ruhr covers an area of 4,590 square kilometres (13·2 per cent of Nordrhein-Westfalen and 1·9 per cent of the area of W. Germany). The population is 5,700,000 (i.e. 35·1 per cent of the inhabitants of the province of Nordrhein-Westfalen and nearly 10 per cent of the population of W. Germany). The population density is 1,238 per square kilometre (compared with 479 per square kilometre in Nordrhein-Westfalen and

224 per square kilometre in W. Germany). The whole area is divided into one central district and four outer districts.

The outer districts to the west, north and east are regarded as development areas. The existing boroughs will be reduced in number and communities with fewer than 5,000 inhabitants will be integrated into larger administrative units. In particular the municipalities closest to the central district will be amalgamated and will contribute towards its expansion. The description that follows will concentrate on essentials in considering central district.

In ground area, the central district of the Ruhr represents the largest concentration of industry not only in West Germany but in the whole of Europe, and has a population density of 2,898 per square kilometre.

In the last hundred and fifty years the population of the central area has multiplied thirty-six times, while the population of the Ruhr as a whole has increased twentyfold. In the same period the population of W. Germany as a whole has trebled. In 1850 there was no large town in the Ruhr; by 1905 there were five, but none with a population exceeding 500,000. In the central district there are today sixteen towns, of which eleven can be classed as large with a population of 3,414,000 between them at the census of 1963. Essen and Dortmund both have more than half a million inhabitants. It is one of the many paradoxes of the Ruhr region that up to now none of these towns has achieved the position of an administrative power centre for the whole of the area. Moreover, only four of the eleven towns with populations exceeding 100,000 have major importance within the area. Duisburg, Essen, Bochum and Dortmund have the structure and the character of large towns, but they suffer from a lack of architectural planning which has allowed industrial buildings to grow up side by side with private dwellings. The other major towns look like extensive industrial suburbs. Even those with more than 100,000 inhabitants give this impression, and seem to have no city feel about them. The towns are continually growing, so that now they are inextricably fused together. Here and there oases of countryside have survived, but the whole area threatened to become one amorphous conglomeration of buildings. Recently an attempt has been made to counteract the economic, socio-hygienic and socio-cultural consequences of this development by proper district planning.

The process of urbanization in the Ruhr was set in motion by the arrival of heavy industry, which then increased at an explosive rate. The result was an industrial landscape. Great power struggles took place among the companies that set up their businesses there, and from the latter emerged the huge chemical firms. Before the Second World War, the whole of Germany's raw steel industry, one-half of her coal production and two-thirds of her coke were concentrated in the hands of six great companies.

A complicated system of interlocking companies had turned the Ruhr into an impenetrable jungle of businesses. There were repeated crises – particularly during the 1929 slump – and most of all in mining. The Second World War hit the Ruhr hard. The chemical industry, foremost in the world until 1939, was crippled by bombing; the coal industry was severely cut back; the iron and steel works, among the largest and most modern in Europe, had to be closed down; the huge web of companies was disentangled. As the restrictions began to be lifted in 1950, rebuilding quickly started. By 1957 however, it became apparent that with the progress of automation, the immense expansion of the chemical industry, the coming of atomic power and the resulting decline in the use of coal, an acute crisis in mining and in the general work situation in the Ruhr was developing.

Four population divisions can be distinguished in the Ruhr: the Ruhr itself in the South, the old Hellwegstrasse and the Emscherweg in the central district, and in the North the strip that runs up to the River Lippe. The old Ruhr is now a region of silent collieries. In this, the oldest of the mining areas, up until 1860 each miner had his small holding, with a field or little garden and a cowshed. As the coal seams were opened up further north, it became usual after 1870 to build blocks of living accommodation, consisting mainly of three-storied rented houses, with no trees or grass in between. Until the turn of the century, these were usually one-family homes; later there came three- and four-family houses. An increasing number of these were built by the colliery companies themselves. In the older mining areas, therefore, there was little social differentiation, and no middle-class stratum appeared. Where the iron industry grew up alongside mining, in the vicinity of existing townships, industrial towns were created where the social differences were more marked. This was particularly the case along the Hellwegstrasse, which runs through the major towns. But here the same thing has happened as in the completely industrial towns along the Emscherweg; the town centres are unpleasantly monotonous, and the industrial quarters have spread out to the peripheries of the towns, so that the whole area has become an unsightly mess.

The destruction of the industrial region in the Second World War drastically reduced living accommodation also. This afforded certain opportunities for improvement in housing facilities. The first thing to clear up was the mixture of industrial and living accommodation, hitherto so inextricably entangled. In some towns, the spread of industrial building had to be halted. In the central area, space for living accommodation had to be found outside the towns or in the outer districts. Densely populated areas could be improved by building satellite centres with their own shopping districts. At the same time care had to be taken to see that communications were maintained with the central business districts in the cities. In other places, it proved necessary to gather the living areas together, so as to prevent depopulation.

Ever since 1875, the Ruhr has had the largest and most complicated road and rail network in Europe. It has been described as 'one unending marshalling yard'. There are four times as many railway lines here as in the whole of the rest of Germany.

A number of canals lead out from the Ruhr, relieving the burden of goods traffic on the two most important railway lines. The existing rail system has long been inadequate to meet the demands of commuter traffic. Every day forty thousand people have to be transported in and out of the central district, and taken to their places of work. In order to relieve congestion and improve the traffic facilities in the central district as a whole, in March 1969 a framework was established for the creation of a central City Road and Rail Company for the Ruhr. A plan for new north–south communications is a particular feature of the new system, along with the building of two hundred kilometres of new and uninterrupted railways.

One particularly vital problem for the Ruhr area planners is to ensure that space is allowed for greenery. In the areas of industrial concentration and heavy traffic, a pall of smoke hangs over the cities, presenting a considerable danger to health. The waterways are polluted by industrial waste. Town-planning authorities are therefore anxious not only to preserve the existing green areas as far as possible, in order to afford some degree of contrast, but also to see that green spaces are allowed for when rebuilding old districts and designing new ones. The development plan for the entire area makes provision for an extensive green belt system.

Social Structures

The immense growth of heavy industry and population in the Ruhr in the last hundred years has given rise to some unusual features in the social structures of the area. In terms of social history, the Ruhr can be regarded as unique.

The drive towards industrialization began in 1840. In those days, before the mighty firms bore the stigma of 'plundering capitalists', they took fatherly care of the needs of their workers. Whether conservative or liberal in outlook, they all subscribed to a fundamental belief in 'order and discipline', a belief which accorded well with the strongly religious upbringing of the mine workers and their mainly peasant ancestry. The miners and foundry workers, who are predominant in the social make-up of the area, have remained essentially peasant-like, home-bound people. Most of the other workers who have come into the area share similar backgrounds, and have to a large extent adapted to the local way of living. It follows, then, that the Ruhr, so modern in some respects, still retains an intensely provincial social image.

One of the explanations for this can certainly be found in the social benefit schemes that the larger firms have run since their inception for their workers. For instance, the firm of Krupp have always built houses for their workers, as well as hospitals, schools, libraries, banks and shops. Another important factor has been the *Knappschaft*, or Workers' Own Welfare Society, which was originally started as a self-help organization and in 1854 was made compulsory by law. The Workers' Society of the Ruhr takes care of the aged miners living on pension, provides work for members' wives, etc. The way of living that has resulted from all this affords happiness to millionaires and pensioners, Catholics and Communists alike. There are no 'democratic cities', like Hamburg, Frankfurt or Berlin, to be found in the Ruhr.

In the Ruhr the numbers of people employed in the fields of agriculture, manufacturing, and service industries are divided in a way which differs significantly from the division of labour in West Germany as a whole. In 1963 it was as follows:

TABLE 1

	Ruhr %	W. Germany %
Agriculture	1·0	13·9
Manufacturing	63·7	53·7
Service industries	35·3	32·4

The Educational Situation

Against this background then of information about the economics, population, communications systems and social structure of the Ruhr, the educational situation may now be looked into. In 1965 a prominent lady politician asserted that while Nordrhein-Westfalen might be the richest of West Germany's eleven Länder, culturally and politically it was one of the most backward. In education, it had fallen behind at every level from kindergarten to university. She believed there were three reasons for this: (1) Until very recently the State had failed to recognize that the Rhineland and Westphalia, originally almost exclusively rural, had developed into fully urbanized industrial areas. (2) After 1945 the struggle for the retention of church schools had hindered much-needed reforms. (3) Practical guidelines for the shaping of new educational methods were lacking.

The framework for a new educational system in Nordrhein-Westfalen was laid down in February 1968 in an Act passed by the West German Parliament. According to this, the system of general education was to be radically changed. From 1968 onwards, all pupils would attend a primary school (*Grundschule*) for four years. They then would go on to one of a number of types of school. They could take a five-year secondary school (*Hauptschule*) course, a six-year high school (*Realschule*) course, or a nine-year grammar school (*Gymnasium*) course. In the high schools and grammar schools, there were to be 'creative' classes as well as the usual classes. The *Gymnasien* would divide from the second form onwards into various fields of education.

The new law contained provisions for the abolition of at any rate most of the so-called 'dwarf schools' (*Zwergschulen*) – schools with either one class only or with very little differentiation in levels. These are to be found mainly in rural districts. The cost of this reform is of course considerable, and to some extent detrimental to the programme for school building in the towns. In 1965 there were in Nordrhein-Westfalen 6,510 eight-year elementary schools (*Volksschulen*), of which 881 (almost 13 per cent) were in the Ruhr. These were divided as follows:

TABLE 2

	In NRW	In Ruhr
One-class schools	622 (9·6%)	8 (0·9%)
2/3-class schools	1,634 (25·1%)	35 (3·9%)
3–7 classes	2,844 (43·7%)	348 (39·6%)
8 classes, completely separated by year	1,410 (21·6%)	480 (55·6%)
	6,510 (100%)	881 (100%)

The Act stated also that primary and secondary schools could be arranged as ordinary community schools, or as denominational schools, according to the requirements of the education authorities.

The change from elementary schools with four-plus-four school-years to secondary schools with four-plus-five school-years took place slowly. As a result of the increasing intake into the high schools and grammar schools, the size of the classes in the secondary schools fell rapidly from the fifth year onwards, and some elementary schools had to be merged in order to produce a workable system.

The percentage of children attending high schools and grammar schools grew higher in Nordrhein-Westfalen as a whole than in the Ruhr (Tables 3 and 4).

TABLE 3

	1952		1964	
	High Schools	Grammar Schools	High Schools	Grammar Schools
In Nordrhein-Westfalen	3·6%	9·0%	5·6%	9·6%
In the Ruhr	3·3%	5·1%	6·9%	6·8%

In 1964 of one hundred children of the same school year, the proportion of six-year high school children to nine-year grammar school children was as follows:

TABLE 4

	High Schools	Grammar Schools
In Nordrhein-Westfalen	11·2%	13·2%
In the Ruhr	10·5%	11·4%

The number of students completing *Gymnasien* courses, based on one year out of the three between the ages of 18 and 21 (leaving aside evening classes and institutes giving special courses for the final grammar school examination) was in 1964: 7·8 per cent in Nordrhein-Westfalen, and 2·5 per cent in the Ruhr.

The educational shortcomings of the Ruhr are therefore self-evident. It is unlikely that they will be improved significantly by the introduction of additional forms in the *Realschulen* and *Gymnasien*, or of special classes in evening colleges, or the institutes mentioned above. In Nordrhein-Westfalen a simplified form of transition from the fourth and fifth school-years to the high schools and grammar schools was instituted in 1964, and the number of pupils making this transition increased by 4 per cent as a result. In the various towns and villages of the province the proportion of these transitions can vary very considerably. They can be regarded almost as a yardstick for the social structure of the local population and its attitude towards education.

While the attendance at the old and new style grammar schools and at the 'dwarf' schools does not vary very much between the Ruhr and Nordrhein-Westfalen as a whole, it is noticeable that in the Ruhr the attendance at the old-style grammar schools is smaller than at the new ones which are oriented towards mathematics and the natural sciences. It is apparent therefore that in the purely industrial areas the tendency is towards the grammar schools specializing in these subjects, while the old-style grammar schools in towns concentrate more on the traditional cultural subjects. Apart from the upper forms of elementary schools, which after the introduction of the nine-year system became secondary schools, the following additional forms are planned up until 1970:

TABLE 5

	NRW as a whole	Ruhr only
High Schools	130 (34% increase)	24 (35·3% increase)
Grammar Schools	72 (13·9% increase)	24 (20·8% increase)
	202 (22·4% increase)	48 (31·1% increase)

From these figures it becomes apparent that the school building programme has been devised with a view to correcting the Ruhr's deficiency in advanced secondary level education.

Apart from the usual forms in grammar schools, the students of high schools and elementary schools can prepare for the final grammar school examination (*Abitur*) by proceeding to a grammar school for three to six years. These special grammar schools tend to specialize in economics and social sciences, in natural sciences, or in the traditional academic subjects. This examination then opens the way to study in the corresponding faculties at universities and colleges. It is these specialized new grammar schools, above all, that will make good the Ruhr's deficiencies in higher level educational facilities.

Along with the growth of the new educational system in Nordrhein-Westfalen goes the development of the 'Second Way to Education', which enables those already in employment to take the final grammar school examination. West Germany now has ten evening grammar schools, of which seven are in Nordrhein-Westfalen and four in the Ruhr. There are also 26 institutes providing courses for the same examination, of which fourteen are in Nordrhein-Westfalen and four in the Ruhr. Altogether, there are in the Ruhr twenty different kinds of course leading to the final examination. This rich choice of secondary education gives Nordrhein-Westfalen a unique position in West Germany's educational system.

Progress in Educational Reform

In most of the German Länder only slow progress is being made with fundamental plans for educational reform. In Nordrhein-Westfalen, however, attempts have been made since 1967 not only to lay down the subject syallabuses to be followed in secondary schools, but also to design more flexible teaching methods and systems of school administration. Special attention has been paid to the dovetailing of essential basic subjects in the secondary school with specialized training for work. The guidelines for this project were laid down by an independent commission, appointed by the Minister of Culture and working under the direction of experienced educationists. It was able to draw on a fund of knowledge gained over many years in schools in the Ruhr and in Cologne, and partly from a series of study groups on 'The School and the Economy'. Recognizing that the processes of industrialization and urbanization must involve constant change and necessitate constant re-thinking on the part of planners, the commission published its findings in loose-leaf form, so that alterations and additions could be made. This method of schools organization differs considerably from that followed previously in the majority of the German provinces, where the responsibility for school policy rests with the education authorities.

Special Problems of Pre-school Education

The industrial and urbanized Ruhr presents particularly difficult problems in the field of pre-school education. In comparison with other parts of West Germany the number of kindergartens and other infant schools is very low. Playgrounds are also lacking, especially in the very thickly populated areas of the large towns. It is noticeable that children from such areas are frequently educationally backward, and therefore attempts have been made recently to arrange some sort of schooling for five-year-olds (compulsory education begins at six in West Germany). Special activity programmes in speech training and the development of the intellect in backward children are at present under way at the University of the Ruhr. The provision of children's playgrounds is also regarded as a high priority in the planning of new building developments, particularly in areas where large educational centres are to be built.

Industrial Training

Industrial training in West Germany differs from that in most other European countries in that students attend part-time industrial training centres, where they receive full instruction in their chosen trades. There are also specialized centres where students can acquire qualifications in industrial techniques, a form of training which until recently was largely neglected. In Nordrhein-Westfalen, and especially in the Ruhr, a complete reorganization of industrial training methods has been undertaken.

A number of alternative methods have been used. Students completing their nine-year secondary school courses can then attend full-time one-year courses allied to their chosen trades, or part-time two-year courses. The opportunity should also be open to them, either then or at a later date, to attend centres for industrial training at higher levels, which can prepare them for qualifying examinations right up to degree standard. This arrangement is particularly beneficial for the Ruhr, since Nordrhein-Westfalen as a whole has up to now been the most backward of the German provinces in terms of student-hours spent in education under the dual system. In 1964, only 21 per cent of a 48 per cent sampling of students at industrial training centres were spending more than eight hours per week under instruction. In areas of dense industrialization only two per cent of sixteen-year-olds are in full-time education (as against about 47 per cent in the mainly agricultural province of Schleswig-Holstein). The only funds available for the improvement of this situation are those which in 1963 were supporting only elementary schools (Nordrhein-Westfalen: 491,000,000 DM; Schleswig-Holstein: 574,000,000 DM). The newly developed methods of industrial training offer at least some compensation for this unfortunate state of affairs, and in the Ruhr attempts at further expansion are being made. Since 1964, for example, Industrie Gewerkschaft Metall have been running their own three-tiered training scheme, and Krupps have had a four-tiered scheme in operation since 1965.

There has been a considerable amount of controversy about the types and status of all the various industrial training schools and their elevation to college level, as well as about their amalgamation into 'comprehensive colleges'. We will have to wait and see whether an Act of Parliament dealing with industrial training, and the drafting of frames of reference for the building and organization of new colleges and universities, can produce satisfactory solutions, perhaps even an integrated policy for co-operation.

Teacher Training

Elementary school teachers receive their training in a six-term course covering both optional and compulsory subjects. Nordrhein-Westfalen has fifteen teacher training colleges, which until 1969 were almost all denominational. In June 1965 five of them became regional colleges, run by three authorities with no denominational attachment, and in 1969 were granted the status of 'academic colleges', with the right to confer degrees.

The entire scholastic system in Nordrhein-Westfalen suffers from a great shortage of teachers. As the number of students rises, and the intake into the higher level schools becomes ever greater, this problem can only become more acute. Teachers of mathematics and science, subjects of vital importance in the Ruhr, are in especially short supply. An attempt has therefore been made to bridge over this gap by recruiting four to five thousand assistant teachers. The serious lack of teachers is further high-lighted by the fact that the average number of pupils in a class in Nordrhein-Westfalen is 37, the second highest in Germany.

It is very clear that because of the high costs being incurred by the Ruhr in respect of school building, teaching materials and teacher training, modernization of the school system and teaching methods is of the utmost importance.

Tertiary Education

In Nordrhein-Westfalen there are a number of universities, some old-established and some which have been recently reopened. Others have been created in the last ten years, to help reduce the burden on the older colleges, universities and institutes. One of the major reasons for the lack of university level establishments until recent times – apart from the particular circumstances which commonly apply to semi-urbanized and over-urbanized industrial communities – was the fact that the Kaiser, in 1892, forbade the building of garrisons and universities in the Ruhr.

Most of the universities built in Germany since the Second World War, and those still in the planning stages, play an important role, not only in improving educational facilities, but also in educational reform. The special resources of Nordrhein-Westfalen, for instance, offer excellent opportunities in terms of research material. The 'University of the Ruhr' at Bochum offers a good example of reform tempered with moderation. It was opened in 1965, on the outskirts of Bochum, as Germany's first campus university. When all the buildings are completed, as well as the faculty and research buildings, there will be living accommodation for forty to fifty thousand people and places for twenty thousand students. Of the 8,200 students attending there in 1968, 69·2 per cent came from the Ruhr district and 12·5 per cent from working-class families. For the first time in Germany, Bochum offered courses in engineering at university level; hitherto engineering could be studied only in technical colleges of university standing or *Technische Hochschulen*. Another innovation was that a principle of inter-disciplinary co-ordination was adopted. A system of departments and central institutes replaced the usual faculties.

In 1969 another new university was founded in the Ruhr, at Dortmund. Originally a technical college, Dortmund's emphasis is on science and technology, and on instruction rather than research. In Essen a medical faculty has been founded by the University of Münster, but later on its place will be taken by a medical department at Bochum. The plans al-ready afoot to bring about a spectacular increase in university places in Nordrhein-Westfalen (in 1939, only 9,135 students from the area had the benefit of university education) make it apparent that economists and politicians alike are anxious to strengthen the cultural life of this materially rich area. It is likely that by 1976 the student population of Nordrhein-Westfalen will have risen to 100,000, and university places available to them within the province will be about 92,000. During this development it is to be hoped that the special needs of the Ruhr will be borne continually in mind, so that the scope of research programmes and teaching facilities can keep pace with the ever-growing population.

Adult Education

The development of adult education in West Germany has made its greatest strides in Nordrhein-Westfalen. In 1965 the province had altogether 378 adult education institutes, of which 41 (9·2 per cent) were in the Ruhr. These were divided into 16 evening colleges (at least one in each large town); 3 home study colleges; and 22 colleges specializing in religious, social or political subjects (11 of these are in Essen and 6 in Bochum).

The state acknowledges and encourages adult education in West Germany, regarding it as an indispensable part of the educational system. On the whole, there is a sufficient number of adult education centres, but again, qualified teaching staff are in short supply. There is a long-term plan in operation to provide all communities with populations over 30,000 with an adult educational adviser. Since 1959 there has been close collaboration in this field with the universities and colleges of Cologne and Münster, and recently a Chair of Adult Education was founded in the University of the Ruhr at Bochum.

As is usual in Germany, evening colleges are attended mainly by middle-class students. The crisis in the coal industry, however, produced changes in the economy and a degree of mobility in work, which in turn brought about a considerable levelling of social differences. Adult education institutes are therefore devoting themselves more and more to the teaching of work techniques. The University of the Ruhr runs a course for this, the 'Third Way to Education', designed to help workers progress towards promotion by means of qualifying examinations.

The first city in West Germany to give a lead in this direction was Marl, on the outskirts of the Ruhr; the adult education centre that was built there served as a model for other institutes in the area. Westdeutscher Rundfunk are in process of planning a television college, with programmes specializing in the field of adult education. Discussions with the German Trades Union Council resulted in 1969 in an experimental course at the University of the Ruhr for workers on sabbatical leave, studying for promotion in their trades.

Changes in the Social Structure and Planning for the Future

The economic changes in Germany's social structure heralded a period of increased regional and social mobility, and plans have had to be made for the solution of problems which have resulted. Changes of function in the industrial sector led to differences in numbers of commuters as well as to different requirements in living accommodation. It therefore became imperative to plan comprehensively for new communication facilities and population movements. In industry, technological requirements also changed; whereas at one time technical qualifications were scarcely needed, they have now become indispensable. Thus people needed to be given access to the means of acquiring these new skills. This is a factor which implies the need for fundamental changes in the whole system of education, and this cannot be achieved without constructive planning. The urbanization of the central district produced great difficulties in the field of secondary education. The introduction of secondary level education into a school system that was already overloaded has in many places brought about a breakdown in facilities rather than an improvement.

This has made the planning authorities the more determined to achieve optimum solutions. The theory is gaining more and more ground that in areas of high population density, large school systems, after the style of comprehensive schools, present the most rational solution to the problem. The *Deutsche Bildungsrat*, or German National Council for Education has therefore set in motion a programme of experimentation, in the course of which about forty such schools will be set up and their progress studied. Four comprehensive schools have been scheduled for Nordrhein-Westfalen, three of which are to be in the Ruhr. These will be at Duisburg, Overhausen and Dortmund, and others are planned for Bochum and Gelsenkirchen.

The Hibernia School in Wanne-Eickel is a forerunner of this development. It bears the distinctive stamp of the Rudolf Steiner Schools, of which there are twenty-seven, but its concepts of organization are quite new. It is a day school, with nearly 900 pupils aged from six to eighteen, mainly from working-class families. It contains a kindergarten, an elementary and a secondary school, an industrial training school and a further education centre. In the main, pupils at the Hibernia School are receiving an education that will fit them later on for their jobs, and in that sense the Hibernia cannot be regarded simply as a comprehensive school in the usual sense but rather as a training school. It is well provided with workshops and can undertake pioneering work, particularly in the new study field of job-training.

The Hibernia School has been developed mainly to meet the special educational requirements of the industrial world. In contrast to this, the comprehensive school planned for Dortmund will meet academic needs that spring directly from the process of urbanization. Dortmund is the largest town in Westphalia and, apart from the three city-states, has the second largest area of any town in Germany. Since the middle of the nineteenth century it has developed into a leading industrial city. This growth occurred without any kind of overall town planning. In the twentieth century the city was divided into sixty municipalities. For all its large ground area, Dortmund always remained very thinly populated. Even now, fifty per cent of its area is still used for agriculture. The city is centripetally arranged, and Dortmund has a radial traffic communications system, connected by transverse intersections. Forty per cent of the working population of Dortmund is in mining and the metallurgical and power industries, eight per cent in other industries and forty per cent in service trades. In 1968, as a result of the coal crisis, only four collieries out of sixty were still open. After the Second World War, seventy per cent of Dortmund had been destroyed (ninety-three per cent in the centre), and the population was 300,000. By 1968 this figure had risen to 650,000. In 1945, seventy-five schools were left standing, with 496 classrooms; in 1968 there were over 200 schools, with more than 3,000 classrooms. There is a long-term plan in progress for another sixty elementary schools, ten high schools, ten grammar schools and ten industrial training schools to be built by 1988.

The project of a new comprehensive school on the outskirts of Dortmund, lying as it does right in the catchment area of the mining industry yet where the land is still mainly agricultural, will be a particularly informative one. The satellite town it serves, Dortmund-North-East, is situated on the site of an old disused mine ('Scharnhorst', 1872–1931). It was designed by the Poelzig Team and built with American aid in 1954–58. The population has risen from 6,000 to about 11,500, but the density is still only about 14 persons per hectare and when the town is completed it will still be about 23 persons per hectare. The new living accommodation area was designed for a population of around 15,000. The satellite town can therefore grow into a section of the city with a population of about 26,000. It will bring prominence to four neighbouring parts of the city, as traffic communications with the centre of Dortmund are improved. A remarkable experiment was made in order to discover the best means of providing educational facilities in an area such as Dortmund-North-East. Fifty-nine experts took part – lecturers, architects, school inspectors, school authorities, building authorities, and town planners – with the object of deciding whether the comprehensive school was the most suitable 'school concept in a major industrial city'. The school intake comes, in fact, from a population consisting of 68·5 per cent industrial workers, 16·0 per cent salaried employees, 1·6 per cent public officials, and 4·4 per cent self-employed (half of them farmers).

A planning group prepared the erection of the comprehensive school; it is to be a day school, and will be closely observed by a research group.

It is to be a decentralized comprehensive school, in that the participating schools will remain separate in the lower forms. Industrial training will begin in the middle forms and the higher forms will take courses leading to university entrance. The total student population will probably be about 3,680–3,780. The whole complex is envisaged as a centre of learning, with infant schools, sports grounds and playing fields, a swimming pool, an adult education college, and buildings for the care of the young and the aged, and the planners hope that this concept will help to bring about an improvement in the present poor educational situation in the suburbs, the result of unfavourable social conditions. It is important also that from now on the changes which are to be expected in the social structure of the suburbs will be paralleled by a corresponding improvement in the rate of building. The building of 65 per cent three-room dwellings, 15 per cent two-room and apartment dwellings, and 20 per cent dwellings for large families, must, after all, bring about considerable changes in social ambiance.

It is an indication of the extent to which education has become conditioned by urbanization that a number of large international exhibitions of educational materials have been held in various German cities since the beginning of the Sixties. Dortmund has been the venue for the *Interschul* exhibitions, held there at intervals since 1960. The second *Interschul* was opened by a prominent member of the German Schools Committee with a speech on 'The Responsibility of our Towns for their Schools', and had as its main theme 'City – Company – School'. The next *Interschul*, in 1972, will again be in Dortmund. Its slogan has already been decided, and in the best urban manner. It is: 'Education for Progress in the World'.

22

New Cities, Educational Traditions and the Future

Mogens Jansen, Jens Bjerg, Anders Leerskov and Peer Mylov

For more than a century an educational ideology has been manifesting itself in Denmark, maintaining that the influence exercised by parents in the home must be considered the most important form of education. This ideology originates from the circles which around the end of the nineteenth century backed the foundation of the Danish folk high school. (Brickman, 1949.) It is one of the main characteristics of the folk high school that it considers education on a voluntary basis, concentrated on developing the interests of the pupils, as a goal in itself so that tests and examinations are not necessary, and believes that education should be a life-long process.

The folk high schools are intended for adults and young people, and a considerable number of prominent Danish people, including many politicians, have declared that they are indebted to the folk high school. This has exercised a direct influence on the Educational Acts determining the structural development of the public school. The Educational Acts and the political debate on the school have been influenced by views and contributions that may be traced back to the ideology of the folk high school: *The parents' right, to the widest possible extent, to decide the length of their children's schooling and the content of their education.*

The parents' influence on the length of the schooling is of prevailing interest within the public school, the school which, incidentally, holds a dominating position as compared to private education. The content of the education is, however, not under the direct influence of the parents or the individual school, but is to a very large extent determined at a more central level.

Compulsory education over a period of seven years is a point that has been maintained in all Educational Acts since 1814. Beyond this period the parents have the right to send their children to school for a further period of from one to six years, provided that this is justified by the interest and ability displayed by the individual child.

The development from rural to urban communities has to an ever increasing extent made people realize that knowledge and exams are a means of social upgrading, and more and more parents, therefore, avail themselves of their *right* to have their children benefit from further education.

Modern Occupational Structure

Up until this last decade the above philosophy and attitude have seemed to form a satisfactory basis for the development of an appropriate educational system. In viewing this situation it must be taken into consideration that the socio-economic standard prevailing within the lowest layers of society has been sufficiently high to make it possible for the intentions expressed in the Educational Acts to be redeemed.

A fundamental factor in this respect is that throughout the first half of the twentieth century, where agriculture – because of the country's lack of natural resources – has been the most important industry, the occupational structure has been marked by a continuous, steady development. During the period 1840–1950 where the rural population remained at a constant figure of about one million, the total population figure increased from about one and a half million to about five million.

Except for the metropolitan area, the individual urban communities are comparatively small, and the slums found in the industrial towns and cities in other countries have been practically non-existent. (The Municipal Reform Commission, 1968.)

By virtue of a thorough rationalization within the agricultural sector, the farmers have been able to increase agricultural output so as to keep up with the other industries developing within the same period. It was not until the middle of the 50s that this development came to a stop, brought about by the difficult marketing situation facing Danish agriculture. In recent years agriculture has witnessed a pronounced migration of farm labourers, but in view of the general favourable conditions within trade and industry, it has been possible for the industrial sector and the service trades to absorb this manpower. Until the 1950s it was taken for granted that agriculture must be considered the principal industry of the country, but since then Denmark has generally been described as a welfare society. This development has been made possible mainly because of rising industrial earnings, and this in spite of the fact that the country actually lacks practically all types of industrial raw materials.

In this situation it has been accepted that money must be invested in the education and training of the people, if the country is to remain competitive, such competitiveness being based on quality, precision and inventiveness. The increased importance which is thus being attached to the school and to education accentuates the community's interest in providing the greatest possible number of people with the best possible education and training. Therefore, the interest taken in educational policy is pronounced as never before, and it is recognized to a greater extent than ever that modern education costs a great deal of money.

In recent years Denmark has been the country in Europe which, next to Sweden and Malta, has had the largest per capita investment in the educational sector. (Sixth Conference of European Ministers of Education.)

In 1956/57 the overall educational expense represented 3·0 per cent of the gross national product, while in 1966/67 this increased to 5·6 per cent. (Goldschmidt, 1968.)

A surprisingly small proportion of this money has, however, been spent on educational research and development. In 1967/68 an amount of barely Dkr. 2 million was set aside for educational research or 0·65 per thousand of the total educational budget. Therefore, there is a lack of tradition, and not enough manpower to take care of this work. This unhappy situation may be ascribed to the fact that certain demands within the educational sector were so obviously urgent that the necessity for research was given second priority in favour of direct action.

Extended Compulsory Education

Concurrently with the investments which have been made in the educational sector, the question arose of extending the period of compulsory education beyond seven years. When this issue was debated in 1967, strong voices against such extension were immediately heard from circles within and close to the folk high school: the extension was undesirable as it was in conflict with the principle of voluntary attendance and represented interference with the rights of parents. The greater majority of the children already attended school on a voluntary basis until the age of 15, and many until 16.

This debate marks a clash between two parties, one basing its arguments on social statistics out of considerations for *the rights of parents*, while the other party is arguing in favour of a dynamic society and *the requirements and offers made by society* – in respect of citizens, including children and young people.

The Bill subsequently presented by the Minister of Education may be described as representing a compromise between these two points of view.

In Denmark the lower age limit for compulsory education is seven, and two of the points included among the various provisions of the Bill were directly aimed at this lower limit. It recommended that:

(1) the compulsory period be extended, starting five months earlier, and

(2) that in addition, parents may demand that their children be admitted to school one year earlier than mentioned under (1).

Among educational experts this Bill is characterized as being determined by party politics; it is maintained that this is a compromise – and a bad one at that – between the government parties' wishes not to let all children attend school too long and the requests from other sides for an extension of the compulsory period. The Bill directly provides a poorly disguised possibility for an extension of the lower limit rather than the upper one; and the traditional educational approach thus still makes itself felt.

The Urban Development and Educational Materials

When social development, in spite of all objections, leads to an extension of the compulsory period and thus also to prolonged school attendance, the questions may be asked: to what extent does the school live up to the requirements of the community? What has been the effect exercised on the educational field work by the new occupational structure and urban development?

Modern educational research, which aims to give a realistic picture of the educational situation, i.e. the classroom situation as close to the individual pupil as possible, gives certain indications in this respect. Systematized educational descriptions could provide some of the necessary details; it might perhaps serve the purpose to emphasize a few background factors, which probably are peculiar to Scandinavian countries and to Denmark in particular.

In Denmark the central authorities make *suggestions* (by means of educational guides) for educational materials and methods to be used when teaching different subjects. Thereafter, educational plans are prepared at local level, a point at which the parents can theoretically exercise a great deal of influence through local, politically elected representatives. The educational plan gives a rather close description of the field or fields to be covered at the various grade levels. But stipulations are nowhere to be found stating how thoroughly the teacher must go into the individual subjects on the educational plan, and the methods to be applied.

The liberty given to the teacher in connexion with his work is thus held within certain clearly defined limits in respect of the subjects to be taught – a limitation which may seem rather confined to people from other countries. Work is not concentrated on 'social studies' or 'science', etc., but the curriculum is divided into certain 'subjects' (geography, biology, history, physics, chemistry, etc.). Within these subjects, certain topics must be covered; in the fifth grade the lessons in geography must, for example, deal with certain countries.

On the other hand the teacher is, from grades 1 to 7, very much at liberty not to give tests throughout the year, including closing tests. In principle, as well as in actual practice, the teacher enjoys considerable freedom as to the choice of method.

Because of these external factors, the teacher will make rather greater use of textbooks, occasionally following them directly, but apart from that these books are a stable and time-saving aid for the teacher.

The fixed curriculum, the comparatively large degree of exemption from tests and the fairly central importance of textbooks, all combine to make a situation where it is possible, through an analysis of the textbook material, to tell a great deal not only about the topics the pupils are studying but also about the way in which most of the lessons are conducted. The fact is that textbooks serve to confine within rather narrow limits not only the subject matter but also the teaching methods.

Within educational research there have been obvious reasons in this situation for paying particular attention to an important part of the educational tools applied by teachers and pupils, viz. educational materials.

The first textbook analyses have already been published, and more are in preparation. It is characteristic that attention has been especially concentrated on an analysis of the teaching of the native language during the compulsory period, the field where the educational development has been most pronounced in recent years.

An analysis of all Danish textbooks used in public schools (Jansen, 1969), in conjunction with an analysis dealing especially with illustrations in these books (Jansen and Mylov, 1968), shows that: the generally accepted time-gap of 20–40 years between research and public school textbooks has a parallel in the gap between the description given in the textbooks of Denmark as being mainly an agricultural community (practical examples are taken from the 1930–40s) as opposed to the Denmark of today, where industries and service trades tend to out-distance agriculture.

This may be seen in the traditional descriptions contained in the ABC-books of the Danish community. Similarly with written language textbooks, readers and arithmetic books and also books on the so-called orientation subjects. Developments throughout the past decade are not reflected in the text or in the illustrations; these illustrations follow the text and thus they fail to depict the community of today. The statistics contained in the textbooks have, however, to a certain extent been kept up to date.

It might perhaps be as well to mention that textbooks are oriented towards foreign countries, especially when compared with many corresponding books from other countries, and this applies both to books on the orientation subjects and those on foreign languages as well as to the translated literature used in the teaching of Danish. It is, however, not known how well the descriptions cover the foreign countries of *today*.

It should be pointed out, however, that an effort is being made to bring many of the textbooks up to date, and the opportunity for doing so is obviously greatest when a popular book is repeatedly reprinted.

Some schools are rather slow at renewing their textbook material and it is possible to come across schools with 20-year-old textbooks, and the situation arises where the pupils in their textbooks read – and to a smaller or larger degree are expected to learn – subject matter which has been obsolete for 20 or 30 years.

With rapid changes in social development this may cause complications as the school is unable to give the pupils sufficient information about the community of today.

Urban Development and Pre-school Education

As a result of increased knowledge gained in the field of child psychology, it has recently been possible, especially in connexion with the youngest age group, to plan the educational programme on the basis of the children's requirements and abilities. Formerly the programmes were planned on the basis of traditional requirements of formal education, aimed at grade levels and higher classes.

In these efforts the school has taken over and developed a philosophy which otherwise was mainly confined to the Danish kindergarten.

Within the same period the kindergarten idea has also gained ground among parents. This must be viewed against the background of urban development brought about by the changing occupational structure. An ever increasing number of married women continue to work away from home, a situation which emphasizes the need for more kindergartens; the rapid growth within urban communities and the resulting higher traffic density, have served to rob the children of a considerable proportion of their earlier playgrounds and other similar facilities.

The fact that too few kindergartens were available to meet the increasing demand and that it would take a very long time before the existing and rather heterogeneous institutions could be sufficiently increased, caused parents to demand the prompt introduction of kindergarten classes at existing schools. A country-wide network of school buildings was available, and the possibility of applying the educational principles of the kindergarten movement was present.

A provisional arrangement now permits schools to establish such classes, the grants-in-aid being on the same scale as for ordinary grades, and a number of schools and educational authorities have availed themselves of this offer. On the whole, this kindergarten within the school is considered a success even though there is a great shortage of classrooms and teachers and in spite of the fact that the short period (2–3 hours a day) during which the children are accommodated at school does not mean any appreciable relief as far as the mothers employed outside the home are concerned.

The existing provisional arrangement, permitting schools to establish kindergarten classes, will probably be superseded by an order at a later date. And if the present expectations of good results with these classes are fulfilled, the situation may very well arise where the educational authorities and some politicians may require that all children must attend a kindergarten class or be provided with similar facilities. Here the old dispute about voluntary attendance versus compulsory education to serve the interests of the *community* will arise again, but with a different background.

The Pre-School Philosophy

An interest is thus taken in influencing the children educationally under some form or other prior to the compulsory age ($6\frac{1}{2}$–7), but at the same time it is desired that any such influence shall be aimed at providing the children with an increasing amount of general experience. It is not desired to anticipate the actual teaching and learning of skills in the three Rs. It is argued that there is plenty of time for the children to learn these skills later.

A review and expansion of the work with children of pre-school age is closely bound up with the attitude taken by society (parents, teachers, educational authorities, trade and industry, etc.) in the discussion going on between psychologists and educationists. When discussing the respective effect of inheritance and environment on 'educational maturity' the extreme views have been expressed by the 'inheritance-oriented' and the 'environment-oriented' participants in the discussion, i.e. those definitely believing in the inheritance factor and those to whom environment is all-important. 'Educational maturity' is here understood to be the ability to cope with tasks set by the school, making it possible for the child to benefit from education.

Though this discussion is still going on in Denmark, as elsewhere – often in connexion with the highly disputable point of the need for con- tinued streaming of pupils at the secondary level – the Educational Acts recently passed must, it is believed, first and foremost be taken as an indication that it is the 'environment-oriented' psychologists and educa- tionists who have been most successful in their argumentation.

The concept that ability is not an unalterable factor is thus gradually gaining ground.

An Integrated Educational Goal

The increasing belief in this theory means that its advocates will demand that children of pre-school age be provided with education to add to their experience level, without any demands being made as to the teach- ing and learning of specific subject-matter.

The idea is further supported by the integrated educational goal which is being currently formulated. Influenced by the general impression that care should be taken not to provide the children with education aimed at any specific occupation, due to the rapid change in social structure, the interest in specific knowledge and specific skills is diminishing, since these skills may be of no use in a few years' time.

Therefore, greater consideration is being paid to ordinary skills such as listening and understanding, ability in the spoken and written language, writing and arithmetic, and knowing how to locate useful information on topics specially selected by the teacher.

Moreover, an effort will be made within the different disciplines of the individual subjects to provide the pupils with a certain elementary knowledge of the terminology and methods used, and to leave possibilities open for the individual pupil to work according to his own interests and abilities.

In the community of the future it must be taken for granted that everybody will normally need further or advanced education. While admitting the reasonableness of this argument, it is also quite clearly realized that the establishment of a kindergarten class closely connected with the public educational system will require considerable, renewed planning, of further sectors of the Danish educational system.

The establishment of a kindergarten class will make reorganization of the primary school necessary, and this again will affect the secondary levels. To provide children of pre-school age with adequate education, the necessary number of teachers must be trained for this purpose. This will require recruiting of qualified teachers and so on.

It is apparent that it is not possible to bring about changes in one sector of the educational system without involving all the other sectors at the same time.

Urban Development and Educational Philosophy

Urban development and the factors connected with it have during the past decade given rise to a discussion on and interest in the *overall* Danish educational system, of dimensions never before witnessed. It is not that the increasing density of the built-up areas has in itself caused any fundamental difficulties as far as the tradition-bound Danish educational system is concerned, for this system could be developed, though with some delay. But concurrently with the influence worked on the community by urbanization and connected factors, a new educational philosophy is becoming evident.

This new philosophy is based on an assumption of the factors that have generated the growth in urban development (the new occupational structure, population increase, etc.); it is made possible by the development with the increased concentration of the population; and it is in

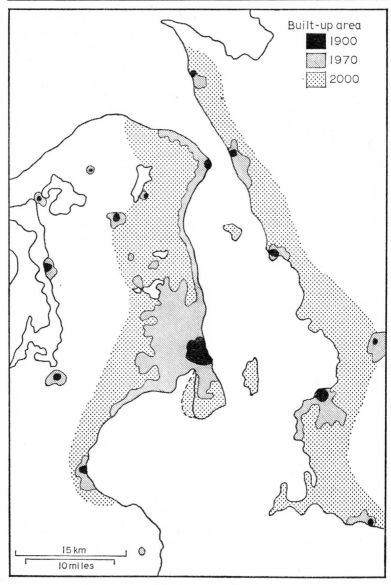

Built-up area
■ 1900
▨ 1970
▒ 2000

15 km
10 miles

The past and future growth of Copenhagen.

harmony with the need brought about by the new social structure for everyone to enjoy a longer period of education.

At the same time a new possibility was found for realization of the democratic principle of equal educational rights for all in Denmark. The urbanization factors constitute a break with old tradition as they have developed so far in Denmark, but at the same time they facilitate co-ordination and differentiation of the educational course, giving children and young people alike greater freedom of choice according to individual interests and abilities.

The principle of freedom for parents to decide how their children should be educated must be viewed on the basis of their own possibilities of introducing the children to an occupation where the requirements were foreseeable, but this provided the young people with comparatively few chances of making their own choice. The planning of integrated and flexible educational courses beginning at pre-school level and continuing from there to university level – and perhaps even further – is a task of such recent date that it is difficult to handle immediately. During recent years the different sectors of the educational system have been discussed gradually one by one as the need for such discussion arose through an essential factor in urban development, i.e. the increase in population. Nevertheless, the educational philosophy of the development period has been predominant as it is no longer desired that only a certain small percentage of young people shall benefit from advanced education.

Within the public school system, streaming has been postponed until about the age of 14, and there is every indication that within a few years it will be postponed for two additional years. The debate around the educational structure is again current in connexion with problems surrounding the contemplated extension of the compulsory period, and the kindergarten class is now being drawn into this discussion. It seems, however, as if less attention can be paid to the development of methods and materials for the time being, but in respect of the highest and lowest grade levels work is proceeding well.

In between the debates on the public school and the kindergarten class the educational course between the public school (from age 6–7 to age 15–16) and the higher forms of education (universities, technical high schools and other colleges) has been developed and differentiated. But the urbanization factors have also made young people conscious of education as a system, and the actual forms of occupational training are now being discussed in connexion with these latter sectors. This development has opened the possibility for young people to exercise their influence on the educational system and has provided them with more alternatives to choose from within the system.

Urban development within the community has created educational institutions, promoting this development. Centralization of smaller units, decentralization of larger units, spread over wider areas away from the most densely built-up districts, follow the trend within trade and industry.

If the market conditions are maintained and the growing interest taken in social planning continues, the Danish educational system can probably benefit from, while also contributing to, a favourable urban development.

BIBLIOGRAPHY

William W. Brickman, *Denmark's Educational System and Problems*, U.S. Department of Health, Education and Welfare, U.S. Government Printing Office (Washington: 1967).

Willis Dixon, *Education in Denmark*, 'Centraltrykkeriet' (Copenhagen, 1959).

Ernst Goldschmidt, 1,000,000 $ til forskning. ($1 mill. for Research), 'Uddannelse 68', 1 edition 1968, No. 8, pp. 272–274.

Mogens Jansen, 'Danske læsebøger, 1–7 skoleår' (Danish Readers and Textbooks, Grades 1–7), Vol. 1 and 2. Copenhagen: Danmarks pædagogiske Institut (The Danish Institute for Educational Research), 1969.

Mogens Jansen, 'Skriftligt arbejde i dansk, 1–7 skoleår' (Textbook material available on the written language in Denmark, Grades 1–7). Registration and Analysis of the mentioned textbooks. Copenhagen: Danmarks pædagogiske Institut (The Danish Institute for Educational Research), 1966.

Mogens Jansen and Peer Mylov, 'Illustrationer i danske læsebøger, 1–7 skoleår' (Illustrations in Danish Readers and Textbooks, Grades 1–7). 'Nordisk Tidskrift för Specialpedagogik', 1969.

The Secretariate of the Municipal Reform Commission. The Secretariate of the National Planning Committee '*Amtskommuner – befolkning, opgaver, økonomi, oplande* (Counties – population figures, objectives, economy, surrounding areas. (Copenhagen, 1968).

Sixth Conference of European Ministers of Education, Report prepared by the Secretariat (Athens, May, 1967).

Ole B. Thomsen, *Some Aspects of Education in Denmark*. The Ontario Institute for Studies in Education (University of Toronto Press, 1967).

23

Czechoslovakia

Rudolf Sturm

General Description

Founded more than eleven hundred years ago, Prague has for centuries been the cultural and political centre of the Czech people living in Bohemia and Moravia who at present number over ten million inhabitants. The city is the seat of the Government of the Czech Socialist Republic and of the Federal Government of both the Czech and the Slovak Socialist Republics. Its many factories make it the most important industrial city in East Central Europe.

Located here is the manufacture of locomotives, railroad cars, tramways, and other heavy machinery, airplane engines, optical instruments, food, clothing, paper, chemicals, and other goods. Agriculture is pursued on the outskirts of the city to a substantial extent. On the Vltava (Moldau) there are port facilities used for a lively barge traffic with Hamburg. The city is linked with the rest of the country with several railroads and many highways; its airport is served by nearly all European and some overseas airlines. Tourist trade, flourishing in particular over the past decade, has helped in the development of large hotel and restaurant accommodation. Prague has fourteen permanent theatres with twenty-two stages, seventy-eight permanent cinemas, a dozen symphony and chamber orchestras, 115 libraries, and several museums and art galleries.

The population, at the end of 1969, is estimated at 1,050,000. Due to Prague's shortage of housing as well as to careful government planning, the increase has for many years been less than 0·5 per cent annually.

Main Characteristics of the Educational System

In Prague, as in the rest of Czechoslovakia, there are no private schools today. The few that existed up to 1948 were owned and operated by various churches and were accredited by the Ministry of Education. In that year, when the Communist Party took over control of the country, education became the exclusive prerogative of the Government. The present educational system is based on the Education Act of December 15th, 1960, and on other laws and governmental decrees. These restate, and in some instances formulate anew, certain basic principles, the more significant of which are the following:

(1) For all citizens of Czechoslovakia education is a right guaranteed by the Constitution. (It should be noted here that in practice children of former factory and land owners or those who opposed the Communist régime were often excluded from higher education, especially in the nineteen-fifties.) The task of the schools is to educate young people and adults alike in the spirit of Marxism-Leninism and to prepare them for socially useful work.

(2) The Government alone can own and operate schools, and it does so mainly through the Ministry of Education. Theological learning is controlled by the Office of Church Affairs in the Ministry of Culture; nurseries and schools of health are administered by the Ministry of Public Health; and military academies, by the Ministry of National Defence.

(3) Education from nursery through graduate school is made available to all free of charge, and is financed entirely by the Government, including school buildings, teachers' salaries, and even textbooks,

(4) To help defray students' room and board and other expenses, the Government grants them scholarships of up to an equivalent of $100 per month, depending on their academic standing, their parents' income, and the number of dependants in their family. (Some 30 per cent of students in both secondary schools and colleges actually receive scholarships.)

(5) All curricula as well as textbooks are decided on by the respective Ministries. The Ministries, either directly or through a lower agency, appoint, promote, and dismiss teachers and administration personnel. They also set salaries and other benefits.

Pre-school and Elementary Education

Pre-school facilities have a long tradition in Czechoslovakia, dating as far back as 1832 when the first kindergarten was founded in Prague on principles formulated by the Czech educator Comenius (1592–1670). To alleviate the burden of working mothers – more than 47 per cent of the labour force at all levels in Prague are women – there are 136 nurseries caring for 6,961 children between the ages of three months and three years. (These and most other figures used in this article reflect the situation as of Spring, 1969.) About 10 per cent of the nurseries are open day and night; the rest are day schools only.

Children between the ages of three and six attend maternity schools. Attendance is voluntary at present, but a plan is under consideration to make kindergarten compulsory for all children from five to six years old. There are 251 maternity schools caring for 22,479 children, and the teacher–pupil ratio is 15, not counting auxiliary personnel.

A small number of nurseries and kindergartens are located directly in factories and state offices where a large number of working mothers are employed. In such instances the employers defray part of the schools' cost. In all the nurseries and maternity schools the only fee paid by parents is about one-half of the cost of food.

Between the ages of six and fifteen, every child in Prague, as in the rest of the country, must attend a Basic Nine-Year School. As a rule these are day schools. In the school year 1968–69, there were 98,000 children attending 162 Nine-Year Schools, with twenty-nine pupils in a class. About 30 per cent of the graduates transfer to a four-year secondary school ending in a *matura* examination; nearly all the rest enter secondary schools with a shorter programme or become apprentices.

If mentally or physically impaired, the child must go to a special school according to his handicap. For the blind, there are three schools in Prague; for the deaf-mute, also three; and for those with a speech impediment, one school. These special schools usually offer education from kindergarten through secondary school, that is, to the age of eighteen or nineteen. Children with delinquent tendencies are placed in two schools with compulsory residence in children's shelters.

Extra-curricular activities for children between nine and fourteen are directed by the Pioneer Organization, a junior division of the Communist Party-sponsored Czechoslovak Youth Union. Although membership is voluntary, non-participation is rather unpopular and is frowned upon by school authorities. Consequently, over 95 per cent of Czech youth belong to the Pioneer Organization. The Pioneers organize rest and recreation (meetings, excursions, theatre and concert attendance, physical education clubs) for the schoolchildren, so that 'socialist education after classes will become an inseparable and organic part of the educational system', as one official publication puts it.

Secondary Schools

A great concentration of industry, transportation, and cultural facilities makes it imperative for the Prague secondary schools to graduate large numbers of prospective college students as well as immediately employable technicians, laboratory workers, foremen, and other personnel of intermediate rank for whom a high-school diploma is the terminal degree. Since demand for high-school graduates greatly exceeds supply, the Ministry of Planning takes great care in apportioning the fifteen-year-olds, after their graduation from elementary school, to the various vocational and academic high-schools. The Ministry knows, or can accurately estimate, the number of new nurses, master mechanics, and also history Ph.D.s or dentists that will be needed in a given future year, and sees to it that this exact number of first-year students is admitted in each respective area, taking account of attrition and similar factors. Admission to all high schools is contingent on entrance examinations in Czech language and literature as well as in mathematics, and in the case of art and music schools, also on a talent test. Psychological testing, introduced in Prague schools in 1966, is used only sporadically.

There are the following types and numbers of secondary schools in Prague today:

(1) *gymnasium* – a school with a four-year academic programme in either the humanities or natural sciences, ending with a *matura* examination. Graduates as a rule transfer to schools of higher learning. There are twenty *gymnasia* here with a student body of 10,017;

(2) secondary vocational school, with a four-year professional programme of study, also ending with a *matura* examination; and a two-year vocational school. Over 17,000 students are enrolled in thirty-six such schools. The following programmes can be studied in Prague: machinery, instruments and automation, electrical technology, technical chemistry, food, clothing, typesetting, construction (including waterworks and transportation facilities), agriculture, general economics, foreign trade, economics of transportation and of services, foreign language correspondence, administration of factory and office cafeterias, health (including X-ray technicians, dental assistants, nurses, maternity school personnel, and dieticians), social and legal work, library science, and others. Each of these disciplines is taught in Prague at a separate school.

(3) Schools for the education of apprentices, usually with two or three-year programmes. There are thirty-three such schools with an enrolment of 25,976 boys and girls.

In addition, there are several thousand adults with regular jobs who are completing their secondary education by taking evening courses, correspondence courses, or pursuing independent studies. They must spend six to seven hours weekly consulting with their teachers and must pass regular examinations at the end of each semester. They receive time off with full pay for both consultations and tests.

As with elementary school children, high-school students too have their rest and recreation activities organized by the Czechoslovak Youth Union, senior division, in which over 55 per cent of students between the ages of fourteen and twenty-six are enrolled. The Union sponsors not only summer camps and gymnastic clubs, but also discussion groups and meetings, for here too stress is laid on ideological preparation.

The average teacher-student ratio in the secondary schools is 15. There is a 6 per cent attrition rate at the *gymnasia* during the four-year programme; the rate is 12 per cent in other secondary schools; nearly 25 per cent of those taking correspondence or independent study courses drop out of these programmes. Some 10 per cent of high-school graduates enter institutions of higher learning.

Higher Learning

If the demands of Prague industry, the state ministries, and cultural establishments for people with secondary education is high, it is doubly great for those with higher degrees. Additional pressure on Prague's schools of higher learning is caused by the steadily increasing need for college and university graduates in the rest of Bohemia.

The most important and oldest (established in 1348) is Charles University, the main source of personnel for non-technical fields. It has the following schools: General Medicine, Public Health, Podiatry, Law, Philosophy (including social sciences, languages, literatures, and education of high-school teachers), Mathematics-Physics, Natural Sciences, Physical Education, Journalism, and Pedagogy (for training elementary-school teachers). In the academic year 1968–69, enrolment was 12,800, of which 7,200 were female students, reflecting the great need in Prague for high-level women employees.

Technical and scientific personnel are educated at the Czech Institute of Technology which grants degrees at its Schools of Construction (including waterworks, transportation facilities, and cartography), Mechanical Engineering, Electrical Engineering, and Technical-Nuclear Physics (including nuclear chemistry). Chemical engineers are educated at the Chemical-Technological Institute, with specialties in inorganic and organic technology, technology of food, and the automation and economics of chemical production. Economists are trained at the Economics University, that includes the School of Public Economics, Economics of Manufacture, Commerce, and Management. Agricultural specialists study at the Institute of Agriculture which comprises the Schools of Agricultural Operations and Economics, Mechanization of Agriculture, and a School for Agronoms.

Political scientists, for whom there is a pressing need in the ministries and other public offices, study at the University of the Central Committee of the Communist Party and at the Law School of Charles University. Education and ideological officers of the Czechoslovak armed forces are trained at the Klement Gottwald Military-Political Academy, while other officers go to Brno, Moravia, to study at the Antonín Zápotocký Military Academy or to Žilina, in Slovakia, to study at the Military Transportation Academy. Future painters, architects, and sculptors attend one of the two Schools of Art. The Academy of Music and Art prepares its graduates for careers in music, theatre, film, and television.

Roman Catholic priests are educated at the Cyrillo-Methodian School of Theology, with its official seat in Prague, but located temporarily in Litoměřice, in northern Bohemia; its enrolment in June of 1969 was 179, but only a fraction came from Prague. Those desiring to become priests of the Eastern Orthodox Church study at the Orthodox School of Theology in Prešov, Slovakia. The only Czech Jewish divinity student, preparing to become the Prague rabbi – the present holder of that office is over ninety years old – is studying in England on a scholarship from the Czech Ministry of Culture.

Protestant theologians of various denominations (Czech Brethren, Lutherans, Calvinists, Methodists, Baptists, etc.) are educated at the Comenius Evangelical School of Theology, while future ministers of the Czechoslovak Church receive their schooling at the Hus Theological School. Each of these institutions has an enrolment of about 50 students.

The University of November 17th holds a special place among the thirteen institutes of higher learning located in Prague. It was established for the training of students from developing countries and received its name to commemorate the fatal day in November of 1939 when the German occupation authorities closed all Czech colleges and universities 'forever' in retaliation for the student participation in anti-Nazi demonstrations. In 1968, there were 836 foreigners studying at the University, most of them from Africa, and 188 Czechoslovak citizens. The foreigners are trained in Czech or Slovak and partly also in social sciences, after which they transfer to other universities to study medicine, engineering, and other technical disciplines. The Czechs and Slovaks studying here are preparing for the careers of interpreters or translators.

Candidates for admission to the Prague schools of higher learning – with the exception of the Univeristy of November 17th, where the admission requirements are somewhat lower – must submit a *matura* diploma from a high school and pass a strict entrance examination. Attrition during the college years is about 20 per cent among men and over 30 per cent among women. It was estimated that in the Fall of 1969 there were 32,000 regular students registered in Prague at the schools of higher learning, while some 10,000 were taking correspondence and other non-matriculated courses. Nearly 70 per cent of regular students received room and board at the schools. The faculty-student ratio was just over six for each full-time teacher.

Compared with the pre-World War II situation, the number and the variety of both secondary schools and institutions of higher learning located in Prague have risen spectacularly. The increase does not reflect any rise in population, which is minimal, but rather the truly revolutionary changes affecting the city's economy as well as the rôle Prague is called upon to play in the highly centralized administration of Czechoslovakia after 1945.

Some of the more salient of these changes are: the introduction of new branches of industry and the resulting increase in transportation facilities; the modernization of production methods; the development of research in natural sciences and the humanities alike; the industrialization of the hitherto little-developed regions of Czechoslovakia for which Prague is to supply both lower technical personnel and executive cadres; the necessity of increasing the length and quality of teachers' education. Also, the ever-increasing number of foreign students in Czechoslovakia and the desire of the Government to assert its influence in the developing countries led to the establishment of the University of November 17th (in 1961).

BIBLIOGRAPHY

1. L'udovít Bakoš, and others, *Školstvo v Československu*. (Bratislava: Výskumný ústav pedagogický, 1966) 254 pp.
2. František Budský, ed, *Education in the Metropolis; Commentary on Hugh Philp's Study 'Education in the Metropolis.'* (Praha: Education Dept. of the City of Praha, 1967) 25 pp.
3. Jaroslav Hartman, *Profily absolventů vysokých škol; seznam studijních oborů a jejich rozmístění na vysokých školách* (Praha: Státní pedagogické nakl., 1968) 220 pp.
4. Bohuslav Kukačka, ed., *Střední školy; informace o denním studiu 1969–1970* (Praha: Státní pedagogické nakl., 1968) 107 pp.
5. Vladimír Pazdera, Václav Tvrdek, and Antonín Wagenknecht, *Odborná učiliště a učňovské školy; informační brožura pro školní rok 1969/70* (Praha, Státní pedagogické nakl., 1968) 103 pp.
6. *Statistická ročenka Československé socialistické republiky 1968* (Praha, Státní nakl. technické literatury, 1968) 608 pp.

24

Milton Keynes: A City for Learning

Roy P. Harding

Milton Keynes is to be a new city in the north of Buckinghamshire, less than 50 miles from London. The population of the designated area is now about 44,000, over half in Bletchley, which has developed from a population of 9,000 in 1948, about 10,000 in Wolverton and New Bradwell, nearly 4,000 in Stony Stratford, and the rest in a large number of small villages. The interim proposals for Milton Keynes published by the Development Corporation in February 1969 provide for a planned growth to a population of over 230,000 in 1989 and over 250,000 in 1994.

The final plan for Milton Keynes will not be published until early in 1970 and therefore there are bound to be uncertainties about the future. For example, the ability of people living in Milton Keynes to choose between alternative services will depend to some extent on the standard of public transport facilities. However, the Development Corporation clearly expect the final plan to be firmly based on the interim report. As far as education is concerned, the interim proposals are based on a more detailed report approved by the Buckinghamshire Education Committee and it seems unlikely, therefore, that there will be any major changes in the final plan. Many seminars were held to examine the goals which should guide the development of the new city. The summary of the interim proposals says of the discussions that the most general conclusion was that Milton Keynes must be planned to give people what they want. 'This idea is not new but it is new to take it seriously'. One attitude fundamental to the approach to all proposals for Milton Keynes is the strong emphasis on flexibility and the provision for choice and change. This emphasis has been from the very beginning in the minds of those who have been planning the education provision in the new city – long before they knew of the same approaches by their colleagues. Perhaps this was inevitable. It is difficult to be certain about the views that will prevail in education arguments one year from now. The planners can assume very little about the views of 1989.

The planning for the provision of education in Milton Keynes has involved many people and at all stages the education service has been looked at in relation to the needs of the whole city and those who will live there. The education service in Milton Keynes will be largely provided by the

County Council, though there will be many opportunities for joint ventures with the Development Corporation, local authorities or voluntary bodies. Members and officers involved in all services which the County Council will provide have worked closely together, as would be expected. In addition, however, there has been much wider collaboration, partly through seminars, with all those who are involved in planning the future city and especially, with the Chairman and members of the Development Corporation, their master planners, consultants and staff.

What education will people want in 1989? It is relatively easy to look at statistics over a period of years and attempt some form of extrapolation. For example, in the last twenty years in Buckinghamshire the proportion of the 15/16/17 age groups in full-time education in schools has increased from just over 10 per cent to over 40 per cent and the total number of further education students has shown a five-fold increase, with a much quicker rate of development in full-time and part-time day provision. Is this rate of increase likely to continue? Many would argue that a similar rate of growth in the next 20 years is unlikely. Will some parts of the education service be restricted whilst others continue to expand? Is it not probable that the needs of industry and commerce will change at least as rapidly as at present and consequently employers and employees need to be kept up to date? Should not more people be encouraged to seek more ways of positive use of increased leisure time? Will the evident demand for nursery education be catered for? The education planners cannot answer these and similar questions. Nor are they so much concerned with questions as to whether local or central government will provide the finance or whether some money may come from the industrialists for the re-education of their employees or from parents for nursery education. They must, however, make planning provision which will allow for these and other developments in the city if the demands exist and the resources are available to satisfy the demands. It has been assumed for planning purposes, therefore, that there will be a large increase in demand for education, almost from the cradle to the grave.

How will education be provided in 1989? Adults and older students might be able to learn many things by individual access, physically or electronically, to data or information banks, which would include all kinds of education programmes, visual as well as aural. The plan for Milton Keynes assumes, however, that most of the best education will continue to come from the interaction of minds. Consequently those who undertake most of their study at home will need some facilities for tutorial work and, perhaps, for laboratory or workshop experience. It is expected that these facilities would be provided jointly with other facilities for full-time and part-time education. In any case the plan assumes that most education up to the age of 18 will be provided in some educational establishment.

What kinds of educational establishment will exist in 1989? Ideas now current are quite different from those expressed in 1949 and there is no reason to suppose they will not alter again. The proposals for schools for the new city suggest transfers at the ages of 8 and 12. First schools will be essentially local schools, probably with a maximum of 60 in any age group, planned in such a way as to allow for the implementation of the Plowden Committee recommendations for provision for the 3–5 range as well as the compulsory 5–8 group. The additional expenditure commonly associated with migration to a new town and setting up a new home could result in a high proportion of working mothers in Milton Keynes. The need for nursery school places is likely to be great, but it seems likely that at least in the early stages of the development of the city there will be very little statutory provision because of the scarcity of resources. It is hoped, however, that the demand might be met by co-operation between the Education Committee, the Development Corporation, voluntary organizations and, possibly, industry.

Middle schools will provide for the educational needs of the 8–12 age group but there are differing views on the appropriate size for these schools. Many argue for the personal contact of small schools. On the other hand the increasing variety of children's needs could make the planned size for middle schools with age groups of up to 120 children too restrictive.

It is much more difficult to forecast how education will be provided for the 12–18 year-olds. Optimists may hope that there will not be a shortage of good teachers in any subject at any level. It has been assumed, however, that it will continue to be necessary to make the most effective use of resources of manpower, equipment and buildings. This implies large numbers of young people on one site, however extensive the use of new aids such as C.C.T.V. (closed circuit television) may become. But the basic groups must not be so large as to be impersonal.

Campus sites are being proposed which could accommodate, in present day terms, three schools for those of ages 12–18, each with an intake of 250–350 pupils each year, together with a shared scarce-resources centre. These centres will provide, for example, very expensive scientific equipment, special physical education facilities, and teaching of subjects for which there is relatively little demand or few teachers of outstanding ability. The present trend towards a longer period of full-time education is expected to continue and provision has been based on at least 50 per cent of the 18 year-old age group continuing their full-time education on the campus sites. Three schools on one site should provide for some measure of choice but it is hoped that a first-class transport system in Milton Keynes will make it possible for children to travel easily to any school in the city, thus giving a freedom of choice between schools that are certain to develop in different ways.

The campus sites will not only allow for flexibility in the organization of full-time education but are each intended as natural centres for many purposes for populations of about 30,000. The educational provision on each campus will include accommodation for adult education, a library, part of the youth service provision and the normal meeting places for most voluntary groups and societies. In addition, however, health, welfare and social services will probably have many of their local facilities on these sites. Those who have been concerned with planning these services are just as keen as the educators on joint provision and maximum co-operation in use of resources of buildings and manpower.

An advanced education campus is provided for and the Development Corporation expect that this will ultimately be the site of a University. The County Education Committee have approval to build new accommodation for the North Bucks College of Education on this campus to replace the temporary accommodation elsewhere. It is hoped that the college will educate not only for teaching but also for a much wider range of careers. These might include careers in many of the social services and the wide range of occupations which are linked to the main stream of education, for example in many aspects of educational technology, communication or ancillary services. In the meantime, however, the headquarters of the new Open University is being established at Milton Keynes and although this is a national institution it is bound to have a considerable influence on the city. Cranfield College, with its specialist postgraduate full-time courses, is situated near the borders of the new city and is likely to widen its range of courses after it receives its charter. Milton Keynes will be fortunate to start with so much potential at the advanced levels of education, but clearly there must be an effective co-ordination of all these resources.

One of the most urgent needs is for provision between the levels of what is now regarded as school and advanced education. Reference has already been made to the demands which the changing needs of employment and increased leisure will make on the education services. At present there is only one small college of further education in the designated area. Considerable additions to the present facilities are needed quickly, for undoubtedly they will help to attract a variety of employers to the new city. Four colleges of further education are planned to meet the needs for all kinds of vocational and non-vocational education and the Education Committee hope to make an early start on the first new college in the Bletchley area. In addition to the youth wings on campus sites, the youth service provision will include some purpose-built youth centres not in proximity to schools and a major central establishment offering specialist amenities of the kind which could not sensibly be dispersed. It seems probable that the Development Corporation may provide some of the major facilities for leisure time occupation (for example, a sports complex or golf courses) but there will be ample opportunity for collaboration in many ways between the Corporation, the Education Committee, local authorities and voluntary bodies.

In the early stages of planning most attention is inevitably given to the services which demand a great deal of space and capital investment. There has been less detailed work on other developments but needs have been defined for provision for those with physical or mental handicaps on the one hand or those with special abilities or interests on the other. Ideas about the ideal provision for the needs of the handicapped havevariedbut special schools for a range of handicaps will be established in addition to the present Educational Subnormal school and for maladjusted children. Special units, e.g. for partially hearing children, will be provided in association with the normal schools. Most child guidance clinics will be on campus sites and the psychological service will operate mainly from the same bases. There will be special opportunities for an integrated approach to the health, welfare and education of children as a result of the recommendation from the Medical Planning Group that general practices should be conducted from Health Centres. Family doctors based on these centres will be supported by a range of Local Authority staff, such as Health Visitors, Social Workers and Speech Therapists, and they would also be involved in hospital work. The Health Centres, which may well be on the campus sites, will be focal points at which will be found much knowledge about individual children which might otherwise be fragmented between general practice and specialist branches of the public health service. It is intended that the team serving the area covering two or three secondary schools and the contributing primary schools will break itself down into units sufficiently small to establish an effective partnership with the staff of individual schools. Clearly a real working partnership between the family doctor, his supporting staff, the parents and the teachers will be a major contribution to creating a sympathetic environment for children coming to live in the new town.

In Buckinghamshire the Library and Museum services are the responsibility of the Education Committee. Obviously, there will be clear links between these services and the schools and colleges. It is intended that education services should be effectively co-ordinated with all aspects of living, in work, recreation or leisure, and every effort will be made to tell those who live in Milton Keynes what services are available, as well as to find out what supplementary provision they would like to have. The interim proposals of the Development Corporation suggest that there is good reason to regard education as a dominant component in future cities and suggest that Milton Keynes could be the first to be planned as a 'City for Learning'.

25

Nottingham

John Newson and Lea Lowinger

Nottingham is a city of some 310,000 people in the English East Midlands. As far as estimates are available, the population is not rapidly expanding at the present time. There is a preference, amongst those who can afford it, to live in the suburban areas, as the houses in the centre tend to be old and lack modern conveniences; as a consequence there is a decaying city centre. The city is thus composed of a central high density area surrounded by a ring of suburban areas. Within the city as a whole a third of the population live in Council-built houses. There is a plan (the Maud Report) for placing the city and county (which contains a number of important suburban areas) under one administration. The figures given in this article refer to the city alone, but obviously the conurbation is more extensive than this; there is, for instance, a higher proportion of working class people in the city than there would be in the whole conurbation.

The age distribution has remained stable since 1951, and the 1966 distribution is shown below:

TABLE 1

Age (years)	0–4	5–14	15–19	20–29	30–44	45–59	60–64	65 and older	
per cent	8·9	14·8	8.3	12·5	18·7	19·5	5·6	11·7	100

The population is not unduly weighted either by young people or by people above the age of retirement.

Over the years there has been a general movement out of the city. The Census also reports that about 6 per cent of the population move to better parts of the city itself in the course of a year. Of all working people, 17 per cent work outside the city – of these 44 per cent travel to work by bus and 30 per cent by car. 47 per cent of those who work in Nottingham go to work by bus and 11 per cent go by car.

The City's Economy

Nottingham has a high proportion of female workers, and this rate of 38 per cent carries with it an illegitimacy rate which is twice the national average. 51 per cent of the population is female. Nottingham is prosperous, having a wide variety of industries; for example, Players the cigarette manufacturers, Boots the Chemists, and Raleigh Industries which make bicycles, mopeds, toys and gears. The city is well-known for its lace trade. Nowadays only 6 per cent of the population work in the declining coal industry. The average salary is £1,101 compared to an East Midland's average of £1,102 and a national average of £1,164 but, as no breakdown of salary by sex is available, all we may deduce is that probably male workers receive a higher salary than the figure of £1,101 indicates. 2·5 per cent of people are unemployed, and this figure is similar to that for England and Wales, but is somewhat higher than that for the East Midlands as a whole. As in the rest of England, there is a surplus of unemployed unskilled labour.

As Nottingham is not in a development area there are financial incentives for industry to move out; nonetheless there are a considerable number of new developments taking place. There has also been much commercial redevelopment in terms of blocks of new offices in the city centre.

The social class breakdown for the city and that for England and Wales is as follows:

TABLE 2

Social Class	Nottingham 1966 per cent	England and Wales 1961 per cent
1 (Professional)	2·8	2·8
2 (Managerial)	10·5	13·4
3 (Skilled Labour)	50·2	43·5
4 (Semi-skilled Labour)	25·1	18·3
5 (Unskilled Labour)	10·5	7·2
Other	0·9	14·8
	100·0	100·0

Although Nottingham has more working class people (i.e. classes 3, 4, and 5) than does the country as a whole, the two sets of figures are broadly comparable. Comparison with previous census figures would appear to indicate that the proportion of unskilled labour in the population of Nottingham has been declining in recent years.

Social Services

The range of social services provided by both local authority and voluntary agencies is reasonably comprehensive. Included are: mental health services, probation work, reform schools, hospital work, education welfare, child care, the welfare of the coloured community, the aged, housing, the poor child and family, and many more.

Cultural Amenities

The cultural amenities of the city are not unreasonable; amongst them are two theatres, one of which, the Nottingham Playhouse, has a national reputation both for its architecture and for the high standard of its productions. The comprehensive library service makes a special effort to appeal to children. A recent survey has shown that 42 per cent of 7 year-olds are library members. There is a gallery of the Midland Group of Artists, and two other art galleries and a museum are maintained by the Corporation. The city does not maintain an orchestra.

Politics

The politics in Nottingham broadly reflect those at the national level; the majority of councillors represent either the Conservative or Labour Party. At present the control is in the hands of the Conservatives, but over the past 10 years the political balance has been mainly in favour of the local Labour Party. The Labour Party has, however, tended to adopt a bi-partisan attitude in that no major policy change is effected without the consent of the minority party. For instance, although the central Labour Party has officially been in favour of comprehensive education for some years, Nottingham still has not adopted any radical plan of comprehensive education. A comprehensive school is one which caters for children of all abilities, and which, as there are no fees within the State system of education, would tend to give children of poor families the same educational opportunities as those from rich families. It also ensures that children who develop intellectually after the age of 11 years are not discriminated against as they tend to be in a two-school (bi-partied) system, that is where a small proportion of children are selected for grammar school education at the age of 11. There is only one comprehensive school at present and that, in fact, is a boys' school situated on one of the larger Corporation housing estates and therefore serving an almost entirely working class catchment area.

Immigrants in Nottingham

An unofficial estimate of the number of immigrants in Nottingham is 15,000, of which approximately 60 per cent are West Indian, 20 per cent

Indian and Asian, and 16 per cent Pakistani and Muslims of Asiatic origin. Within each group there is much in-fighting for social dominance and this has a retarding effect on the absorption of the minority culture into the majority one. In 1958 there were some 'race riots' in Nottingham, but it is considered that these were magnified out of proportion by the press and television. A few minor ghetto areas have developed within the city.

Poverty in the City Centre

The areas known as 'The Meadows', 'Radford' and 'St Ann's' constitute Nottingham's zone of decay; the latter area has been the topic of much controversy, and a film on poverty in St Ann's was shown in 1969 on Independent Television. Thus we shall discuss mainly St Ann's, because although no older than the other parts of the decay zone, the homes are in poorer condition and much research has been conducted since 1966 on this area by the Social Sciences Department of the University of Nottingham. St Ann's is overcrowded, having 62·6 persons per acre, whereas the city as a whole has a density of 17·0 persons per acre.

Within the zone of decay the problems of poverty and immigration overlap. The fact that many West Indians are forced to live in multi-occupied tenements may partially account for the appallingly high incidence of infant mortality shown in the table below.

TABLE 3

National Rate	19·0 Deaths per thousand
Nottingham Rate	27·38 Deaths per thousand
West Indian Rate	52·02 Deaths per thousand

St Ann's is classed as a re-development area, and the policy is for 10,000 homes to be demolished by 1976. If one takes into account that the number of houses here is equivalent to those in a whole small town, one wonders how likely it is that this ambition will be fulfilled. The Government refused to sanction the contract for the first phase of the demolition process because it had not formally been given out to tender, and this has already led to some delay.

Poverty may be defined as 'existing in a family where the income is not more than 40 per cent above its entitlement from the Ministry of Social Security'. It is of note that half, i.e. 5,000, of the 10,000 poor people in St Ann's (by this definition) are children, and also half, again 5,000, of all the children in St Ann's are poor. In St Ann's about 10 per cent of people live in overcrowded conditions, but again this figure includes a disproportionately high number of children.

Education in Nottingham

According to the Department of Education and Science, Nottingham qualifies as an educational priority area by having at least 6 per cent immigrants and 2 per cent overcrowded homes. Because of this the Government has recently granted 300 extra nursery places to the city.

17 per cent of the population of Nottingham is at school. In January 1968 there were 33,625 children at Primary and Special schools, and 20,306 children at Secondary schools. For 1968/69 there were:

  4 Nursery Schools (2–5 years)
113 Primary Schools of which
  42 were Infant (5–7) years
  40 were Junior (7–11 years)
  19 were Junior and Infant and
  12 were Voluntary (all being denominational, 11 being for Juniors and Infants, and 1 being for Infants)
9 Special schools (e.g. for subnormal pupils, physically handicapped children, etc.)
26 Bilateral Schools (3 being denominational, 11–16 years)
4 Secondary Modern Schools (11–15 years)
8 Grammar Schools (2 being denominational, 11–18 years)
2 High Schools (11–18 years, fee paying)

At the high schools a number of pupils are supported on scholarships provided by the Local Education Authority (L.E.A.). A few of the Infant schools have nursery classes for 3- to 5-year olds.

Expenditure on Education

Expenditure on education must first be sanctioned by the Government. To quote from a national newspaper,[1] 'Officials in Nottingham City feel that the squeeze on school buildings (in reply to the Maud Report) is making nonsense of their hopes for reorganization; in three years they have had the Department's approval for only one secondary project worth a mere 150 places, and by 1970 they could be 6,000 secondary places short.' Eighteen schools have been requested, and the city expects to get four. The raising of the school leaving age to 16 years would add 2½–3,000 pupils to the roll, this and the peak in births in 1964 lead to the figure of 6,000 places needed.

The gross estimated expenditure for Nottingham for 1969/70 is about

---

[1] *Guardian*, 25th January, 1969.

£23 million, of which approximately £12½ million is to be spent on education. The estimated breakdown of this expenditure on education is:

TABLE 4

	per cent
Pure administration, inspectors etc.	1·8
Contribution to L.E.A. pool	0·4
Primary education	25·2
Secondary education	27·2
Further education	36·8
School meals (12 per cent of children have free meals)	6·2
School Health including child care, psychologists, speech therapists	1·2
Repairs, Renewal Fund, Revenue contribution to capital outlay	1·2

£12,448,630 = 100·0

(Total expenditure on teachers' salaries, including remedial teachers, comes to £4½ million.)

It can be seen that more than a third of the expenditure is on Further Education, from which, of course, not all children benefit. In common with other L.E.A.s, Nottingham receives financial help for Further Education from other L.E.A.s via the pool. For instance, the sum of £4,583,000 for Further Education includes a 20 per cent grant by Nottingham's L.E.A. for the Regional College and the College of Art and Design, but the remaining 80 per cent is provided by the pool. Thus, in the end, Further Education gets an even larger proportion of the total than the above suggests.

Selection of Children to Secondary Schools

To understand the function of secondary selection, it is necessary to appreciate the distinctions between the different types of secondary schools which are available. At the top of the hierarchy are the grammar schools and the independent high schools which specialize in preparing children for Advanced Level ('A' Level) examinations, which are a necessary prerequisite for entrance to all universities, and for the better technical and teacher training colleges. All children at grammar schools are automatically entered for the Ordinary Level ('O' Level) examinations, which precede study for Advanced Level. It is also true that 'A' level qualifications are required for most management training schemes in industry.

The bilateral schools, although they do not prepare children for 'A' level, do allow pupils to sit for the 'O' level examinations. If they pass these in a sufficient number of subjects, the children become eligible for transfer to grammar schools where they can take 'A' level examinations.

However, the staff are usually less well-qualified than those in grammar schools, and the academic facilities are generally somewhat poorer, so that in practice this route is only followed by a small minority of children.

The secondary modern schools do not in general prepare their children even for 'O' level examinations. The majority of children in the secondary modern and bilateral schools leave at the statutory school leaving age of 15 years.

A comprehensive school is similar to a bilateral school except that it has facilities for sixth-form study, including preparation for 'A' level examinations. Within the lower age ranges it is geared to cope with children of all levels of intellectual ability, but those who succeed well academically can stay on up to the age of 18 years as in a grammar school.

It must be understood that for a child of given intelligence, the route to higher education is much easier via a grammar school or one of the independent high schools, and in consequence the question of selection has been one of ardent political debate.

Selection of grammar schools is still largely based upon verbal reasoning tests. All children in their last year at primary school take two tests, on the basis of which each primary school is allocated a number of places at grammar schools. The actual verbal reasoning quotients obtained are known to the head-teacher, but the pupils are not named. On the basis of his knowledge about each child's abilities and attainments, the head-teacher must then make the decision of which children are allowed to go to grammar school. In practice the same children appear to be chosen by both the head-teachers and the test, since it is claimed that there is a 96 per cent agreement between the two. However, if the parents are dissatisfied, the child is referred to an educational psychologist who is empowered to review the decision.

Parents are sent a form from the Director of Education on which they indicate which type of secondary education they would like their child to be considered for, i.e. grammar, high school, bilateral or denominational. The wording on the form is such that parents are led to believe they have no choice between schools. Their attention is not drawn to the 1944 Education Act which permits a choice; even if their child is selected for grammar school, parents are only told to which school he has been allocated. The L.E.A. says that should there be good reasons for a parent wishing his child to go to a particular school then this would be allowed.

Of the pupils at L.E.A. schools, approximately 18 per cent are at grammar schools, 7 per cent at the comprehensive, 5 per cent at secondary modern schools and 70 per cent at bilateral schools. In practice, schools located in middle class residential areas send a much higher proportion of children to grammar schools than those located in the poorer areas. For instance, in one residential area 60 per cent of children go to grammar schools.

Since the majority of children are in bilateral schools, greater equality of educational opportunity could be achieved by the provision of sixth-form colleges for all children who wish to continue their studies beyond 'O' level. This is part of the city's long-term plan for education, and if it was put into effect, the grammar schools would cease to function in the way they do now. No sixth-form colleges exist at this time in Nottingham. The tendency for children in Nottingham to stay on at school beyond 15 years is shared with other parts of the country. Another aim is to develop vocational and non-vocational courses in higher education for the age range 16 to 19 years out of school; the L.E.A. hopes that this will take place during the next ten years, and claims that it has not rushed in to the comprehensive system in order to allow itself time to prepare the ground.

Further Education

Once children have left school there are a variety of institutions for further education which may be attended voluntarily or as part of day-release schemes for young people in employment. The People's College and Clarendon College provide 'O' and 'A' level General Certificate of Education courses together with a number of more specific vocational ones. At a slightly higher level there is the College of Art and Design and the Regional College. The latter includes a teacher-training department and a school of town and country planning. These two colleges are to be re-designed as a Polytechnic to start in January 1970. This will obviously constitute the next major administrative problem for the Educational Authority.

The University of Nottingham is not under the control of the Education Authority; its finances come mainly from the Central Government via the University Grants Committee, but the local authorities do pay fees for students from their areas to whichever University they attend. Like other civic universities Nottingham tends to draw its students from all over the country. In a similar way, the Nottingham College of Education at Clifton enjoys a national reputation as a teacher training college and is not under the direct control of the Nottingham L.E.A. Some non-vocational adult education courses are organized by the Workers' Educational Association in conjunction with Nottingham University's Extra-Mural Department, and other courses are run by the L.E.A.

Education and Immigrants

The impact of immigrants on schools would not be great if they were equally spread, but they do tend to cluster in a few areas. Thus there are some schools with a very high proportion of immigrants. There is a feeling amongst some white people that the presence of coloured children depresses the standard of schooling. Immigrants, especially those from the Punjab, do have considerable problems if English is not their first language.

Official L.E.A. figures state that at primary and special schools 7 per cent are coloured pupils, at secondary schools 5 per cent, but these figures are underestimates because they exclude coloured children born in the U.K. whose parents came to the U.K. before 1958, and they also exclude children of mixed immigrant and non-immigrant parentage. The universal problem is for teachers to appreciate the cultural shock experienced by immigrants, and it is unfortunate to find that in 1969 only two teachers in Nottingham took advantage of the opportunity provided by the Department of Education and Science of a course in the methods of teaching immigrant children.

The cultural difference between children of West Indian and Indian/Asian parents is of some importance. The latter children tend to make better academic progress at school than do the West Indian children, whose parents favour the traditional formal approach to schooling. This could be because in India, unlike the West Indies, higher education has been established for a long time.

Education and the Zone of Decay

There have been a few recent studies on poverty in the zone of decay – one of these relating to St Ann's suggests that only 1·5 per cent of the child population is accepted for grammar schools, compared with 18 per cent of all children. Also, as many as 91 per cent of primary school leaving children in St Ann's go to secondary modern schools, compared to 5 per cent of all children. It has also been suggested that in this area 40 per cent of the children come from broken homes. A project in the Meadows area showed that, in one school, 65 per cent of pupils lived in homes in which their families shared accommodation with other families, and of the 96 children taking school meals, 55 were qualified to take them free of charge.

Many of the schools in the decay area are in dilapidated and old-fashioned buildings. The teachers tend not to live in these areas and there is a high rate of staff turnover. These are among the facts which contribute to poor academic progress, particularly in relation to reading ability at the primary school level.

Teacher Training

It must be stressed that any problems of teacher training and facilities etc. should be looked at on a national level. The organization of teacher training is a central process. Money is allocated direct from the Government from the teacher training pool to which every L.E.A. contributes. Nottingham does well out of this – the contribution to the pool is £45,000, and the upkeep alone of one of Nottingham's teacher training colleges comes to £750,000 per year.

The College of Education at Clifton previously referred to is one of the newest and largest of 164 such establishments in the country. In addition, the Regional College has facilities for teacher training, and this will have its first output of teachers in 1970. The course here is encouraged by the Department of Education and Science as part of a drive to recruit mature married women back to teaching. At the Regional College and at Clifton the staffing ratio is about 1 to 10. There could be a problem in 1970 in that new teachers from the Regional College in Nottingham might be competing for jobs against those newly qualified at Clifton. As married women teachers are not mobile, they are thus likely to be given preference.

All colleges of teacher training are now allowed to teach for a degree awarded by the local university. There have consequently been enormous changes in the curriculum and in the level of work undertaken. Before 1960 the basic training took two years, in 1960 it became a three-year course and in 1965 the first B.Ed. courses started. Hence it is understandable that there has been considerable extra administrative work.

The supply of teachers in Nottingham is more than adequate; unfortunately there is not enough classroom space for new teachers in the schools which need them most. The overall ratio of teachers to pupils is approximately 1 to 24, but primary classes of 38 children are not at all uncommon.

In conclusion, we can do no better than to quote Professor D. V. Donnison of the London School of Economics. In an article recently published in a national newspaper[2] he said 'The next twenty years will tell whether we succeed or fail in arresting the tendency of urban industrial societies to disintegrate into increasingly affluent suburban majorities living around the fringes of deprived minorities, increasingly degraded (and who knows) ultimately violent'. The problem Nottingham faces is to provide as adequate education for children left in the decaying city zone as is obtainable in the better city suburbs.

MAIN SOURCES

Census figures – England and Wales 1951, 1961 and 1966.
Ministry of Employment and Productivity – Nottingham Exchange Area figures.
Ministry of Technology – Board of Trade.
Ken Coates and Richard Silburn 'St Ann's' Nottingham University, Department of Adult Education, 1967.
1965 Report of the Medical Officer of Health.
City of Nottingham Committee 1968/69 Handbook.
City of Nottingham Education Committee Return of Immigrant Pupils, January 1968.

---

[2] *Guardian*, 12th January, 1969.

26

Rotterdam and Its Educational Reforms

J. H. N. Grandia

History of Rotterdam

The social structure of the population and the social life of Rotterdam are largely determined by the fact that this town is a world port and exists on world trade. First records show that Rotterdam started as a fishing village about the middle of the thirteenth century A.D. Town rights were probably granted in 1328 and from 1340 onward, Rotterdam developed into a sea port. Trade and shipping flourished in the sixteeth century and the ports were greatly extended.

A century later, both the United East India Company and the West India Company established offices and warehouses in Rotterdam. The further development of the town was stimulated about 1870 by the opening of the Suez Canal, by the prosperous state of affairs in the Dutch East Indies, by the unification of Germany and by the emergence of the Ruhr area. In 1872 the *Nieuwe Waterweg* (i.e. New Waterway, a specially dug canal) was opened and provided Rotterdam with direct access to the sea.

The Harbours of Rotterdam

Until the middle of the nineteeth century, the man-made harbours in the town could cope with the shipping traffic. However, the increase in length and in draught of sea-going vessels necessitated the digging of new harbours after 1850. Since the end of World War II, the port and industrial areas have been extended at an ever-increasing pace, especially through the opening-up of the Botlek and Europoort areas.

The Economic Structure of Rotterdam

Opportunities for employment are to a great extent determined by the port industry. Rotterdam is a transit port to and from the Ruhr area and it is also an oil port, as well as the most important home port for Dutch inland shipping. The port activities have stimulated the growth of ship building and ship repairing yards and also the metal industry. Further developments led to coal and oil bunkering facilities and a chemical industry.

Geographical Expansions

It is said of Rotterdam that it is a collection of annexed villages; indeed, during the nineteenth and twentieth centuries a great number of previously independent communities were annexed by Rotterdam.

Destruction and Reconstruction

On May 14th, 1940 the centre of the town was virtually obliterated by German air force bombing. More than 400 acres of built-up area were destroyed, including some 250 acres of roads, squares and city parks. Four days later, on May 18th, 1940, the Corporation ordered a plan to be drawn up for the reconstruction of the city centre. Compared with the previous centre, the present one is more characterized by a commercial and banking atmosphere, big industrial concerns having moved out.

Population

Up to 1960 there was a steady, sometimes spectacular, increase in population; e.g. 8,000 inhabitants in 1550, 50,000 in 1800, 332,000 in 1900 and 729,000 in 1960. Since then, however, a small decline has set in, chiefly due to better-off people moving out of the central town to more rural villages in the district.

In 1968 the religious classification was as follows: 25 per cent Roman Catholics, 46 per cent Protestants, 4 per cent other religions, 25 per cent not belonging to any denomination.

In the same year the social structure of the population was roughly as follows: 65 per cent lower class, 30 per cent middle class and 5 per cent upper class.

Housing Conditions

The economic revival and the industrial expansion since the second half of the nineteenth century have stimulated the opportunities for employment in Rotterdam. Great numbers of workers were needed for the digging of harbours, the loading and unloading of ships, etc.; these workers were drawn from nearby and outlying districts. Also, the agricultural crisis from 1878 to 1895 induced many labourers to look for work in the town. To cope with this flow of immigrants, extensive blocks of houses were built without any specific architectural plan in mind, thus giving a rather disorderly impression. The uncontrolled building of houses led to many unhappy situations, such as communal bedrooms in the lofts of houses. Later, the alcove system was used to house as many people as possible in cramped conditions. For a long time there were, and to a certain extent there still are, some miserable housing conditions.

An 1899 census showed that 58 per cent of the Rotterdam population lived in one-roomed habitations. In a social and pedagogical sense it is highly unsatisfactory that unfavourable housing conditions still exist in our present time, in spite of newly built residential districts. A recent sociological survey, made in an old district near the centre of the town, shows that out of 145 habitations, 82 had one room, 41 had two rooms, 13 had three rooms, 6 had four rooms, 1 had five rooms, 1 had six rooms and 1 had seven rooms. Of these 145 habitations, only 67 had a separate kitchen and their own toilet. Baths or showers were virtually non-existent. It was also clear from the survey that due to lack of space, children had to sleep on the floor or in one bed with their parents. From a pedagogical viewpoint this is a serious matter, because the children become acquainted at too early an age with the sexual life of adults; therefore, because they have not generally learned how to control themselves, these children will soon proceed to sexual contact themselves, leading to psychical damage.

The irresponsible house-building during the second half of the nineteenth century resulted in dreary residential districts for workers, with dismal roads and houses. Because of the specific sub-culture that has developed among the inhabitants of these districts, they seldom avail themselves of the educational and cultural provisions of the town.

The Social Rearguard

The term 'social rearguard' means that adults in our community who have grown up in a simple workers' environment have been socially retarded through pedagogical neglect in their childhood and years of adolescence, and also because of economic circumstances which make it difficult for them to educate their children in conformity with the requirements of modern citizenship. This social rearguard is partly formed by unskilled labourers and their families, as well as street vendors, small traders and, occasionally, skilled labourers who could not or would not break away from this environment and who will remain within this group on account of their ideas and mode of life. It is this social rearguard that lives in the poor districts and slums of the nineteenth century.

What does it mean pedagogically for the child to have to grow up in these conditions? The streets are narrow and dirty; usually there are no playing grounds or sports fields, nor any enclosed spaces where the little ones can play. The neighbourhood offers little or nothing to satisfy the urge for exploration, the desire for adventure, and for being engaged in something without being disturbed at it. As the cramped living space offers little or no opportunity for playing, the child will become bored and may revert to hooliganism and vandalism. It is not imaginary that the mental poverty of these young persons, in view of their restricted and superficial interests, is the result of their having been 'homeless' in earlier years, rather than of inferior talents. After all, they have not had the opportunity to explore, so that qualities such as imagination, insight, concentration, etc. have not been activated enough and have not developed sufficiently. This is why it is stressed among pedagogues that the child's own living space and its own world to play in are so important. If these are lacking, the individualization of the person to be educated (essential for a differentiated personality structure) cannot take place in a satisfactory way.

Work for Neglected Children

The circumstances in which children grow up in the slums of Rotterdam led local residents to found an institution for neglected children as early as 1853. This institution was a success, so that in 1894 a new school was opened with 10 classrooms for 50 pupils each, and also a gymnasium and a bathroom; rather progressive thinking for those days! Tuition was daily from 9 a.m. to 4 p.m.; the girls then stayed behind for another two hours to learn sewing and knitting. On Saturdays, the boys received lessons in repairing shoes and mending torn clothes. According to the head of the school, these boys would be dock-hands in due course, but they would at least be able to repair the shoes and mend the clothes of the family. As the children were physically under-developed, they received lessons in gymnastics. To instil a feeling for neatness and cleanliness a barber came to the school once a week to cut the children's hair, and they had a weekly bath. Also, hot meals were provided during the midday rest. Changing social circumstances and the increase in prosperity led to a drastic drop in the number of pupils, so that the institution is now closed.

The Descendents of the Neglected Children

The descendents of the neglected children from the nineteenth century live in the antiquated popular districts of Rotterdam. Socially and culturally speaking, these inhabitants lead more or less isolated lives as their social contacts are limited and as only few of them participate in corporate life. It is very difficult for them to get a clear picture of the society structure because they are not able to obtain objective information and to make use of the social provisions supplied by the city, such as a vocational guidance bureaux or evening schools. As a result, the young people growing up in this environment know little about the possibilities outside this circle and, like their parents, show very little ambition. They start their social careers as unskilled labourers.

Among the families of this social rearguard, because of the low level of development of the parents, one finds very little interest in the activities of the children at school. This is not conducive to the work of the children, nor to their attitude to study. Besides, there is insufficient room for them at home to do their homework properly. And the parents, because of their ignorance and inner uncertainty, cannot discuss with the teachers the progress of their children and their possible careers. For these children, normal primary schools are inadequate because not enough consideration is given to their environment, their unfavourable educational circumstances, their defective and limited command of language, their lack of wider social and cultural interests, and the absence of plans for the future. Moreover a considerable ignorance exists among these people of the possibilities of any further education, because ideas of education in general and of further education in particular, are beyond their grasp. Consequently, vocational training for these young people is not a reality, or if they do get any training it is very incomplete. Neither are they prepared for the life of a trained worker, and their further social education is also wholly neglected. As a result, there are great differences between the educational circumstances of children in the lower strata of society and of children in socially higher levels. In our society not everybody gets equal opportunity in respect of:

(1) The possibility of attaining an all-round development of his or her personality.
(2) The right kind of education.
(3) Knowledge of how to spend one's free time.
(4) Choice of trade and profession, and the necessary training and study.

This social neglect is highly unsatisfactory because a democratic society in which all adults get the right kind of opportunities for development, is attacked in its basic conditions, as society is dependent for its existence on the insight and social responsibility of its citizens. Society may not tolerate, therefore, the neglect of talents which can support and stimulate personal responsibility. The Rotterdam authorities, therefore, have set themselves the task of improving the educational situation, the training possibilities and the perspectives of the future, by taking certain social-pedagogical measures and provisions.

A Social-Pedagogical Project

It has been found that the young persons of the antiquated districts in Rotterdam receive little or no further education, because, among other factors, of poor achievements at lower school levels and of their parents' not realizing the significance of education for the formation of personality and the social future of their children.

However, educational experiments have shown that, for children whose father has a low professional status and who live in the city popular districts and slums, it is also possible to bring about a more positive approach toward school life and to increase the ability to learn. Increasing the child's ability to learn, as well as the parents' realization of the importance of further school education, can considerably promote the socialization of education, i.e. there will be a greater participation from the socially lower strata in secondary level and university education.

These viewpoints have led to a social-pedagogical project, the aims of which are as follows:

To influence in a positive way the educational situation of these children.
To increase their ability to learn.
To promote participation in further studies and the completion of these studies.
To help them prepare for a professional career.

Explanation of the Aims of the Project

Generally speaking, among families in the socially lower levels there is little understanding of the demands made on pupils by schools. Proper guidance can improve the education situation for the child in such a way that the parents will not only acquaint themselves with the child's progress of study, but they will also be prepared to co-operate so that the child may perform his educational duties as well as possible.

The improvement of the educational situation of the children should take place at school. Among other things, efforts will be made within the framework of current legislature to break through the classroom system so that the pupil may receive more personal attention. Opportunity should also be given to do homework at school.

Increasing the child's ability to learn can be effected by increasing linguistic ability and study concentration, by strengthening a sense of order and discipline as well as study motivation; however, this is a matter to be taken in hand by the child itself, by the family looking after the child and by the school attended by the child. Many factors will have to co-operate in order to arrive at satisfactory study achievements. Children should not participate in secondary level education as a mere means of attaining school-leaving age, but in order to complete an advanced training. Therefore, pupils of primary schools should be given such a picture of life that they will think it only natural for them to progress towards secondary level education. In contrast to middle groups and socially higher levels, it is not a matter of course in the socially lower environments to take secondary level education.

In spite of all efforts made by the teachers at primary schools, a number of pupils will not be willing or able to take secondary education. During their last year at school, these pupils should be offered a social-cultural education that will not only facilitate their entry into society, but also influence the way in which they spend their free time. In order to realize the aims outlined above, the following points have been considered:

(1) Drawing up a 'play-study' plan for pupils at infant schools situated in typical popular districts where most of the pupils will come from the socially lower levels; this will prepare the children better for the time when they move on to primary school.

(2) By way of trial, the formation of small classrooms at infant schools for 3-year-olds, in order to examine the possibilities of stimulating the acquisition and usage of language by children of this age.

(3) Involving the pupils' mothers in the work done at the infant schools to give them more insight into the significance of play in respect of the emotional and intellectual development of the child, and also to inform the mothers of the possibilities of play for these infants within the family.

(4) Drawing up a flexible study plan in order to increase the ability to learn, to reduce drastically the incidence of 'staying down', and to make the child familiar with the thought of continuing its studies after having attained school-leaving age.

(5) Observing and analysing the school career of the pupils, from infant school to secondary level.

(6) A regular co-operation between infant and primary schools and between primary schools and institutions for advanced studies.

(7) Contact, discussion and co-operation between families, schools and institutions for social-cultural development, in order to achieve a favourable climate of education for the child.

(8) The ultimate target is that, after ten years of didactic conduct of the pupils and influencing the parents in a social-pedagogical way, 30 per cent of the children will move on to advanced general education and 60 per cent to lower professional education. The remaining 10 per cent will not take any further education. It is expected that 10 per cent of the children will finish the advanced general education prematurely, i.e. without school-leaving certificate; for the pupils at the lower professional education this is expected to be 20 per cent.

Choice of Residential Areas

After careful consideration it has been decided to start with this project in two city districts. They are antiquated popular districts, whose inhabitants are mainly unskilled and untrained labourers, working in factories, the ports or in transport. For many years there have been district club houses so that contacts do exist for the start of discussions between the schools in these districts and the social-cultural institutions there. These districts have not yet been earmarked for slum clearance. It is, therefore, important to be active socially-pedagogically there, in order to prevent further impoverishment.

Size of the Project

Six infant schools and ten primary schools will participate in the project. An estimated 2,000 pupils (1,000 families) and 85 teachers will be involved. Others involved will be the writer of this article as project leader; a sociologist; four didacticists; two visiting-teachers; a 'social contact' man and an administrator. The cost will be met by the Government and by the Rotterdam Corporation.

Project Schools and Evaluation Schools

The name of 'project schools' will be given to the six infant schools where work will be done along the lines of a 'play-study' plan, and to the ten primary schools for which an experimental study plan will also be drawn up. At the same time, other infant and primary schools, similar in respect of the social composition of the pupils, study means and study level, will be chosen. To these schools the name of 'evaluation schools' will be given. They will not be didactically conducted and no influence will be exerted on day-to-day progress at these schools. It is the intention to compare annually the results of the pupils at the project schools with those at the evaluation schools. Investigations will be made as to the percentage of pupils progressing to advanced education and the level of this education, in order to compare these figures with those at the evaluation schools. It will then be possible to form an impartial opinion about any progress made through didactic conduct of pupils and teachers, in what form this progress was made, and to determine what factors have been of decided stimulating importance. It will have to be borne in mind that the evaluation schools will also be subject to changes, and may adjust themselves didactically to new ideas.

Co-operation between Family and School

Surveys have shown the great importance of regular discussions between families and schools. It has also been shown that parents who belong to the social rearguard as far as their professional level, their residential district and their mode of life are concerned, cannot adequately discuss the educational problems of their children with the teachers. They have also little understanding of the effort required from their children if they are to do well at school. Lack of room and time to study at home make it much more difficult for the child, especially at secondary school level.

The above considerations suggest that it is socially-pedagogically important for the child to know that a more or less 'institutionalized' contact exists between family and school through visits to the parents' homes. This contact is not only intended to learn to know better the family environment of the pupils, but also to involve the parents more intensively in the school life of their children. These visits will be made by specially appointed pedagogical advisers, after full discussions with the schools in question; this is done so as not to overburden the teachers connected with the project. These pedagogical advisers must have had some years' teaching experience, and should inform the teachers of the domestic and personal circumstances of their pupils.

Co-operation between Schools

To realize a 'play-study' plan for the infants, it is desirable to have a close co-operation and regular contact between the teachers of the schools to be chosen for the project. It is also necessary that the teachers of the primary schools should have regular contact and should work closely together as far as the execution of the experimental study programme is concerned.

As the essential facet of this project is to prepare the infant for school and to facilitate the move from infant school to primary school, it is advisable to bring about discussions and co-operation between the teachers of the infant and primary schools chosen for the project.

Co-operation with Institutions for Social-Cultural Education

The aim of this project is, in fact, to remove the social rearguard and to prevent the social backwardness caused by insufficient participation in advanced studies. The socially lower levels in particular do not realize the 'key function of the schools' for developing and enriching the personality and for acquiring a social position. This backwardness is not always the result of intellectual inability, but is also caused by social-cultural factors. It has been proved that the way of life of a family may be of great significance to the child in this respect. That is why institutions for social-cultural education are trying to influence the way of life of families in order to improve the children's educational situation so that they may have more opportunities for personal and social development. For this reason, efforts will be made to bring about contact and discussions between the schools involved in the project and the institutions for social-cultural education active in these districts. It will then be possible to achieve a more comprehensive influence on the educational situation of the children from the social rearguard.

27

Rome

Anacleto Benedetti

Anyone who has to deal with the administrative problems of the City of Rome must first overcome a psychological difficulty. A city in bonds to centuries of admiration and affection from the whole world, a unique treasurehouse in the context of the history of human development, Rome seems ill-adjusted to be considered as merely an urban complex set within the framework of the economic development of its environment. The Rome pictured in literature and carried in the imagination of those visitors who have sought devotedly to discover its real spirit and strength, still overlays the image of the Rome of today, with its heterogeneity and its confusion, in search of its own identity as a modern metropolis.

This difficulty in approaching the real Rome may be seen not only in the state of mind of the individual observer. It is also reflected in the course taken by the city in the analysis and understanding of its own problems.

The problems which Rome confronts as a result of its cultural heritage and of the fact that it belongs to all the world are not easily found to be commensurate with the problems deriving from its position as capital of Italy, and therefore as a national and regional centre of administration. The difficulty the city encounters in keeping the 'evocative' atmosphere dear to its visitors, and at the same time in attaining the efficiency demanded by its demographic development and its function as a capital, is the source of many problems. Rome has not succeeded in establishing a proper relationship with both its own region and the country as a whole to which as a capital it should give unity and expression. It appears in fact to be isolated from both. The inability of the city to answer to these exigencies sometimes makes the Italian citizens feel deluded and resentful, especially those living in the northern cities who are used to a higher standard of industrial efficiency and are intolerant of the capital's bureaucracy.

The city is located in a region which has not yet brought to full fruition the process of industrialization. In the formation of the gross national product, the contributions of its industry and agriculture are below the national average. Above average, on the other hand, is the rate of employment in tertiary activities. Rome lives largely from tourism.

As a centre of public administration and political life, it has a strong power of attraction extending over the whole metropolitan area which demands that the city provides new opportunities for economic development. The rate of immigration towards the city is always increasing. Rome has not yet succeeded in absorbing these immigrants productively, nor in establishing a healthy economy other than tourism. In fact, its urban expansion seems a phenomenon out of all proportion to the process of economic development within the region; the latter has therefore not developed according to any preordained planning but with much unevenness and incongruity. By itself Rome cannot solve its problems as a city and a capital. The city's income is poor both because of the many diplomatic immunities and because of the low level of contribution made by the immigrant population. It hardly covers the salaries of the personnel indispensable to the public services as well as interest on loans previously made.

This lack of equilibrium between demographic size and territorial extent of the city and its resources, taking into account its needs for national and international representation, explains why the City Council of Rome is one of those most in debt in the world. Already some years ago the *Financial Times* of London interested itself in this complex human and economic phenomenon. To financial indebtedness one must also add a hidden debt consisting of the large mass of indispensable public works which have not been carried out. The city's local authorities have therefore requested the help of the State, declaring that the efficiency of its administrative machinery is of the greatest importance to the whole country. They requested state assistance not to meet the debt, but as an investment in an economic expansion which could accelerate the city's attainment to some degree of self-sufficiency.

The particular economic structure of the area, its lack of equilibrium in terms of population and income distribution create some specific problems in the field of educational policy. There is an obvious disproportion between the economic resources which can be produced locally and the educational services which a heavy demographic concentration renders necessary. This problem is particularly acute in the sector of school buildings.

Both demographic expansion, which orientates any new building programme towards the periphery of the city, and the extension of the obligatory school-leaving age, pose problems with which the authorities concerned are not always equipped to deal. Such problems are also aggravated by the uncertainties caused through the division of responsibility among the various decision-making organizations involved in the different phases of education programmes.

In Italy the schools are mostly state-run so far as their financing, direction and control are concerned, but decisions as to the areas and places in which individual schools operate are within the competence of each local authority. The various authorities concerned do not always succeed in completing their respective duties and projects within the allotted time and according to the method imposed by the established programmization. Channeling of the various programmes is unfortunately both long and complicated. This fact renders both costs and gestation periods for school building programmes particularly unsatisfactory, given the complexity of the administrative channels which any official business must follow.[1]

Legislative Difficulties

These difficulties, juridico-administrative in character, which are perhaps common to other great cities, are aggravated in Rome because of special legislation drawn up to protect Rome's exceptional artistic heritage.

The legislation requires, besides preliminary archaeological investigations, that there shall be official agreement before any construction is put in hand; and this renders extremely difficult or makes virtually impossible any kind of adaptation of the existing buildings to new functions. The procedure required in order to obtain such authorization is complex and sometimes discouraging. The time and costs for fitting out a building are long and complicated with a resulting increase in costs.

On the basis of the agreed town planning scheme for the city of Rome (3·65 square metres per person) 2·400 acres should have been set aside for the use of schools (excluding universities). Given the present census of population, the deficit in this respect is very great: more than 400 acres. A special working team has been set up to determine the actual area of the city already allocated to educational use and to search for new places. It is not unlikely that changes must be made in the town planning scheme if the deficit is to be met while still maintaining in force the accepted standard of 3·65 square metres per inhabitant. The average cost of a school building within the city boundaries is estimated at 17 million lire including the cost of the land itself and interior decoration; 12 million lire of this is required for the construction costs alone (1969 figures).

Specialized study commissions, appointed within this framework by Rome's City Council, are seeking to establish a realistic correlation between the rate of urbanization and the school population and the specific educational requirements as regards the building programme. In parti-

---

[1] When the projected school buildings are not ready in time, the education authority has to rent adjoining apartments and adapt them. The result is that many classes have to be divided in two to allow such premises to be utilized; so the number of teachers must be increased, with a further financial burden to be met. Sometimes classes which should contain 25 scholars contain 40 in the congested areas of the periphery, and only 12 in the central residential areas which are in the process of depopulation.

cular, experiments are to be carried out over a limited pilot area to ascertain the optimum type of educational organization.

In this respect, as it concerns the upper-middle school sector, a plan has been prepared by the city and provincial authorities acting in association, for the administration of a special school city which will function as a social centre in the afternoon. This project will be financed by city funds. The administration of the services available – sporting facilities, cinema, theatre, students' hostel – will be entrusted to a body consisting of the representatives of the city, the provincial authorities, the education authority and the students. Modification in the standard of school buildings is foreseen with regard to the eventual requirements of the lengthening of the obligatory period of school hours, either by the day or over the year.

The criterion to which the school building programme in Rome tries to conform is that of creating educational centres, open to the surrounding world. The idea behind this is to make the school a useful link with economic and social life, a centre offering educational services in which various extra-educational activities can take place, even on a professional scale.

A more detailed view of the educational problems confronting Rome as a result of urban expansion can be gained with the help of the following information. In an attempt to trace the general lines for an educational programme, the local education authority (*Provveditorato agli Studi*) has drawn up a 'plan' which by an analysis of the changes in the state of the school population in the last three years, makes a projection up to 1970. The increase in the school population of Rome was 10,000 pupils in 1966/7, 12, 000 in 1967/68 and 15,000 in 1968/69. If this rate of growth continues, the increase in the next few years will be in the order of 20,000 per year.

The number of new school entrants according to the Registry Office was 44,011 children for the year 1968/69. In 1968, 26,711 scholars took the middle school leaving examination and 18,309 the examination for a technical diploma.[2] Some of these children belong to families who have immigrated from the south of Italy and who are not yet established as part of the city's population nor fully assimilated.

In particular the school population in the higher grade schools increased

---

[2] The scholastic population of the City of Rome in the year 1967/68 was divided as follows:

Kindergarten	76,615	(City of Rome)
	18,900	(Province of Rome)
Elementary	165,736	(City of Rome)
	57,897	(Province of Rome)
Lower middle (*media I° ciclo*)	90,468	(City of Rome)
	+ 27,059	(Province of Rome)
Higher middle (*media II° ciclo*)	80,911	(City of Rome)
	11,970	(Province of Rome)

from 74,421 in 1964/65 to 89,144 in 1966/67. This increase of 19 per cent shows that the tendency towards the continuation of studies by those who have completed the obligatory stages of middle school education is an established phenomenon which can be based on uniform percentages, varying between 99·2 and 99·8 per cent. The size of the phenomenon is such that, according to the local authorities, it cannot be considered merely as a local problem.

Demographic Expansion

The following are the most significant indications of demographic expansion, as it concerns the educational planning in the various sectors:

(*a*) Fifteen classical grammar schools (*Licei Classici*) had 15,981 scholars divided into 545 classes. This sector has an annual increase which appears to vary between 400 and 500 pupils. What is wanted here is not so much new schools but rather research into a better way of sorting out the existing students and dividing them among the institutes in a different way. Within the historic centre of Rome there are several overpopulated institutes operating with 1,200 students divided among 40 classes.

(*b*) Scientific grammar schools (*Licei Scientifici*) had 10,000 students divided among 326 classes. In the last triennium the increase in numbers has been from 1,000 to 1,200 students per year. This increase has forced the education authority to use 40 classrooms for extra tuition in the afternoons. In this sector there is a need to open five new schools, both in order to make provision in zones which are lacking such institutes and to reduce the school population of those institutes (four out of every seven) which are operating with more than 1,000 students. (The new schools could be located in the districts which have the highest output of school-leavers per year. There are Roman districts with an average of 3,000 school-leavers per year.)

(*c*) The sector of grammar schools specializing in elementary teacher training (*Istituti Magistrali*) had 6,191 students divided into 192 classes. The annual increase is estimated to be between 700 and 800 students. Thirteen classes are given as extra tuition in the afternoons. Two schools have more than 1,200 students. In the province of Rome the increase is about 136 pupils per year and the existing schools are full to saturation point: 1,148 students in 41 classes. In this sector it seems necessary to provide two more specialized schools to assist those which at present have too many students.

(*d*) Fourteen technical and commercial institutes had 18,840 students divided among 637 classes. The annual increase is estimated to be 1,000 students. (The size of the phenomenon seems to be due to the decline of the technical institutes for girls and of the professional institutes which recruited only 6,278 students.) Since six institutes are operating with 1,300 students it would be necessary to establish seven others in zones which are still not provided with them.

(*e*) Eight technical industrial institutes had 14,804 students divided between 464 classes. The annual increase is estimated at 870 pupils. There is a need for four new institutes, both to relieve congestion (six institutes operate with more than 1,400 students) and to face the future expansion.

(*f*) Five technical institutes for girls had 1,318 students in 64 classes. The sector shows an alarming decline despite various attempts to introduce new subjects to encourage the admission of new students.

(*g*) Fourteen professional commercial institutes had 6,278 students in 292 classes. This sector is in decline; indeed one institute should cease to function. The only problem is a redistribution of the school population within the sector.

(*h*) The professional institutes for industry and handicrafts recruited 2,709 students into 183 classes. The annual increase estimated at 150 pupils can be absorbed by the existing structure.[3]

Given the above data, which are still insufficient to picture the demographic expansion, it is understandable that the gravity of the educational situation is such as to make it impossible in practice to draw up a programme based on choice by priority. Choice is possible only on a basis of emergency.

The task of making Rome a large city capable not only of maintaining the spirit it derives from the unique spiritual heritage which it preserves, but also for providing better conditions of life, work and education for its citizens, is a complex one requiring the patience and work of generations. Probably the problem has not been posed in correct terms in the past, since the power of Rome's attraction over its surrounding zones was not perceived in time. Up to now the problems of the city of Rome have not been resolved.

The idea of a capital city as a centre given entirely to administration and tourism, and therefore with merely consumers' facilities, is out of date. Only a fully developed metropolitan area may provide the solution of the present difficulties of a city which is rapidly moving toward 3 million inhabitants and within a few years will have 4 million. A specific investment policy is required which can give to the city and its surrounding region the vitality necessary for it to absorb, upon a correct economic

---

[3] A separate analysis should be made of the problems of the University of Rome, both as regards the pressure caused by an overlarge student population and the modernization of its structure as well as its special human problems all of which have disturbed its regular functioning in the last months. Only the Faculty of *Magistero* lies within the competence of the local authority. As regards the project for expansion of the University, there has been much controversy about the site on which an option has been taken. This site which was provided for in the town-planning scheme for Rome has not received the agreement of the Ministry of Public Works which has put forward its right to protect the zone.

basis, a flow of migrants which shows no signs of diminishing. Only a correct solution of its economic problems can permit Rome to develop its proper function both as an idea and a symbol of a great cultural heritage and as a great metropolis which can meet the requirements of those administrative services which every country expects to receive from its capital city.

BIBLIOGRAPHICAL NOTE

The data are taken from: *Schema di programma per l'assestamento e l'istituzione di scuole secondarie di secondo grado nella Provincia di Roma, per il triennio 1967/70.* (Rome: Educational Authority 'Provveditorato agli Studi' 1967); *La scuola romana di fronte al nuovo anno,* by the Educational Authority (Notes reserved to the Press), October 1968; A. Frajese, *Memoria per il Consiglio Comunale e la stampa cittadina. Comune di Roma, Assessorato IX Ripartizione, 1967.* – *Un piano per Roma,* Editoriale Romana, 1966 (Dei Discorsi e scritti di Amerigo Petrucci).

28

Sofia

John Georgeoff

Introduction

Sofia, the capital of Bulgaria – a Balkan nation of about 8,000,000 people –
is located in the southwestern part of the country on a plain approximately
1,830 feet above sea level. It is surrounded by lofty mountain ranges which
shelter it from the winds of northern Europe so that the city has a rather
pleasant climate with an average temperature of $-2 \cdot 1°$ C in January and
$21 \cdot 0°$ C in August.

The city is located strategically on the Balkan peninsula, a fact that has
contributed to many of its problems in the past, but also to its rapid
growth in the latter part of the nineteenth and present centuries. Sofia lies
almost exactly in the centre of a line drawn from the Black Sea to the
Adriatic Sea. It is approximately 200 statute miles from each of three
other Balkan capitals: Belgrade (Yugoslavia), Bucharest (Romania), and
Tirane, Albania; and both Athens and Istanbul are approximately 320
statute miles from Sofia. Thus, the city, located along one of the important,
historic East–West routes, has been subject to many conquerors: Mace-
donian, Roman, Hun, Byzantine, Bulgar, Crusader, and Ottoman Turk.
In modern times, this same important location brought the railroad which
helped to make Sofia not only the most important commercial and manufacturing city of Bulgaria, but also one of the most important industrial
cities on the Balkan Peninsula.

In a sense, Sofia is an old city. Its history as a settlement dates back to the
Thracians in the fifth century B.C. Since this time, it has borne several
names: Serdika, Sredets, Triaditsa, and finally Sofia. Its population has
fluctuated with its fortunes. Bulgarian historians estimate that in the
seventeenth century Sofia had a population of about 40,000; but at the
time of Bulgarian independence in 1878, the city's population had
dwindled to somewhere near 16,000, of whom 13,000 were Bulgarians,
the remainder being mostly Turks and Jews. Today, less than a century
later, its metropolitan population has grown to over 800,000 (see Table 1).
In another sense, therefore, Sofia is a very new city.

TABLE 1

POPULATION GROWTH OF THE CITY OF SOFIA, BULGARIA, 1880 TO 1965*

Year	Population of Sofia	Interval period between censuses	Numerical increase of population during interval period	Per cent of increase of population by year during interval period
1880	20,856			
1887	30,928	1881–1887	10,072	4·7
1892	46,593	1888–1892	15,665	6·7
1900	67,789	1893–1900	21,196	4·5
1905	82,621	1901–1905	14,832	3·6
1910	102,812	1906–1910	20,191	3·9
1920	154,025	1911–1920	51,213	3·3
1926	213,002	1921–1926	58,977	4·6
1934	287,095	1927–1934	74,093	3·2
1946	366,925	1935–1946	79,830	1·8
1956	644,727	1947–1956	277,802	4·3
1965	800,953	1957–1965	156,226	2·2
		1881–1965	780,097	

* Bulgaria. Tsentralno statistichesko upravlenie pri Ministerskiya s″vet. *Demografska statistika, 1960* (Sofia: the author, 1962), p. 223. It should be noted, in examining the above data, that the interval periods between censuses are not equal.

The Growth of Sofia

In comparing the growth rate of Sofia with the growth rate of the country as a whole (Tables 1 and 2), one can see that Sofia's growth has consistently been greater. Although Sofia grew most rapidly in the 1880s and 1890s after it had been made the capital city (during 1888 to 1892 it grew 6·7 times faster than the country itself), it has had significant spurts in growth after each world war. Even during the great world depression of the 1930s it continued to grow faster than the rest of the nation. Stated another way, the census of 1892 showed the population of Sofia to be more than double that of the 1880 census – the first census after independence. The population again doubled by 1910 and still again by 1926. In 1956 the census showed that this time the population had more than trebled in the preceding thirty years. The present population, therefore, is about twenty times greater than that of 1880.

In years past, migration from the rural villages and smaller towns was responsible in large measure for the city's rapid growth. The percentage of residents born in Sofia was 55·6 per cent in the first general census of 1880, 38·4 per cent in 1900, 34·1 per cent in 1920, 32·2 per cent in 1926, and 31·5 per cent in 1934 (the last nation-wide census before World War

TABLE 2

POPULATION GROWTH OF BULGARIA, 1880 TO 1965*

Year of census	Total population	Interval period between censuses	Numerical increase of population during interval period	Per cent of increase of population by year during interval period
1880[1]	2,007,919	1881–1887[1]	185,515	1·3
1884[2]	942,680	1885–1887[2]	18,261	0·6
1887	3,154,375	1888–1892	156,338	1·0
1892	3,310,713	1893–1900	433,570	1·6
1900	3,744,283	1901–1905	291,292	1·5
1905	4,035,575	1906–1910	301,938	1·5
1910	4,337,513	1911–1920	509,458	1·2
1920	4,846,971	1921–1926	631,770	2·1
1926	5,478,741	1927–1934	599,198	1·3
1934	6,077,939	1935–1946	951,410	1·4
1946	7,029,349	1947–1956	584,360	0·8
1956	7,613,709	1957–1965	612,855	0·9
1965	8,226,564	1888–1965	5,154,375	

(1) Northern Bulgaria only.
(2) Eastern Rumelia only. This region was united to the rest of Bulgaria in 1888.

* After: Bulgaria. Tsentralno statistichesko upravlenie pri Ministerskiya s″vet. *Statisticheski godishnik na Narodna republika B″lgariya, 1967 (Sofia:* the author, 1967), p. 13. These figures include population changes as a result of territorial adjustments.

II).[1] This trend has continued during the post-war period as indicated in Table 3, which presents data regarding migration to Sofia from other parts of the country. It bears noting that during the peak year of this period there was a net gain of 48,294 residents to the city.

In 1961, of 725,838 inhabitants of Sofia, 697,450 were native Bulgarians, 8,103 were gypsies, 4,052, Armenians, 3,592, Russians, 3,442, Jews, 2,935, Macedonians, 1,482, Turks, 1,475, Greeks, and the rest Czechs, Slovaks, Serbs, and other small national and ethnic groups.[2]

As a result of its rapid growth, Sofia's suburbs now reach what once were distant villages. The city limits presently extend east and west a distance of about fifteen kilometers and north and south about ten kilometers. The population density in 1966 was 881·4 persons per square kilometer, the highest of any city in Bulgaria and nearly eight times greater than that of Plovdiv, the city with the second highest density.

The rapid growth of Sofia after World War II resulted in a serious

[1] Bulgaria. Glavna direktsiya na statistikata. *Statisticheski godishnik na Tsarstvo B″lgariya, Godina XXXIII* (Sofia: the author, 1941), p. 49.
[2] Dimo Kazasov. *Sofiya: P″tovoditel* (Sofia: Meditsina i Fizkultura, 1962), p. 23.

TABLE 3

MIGRATION TO AND FROM SOFIA, 1947 TO 1960*

Year	Migration to Sofia	Migration from Sofia	Net gain or loss
1947	15,895	1,293	14,602
1948	11,713	5,135	6,578
1949	11,015	3,436	7,579
1950	11,605	2,624	8,981
1951	15,032	1,296	13,736
1952	17,874	1,015	16,859
1953	51,177	2,883	48,294
1954	15,906	1,120	14,786
1955	13,282	1,211	12,071
1956	14,176	914	13,262
1957	7,543	1,490	6,053
1958	7,375	658	6,717
1959	8,829	532	8,297
1960	7,300	572	6,728

* After: Bulgaria. Tsentralno Statistichesko Upravlenie. *Demografska statistika, 1960* (Sofia: the author, 1962), p. 304.

housing shortage. The situation was intensified because sections of the city had been destroyed or severely damaged by air raids during the war. These buildings were repaired or rebuilt to meet the needs arising from the influx of population. In addition, construction was begun on a number of large apartment house projects.

The growth of the city of Sofia has been due to several factors. Its strategic location, already mentioned, led to the selection of the city as a stop along the East–West international railroad line that runs from Constantinople to Vienna and then to the rest of Europe. The building of this line was completed in 1883 and contributed greatly to the early and rapid growth of Sofia as a commercial and trading centre.

The fact that Sofia was selected to be the capital of Bulgaria in 1878 by the Russian military government of occupation, and confirmed later by the Bulgarian Constitutional Assembly, is another factor. Historically, the cities of Pliska, Preslav, and Turnovo had been the capitals of ancient Bulgarian kingdoms; and at the time of Bulgarian independence, Plovdiv, Shumen (Kolarovgrad), Rousse, and Varna all had larger populations than Sofia. The selection of Sofia as the capital brought administrative machinery of government and additional population to the city and contributed to its early growth.

The proximity of Sofia to the rich coal fields around Pernik has helped the growth of industry – a significant factor almost from the time of

Bulgarian independence, but one of accelerating importance after the turn of the present century. Today, more than 250 establishments, 22·2 per cent of all the industrial enterprises in the nation, are located in and around Sofia; and of the city's population of 725,838 in 1961, 134,092 were gainfully employed in these establishments – or 19·6 per cent of all the industrial work-force of the country.[3]

Importance of Sofia

Sofia is the cultural centre of Bulgaria. The Bulgarian Academy of Sciences is located here, with its fifty-six research institutes of various sizes, as well as the archaeological, ethnographic, and natural history museums which are under its jurisdiction. Here, also, is Sofia State University, the only university in Bulgaria. The city is the home of the Vasil Kolarov National Library, a dozen theatres – including the National Theatre – a ballet company, a symphony orchestra, and the National Opera. Several teacher-training institutions, the most important Bulgarian art academy, music conservatory, and schools of ballet and folk-dancing also are all found here. Eight daily papers are published in the capital, which are then distributed throughout the country. Seventeen of the nation's nineteen book houses – all of which are nationalized now – have their offices in Sofia. The National Film Board is located here; and the radio station for the entire nation is Radio Sofia.[4] Finally, the city is the headquarters of a number of other cultural and educational groups, such as the Federation of Bulgarian Writers, the Federation of Bulgarian Artists, and the Federation of Composers, Musicologists, and Performing Musicians.

Politically, Sofia is an administrative centre in three important respects. As the capital, it is the administrative centre of the national government and of the country's Communist Party. At the same time, it is also the local administrative centre, with the city possessing the same functions as the larger territorial, political subdivisions known as *okr"zhi*,[5] the only Bulgarian city so constituted. Sofia is the seat of the National Assembly and its permanent organ, the presidium. In the city also are located all the ministries, committees, and commissions of the national government and the Supreme Court. The Bulgarian Communist Party maintains its national headquarters here, including the offices of the nation's Party Central Committee which makes most of the important political policy decisions.

---

[3] ibid., p. 25.

[4] Although there are three regional broadcasting stations elsewhere in the country, these transmit only two to four hours of independent programmes a day, the rest of the time re-transmitting the emissions of Radio Sofia.

[5] The singular form of this word is *okr"g*.

At the local level, the Sofia city council, having the same responsibilities as an *okr"g* council, administers all of the collectivized establishments (practically all are now collectivized) and most institutions in the city – except the cultural, social, and political ones functioning strictly at the national level. Hence, the council administers all elementary and secondary schools, cultural institutions, such as libraries, museums, and theatres, and the health facilities (hospitals and clinics). It is also responsible for retail stores and other places of business and commerce in the city, for the output of factories and plants, and for the quotas of the agricultural enterprises. The problems of the council are especially difficult in view of the fact that so many of the industrial, commercial, cultural, and political activities are located within its territorial jurisdiction, resulting in the high population density (relative to Bulgaria) – and its by-products: housing, health, educational, and transportation problems. For administrative purposes, therefore, Sofia is subdivided into six *rayons*, with the city council co-ordinating the work of these units.

Educational Problems of Sofia

For several reasons, Sofia has a number of educational problems: the city's rapid growth and high population density, its position as the cultural and educational centre of the country, insufficient school finances, the proximity of the educational institutions to the political and educational power centre of the country, and inadequately trained teachers. Certain religious problems are also present and, to a lesser extent, ethnic ones. All of these factors will now be reviewed in greater detail.

The rapid growth of the population of the city has sorely taxed its educational facilities. In 1966, there were in Sofia 188 elementary and secondary schools, attended by 125,875 students,[6] making an average enrolment per school of 669·5 pupils. As a result, the schools in many cases simply do not have a sufficient number of classrooms to accommodate all the pupils within their district at one time, the situation being especially acute in the higher density areas of the city. Further, the expansion of the city into the suburbs and the building of new apartment complexes has necessitated the construction of new schools in these developing sections. This has placed a drain upon the economy of Sofia at a time when state plans call for a concentration on aspects of the economy relating to

---

[6] Bulgaria. Tsentralno statistichesko upravlenie pri ministerskiya s"vet. *Statisticheski godishnik na Narodna republika B"lgariya*, 1967 (Sofia: the author, 167), pp. 494.

Of the 188 schools above, 21 were primary schools, 5 *progymnasiums*, 124 were full elementary schools, 16 were *gymnasiums*, and 22 were complete middle schools. Altogether in 1966–1967 Sofia had a total of 280 educational institutions, of which, in addition to the 188, there were 9 special schools for the blind, deaf and mute, slow learners, and 'hard-to-discipline youths' (i.e., reform schools), 27 professional technical schools, 38 technicums, including schools of the arts, 4 semi-higher schools, and 14 institutions of higher education.

production. In 1966, as a typical instance, only 7,400,000 *leva* out of a total budget for capital investment of 324,883,000 *leva*, or a bare 2·3 per cent, were spent by the city council on matters relating to education, culture, and the arts.

Increasingly, moreover, working parents are taking advantage of a special educational plan known as the *zanimalna*, under which students are cared for the entire day by the school, from early morning when their parents leave for work until the early evening when they return. The plan includes independent study by the pupils, special tutorial help by the teachers, and guided recreation. Since these children remain in school all day, the number of classrooms available for use by other class sections attending only part of the day is therefore limited. To alleviate what would otherwise be an impossible situation, a large number of the schools in the city (the exact number was unavailable to the writer) are operated in two or even three shifts.

Sofia's position as the nation's cultural and educational centre is a mixed blessing, for this is the cause of another of the city's educational problems. Until recently, the only university in the country was located in Sofia, and even now, the three other regional higher educational institutions are affiliates of this one. Moreover, when specialized higher schools are considered, such as those in agriculture or engineering, fourteen of the twenty-six institutions functioning in the country (i.e., over half) are located in Sofia. In terms of the number of students enrolled in these schools, 59,130 out of a national total of 82,573 (nearly three-quarters) are enrolled in the institutions of Sofia.[7] Since the higher educational institutions of Sofia serve the entire nation, it is obvious that a large number of the students enrolled in them are from other parts of the country. The potential magnitude of the problem, especially in terms of housing which already is so critical, can be seen when the present enrolment of students in the higher schools of Sofia, which stands at 59,130,[8] is compared to that of 1941, which was 9,242.[9] To lessen the problem new dormitories have been built for students and special cafeterias have been opened for them in the student quarters of the city.

However, the real solution to the problem is found in an educational approach adopted by the university and higher schools after World War II.[10] Although students are enrolled officially in these institutions, their enrolment may be of an extra-mural kind, so that they continue at their respective occupations wherever they are located throughout the country,

---

[7] ibid., p. 495. These data are from official statistics issued by the present Bulgarian government. There is obviously no way to verify the data.

[8] ibid.

[9] Bulgaria. Glavna direktsiya na statistikata, op. cit., p. 732. Here again, there is no way of verifying these figures.

[10] The schools of medicine excepted.

but study their university course work through a series of specially prepared lesson materials and a list of assigned readings. Whenever they have completed their studies and feel themselves to be sufficiently prepared, they apply to take the examinations which are given periodically at their particular institution. At least a third of the students enrolled in the higher schools of Sofia are enrolled under this plan. Theoretically, there is no difference between the level of achievement of the students studying extra-murally and those that are regularly enrolled at an institution; and the rights and privileges of both groups with regard to employment opportunities and advancement are supposedly the same. Many Bulgarians feel, however, that the level of achievement of the extra-mural students, even of those studying in a field closely related to their regular occupations, is generally not as high as that of the regular students. This is a problem that has yet to be adequately solved. In some instances, 'extension professors' are sent to certain newly-established centres in larger cities who work with the extra-mural students for a period of time prior to their taking the battery of examinations. These professors answer questions that the students may have about the material that they are studying, assist them in reviewing the most important points, and in other ways help them to prepare for the examinations. Students studying under the extra-mural system receive a certain amount of paid time off from their places of employment in order to get ready for the examinations. Whether the economic and educational advantages of this plan of study are great enough to warrant its continued use has not been officially questioned – and probably will not be while there are insufficient housing and educational facilities in Sofia for full-time students or while, as a result of the expanding economy and industrialization of the country, the requirements for trained manpower are so great that they cannot be met solely through direct university study.

Proximity to the Nation's Power Centre

The proximity of Sofia's educational institutions to the educational and political power centre of the country also poses problems. Schools of Sofia are often used by the Ministry of Education and the Todor Samodumov Pedagogical Research Institute, an affiliate of the Ministry, for research and experimentation, sometimes disrupting the class routine. Sofia schools are also most likely to be used for demonstration purposes when native educators come to the city to visit the Ministry of Education, or to attend the conferences for practising teachers of the special teacher-training school that exists in the capital; likewise, these same schools often are the first ones to be shown to educators from abroad. For these very reasons, though, Sofia schools selected for the above purposes are likely to be better financed and equipped, to have better-trained teachers, and to have a classroom curriculum – albeit with the framework of the national course of study – that is more frequently reviewed and revised to meet local needs.

The fact that these schools are situated in the capital, the nation's political power centre, adds still other dimensions to education in the city. Both educators and the children they teach must possess greater 'political consciousness' and be more active in political affairs. Students of Sofia, together with their teachers, are likely to participate in political rallies, parades, and demonstrations more frequently than their counterparts away from the capital. They are more likely to be found at required meetings in honour of national and party leaders (who often are the same persons) or of visiting foreign dignitaries, for such meetings are more frequent in Sofia just because it is the capital. Their work also in the political youth organizations, such as the Dimitrov Young Pioneer Organization (for elementary pupils) and the Dimitrov Young Communist Youth League (for secondary and older students) is more likely to come under scrutiny. On the other hand, the educational opportunities for youth are much greater in the capital, if for no other reason than the number of different schools that are there; and recognition and advancement probably is greater and more rapid there for both pupils and teachers who do exemplary work, either educationally or politically (most often both).

Lack of Adequately Trained Teachers

As the educational centre of the nation, Sofia is the focus of government attempts to improve teacher education. Until recently – and in many parts of the country even now – the only training available to secondary school graduates desiring to teach in the primary grades was a three-year teacher-training course. Now, a university programme has been inaugurated and prospective primary school teachers of Sofia are urged to complete it, plans already having been made to phase out the existing three-year teacher-training school in the city. For older teachers lacking adequate professional training, for those in need of refresher courses, and for those persons with industrial or shop experience wishing to become instructors in their field, a special school exists called the Institute for the Improvement of Teachers. It provides special intensive courses of several weeks' length during vacation periods for teachers who are currently practising their profession. Other courses, of a year or more in duration, are provided for those individuals who wish to become teachers of vocational subjects, or who desire to become leaders of the Pioneer and Young Communist League Organizations in some school.

Ideological Conflicts

The schools of Sofia – institutions in a city of a nation led by members of a Communist Party – are patently anti-religious. Yet, at the same time, many of the parents of the children attending those schools hold religious beliefs, and in the home attempt to sway their children to their point of view. Further, many parents are not in sympathy with the political objectives of the country and may express their feelings at home. To counteract any religious training that children might receive from their parents, the schools conduct anti-religious campaigns and activities, attempting to persuade the children that atheism is the 'reasonable and scientific' attitude and that religious beliefs are 'relics of an unscientific and superstitious past'. Similarly, political work in the schools is intended to bring about the creation of the 'new socialist man' – loyal to the Party and its principles and economically competent, able to add to the welfare of the state in some productive way.

Minorities

The problem of minorities, though a significant factor in education elsewhere in the country, is of less importance in Sofia. Most of the Jews – at one time a significant element in the population of the city – were permitted to leave for the new State of Israel after World War II; and most of the Turks, who also were once an important part of the population, left for Turkey. Only the gypsies remain an important minority group in the capital. Those who have accepted the new policies of the communist government, despite any of their opposing cultural traditions, have been permitted to remain in Sofia and still mainly reside in the historic part of the city known as the 'gypsy quarter'. An elementary school for their children was built by the city council in order that they might more easily comply with the compulsory school attendance laws. However, those clans which refused to accede to government policies were forcibly transported to Northern Bulgaria to work on state farms, and their children were made to attend school, either in the communities where they live, or away in some boarding-school.

Thus, Sofia has not been without its educational problems. Its rapid growth, its role as a cultural and political centre, the lack of sufficient finances to meet seemingly ever-expanding needs, and other factors place severe burdens upon the schools of the city. At the same time, responses have been developed by educators of the city which permit the schools to function – more or less adequately – under the existing conditions.

BIBLIOGRAPHY

Mikhail P. Arnaudov, *Istoriya na Sofiiskiya universitet sv. Kliment Okhridski prez p"rvoto mu polustoletie, 1888–1938* (Sofia, 1939) 647 p.

Sofiiski universitet sv. Kliment Okhridski; kratka istoriya za 50 godishninata ot osnovavaneto mu (Sofia, 1939) 77 p.

Balkantourist, *Guide to Sofia* (Sofia, 1958) 58 p.

Atanas Bozhkov, *B"lgarskata khudozhestvena akademiya* (Sofia: B"lgarski khudozhnik, 1962).

Bulgaria, Glavna direktsiya na statistikata. *Statisticheski godishnik na Tsarstvo B"lgariya* (Sofia: The author, 1909–1942).

Bulgaria, Tsentralno statistichesko upravlenie. *Demografska statistika, 1960* (Sofia: The author, 1962).

Dvadest godini sotsialistichesko stroitelstvo v tsifri (Sofia: Nauka i izkustvo, 1964) 289 p.

Spetsialisti s visshe i sredno spetsialno obrazovanie v Narodna republika B"lgariya; statisticheski sbornik (Sofia: Nauka i izkustvo, 1959) 126.

Statisticheski godishnik na Narodna republika B"lgariya (Sofia: The author, 1947/ 1948+).

B"lgarska akademiya na naukite, Sofiya. *B"lgarskata akademiya na naukite sled 9 septemvri 1944; spravochna kniga* (Sofia: the author, 1958) 323 p.

Arkelogicheski institut, *Materiali za istoriyata na Sofiya prez XIX vek do Osvobozhdenieto na B"lgariya* (Sofia: The author, 1937).

Komitet za istoriya na Sofiya. *Iubileina kniga na grad Sofiya* (Sofia: Pechatnitsa Knipegraf, 1928).

Institut po filosofiya. *Izgrazhdane i razvitie na sotsialisticheskoto obshtestvo v B"lgariya* (Sofia: The author, 1962) 488 p.

Institut po pedagogiya. *Politekhnichesko obuchenie; sbornik ot statii* (Sofia: The author, 1955) 158 p.

Naiden Chakurov, and Zhecho Atanasov, *Istoriya na obrazovaniento i pedagogicheskata mis"l v B"lgariya*. 2nd ed. (Sofia: Nauka i izkustvo, 1962) 432 p.

Dimo Kazasov, *Sofiya; p"tevoditel* (Sofia: Meditsina i fizkultura, 1962) 180 p.

Ulitsi, khora, s"bitiya; Sofiya predi polovina vek (Sofia: Nauka i izkustvo, 1959) 379 p.

Nikola V. Mikhov. *Sofiya do osvobozhdenieto; bibliografskostatistichna skitsa* (Sofia, 1942) 61 p.

A. Monedzikova, *Sofiya prez vekovete* (Sofia, 1946) 393 p.

Iordan Nikolov, *Boiniyat p"t na b"lgarskotot uchitelstvo* (Sofia: Narodna prosveta, 1965) 271 p.

Sofia. Naroden s"vet. *Ukazatel za utilsite, bulevardite, ploshtadite, mestnostite, kvartalite na Sofiya* (Sofia: Formuliari i registri, 1957) 188 p.

Universitet. *Iubileini turzhestva mai 1939 po 50-godishninata na Universiteta, 1888–1938* (Sofia: The author, 1940) 366 p.

Sofiya; vodach za istoricheskite i kulturnite zabelezhitelnosti (Sofia: Nauka i izkustvo, 1959) 186 p.

29

Ankara

Fatma Variş

Rural exodus towards the shanty-towns of the big cities is a crucial problem today in Turkey. In 1968, the number of shanty buildings in certain big cities of Turkey was approximately 465,000 with a population of 2,225,000, accounting for 20 per cent of the urban and 7 per cent of the whole population of Turkey. In Ankara, 65 per cent of residential housing consist of the so-called *gecekondu*[1] while in Istanbul, Izmir and Adana the *gecekondu* constitute 40 per cent, 24 per cent and 43 per cent, respectively. In Ankara 53 per cent of all inhabitants live in *gecekondu* settlements; 45 per cent in Istanbul, 33 per cent in Izmir and 45 per cent in Adana.

Ankara, the capital of the Turkish Republic, has for the last two or three decades been one of the cities which has most strongly felt the multifaceted impact of rural mobility. Situated on the once dry steppes of the north-western part of central Anatolia, it has three distinct types of residential areas – the old, the modern and the 'spontaneous' (*gecekondu*). All three areas need to be studied interdependently to determine the whole educational policy required to expedite the adjustment of a rural population to an urban setting. And it is with this end in view that I shall undertake here to examine the interrelated development of the modern, the old and the *gecekondu*.

From the Old Citadel to a Modern Capital

Turning first to the old city of Ankara, it will be recalled that it boasts a rich history; there is evidence of its conquest and occupation by Lydians, Persians, Macedonians, Galatians and Romans. It was built originally as a citadel-city on a high hill overlooking flat land, and this nucleus still survives, forming the old section of the present city. Medieval Ankara, once an important Roman city, fell under the rule of the Byzantines until 1073 when the Seljuk Turk conquest heralded once again the beginning of the Turkish reign. The city was annexed to Ottoman lands by the middle of the fourteenth century. The records show that in 1522 there were around

---

[1] 'A construction hastily made in one evening, without permission from the municipality', see Fehmi Yavuz, *Dorduncu Iskan ve Sehircilik Haftasi Konferanslari*, SBF Yayinlari, Ankara, 1961, p. 49.

3,150 houses in the city of Ankara.[2] At the beginning of the eighteenth century the population of the city was 45,000 of which 40,000 were Turks.[3] In the Provincial Annual (*salname*) dated 1902, Ankara is recorded as a city of several large districts such as Kayseri, Yozgat, Kirsehir and Corum with a population of 1,210,140.

During the years of the fight for national independence (1919–23) Ankara became a centre of attention as the hands of protest of the Turkish people against the invaders joined in Ankara. Thus on April 23, 1920, the first national assembly convened. Ataturk led the move to establish the Turkish Republic within the national territories and as an independent member of the family of nations. Ankara was proclaimed the capital on October 13th, 1923 and on April 20th, 1924, the districts within were made separate provinces. Today Ankara covers an area of 30,939·45 square kilometres and as the second largest city in Turkey with a population of 1,644,300[4] has developed rapidly in the last four decades to reach the dimensions and facilities of a major capital city.

Demographic Changes

Continuous increase in the population relates, on the one hand, to Ankara's role as the capital of the Republic and on the other hand, to the demographic mobility from rural areas towards cities. The results of the population census, regularly held after the year 1927, illustrate the population increase in the city.

The population increase between 1927 and 1935 was 32 per cent. Succeeding census reports indicate variations between 13 per cent and 38 per cent until 1956; while the highest rate was 38 per cent between 1950–5.[5] This increase is explained by the introduction of a systematic neo-liberal economic policy at the time, the implications of the Marshall Plan and by the gradual mechanization of agriculture. This partial mechanization in farming caused many non-landowners to move into the cities. The improved communications, the increase in credit facilities and public and private investment in industry were among the main reasons for rural gravitation towards cities. While experts in urbanization point out the urgent need for a national programme in urban planning,[6,7] the move is still towards certain big cities, reinforcing the well known Turkish adages 'However poor you may be, be close to a city' and 'If you are to drown, let it be in a big pond rather than a small one!'

[2] A. Galanti, *Ankara Tarihi*, Cilt 2.   [3] *La Grande Encyclopedie* (see Ankara).
[4] *Il Yilligi Ankara*, 1967, p. 104.   [5] *Il Yilligi Ankara*, 1967.
[6] R. Y. Keles, *Sehir ve Bolge Planlanmasi Bakimindan Sehirlesme hareketleri*, SBF Yayinlari 122, Ankara, 1961, 7B1-Kisim 3.
[7] R. Y. Keles, *Turkiyede Koylu Nufus ve Sehirlere Akin*, V. Iskan ve Sehircilik Haftasi Konferanslari, SBF Yayinlari No. 139, Ankara, 1962, p. 45–50.

Gecekondu (Spontaneous) Settlements

The factors mentioned above partially account for the migration from rural areas to the cities. The result of this exodus was the development of massive slums on the peripheries of urban areas. The *gecekondu* implies a sub-area full of shelters hastily constructed overnight, without any permission from either the municipality or from the owner of the land. At present, there are 113 *gecekondu* quarters in the total 187 administrative districts of Ankara.[8] Those living in these small houses of one or two rooms have managed to preserve some of their traditions, as well as adapting themselves to a new way of living. Because of the rapid growth of urbanization after 1949, adjustment of these newcomers to the city-culture could not be completely realized because of the continuing mobility among still unurbanized *gecekondu* dwellers. Consequently a different group, a sub-culture confined to the *gecekondu*, came into being. These people form a transitional group between the old and the new residential sections of the city of Ankara. Even though they may come to these quarters from different regions of the country, these *gecekondu* people share similar cultural elements such as dress, cooking, entertainment and hygiene. They also share common values and have similar aspirations.

The *gecekondu* settlers constitute the lowest stratum of the city population. This layer is rather different from the people in slum areas in the modern industrialized Western countries. Because of the continuing mobility within its socio-demographic structure, some call it 'the classless class' others call it the sub-proletariat.[9] On arrival in the city, they have to live in inadequate housing and in the cheapest rooms; they are underfed and underpaid. Moreover, it is a customary practice to send for their family as their conditions improve. The economic situation further improves as all the members of the family find work. They then start looking for better jobs and eventually decide on a permanent vocation. They seem to be happier living together as a family. They are more or less settled. Their ways of dressing, speaking, behaviour, aspirations are modified. It is not only an adjustment to the superficial elements of the culture; it is a deep psychological process that takes place in the adjustment of the individual as he gradually adopts the new city-culture.

As they adopt new values, links with relatives in the villages weaken. Migration has on the one hand caused the break-up of large families and, on the other hand, has introduced a closer co-operation within the nuclear family unit. Besides these small family units, however, there are those

---

[8] I. Yasa, 'The Impact of Rural Exodus on the Occupational Pattern of Ankara', article, *SBF Dergisi*, March 1967, No. 2 st. 151.

[9] I. Yasa, ibid.

who have temporarily moved to the city to find a job, leaving wife and children with their grandparents, as is seen in Sün, Elazig.[10]

The *gecekondu* quarters are not confined only to those from the rural areas; 10 per cent of those living in these settlements are employees with very low incomes who rent the house from its owner. In fact 57·31 per cent of these houses were built by those who really needed them and 35·87 per cent by the speculators who built them for income (6·82 per cent is unknown).[11] Consequently, the population in *gecekondu* settlements is diversified: 65 per cent are qualified workers, 11 per cent are small tradesmen, 10 per cent civil servants and 14 per cent domestic servants.[12] A recent survey indicates that 36 per cent of technical skills and occupations are learned in the city.[13] While parents endeavour to climb the socio-economic ladder through their personal efforts, they hold higher aspirations for the education of their children and their future vocations. This brings us to the educational problems of these transitional groups.

Educational Issues in Gecekondu Settlements

Educational issues in such quarters of big cities can hardly be isolated from the educational problems of the whole country.

The Turkish Republic has considered the school as the most significant agency contributing to social development. For almost forty-five years, Turkish schools have been responsible for educating the youth in accordance with the principles of the Turkish reforms.

The leaders of the Republican regime realize that the success of reforms of every type depends upon the education of enough people to assimilate and implement these reforms. Therefore, in the struggle against the medieval guild, Turkey has depended on her rising generations to integrate aspects of the inherited culture with the rapidly advancing contemporary world. The role of school in making the Turkish reforms a reality is also confirmed by Smith, Stanley and Shores:

> ... Advocates of this criterion – criterion of social development – point to the part played by the schools in the social progress of Mexico and Turkey to indicate that the view that the school cannot help with social development is no longer tenable. That the schools alone cannot bring about desirable social growth is granted at once. But callous indeed is the person who still insists that the school cannot exercise a major influence upon social change.[14]

After the declaration of the Republic, the Ministry of Education offered free education to all children and young people. Because the elementary schools assumed responsibility for increasing the number of literates, as

---

[10] N. Erdentug, *Sün Köyünün etnolojik tetkiki*, D.T.C.F. Yayini 1956, Ankara.
[11] Ankara, ibid.   [12] Ankara, ibid.   [13] I. Yasa, ibid.
[14] O. B. Smith, W. O. Stanley, and H. Shores, *Fundamentals of Curriculum Development* (Yonkers-on-Hudson: World Book Co., 1956), p. 148.

well as preparing the children for further schooling, the first five years of schooling were made compulsory.While the rate of literacy is 48·1 per cent in the country, this rate rises to 65·2 per cent in the province of Ankara and to 77·9 per cent in the city of Ankara.

If the trend in democratic Turkey is to provide not only education for all but also *good* education for all, it is apparent that special attention must be placed on manpower development. This means that not only should equal educational opportunities for both rural and urban children be provided, but it also means equal opportunities within the different quarters of cities for the attainment of objectives of national education.

Needless to say, the rural school in Turkey is underprivileged so far as the material and community resources are concerned, when compared with the urban school. The schools in *gecekondu* quarters are less privileged than the schools in the new or old quarters of cities, in general, because of the two main factors: the cultural background of the children and lack of community resources. It is important to note that the schooling in *gecekondu* quarters is probably of better quality than that in rural areas, and therefore the migration from rural areas to urban districts in general helps the mobile group to meet their rising aspirations in terms of more and better education for better social and economic status.

No longitudinal study has been carried out in *gecekondu* quarters to find out how much upward mobility takes place in terms of social status through education. However, in addition to a study as indicated above, the increase in opportunities for education and the positive attitude of families towards the education of their children but 'more for the boys than the girls' needs to be systematically studied. According to a study carried out in Ankara in 1957 in a specific *gecekondu* headquarters, 247 out of 679 children went to school; the rest were either too young or could not afford to do so.[15] Another study indicates that in a specific quarter 70·59 per cent of men and 29·40 per cent of women are literate.[16] In another *gecekondu* quarter, this percentage rose to 75·79 per cent for men and 39·10 per cent for women. This is a good rate when compared with the literacy rate of the country as a whole but the rates are low when compared with those for the city of Ankara.[17] Many adults have learned to read and write at their places of employment and through organized courses arranged by the district adult education bureau, and also by voluntary social organizations such as the Association of Turkish University Women and others. As a result not only do the parents have

[15] I. Ogretmen, *Ankarada 158 Gecekondu*, SBF Yayinlari, No. 3, 1957.
[16] Ankara *Cincin baglari Gecekondu Arastirmasi*, Imar, Iskan Bk gi, Mesken Genel Md. Gu, 1965, Ankara.
[17] T. Yorukan, *Gecekondular ve Gecekondu Bolgelerinin Sosyo-Kulturel Ozellikleri*, I.I.B. Mesken Gen Md. 1965, Ankara.

opportunities for better jobs themselves, they also become conscious of the importance of education for their children, for gaining social status. Consequently more children go to school in *gecekondu* quarters and schools have to run two and sometimes three sessions a day with classes of 60–70 children. The actual situation today indicates the need for *long-term demographic and socio-economic planning, together with educational work-plans on the national, provincial and district level.*

Problems of Adjustment and Role of the Schools

Although those coming from the rural areas generally live in *gecekondu* quarters, there are many who live in the city as door-keepers of the big block buildings or other state buildings whose children do not necessarily attend the *gecekondu* schools, but go to the nearest school in the city. Therefor when the writer tried to gather data about the problems of adjustment of rural children at schools, both city and *gecekondu* quarters were surveyed.

In schools in *gecekondu* quarters, differences between the intonation and pronunciation of the newly arrived group and the already settled group of pupils causes the former to feel self-conscious. However, after a period of cultural shock, the child generally adjusts to the whole school environment, although difficulties of adjustment to the group sometimes arise from the child's wish to continue playing the games he learned in his village. In city schools the main problem of adjustment arises from the acceptance of these children by the group. The first step usually is the phase of perplexity and loneliness followed by introspectiveness.

According to teachers working in *gecekondu* quarters, the adjustment of the rural child to learning activities depends on the attitudes he has gained in his previous school as well as his individual capacity. Behavioural changes depend on the approach and attitudes of teachers as well as the intelligence of the children. These newcomers, accustomed to village life, have difficulty in adjusting to the more sophisticated reading, concept formation and oral expression expected of those in urban schools. City school teachers have pointed out that the adjustment of newcomers depends on the intellectual ability of individuals as well as the previous experiences of individual pupils. They also point out the need for remedial and individualized teaching for these children from rural areas.

In general, the aspirations of parents towards upward social mobility urge them to make financial sacrifices for the education of their children. In most cases they are supported either by the school or by their well-to-do neighbours.

One specific problem arises from overcrowding in their houses: the fact that the whole family has to sleep in the same room leads to early psycho-sexual development and resulting problems.

In the *gecekondu* schools as well as in city schools, the behavioural changes take place in four to five years. These changes are observed as improvement in cleanliness and socialization. The children usually develop an ideal of what they want to do and to be at the end of their elementary schooling.

The above observations made in elementary schools in six districts of Ankara[18] and contacts with twenty classroom teachers, clearly point out that the problems of adjustment can be minimized through action taken by the city superintendent of schools, the school director and most important of all by the classroom teacher. It need hardly be said that the gap between the opportunities of city schools and rural schools are to be bridged through a national policy of education to minimize the problems of adjustment resulting from mobility.

It is within Turkey's power to meet the educational needs of the incoming rural population, since there is little difference in factors affecting education such as in oral and written language, e.g. in groups living in different regions of Turkey.

---

[18] Interviews in elementary schools, Bahcelievler, Aydinlikevler, Cankaya, Altindag, Akdere, Cincin.

Section V: Introduction

The Near, Mid and Far East

Brian Holmes

The cities of Asia show such diversity that a comparative study restricted to this area would be well justified. To the west of this vast territory, Haifa presents a revealing case study. Since the foundation of Israel there has been a flood of immigrants from Europe and Araba countries (p. 335). As Jews they shared a common culture but came from different backgrounds of habits and values. In particular, many Oriental Jews were practically illiterate and unused to living in an industrial society (p. 335). All immigrants have to learn a new language, Hebrew. The population has exploded but the proportion of people living in rural and semi-rural areas has remained steady (p. 337); the educational problem is that of helping town-bred immigrants to live and work together in a modern democratic state. The introduction of comprehensive schools (p. 340), and the strengthening of youth movements and adult education, including vocational courses, are among the policies designed to achieve this goal.

In India, by contrast, most of the teeming millions still live in rural areas, but cities such as Bombay, Delhi, Ahmedabad and Bangalore, have more than doubled in size in the last thirty years (p. 345). The jumble of ancient and modern forms of transport (p. 343), the many refugees, the temporary stay of many immigrants (p. 345), the over-supply of graduates (p. 348), and the appalling conditions of life on the pavements or in *bustee* huts, without adequate water, sewers or minimal sanitation (p. 345), characterize these cities. Conditions in Udaipur seem somewhat more hopeful despite refugees and constant movements of workers and tourists. The educational picture suggests that few primary, middle or secondary schools are properly housed (p. 356), but that facilities for higher and professional education are much better. New buildings and hostel accommodation enable the city to meet the needs of a large number of students amounting to one-third of its total population (p. 354). In Calcutta the unplanned growth of private schools, which enrol some two-thirds of the children attending primary school (p. 346), cannot meet the needs of a city in which more than 50 per cent of the population is either illiterate or semi-literate. New immigrants need to be educated into the ways of city life, there is a grave shortage of buildings and teachers and the accommodation available is very unsatisfactory. The extremely rapid rate of population growth adds new dimensions to intractible problems.

The impression gained from the case studies of Colombo and Bangkok-Thonburi is that cultural diversity is the key to their problems. The immigration of foreigners into Thailand is controlled (p. 376), but there are several minority ethnic groups, the largest of which are the Chinese, most of whom live near the capital and who dominate the commercial class (p. 378). The assimilation of the Chinese with the Thai *élites* is expected to continue. Poor housing, the influx of students and the widening gap between rich and poor constitute problems but education plans seem directed more specifically towards skilled and semi-skilled manpower needs (p. 380). In Ceylon emphasis seems to be given to promoting a cultural renaissance in a newly independent country. The mother tongue has been adopted as the medium of instruction thus opening up primary and secondary education to the masses. Two ancient Pirivenas were raised to university status in 1959 to meet the ever-increasing demand for higher education (p. 365). Proposals have been made that the University of Colombo should specialize in courses meeting the socio-economic needs of a metropolitan area (p. 366). Some success has been achieved in giving prestige to skilled labour (p. 367) and new leaders are likely to emerge from among the workers (p. 368). A clash of cultures remains in the City of Colombo which is the centre of cultural life, government and economic activity and its chief port (p. 362). Overcrowded schools are inevitable and under the Greater Colombo Plan a ring of elementary schools to feed a secondary school and a number of secondary schools on the periphery of the city have been established.

Language difficulties (p. 398), the fragmentation of the metropolitan area (p. 393), the large number of inadequate private schools (p. 396) and rural immigrants (p. 394), create problems for educationists in Manila.

China offers a fascinating case study. There in a typically peasant-agricultural country, the communists embarked in 1949 on an industrialization programme (p. 386). The expansion of education was largely town-based (p. 386) and manpower needs were stressed. These and other social changes drove people to the towns. During the Great Leap Forward (1958–60) an attempt was made to reorganize life in the cities (p. 390), but since 1952 a number of campaigns to move people from the cities back to villages have been launched (p. 391). Graduates have been persuaded to go out into the countryside (p. 393), and while training for industry remains important, the main emphasis has been given to finding ways of educating people for a future in which a large majority will work in rural areas. The outcome of these attempts will be watched with interest everywhere.

30

Haifa

J. S. Bentwich and M. Rinott

Demography

The first problem of education in Israel has been the enormous increase of the school-population in the last 20 years since the establishment of the State in 1948. This has been due primarily to *immigration*. In the early years, there was a flood of immigrants, mainly refugees from Arab countries or homeless remnants of the holocaust in Eastern Europe. Immigration still continues, though on a smaller scale. Further, the high birth-rate among the immigrants, coupled with low infant mortality consequent on improved health services, has resulted in a 'population-bulge' spreading upwards from the first age-groups (4–5) to the latter teens (15–20).

The total population in 1968 was 2,800,000, of whom 400,000 were Arabs. This represents an increase in the ratio 3·5:1 in the last 20 years. Owing to the 'bulge', however, the school population increased from 141,000 in 1948 to 776,000 in 1968 – an increase over fivefold. The main problem, however, is not that of numbers, but of *social and cultural integration*. All migration is an uprooting and entails re-adaptation to a new society; and so most of the immigrants and their families have had to accept radical changes in their way of life. Although, as Jews, they had much in common, the general culture in their countries of origin was usually very different from that of Israel, a modern democratic state. This applies particularly to the Oriental Jews – i.e. those coming from Arab countries of North Africa and the Middle East. Many of these were practically illiterate and unused to modern standards in industry and government; many of them were at first poorly housed, with large families crowded in 1–2 rooms. Over 50 per cent of the children in elementary schools are to this day of Oriental parentage – 'Half our future'. And all immigrants have to learn what for them is a new language, Hebrew – new, at least, as a language not only of the synagogue but of daily converse and adapted to express modern terms and concepts. They come with different traditions, different values – East and West – different habits and ways of thought. How to weld this heterogeneous population into a united nation, proud of their past and of their common destiny, willing to work together, to suffer danger – this is no small task.

The Educational System

Under the British mandate, there was no compulsory education. Among the Jewish population, elementary education was indeed nearly universal; but among the Arabs – by no means.

One of the first acts of the new State was to institute free and compulsory education for Jews and Arabs equally, from the age of 5 to 14, comprising one year of kindergarten and 8 years of elementary school. At the time, owing to the great influx of immigrants, implementation of the Act was not easy; there was a shortage of teachers, a shortage of buildings; and among the Arabs and many of the immigrant families, not accustomed to formal education, school-attendance was irregular. These primary difficulties have now been largely overcome; attendance is close to 100 per cent.

The responsibility for compulsory education is shared between the central authority – the Ministry of Education and Culture – and the Local Authority – the Municipality, or the Local Council. Generally, the Ministry appoints the teachers, pays their salaries and supervises the curriculum, while the Local Authority has to provide buildings and equipment and, with government help, all the ancillary services such as health, food, child care, youth services and the like.

Secondary schools, normally admitting at the age of 14, have been established hitherto, some by the Local Authorities, some by independent bodies. Fees are charged, but are normally graded according to income, the balance being covered by a Government grant; in 1967-8 over one-half of the pupils in secondary schools had their fees remitted altogether. Generally speaking, fees have not been an obstacle to a child continuing his or her education after completion of the elementary school. In the Jewish population, over 80 per cent of the 14-15 age group continue in secondary schools, and roughly half of these stay on till 18.

Nevertheless, the present system has long been regarded as inadequate for a modern State. In 1969, a new Education Act was passed, extending compulsory education to the age of 15 as a first step (to be implemented in the period 1969–72) and subsequently to the age of 16 (to be implemented in the period 1972–75). This lengthening of compulsory education entails, and will be accompanied by, a radical reform of the educational structure, from 8 + 4 – i.e. eight years of (compulsory) elementary education, followed by (voluntary) secondary education of four years – to 6 + 6 – i.e. six years of primary education, followed by six years of secondary education, of which the first four years will be compulsory and free. It is planned that all secondary education should be, as far as possible, *comprehensive*.

Urban Development

During the period of Turkish rule, before the First World War, Palestine was mainly agricultural; and most Jewish immigrants in those days, imbued with the ideal of a 'return to the soil', turned to agriculture; although town-bred, they learnt to become quite good farmers. In the period of the British mandate, however, industry and commerce developed rapidly, and now account for the bulk of the national income. Agriculture has indeed developed too; by irrigation and drainage, by new methods and new crops, large areas, previously barren, have now come under cultivation; but owing to mechanization relatively less man-power is required. It might have been thought, therefore, that there would be, as in other developing countries, a drift of rural population to the cities. In Israel this has been prevented by a planned policy of dispersal of the population, (*a*) by encouraging local industries, and (*b*) by setting up new town-centres in rural areas. As a result, while the proportion of the Jewish population engaged in agriculture is now barely 10 per cent, the proportion residing in rural or semi-rural areas has remained steady at approximately 20 per cent. The cities have grown, but not at the expense of the countryside. One can speak of *urban development* rather than *urbanization*.

The main educational problem, therefore, is not that of helping peasants, uprooted from their villages, to adapt themselves to industry and town life, but of helping immigrants, mostly town-bred but coming from different countries and with different traditions and mother tongues, to work and live with one another, and to bridge the gap between their previous habits and values and those required in a modern democratic state.

Development in Haifa

Haifa is the third largest city in Israel, with a population in 1969 of somewhat over 200,000. It is the principal port and railway terminal of Israel, being favoured with a natural harbour, formed by the spur of Mt Carmel jutting into the sea. Under the British mandate, the Iraq Petroleum Company made it the outlet of their oil pipeline from Iraq, and set up the refineries which, to this day, supply most of the country's needs, and serve also as the basis for a growing chemical industry. The outskirts of Haifa, extending almost all the way to Acre, 10 miles north-east, contain a large industrial area, with iron and steel works, automobile plants, a cement factory, and a wide variety of light industries: textiles, glass, ceramics, plastics, soap and fats, etc.

The residential areas may be divided roughly into 5 zones:

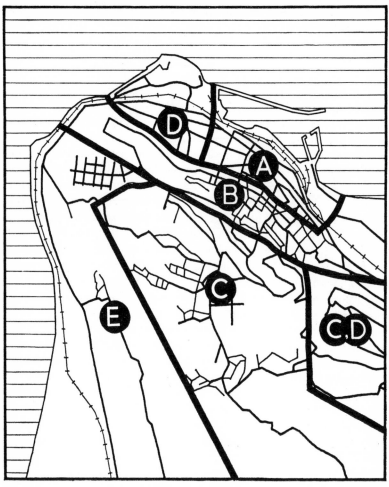

Residential Areas in Haifa.

(A) The old city and down-town areas, at or near sea-level;
(B) The slopes of Mt Carmel facing the harbour;
(C) The ridge and spurs of Mt Carmel itself;
(D) The housing estates on the northern outskirts;
(E) The housing estates on the southern outskirts.

Very roughly speaking, (A) is the poorest zone, mainly occupied by oriental immigrants; (B), developed in the mandate period, is middle-class; (C) middle- and upper-class; (D) and (E) mainly immigrants, the majority lower middle-class, with a considerable proportion of Orientals.

This social stratification, however, is being more and more blurred, purposely, by new housing schemes aiming at slum-clearance, with transfer of families to new buildings in 'better' areas.

Elementary Education

The number of children in elementary schools in 1968/69 was roughly 30,000, and, now that the 'bulge' has passed up, is relatively stable. Of these, roughly 25 per cent coming from low-income immigrant homes are classified as *disadvantaged*, and, to overcome the handicap of their deficient home-upbringing, are given *special attention*. This takes various forms: supplementary instruction, especially in Hebrew, supervised individual study, remedial work, etc. The classes in schools for these children are smaller; and the teachers receive guidance from special counsellors. Some of the schools have a 'long day' – i.e. from 8 a.m. to 4 p.m. – as against the normal school day which is held in the mornings only, making possible the organization of recreational activities as well.

There is no 'streaming' in Israeli elementary schools; but, in the upper grades, there are *sets* for Hebrew language, English (taught as a second language from the age of 10), and mathematics. Here, again, the lowest set is smaller in numbers, to facilitate individual attention.

Pre-school education in the kindergarten is at present compulsory and free for one year only, from 5 to 6. But it has long been realized that disadvantaged children need a longer preparation for formal schooling. And so the municipality has, since 1969, opened kindergartens in the poorer quarters for children of 3 and 4 years of age, free of charge. These are attended by some 25 per cent of the age-groups – roughly the same 25 per cent of children classified as 'disadvantaged' in the elementary schools. The goal is to increase the number of kindergartens so as to include all the 4-year age group.

Secondary Education

Previous to the establishment of the State, secondary schools were mostly private, fee-charging, and of academic grammar-school type, leading up to higher education; hence selective and limited in the main to children from middle-class homes. There was indeed a Technical School attached to the Institute of Technology; but this too was fee-charging and selective. Children from working homes, on completion of the elementary school, had to begin to earn or, as apprentices, to learn a trade.

This has now been completely changed. The Haifa Municipality initiated many years ago, with Government help but long before the new Education Act, a policy aiming at *secondary education for all*. To make this practical for the greatly enlarged and heterogeneous child-population, secondary schools of varied types were established, selective and non-selective, and with emphasis on vocational training, including a large agricultural school, a nautical school and an aeronautical school. Special courses were introduced for boys who would not reach the standards normally required even for apprenticeship. In addition, in order to lighten the fees – even if graded by income – a system of savings was introduced, whereby the parents pay a small annual premium from childhood, and so, when the child reaches secondary school age, there is little additional burden. As a result of these measures, over 85 per cent of children completing the elementary school in 1968–69 went on to full-time secondary education, academic or vocational; or, if one includes those attending night-school or part-time courses – even 92 per cent. Of the boys, one-half attend vocational schools; among girls the proportion is less.

Under the new Education Act, all children will receive secondary education, free, up to the age of 16. In this reorganization, radical changes are being planned. Secondary schools will be admitting children from the age of 12 instead of 14, and will be non-selective, and as far as possible *comprehensive* in type. The existing secondary schools, which are usually sharply defined as academic or vocational, will have to be reorganized so as to include at least a comprehensive junior department up to the age of 15; and it is hoped that many of them will become fully comprehensive later on, so that children admitted at 12 will be able to continue till 18 without need to transfer to another school.

An important aim of this reorganization is the social integration of children from various communities. Elementary schools have to be near the homes, and are therefore often confined to children of one community. The new secondary schools are being planned to mix children from various communities; thus children from zone A, down-town, will be conveyed by bus or train to schools in the 'better' zones B and C.

Another important factor in social integration is the *Youth Service*. *Youth Movements* have a long tradition in Israel, going back to the early 20s; from them the kibbutzim were largely recruited, and they still attract nearly one-half of the youngsters in their teens. Not less important are the *Clubs* attached to schools and the Municipal *Youth Centres* serving a whole residential area. In those clubs and centres, young people of all communities mix on equal terms, are directed towards positive activities and receive a training in citizenship.

Further Education

An important element here is classes of *Hebrew* for immigrants. For those who are still illiterate, small study groups of 5–6 are held in their homes. The personal contact with the teacher is often not less valuable for them than the material learnt.

Then there is a wide range of *Vocational* courses, usually in the evenings, both for adults and working youth. Apprentices get day-release for one day in the week, but usually attend classes in the evenings as well.

Lastly, there are four *Community Centres* with a total membership of close on 10,000 for young adults, offering a wide variety of courses – literary, artistic, hobbies – besides cultural activities – lectures, concerts, drama and the like. One of these, situated on the border between Arab and Jewish quarters, conducts many activities in which Jews and Arabs participate jointly.

Higher Education

With the expansion of secondary education, there has been a growing demand for higher education. In the past, students from Haifa had to go to Jerusalem for this purpose. In 1964, the Municipality founded the Haifa University College, at present academically affiliated to the Jerusalem University but growing towards independence, and serving the whole Northern District, the Haifa area in particular. It has a magnificent site on the Carmel ridge, and is rapidly expanding. Its enrolment for 1969/70 was 3,000, including over 200 Arab students. The Institute of Technology, built before the First World War, but opened only in 1925, serves the whole country. It has an enrolment of 5,600, turning out over 1,000 engineers every year, besides conducting courses for technicians and for skilled craftsmen. There are also four teachers' training colleges in Haifa and vicinity with an enrolment of 800, including one for Arabs, which serves the whole country.

Arab Education

Haifa has a settled Arab population of 12,000. For elementary and pre-school education, they have their own schools, conducted in Arabic, with Hebrew as a second language – though some children attend Jewish schools in their neighbourhood. The provisions for compulsory education are the same as in Jewish schools, and similar ancillary services are provided by the Municipality.

For secondary education, some attend Christian parochial schools, others attend Jewish schools, academic or vocational. In one of the Municipal secondary schools, there are parallel classes for Arab students, with most of the subjects taught in Arabic. Some of the subjects, however, are taught in Hebrew; and Arab and Jewish students participate equally in clubs, sport, social activities and the like.

Summary

The above is only a highly condensed sketch of a much more varied and multi-coloured reality. It will be seen that some of the problems indeed are not very different from those in other cities elsewhere: the differences of wealth and social background, the endeavour to give all children an equal chance, even to give additional help to those who come from poorer homes in order to offset their initial handicap.

But there are problems peculiar to Israel. Haifa, like Israel generally, has a very mixed population, with communities of different origins, different traditions, different mother-tongues. To iron out all the differences is not desirable. The task of education is, while maintaining what is good in the various traditions, at the same time to help the children to grow up together as useful and loyal citizens in the new State. What has been achieved in 20 years is considerable; but much still remains to be done.

Government planning in education is of course of major importance. But educational planning, going hand in hand with general urban development in a town like Haifa, shows the possibilities of local initiative, even in a country with centralized educational administration, such as Israel is today.

31

Calcutta

K. C. Mukherjee

Western problems of urbanization today differ greatly from the complexity of modern urban problems in an underdeveloped country like India. For example, in Calcutta and Delhi, in addition to modern motor vehicles one sees the jumble of camel carts, ox carts, thousands of tongas (two-wheeled horse carts), bullock carts, hand carts, cycle rickshaws, scooter rickshaws, *neharas* (two wheeled horse carts for carrying goods), man-drawn rickshaws, cycles, trams, decrepit taxis, trucks and thousands of pedestrians going all over the cities in a congested flow pattern producing apopletic dismay among visiting foreign traffic experts.

This is in great contrast to the transport system with which the peoples of the West are familiar. In cities like Calcutta dirt, over-congestion and confusion have intensified as the population has increased. In 1948 there were three million people living there. Today there are more than seven million, of whom 300,000 are refugees living in the most appalling conditions. Thousands live on the open footpath in degradation and misery unimaginable to many of the rich countries. Housing and sanitary conditions in Calcutta, Delhi, Bombay and in many of the larger Indian cities are appalling, water supplies are inadequate and the railway stations are hopelessly congested. There is also a lack of space for new industries, traffic bottlenecks, power shortages and a vast unsolved unemployment problem. Calcutta is suffering from the kind of sickness which is rotting the soul of urban India.

In 1961, Nehru expressed his grave anxiety about the city when he said: 'Calcutta is the biggest city in the country. Its problems are national problems – quite apart from problems of West Bengal, and it is necessary that something special should be done. If the whole city went to pieces, it would be a tremendous tragedy.'

Yet Calcutta is a city of the first magnitude, a real metropolis. Few urban concentrations in the world are so populous, probably none is so congested at the heart of the city and none, perhaps, exerts so extensive a range of urban influence. It is also a city of many splendours. It has parks, green lawns, art centres and numerous theatres, museums and cinema houses that are floodlit at night, glowing with a seductive amber brilliance.

Its night life does not debauch the innocents. This is also a city of commerce and manufacture, with a famous seaport and railways of vital national significance. It is the political, commercial and economic centre of the whole of eastern India, which includes West Bengal, Orissa, Bihar, Assam, Manipur, Tripura, Nagaland, N.E.F.A. and the eastern districts of Uttar Pradesh – a total population of 160 millions. The Calcutta Metropolitan District is the conurbation formed around villages and towns along both banks of the Ganges (River Hooghly). The metropolis itself has a population of approximately eight million in an area of 490 square miles. It is India's first city, and also one of the largest cities in the world in terms of population.

The port of Calcutta clears 42 per cent of India's exports and 25 per cent of imports; the metropolitan district accounts for approximately 15 per cent of all India's manufactures and handles about 30 per cent by value of India's bank clearances; and Calcutta's educational institutions provide higher education for 13 per cent of all India's students.[1]

A vast hinterland is closely bound to Calcutta by strong economic ties and looks to it for a host of essential urban services. This hinterland is rich with the natural resources so vital to Indian economy. Besides abundant supplies of coal and mineral deposits in Bengal, Bihar and in Orissa, great iron and steel complexes and concentration of ancillary engineering industries have formed the basis of growing industrial centres. Here at the centre of Calcutta's hinterland is the great Ruhr of developing India. The heavy engineering factories of Jamshedpur, Rourkela, Burnpur, Durgapur, and Asansol and the locomotive works of Ranchi, Chittaranjan, Calcutta and Howrah provide the major foundations of India's industrial progress.

The key role and importance of metropolitan Calcutta is immense. It acts as the main producer and distributer of commodities and services, a financial source of numerous public and private organizations and as the centre for advanced medical services. Its Renaissance palaces provide a source of inspiration to changing ideas and attitudes related to the cultural development of the nation. It is nevertheless evident that the urban development of the metropolis, its essential functions and regional services have not developed for decades. As a result Calcutta now is a city in crisis.

The Calcutta Metropolitan Planning Organization stated in their *Report* of 1966 that although over the past two hundred years many commissions have issued reports calling for urgent action, only piecemeal, sporadic and inadequate steps were taken to meet the needs of the rapidly developing population. Obsolescence has not been matched with appropriate maintenance and new investment. Proper expansion and reorgani-

---

[1] Basic Development Plan of Calcutta, 1966–1986, p. 1. Published by the Calcutta Metropolitan Planning Organization.

zation of utilities and services have not kept pace with population growth. As a result the city has grown haphazardly and unsystematically. Calcutta's population is increasing every year and by 1986 the estimated population will be about thirteen million. This figure is a crude indication of magnitude of the problems the city will face in future. The problems of other Indian cities are also staggering. For example, in the thirty years between 1931 and 1961 Calcutta Metropolitan District grew by 165 per cent, but in the same period greater Bombay grew by 218 per cent, Delhi by 424 per cent, Madras by 167 per cent, Ahmedabad by 284 per cent, Bangalore by 288 per cent. Evidently the city of Calcutta had a growth rate which was the slowest amongst all the major cities of India. It was probably because conditions in the large parts of the two central cities of the conurbation – Calcutta and Howrah – had reached saturation point, and could not absorb population growth. Metropolitan growth has taken place outside the most densely settled parts of the central city complex, within the fringe areas of Calcutta and in the municipalities bordering the city.

A very substantial proportion of the population growth in the city district has been due to migrants who come from all over India, particularly from the hinterland, and the refugees who come with their families in search of a home and a new life. In the 1961 census, about 800,000 were counted as having come to Calcutta sometime during the preceding ten years. During the same period about 300,000 were reported to have come from East Pakistan as refugees. The Calcutta Metropolitan Planning Organization rightly pointed out that the continuous flow of migrants into the city has reinforced its heterogenous cosmopolitan character and has had enduring effects on the demographic and occupational structure of the metropolis. More than half of the total working population are non-Bengali, employed in the jute industry, the engineering industry, the tramways and construction work.

In their *Report,* the Calcutta Metropolitan Planning Organization pointed out that the majority of the migrants are social liabilities. They remain outsiders – sleeping on the pavements or huddled in ramshackle *bustee* huts, on jute lines in apalling sanitary conditions, or living and sleeping inside the shops and offices, hotels, docks, factories where they work.

They consider their stay in the city as essentially temporary, dominated by the hard struggle to survive, to save whatever part of their earning they can to send to their families in the village home . . . . For many migrants there is little stake in the city as such and little concern for civic progress or civic pride . . . . The refugees and the migrants have joined the population created by natural increase, to strain the city's services in health and hygiene to the point of breakdown. They have contributed to the continuing high level of illiteracy and have helped create a well-nigh insoluble problem of housing and rural slum in the heart of the city—intolerable to migrant and original resident alike.

Educational Problems

Calcutta's schools and colleges are overcrowded and in spite of various efforts made by the Bengal Government, there are thousands of illiterates in the metropolitan district.

In 1961 at the beginning of the third Five-year Plan only 67 per cent of the primary school children (age-group 6 to 10) were at school in the city, and only about one-third of these children attended free schools. The majority of the schools are conducted by private bodies and the Calcutta Corporation provides only one-third of the primary schools. Both the private and municipal schools are hopelessly inadequate and their dismal picture of 50 to 60 children in each class cramped into dilapidated and unhygienic buildings is pathetic. Most of the school buildings are un-suitable – usually rented – with inadequate toilet facilities and no playing grounds. Apart from the dilapidated school buildings, in 1961 about 100,000 children of the primary school level and an additional 90,000 at the secondary level had no schooling at all. This was in the city proper. In the metropolitan district 32 per cent of the primary age-group and 56 per cent of the secondary age-group children received no schooling.

By the end of third Five-year Plan in 1966, in spite of the progress made, there were still 260,000 children between the ages of 6 and 10 years (about 30 per cent) who did not attend any kind of school. This slow progress in primary education is due to lack of adequate finance for school buildings, shortages of land and the absence of systematic educational planning. The enrolment in 1966 in junior secondary education classes (VI to VIII, ages 11–13) was estimated at 60 per cent for the city and 55 per cent for the metropolitan district, leaving 211,000 children of the total age-group who were not receiving any schooling. At the higher secondary level (class IX to XI, age-group 14–16) only 30 per cent of the children were receiving some sort of schooling.

The national goal of compulsory and free education for the age group 6–13 years by 1986 is 100 per cent and for higher secondary education 45 per cent. To reach this target the additional number of children who need to be brought to school in the Calcutta Metropolitan District at each educational level to meet existing deficits and the expected population increase would be:[2]

Primary Education	Classes I–V	670,000	100 per cent target.
Junior Secondary	Classes VI–VIII	471,000	100 per cent target.
Higher Secondary	Classes IX–XI	177,000	45 per cent target.
		Total 1,318,000	

---

[2] Basic Development Plan of Calcutta, 1966–86, p. 31.

The development planners for Calcutta agreed that to fulfil the educational obligations the city needs a progressive, well-organized and adequately equipped education system conducted directly by the government. Although private contributions have been valuable they are mostly unplanned. Education should also be compulsory and free, at least at the primary stage, as many parents and guardians are not in a position to pay the school fees for their children. Many new schools have to be established in order to obtain the target of 100 per cent enrolment at the primary level. The Calcutta Corporation has introduced a scheme for utilizing existing secondary school buildings for early morning classes at the primary level, but if all children are to be provided with free compulsory education, then at least one hundred new schools must be opened every year until 1986. For secondary education, with an average secondary school size of 650 students, at least 1000 new secondary and technical schools will be required during the same period – without any allowance for the replacement of the existing large numbers of unsuitable school buildings that now exist.

This is obviously a formidable task and the massive developmental effort now being planned needs governmental resources in order to be fulfilled. Then there is the urgent need to raise the quality of education, for the provision of school buildings is only one aspect of the education problem. The Calcutta Metropolitan District will also require an additional 15,000 primary school teachers (at a teacher/student ratio of 1:45) and 26,000 secondary school teachers (at a teacher/student ratio 1:25) by 1986. Present teachers might be required to work longer hours for additional pay and more teachers will have to be trained – for this the city will need many more training institutes. Again, the massive backlog of adult education has to be made up. In 1961 about 64 per cent of the adults of the city were either illiterate or semi-literate. The literacy standard of the industrial workers was also far from satisfactory – about 40 per cent were illiterate and an additional 36 per cent were semi-literate.

The problem of primary and secondary education and that of adult illiteracy must be taken on by the community as a whole, backed by government administration and finance. The basic Development Planners in 1966 rightly said that the problems of technical education as well as higher education must be tackled as an integral part of the manpower required to run the various economic functions of the society: 'Planning for the provision of trained personnel must be combined with a review of the present wasteful expenditure of human and material resources on those aspects of higher education that have less immediate relevance, now or in the foreseeable future, to socio-economic improvement'.

Shortage of Teachers and Equipment

In urban India, education is often characterized by a shortage of trained teachers, buildings, books and other facilities. More opportunities should be provided for vocational training which, by and large, tends to be insufficient in the urban context. This is very important because of the necessity of the agricultural worker to convert himself into a person who can apply his skills to technical and other urban types of professions. Although urban educational opportunities do exist in limited numbers, they are more likely to be available to the permanent residents of the city than to the new ones. The new migrant in Calcutta also may not be qualified by residence or be familiar with the rules and regulations by which he can avail himself of whatever educational opportunities exist.

In India there is an over-supply of university graduates, thousands of whom are unemployed. A small, newly developing country in Africa may not be bothered by this serious problem but India finds herself in a position where she has a huge surplus of university-educated young persons who, because of the present state of development of the economy, do not have an opportunity to utilise their skills. An Indian university graduate may move from city to city, living with relative after relative in a desperate attempt to find a post in which he can use his higher training. This is a situation which is expected to change as the country gradually becomes industrialized, but at present in India over-supply of university graduates has been one of the main causes of unrest in the country. The problem of the educated unemployed is due to the failure of the Congress Government to provide opportunites for middle-range positions and also partly due to the failure of Indian universities to train appropriately the persons who are needed to staff those positions. The Indian unemployment situation reflects not so much the shortage of educated people as the shortage of appropriately trained personnel. The unemployment problem is very acute in the cities like Calcutta, Delhi and Bombay.

The State governments are exposed to various strains. It is true to say that much larger demands for services are imposed upon them than they can cope with. Urban governments in almost all the underdeveloped countries are under-financed and they have not the resources to tackle the scale of problems with which they are confronted. This lack of resources results in a series of vicious circles: inadequate finance, equipment and direction to cope with the sanitation facilities, for example, lead to increased disease, which in turn, necessitates more governmental spending on medical care. The great mass of the urban population is poor and cannot pay sufficient taxes to the city corporations to enable them to cope effectively with such urgent necessities as the provision of an adequate sewage system.

Leonard Reissman pointed out that underdeveloped countries today present a picture that is reminiscent of Western society in the past. But the process of industrial urbanization today is more rapid than was the earlier urbanization of the West. During the nineteenth century Europe's urban population increased from 5·5 million to 48 million – a rise of 43·5 million. In Asia from 1900 to 1950, the urban population increased from 19·5 million to over 105 million – an increase of 86 million in fifty years. What is happening today in countries like India happens faster and even more catastrophically. Still, it is reminiscent of the process that occurred earlier in the West; for example, the changing pattern of social stratification, the importance and leadership of the middle class, the creaking nationalism, the ecological pattern of the cities and the strong pull extended by the rising metropolises. It is the comparability of these phenomena that makes the study of urban growth in the developing societies so important. India's case is a little different in the sense that until recently, the caste system in India was not seriously modified and the Indian middle class was still in a minority, but the change since independence is now noticeable, although progress is very slow. It should also be borne in mind that the massive urban concentration in India, particularly in cities like Calcutta, Bombay, Delhi and Madras, still only forms a small proportion of a population that is estimated to exceed 550 million persons. But the significant increase in India's urban population before there is sufficient industrial growth to provide employment and housing has only exacerbated misery verging on disaster.

Ronald Segal rightly said that the problem is formidable enough, and no government, let alone the distracted and irresolute one that Congress offers at present, would find it easy to solve. Again the ageless character of Indian custom must be changed, it must come out of the world of taboos and the horoscope to the world of planning and development. It means that India must move from the past into the present, to the living and the dying from the dead. And this can come with scientific planning, with the will to live and the upsurge of desire, with the turning from apathy, indifference and submission to rejection and demand. It must come through education which will widen the mental horizon because the alternative is unthinkable.

32

Udaipur

L. K. Oad

The present city of Udaipur was founded by Maharana Udai Singh in 1560 A.D., although recent archaeological excavations have discovered the existence of an ancient city dating back to 2000 B.C. Udaipur is situated in the southernmost part of the present State of Rajasthan. Before the merger of the native states into the Indian Union, it was the capital of Mewar. It is still an administrative, economic and social centre of Southern Rajasthan.

Besides railway and road connections, there is a daily air service which links Udaipur to some of the important cities of the state and the country, such as Delhi, Jaipur, Ahmedabad, Jodhpur and Bombay.

Population

The population of Udaipur has increased slowly but steadily since the beginning of the century. It occupied the sixth place among the towns of Rajasthan in 1901, and it still occupies the same rank, although its population has more than trebled during this period.

Out of the total population of 111,139 in 1961, 66·6 per cent were Hindus, 18·4 per cent were Moslems, 10·5 per cent were Jains, 2·8 per cent were tribal people, 0·4 per cent were Christians, 1·1 per cent were Sikhs and 0·2 per cent were Parsees. Among the Hindus, 15·07 per cent of the total population belongs to Scheduled Castes.[1]

Between 1946 and 1950, 7,735 immigrants came from Pakistan and established their colonies in various parts of the city. About 15,000 students come from neighbouring areas to get university and professional education. Nearly 10,000 labourers come to work in Udaipur seasonally. About 1,200 persons move daily to and from Udaipur for various purposes such as attending the court, marketing or attending secondary schools.[2]

Udaipur is also a centre of attraction for tourists, because of its historical monuments and scenic beauty. Because of its 'bowl shape' physical setting, it contains a number of beautiful lakes, and lake islands. Most of Rajasthan consists of deserts, but Udaipur is just the opposite – it is known as the city

---

[1] *Census of India 1961*, Vol. XIV, Part II A.

[2] N. N. Meena, *Morphology of Udaipur City*, unpublished dissertation of Udaipur University, 1966.

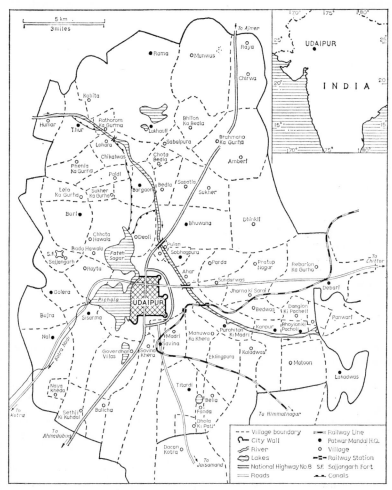

The city of Udaipur and its surroundings.

of lakes. The number of tourists (native as well as foreign) visiting Udaipur has been increasing every year. In 1951 only 80,500 tourists visited the city, but in 1962 their number had reached 348,000.[3]

The municipal area of Udaipur city is 9·72 square miles, but, if the suburban areas are also included, it comes to 13·89 square miles. Nearly 67·5 per cent of the population is concentrated in one square mile in the old walled city. In this part the houses and shops are congested and the roads are very narrow. Outside the city walls, the distribution is also

[3] ibid.

uneven. Nearly 38 per cent of the total population is confined to only 17 per cent of the total area.

Occupational Structure

The following table presents the occupational structure of Udaipur city in 1961.

TABLE 1
OCCUPATIONAL STRUCTURE OF UDAIPUR CITY IN 1961

Workers	Male	Female	Total	Per cent of the total
1. Cultivators	596	353	949	0·8
2. Agricultural labourers	116	45	161	0·1
3. Mining and Orchards etc.	393	162	555	0·5
4. Household Industry	975	839	1,814	1·7
5. Manufacturing	3,693	199	3,892	3·5
6. Construction	3,176	664	3,840	3·5
7. Trade and Commerce	5,408	735	6,143	5·6
8. Transport and Communication	3,411	28	3,439	3·1
9. Other services	11,723	2,396	14,119	12·7
10. *Non-workers	30,793	45,434	76,227	68·5
TOTAL	60,284	50,855	111,139	100·0

* Non-workers include students, women engaged in household work only, old retired people and unemployed persons.

During the period 1941–61 the percentage of persons engaged in agriculture has decreased by nearly 6 per cent, indicating the growth of urbanism and the growing trend of occupation other than agriculture. The significant rise in the percentage of people engaged in productive work other than agriculture on the one hand, and in transport and communication on the other, clearly indicates the growing urban occupational milieu of the city. In 1961 only 3·2 per cent of people were engaged in agriculture, while the majority earned their livelihood from such sources as miscellaneous services, productive work other than agriculture, trade, commerce and transportation.

Dual Control of Education

In Udaipur city, all educational institutions, except the University, are either under government control or are maintained by voluntary organizations. The Municipal Council does not maintain any schools. This position is due to the legacy of the former Mewar State. Among government institutions, a railway training institute is under the control of the Central Government, while the rest are directly under the control of the state government which maintains these schools through its bureaucratic machinery. The Inspector of Schools performs the administrative and academic functions for school-level education while the State Directorate of College Education or the University of Udaipur is responsible for higher general education.

Ministries at the state level are responsible for various types of training institutions. Some voluntary institutions are aided, while others are un-aided. The aided institutions receive grant-in-aid from the state government. They enjoy greater autonomy than government schools, although they are also subject to supervision by the appropriate government authority. The unaided institutions charge heavy fees and try to meet their running expenses from fee receipts.

Some voluntary institutions are denominational, but their student population comes from all sections of the community. For example, in three Catholic institutions, the student population is 2,383, but there are only 31 Christian students studying in them – the rest are non-Christians. The same situation obtains in some Jain institutions. The only exception is a Moslem School, which has boys and girls belonging to Shiya Moslem community only.

Dual control of education by government and voluntary organizations has not created any serious problems in Udaipur city. The system, on the whole, has worked satisfactorily.

Transport Problems

In the development of educational facilities, the major handicap of Udaipur has been its physical configuration, which powerfully affects road patterns. It is because of this factor that the city even to this day has not been able to possess convenient road connexions with the surrounding regions. The result is that although the city of Udaipur is educationally the most advanced in the whole state, the over-all educational level in Udaipur district is very low. According to the 1961 census the percentage of literacy in Udaipur was 51, the highest in the whole state, but if it is calculated on the total population of the district it comes down to 13·73.[4] Children from the villages situated within a radius of ten miles from Udaipur come to attend secondary schools in Udaipur city. As far as university education and higher professional education are concerned, students come not only from the whole state of Rajasthan, but also from many neighbouring states and even from Africa and south-east Asia. So far as university students are concerned, it is assumed that they are financially able to pay for their stay in Udaipur, and therefore good hostel accommodation is available. Some professional institutions have made it obligatory for their students to live in the hostels provided. The real difficulty lies with secondary school boys

4 Pragatisheel Rajasthan Udaipur 1967. Published by the Directorate of Public Relations, Rajasthan Jaipur, p. 37.

and girls, who reside in the neighbouring rural areas. Some of these areas are not linked with the main roads and therefore children have to walk long distances or go on bicycles to attend schools. The government provides neither school buses for transportation of pupils to state schools nor hostel facilities for their residence. Some voluntary institutions do provide hostel facilities for outsiders and transport service to fetch children from the city, but these schools are so expensive that most people cannot afford to send their children to them. The problem is all the more acute in the case of girls. Socially, adolescent girls are not permitted to walk or cycle for long distances to attend secondary school and so most of them have to remain without secondary education unless their parents decide to live in the city while they are being educated. Thus Udaipur's physical situation has been a great obstacle in the development of education in the district. For the city students also, the problem of transport is not easy. The streets in the walled city are too narrow for two large vehicles to pass easily, and because of its situation in a valley, the streets are full of ups and downs. To add to this problem, children's houses are situated in narrow lanes, some of which are not more than five feet wide. Even those children who are studying in voluntary schools have to assemble on the roadside to take the school buses. They are usually picked up from their homes or fixed places on wider roads.

Expansion of Education

After independence, Udaipur became a centre of general and professional education; it is not an exaggeration to say that Udaipur is a city of educational institutions. In 1965–6, the total number of students in the various types of institutions of general and professional education was 40,632 when the total population of the city was estimated to be 120,000. In other words, one-third of the total population of Udaipur consisted of students. The number of students has been steadily increasing and at the time of writing it is estimated that the figure has reached 45,000. The anomaly of this situation is that out of 3,047 students pursuing general higher education, about seventy per cent must be from outside, and from amongst 10,359 students undergoing professional training more than eighty-five per cent are from outside. So far as secondary education is concerned, a significant number of pupils come from the neighbouring villages. Thus Udaipur caters to the manpower needs of other parts of the country. It is not possible, however, for Udaipur city or even for Udaipur district to absorb all the trained personnel produced by various educational institutions. The sudden rise in the number of educational institutions can be attributed to the following factors:

(1) Udaipur was a tourist centre in the past, and was very backward economically, although rich in mineral wealth. Industrialization, particu-

DEVELOPMENT OF EDUCATION IN UDAIPUR CITY FROM 1947 TO 1965

Class of institution		Number of institutions		Enrolment					
		1947–48	1965–66	1947–48			1965–66		
				Boys	Girls	Total	Boys	Girls	Total
Pre-primary education (3 to 5 age cohort)	Government	—	—				49	36	85
	Voluntary	—	4				226	210	436
†Primary (6 to 10 age cohort)	Government	4	51	1,000	200	1,200	3,282	3,146	6,428
	Voluntary	8	11	400	200	600	1,548	991	2,539
Middle (Higher Primary) (11 to 14 age group)	Government	8	12	800	200	1,000	3,585	2,061	5,646
	Voluntary	5	14	1,400	600	2,000	1,615	1,146	2,761
Secondary, Higher Secondary and Multipurpose higher secondary (15 to 17 age group)	Government	1	5	800	—	800	2,965	1,321	4,286
	Voluntary	1	12	200	30	230	2,638	1,967	4,605
Colleges of general education	Government	1	5	250	10	260	1,919	428	2,347
	Voluntary	—	3	—	—	—	628	62	690
‡Professional Vocational and Special Education	Government	—	13	—	—	—	9,427	247	9,674
	Voluntary	1	5	60	5	65	655	30	685
Unclassified institution	—	—	—	—	—	—	—	—	450

Grand Total 40,632

* The data is compiled from the Annual Administrative Reports of the Municipal Council, Udaipur, for the sessions 1958–59 to 1962–63 and for 1965–66.
† These schools have grades I to V. Some of them have K–G sections also.
‡ Under professional and vocational education are included institutions of teacher training, medical college, agriculture college, railway training school, institute for engineering and technology, institute for fishery, tribal and orientation training centres, Patwari training centre, training institute for social workers etc.

larly mining, has started only recently. There was great scope for expansion and plenty of unpopulated space in the valley and on the low hills was available. Moreover, there was an abundance of water, which was scarce in other parts of Rajasthan. Therefore Udaipur was considered to be the most suitable place for educational institutions to grow.

(2) In the pre-independence period, Udaipur had been a leader in educational matters, and several bold experiments in education had been conducted by voluntary institutions. Therefore Udaipur possessed good traditions of education.

(3) Udaipur has provided the state and the country with political leadership, and so political pressure was also partly responsible for the educational development of Udaipur city.

Problems Arising from Expansion

One more anomaly about the educational development in this city is that the higher the stage of education, the better the facilities and vice versa. All the institutions of higher and professional education are located outside the walled city. The buildings are new and constructed for the purposes of particular institutions, and most of these buildings have spacious classrooms. Many of them also have playing fields. There are hostel facilities for students coming from outside, while some institutions are entirely residential.

The picture at the secondary level is gloomy. Only two of the government secondary schools are housed in proper school buildings; all the others are using buildings which were constructed for purposes other than educational. For example, one higher secondary school is in a palace which was built for the heir apparent some time in the nineteenth century, and a girls' higher secondary school is housed in a building which was constructed for the Viceroy's agent in Mewar. But these two are better off than many others which have to make do in old fortresses, private houses or monasteries. Except for three or four secondary schools, all others are situated in the walled city in congested areas.

Middle and primary schools are the worst sufferers. There are hardly any government-owned school buildings. Most of them are housed in temples, monasteries, *dharamashalas* and private houses, and all of them are situated inside the walled city. None of the schools – whether secondary or primary – situated in the walled city has any playgrounds, because the area is so congested that there is hardly any space available either for expansion or for playgrounds. Some schools are in slum areas, and the school buildings are in no way better than the residential buildings. Because of physical limitations, it is not possible even to provide minimum lavatory and washing facilities. Unless these schools can be moved to places outside the city walls, there is no hope of improving their lot.

Expansion of education has been more rapid than finances available for education. As stated earlier, Udaipur schools are maintained either by the state government or by voluntary organizations. The Municipal Council neither maintains any educational institutions, nor does it impose any educational levy. Philanthropic voluntary organizations are concerned to construct and improve their own school buildings, rather than provide school buildings for government institutions. On the part of government, the first priority in education is given to teachers' salaries and other recurring expenditure rather than investing a huge amount in school buildings. Moreover, Udaipur city is one small part in the whole state, and therefore it can have only a small share on an equalization basis. The condition in other parts of the state is in no way better than in Udaipur.

The over-all effect of this is that some well-to-do voluntary schools possess good school buildings, spacious playgrounds and other student-welfare facilities. On the other hand, there are some voluntary schools, which are no better than government institutions. Some of them, in fact, are very poor indeed.

The age structure of the population of Udaipur city is such that demand for primary and secondary education will continue to grow in the next decade. The ratio between boys and girls in the school is 8:5. Now parents are becoming conscious of the need to educate their daughters also, because of matrimonial pressures and social change. If Udaipur has to cope with the demands of school education, many more primary and secondary schools will have to be opened, particularly girls' or mixed type schools. The walled city has reached saturation point and therefore new schools will have to be opened outside the walled city. Old values are changing, and in the future, girls will have the freedom to walk to schools situated outside the walled city.

The moot question is – who will open these schools? Where will the funds come from? It appears the dual control will continue. Political pressures will force government to open new schools – particularly secondary schools. The burden of maintaining primary schools will ultimately have to fall on the Municipality, which has been free from any educational responsibility so far.

Teachers and Teacher-training

Udaipur is a centre of teachers' professional training. There are two teacher-training colleges for preparing secondary school teachers. One of them is situated in the municipal area and another in the suburban area. There are three training institutions for primary school teachers – one situated in the municipal area and the two others in the suburban area. In addition, there is one training institute for science teachers, one for teachers of handicrafts and one for in-service teacher-education. The full-time teacher-training institutions produce about 1,000 teachers every year. As all of them cannot be absorbed in Udaipur city, some are employed in different parts of the State.

In Udaipur city, there is no scarcity of teachers, except in certain subjects. Udaipur provides amenities of urban life, it is a centre of education and so all the teachers serving in the rural areas or in small towns wish to be transferred to or posted in some Udaipur school, to enjoy the facilities of education for themselves and for their children. Some schools however, do find it difficult to get teachers (particularly women teachers) of physics, chemistry and mathematics, although there are so many teachers of humanities and social sciences that the headmasters cannot find adequate work for them.

Changing Values and Student Problems

Until the 1950s, Udaipur remained a comparatively closed cultural pocket. People were not exposed to external environment. Life was simple. There was little sophistication. People were honest and straightforward. Students were meek, humble and modest. Although co-education prevailed, boys and girls seldom mixed with one another. In the classroom also, girls used to sit in a separate row. (This practice still continues in most of the co-educational institutions.)

With the development of industry and linking of Udaipur to other developed cities of the country, people have come directly in contact with other people. With the expansion of education, a large number of students and teachers from other parts of the country came and brought with them the social milieu of urban life.

After 1950, Udaipur became a centre of tourist attraction for foreigners. Europeans and Americans sought employment in educational institutions on an exchange basis, and Udaipur teachers went for higher education to Europe and the U.S.A. Thus Western values were introduced and the past fifteen years have been a period of value-transition.

In Udaipur, problems of student unrest had never been experienced. Now strikes in schools, colleges and the university have become frequent. This upsets older teachers facing the problem for the first time. There are more chances for boys and girls to meet socially and pre-marital relations, absent today, may develop in future.

The rural youth who comes to attend the university for the first time is very ill-adjusted. Either he becomes too urban or feels shy in the company of other urbanized youth. Many things which were considered vices some time ago are the accepted norms today, e.g. smoking among the university students, or defying authority are becoming common features. Juvenile delinquency, which is a curse of industrialization, is bound to grow.

33

Colombo

U. D. I. Sirisena

The phenomenon of urbanization as it exists in cities like Tokyo, Berlin, Paris, London and New York in the advanced and industrialized countries of the world does not occur in Ceylon, which until recently was regarded as a land of villages. Even though, in the world at large, the last few decades have witnessed a rapid increase in the rate of urbanization, Colombo continues to be the only place that can be described as a city in Ceylon, concentrating within it a population of a little over half a million, or just over a twentieth of the total population of twelve millions inhabiting the country.

The Origins of the City

The available records show that the city of Colombo was known to Arab merchant sailors from as far back as the ninth century A.D. In their search for commodities of trade, they found it a useful port of call lying astride the trade routes and destined later to become the city and port of Colombo. It was not long before there was set up a flourishing settlement of Arabs in what was still little more than an exposed bay of the Indian Ocean situated between the mouth of Kelani river and the rocky barrier of Gal Bocca (Anglicized corruption into the present Galle Buck). The site was peculiarly suitable for the first settlers, being isolated from the rest of the country by the sweep of the Kelani river on the north and the north-east, and by a little river flowing sluggishly through swamps and marshes to the south and east, which later was cleared and dredged by the Dutch into the system of canals centred round the Beira Lake. The Sinhala rulers left these settlers undisturbed since they supplied them with a market for the Island's spices and were at the same time a convenient source of procuring the cloth, horses and incense which they needed for their own use.

The arrival of the Portuguese almost by accident in 1505 A.D. was the Island's first contact with a European sea-power. The friendly reception accorded to them by the king did not please the Moors (as these Arab settlers were called) whose ubiquitous trade rivals they were throughout the Mediterranean and the West Atlantic seas. The Moors grew still more alarmed when visitors were given permission to build a trading centre at

St Laurence's Point. The relentless opposition of the Moors combined with the hostility of the Sinhalese population in the surrounding area, forced the Portuguese at length to erect a fortress on the site. In the ensuing struggle for the throne of the Kingdom of Kotte, the Portuguese and the Moors aligned themselves on opposite sides as suited their convenience, and when the conflict was finally resolved by the death of king Buvaneka Bahu and the accession of his grandson, Dharmapala, whom the Portuguese had supported, the Moors lost their foothold in Colombo to the Portuguese.

Colombo Under Foreign Rule

After the battle of Mulleriyava (1561) the city of Kotte lost its pride of place as well as its commercial importance as the capital city of the Low Country, and Colombo became the principal city, offering as it did, the chief anchorage for ships and the acknowledged centre of the Island's trade. From here the Portuguese steadily established their ascendancy over the coastal regions of Ceylon.

In Europe, this was a time of great religious activity, and the discovery of the New World and the opening of new trade routes fired the missionary ardour of the European powers to bring the 'blessings of Christianity' to the 'heathen'. It was, therefore, natural that the Portuguese, from the very outset of their occupation, devoted themselves to the work of proselytization as much as to that of trade. With this end in view, they established schools, first in Colombo and later in the more distant areas under their control. Almost the only residents of the Fort of Colombo in these early days were the leading Portuguese administrative officers, and army and navy personnel, while on the outskirts of the city there lived a fair number of Sinhala princes and chieftains who supported the Portuguese regime. They sent their children to the schools set up by the Portuguese Jesuits and Fransciscans. By the time the Dutch arrived in Ceylon (1648), there were five such institutions in the city of Colombo.

The excesses, corruption, and lethargy of the Portuguese administrators very early caused the Sinhala rulers to look for ways and means of getting rid of them. It was not, however, until the appearance of the Dutch that the eagerly awaited opportunity presented itself. The simultaneous expansion of their eastern commercial empires inevitably led to a confrontation between the Dutch and the Portuguese. Fortune made Ceylon the venue of the conflict. King Rajasinha II invited the Dutch to assist him in ousting the Portuguese and the former, welcoming the opportunity it offered, readily agreed. Jointly they laid siege to the Fort of Colombo and succeeded in capturing it in 1656. With the fall of Colombo, the Portuguese were finally driven out of the Island.

The possession of Colombo by the Dutch now secured them against intervention by any foreign powers, and they were able to enter into treaties with the Sinhala kings, giving them a monopoly of trade in return for their assistance, services and protection in the event of foreign aggression. The Dutch soon discovered that schools greatly facilitated the administration of government, and in a very short time they established a well-organized network of schools over the area they controlled, with Colombo as the main centre.

The last of the major sea powers to come to Ceylon were the British. Their advent was due partly to events in Europe and partly to the rapid expansion of British trade in the East. The clash of the commercial interests of the two East India Companies was inevitable. Towards the end of the eighteenth century, the incessant friction between the Sinhalese and the Dutch erupted into open war and the Sinhalese rulers courted the help of the only other power in this part of the world which could supply it. The British were only too ready to avail themselves of the chance of gaining so valuable an accession to their trading empire, and speedily sent armaments and troops. Once more it was the capture of the city of Colombo after a short siege in 1796 that brought the struggle to a close. The Peace of Amiens in 1802, which terminated the Napoleonic Wars in Europe, gave Ceylon to the British, and with the fall in 1815 of the hill capital of Kandy, where for three centuries the Sinhalese had held at bay three of the leading maritime powers of the West, Colombo became for the first time the capital city of the whole of Ceylon.

Population

During the first years of British occupation, according to a contemporary account:

the Fort was chiefly occupied by British residents, the Pettah by the Dutch and the Portuguese; and the suburbs by Sinhalese, Tamil, and Moorish population.

Colombo contained upwards of fifty thousand inhabitants. Captain Robert Percival, a British officer of the time observed that:

Colombo taken altogether is for its size, one of the most populous places in India. There is no part of the world where so many different languages are spoken or which contains such a mixture of nations, manners, and religions. Besides Europeans and Cingalese, the proper natives of the island, you meet, scattered over the town, almost every race of Asiatics: Moors, Malabars, Travancoreans, Malays, Hindoos, Gentoos, Chinese, Persians, Arabians, Turks, Maldivians, Javians, and natives of all the Asiatic isles; Parsees or worshippers of Fire . . . There are also a number of Africans, Caffres, Buganese . . . ; besides half-castes, people of colour, and other races which proceed from the mixture of the original ones.

The first survey of the population of Colombo in 1827 revealed that Colombo Fort had 734 persons, Pettah, or Colombo within Kayman's

Gate had 4,979, and there were 25,475 persons living beyond Pettah. Table 1 gives the statistics from 1871 to the present day.

TABLE 1

Census year	Area (sq. mi.)	Population	Density	Percentage increase	
				Colombo	Whole Island
1871	9·45	98,843	10,460	—	—
1881	9·45	110,502	11,693	15·3	15·0
1891	9·45	126,825	13,350	14·8	9·0
1901	10·50	154,691	15,469	22·0	18·6
1911	11·93	211,274	17,698	36·6	15·2
1921	12·93	244,163	18,872	15·6	9·6
1931	13·00	184,155	21,858	16·4	18·0
1946	13·27	362,074	27,852	27·4	25·4
1953	13·87	425,881	30·694	17·6	21·6
1963	14·32	511,639	35,729	19·9	31·2
1968	14·32	559,390	39,064	9·3 (estimated for 5 years)	

The growth of the city was closely connected with the growth of population – such growth being the result of natural increase, the influx of migrants, and the extension from time to time of the city's limits. The last factor has little significance as the increase in the area since 1871 has been only 4·87 square miles. Though the area of the city has increased by a little less than 50 per cent over the last fifty years, the population has more than doubled itself. Colombo today is more than a hundred times as densely populated as the rest of the Island, where the density is just over 325 per square mile.

While the sharp rise in the percentage increase in the density of the population of Colombo in the period 1901–11 (the rate being more than double that for the whole of the Island), was partly due to the expansion of the city limits from 10·5 square miles to 11·3 square miles, the more important cause of this increase was the acceleration in the tempo of urbanization. The reasons for this are easy to find; the last two decades of the nineteenth century witnessed a number of epoch-making events, the impact of which began to be felt in Colombo and Ceylon in the first decade of the twentieth century. Between 1865 and 1885 the opening of the Suez Canal caused a sharp decline in the importance of Galle as a sea port, and thereafter Colombo became the principal port in Ceylon. Work on the development of the harbour was begun and by 1881 the tonnage of ships calling at Colombo had exceeded three million per year. About the same time the Municipality of Colombo came into existence, and the first railways, telephones, and tramways were installed. The inauguration of a pipe-borne water supply from Labugama reservoir, followed by a system of water-carriage sewerage, made Colombo one of the most progressive cities in the East from the point of view of health services. Hence it came to pass that by the turn of the present century, Colombo was so well served by amenities and facilities that a large number of people were attracted to it. The change in the trend of the percentage increase in population density after 1931 would seem to indicate that the process of urbanization is coming to an end and that the figures reflect the natural increase of population.

The 47 wards into which Colombo is now divided are not equal in area or in the numbers or social status of their inhabitants. The heaviest concentrations are in those wards where the inhabitants are poorest, while the comparatively affluent live in the southern parts of the city, where there is a low concentration of population. The low density of population in the Fort is due to the fact that the buildings there are mainly business houses or offices and not residential. The increase in population of the city has not led to any movement of population away from the more densely populated areas, so that the pressure on housing accommodation has intensified greatly in many wards. The spread of education and the spread of population throughout the city are thus closely interconnected, and the quality of education provided is intimately bound up with the social and cultural background and outlook of the community that is being served.

From the figures given in Tables 2 and 3, it would appear that the nature of the population of Colombo in the early years of British occupation is as nearly true today as it was then: it is polyglot, multiracial, multireligious, and covers a wide spectrum of the community.

In the process of unification of such a heterogenous agglomeration of people into a civic-conscious society, it is evident that education has an all-important part to play. In the absence of education, it would be a difficult task for people even to understand their fellow citizens, to discover a comity of ideas and ideals with them or even to gather some idea of what it means to belong in common to a city or a nation. They will have little influence on public affairs unless they are literate.

The Beginnings and Growth of the Present School System

In Ceylon, as in most countries with a single large capital city, secondary education was almost entirely concentrated in Colombo. By the beginning of the present century most of the larger schools existing today had already been established; they were a legacy from the missionaries who had flocked to the Island particularly under the British. These schools tended to be set up in areas where the affluent classes of contemporary society

TABLE 2

PERCENTAGE DISTRIBUTION OF THE POPU-
LATION OF COLOMBO BY RACE (1963)

Race	Percentage
All	100·0
Low Country Sinhalese	47·2
Kandyan Sinhalese	3·9
Ceylon Tamils	17·2
Indian Tamils	6·6
Ceylon Moors	17·4
Indian Moors	1·4
Burghers and Eurasians	2·6
Europeans	0·3
Malays	2·2
Others	1·2

TABLE 3

THE NUMERICAL AND PERCENTAGE DISTRIBUTION
OF VARIOUS RELIGIONS IN THE CITY OF COLOMBO
(1963)

	Total	Percentage
All Religions	511,644	100·0
Buddhists	211,047	43·2
Hindus	78·737	15·4
Muslims	109·771	21·5
Christians	100,999	19·7
Others	1,090	0·2

resided. With the development of the harbour and the concentration of commercial and government offices in the Fort and Pettah there was a shift of these classes towards the more salubrious districts in the south of the city. They were followed by the schools that catered to their needs: Royal College shifted from St Sebastian to its present site, St Thomas' College moved from Mutwal to Mount Lavinia, Wesley College moved from Dam Street, and Ananda College from Pettah. Others like St Benedict's College, the Good Shepherd Convent, and Prince College remained in Kotahena, as they were closely attached to places of worship. These were for the most part English secondary schools, established by various religious bodies and receiving the support and favour of the government. Modelled on the great Public Schools of England, they had a highly academic curriculum, aimed at character training rather than preparation of their charges for life in a community. The government policy of making a knowledge of the English language a compulsory requirement for employment in the public service and the prestige attached to the English way of life ensured the success of these institutions. The products of these schools remained for long a privileged *élite* holding positions of power and influence in society. Even schools like Ananda College, Nalanda Vidyalaya, Museaus College and Zahira College located in the city and several of the larger colleges in some of the provincial centres and in the north of the Island that came into existence as a result of the great religious and national resurgence in the last quarter of the nineteenth century, followed the same pattern in regard to organization as well as curricular and extra-curricular activities.

English education, therefore, became for the most part available only in the urban areas, especially in Colombo, and was imparted in private fee-levying schools which catered to the needs of the affluent classes. Elementary education, taught in the vernaculars in the non-fee-levying schools failed to receive either the support of the *élite* or social recognition.

This dichotomy persisted until 1945 when secondary English education, which at first had been mainly an urban phenomenon, was made free and available to all without discrimination and the mother tongue was adopted as the medium of instruction throughout the schools. The once despised vernaculars now became a part of a single unified system. These two measures destroyed the barriers that stood in the way of universal education, particularly at the secondary level, and education for the masses became a reality through the new central schools established in rural areas, although their organization and curricula continued to be influenced by the models found in the main city; so much so that in 1947 only 27 out of the 54 central schools had practical departments and the Kandyan Peasantry Commission in 1951 reported that in all the schools visited there was a complete absence of an agricultural bias in education. This shows the extent to which the traditions of long-established urban English schools had influenced these new institutions.

The expansion of the secondary education system was accompanied by a vigorous demand for higher education with which the University College, founded in Colombo in 1921 to meet an urban middle-class need, could not cope. The first step to deal with the problem was to combine the University College with the Medical College, founded in 1870, to form the nucleus of the University of Ceylon in 1942. The existing buildings in Colombo were used at first, but in accordance with an earlier decision influenced by a powerful urban middle class that the new university should be the focus of a cultural renaissance, it was shifted to a site close to the ancient capital city of Kandy. In an effort to satisfy the ever-increasing demand for higher education, two ancient Pirivenas of Vidyodaya and Vidyalankara in Colombo were raised to university status in 1959. This for a time completed the educational pyramid in the city.

Today there is a network of some 180 schools in the city distributed as indicated in Table 4, in addition to several institutions, some giving pre-school education not recognized by the government and others providing higher education and technical training.

TABLE 4

Management	Elementary	Secondary
State	87	60
Private	7	26

Although it is true that what was in effect a revolution in the sphere of education had taken place during the last twenty-five years, changes in the content of education did not keep pace with the expansion of educational facilities. The type of education with a heavy academic bias introduced by the British rulers to cater to an urban population to meet urban needs failed to foster and develop the latent skills found in the community. This pattern permeated the entire educational structure despite some sporadic attempts made to diversify the curriculum at the secondary level. It was in recognition of this major defect in the higher educational organization that the National Council of Higher Education invited Professor Frank Thistlethwaite, Vice-Chancellor of the University of East Anglia, to advise on the creation of a Colombo Campus in 1967.

Professor Thistlethwaite quite pertinently observed that the University of Colombo as the Metropolitan University should not merely duplicate such courses as were available at other universities but try to contribute to the characteristic activities of a capital city. It should specialize in the education of recruits for such occupations as administration and govern-ment, diplomacy and international affairs, law and finance, trade and commerce and communications. The implications of these recommenda-tions would seem to be that the old idea of a university pursuing knowledge for its own sake should be modified, and that a university should not re-flect but actively cater for the socio-economic needs of the milieu in which it exists. In the case of the University of Colombo, there should be an especially strong concentration on subjects with a metropolitan flavour.

Some Socio-Economic and Cultural Outcomes

One of the more significant results of the present system of education in the city is the emergence of a new middle sector in society. The con-tinuing traditions of the land that goes back for over 2,500 years, fixed the pattern of society according to birth and vocation; the period of foreign occupation added the factors of English education and wealth. Universal franchise, free education, the adoption of the mother tongue as the medium of instruction and political independence coming in quick succession have brought about a social revolution; the old customs and standards are being challenged and new values and attitudes are being sponsored. While equality of opportunity has increased social mobility, the demand is now for greater equity of opportunity and social justice. This is the direct result of the present educational policies. Nascent industries have been creating a demand for new skills and this is being met through training from among classes in contemporary society whose horizons were hitherto restricted to the ranks of unskilled or semi-skilled minor employment. While white-collar jobs still command respect, the emergent middle sector has succeeded in giving prestige and status to skilled labour, especially in the field of modern industry. Table 5 gives a census of employment in the city of Colombo in 1963.

TABLE 5
EMPLOYMENT IN MUNICIPALITY OF COLOMBO—1963

	Males	Females
All Occupations	155,066	20,338
1. Professional, Technical and Related Workers	8,448	4,356
2. Administrative, Executive and Managerial Workers	6,276	254
3. Clerical Workers	22,868	1,715
4. Sales Workers	25,312	196
5. Workers in Agriculture, Forestry, Hunting and Fishing	2,034	240
6. Miners, Quarrymen and Related Workers	25	23
7. Transport and Communication Workers	12,147	295
8 and 9. Craftsmen, Production—Process Workers, and Labourers N.E.C.	49,643	3,724
10. Service, Sport and Recreation Workers	28,313	9,535

Another significant feature is that with the increasing literacy consequent on the expansion of educational facilities almost every individual is actively interested not only in the narrow parochial affairs of day to day life in the city but also in what is occurring in the world outside. The impact of mass media like the newspapers, the radio, and the cinema is most strongly felt among the city dwellers; though, therefore, the urban population is an agglomerate of several different elements, the convergence of interests where political issues and trade unionism are concerned brings about some degree of cohesion. Projects that promote urban growth, facilitate inter-communal harmony, and the secular aspects of social activity find ready acceptance. To the present policy of educational provision and opportunity may be ascribed the fact that leadership and guidance of the once privileged English-educated affluent *élite* is no longer courted or even accepted and that the present trend is more and more to find spokesmen and leaders from among the workers themselves or from among those who actively sympathize with their needs and aspirations.

The impact of education on urban growth and the resultant lowering of social barriers are not without their implications. Perhaps nowhere is this more evident than in the university campuses, where there is a cross-section of the whole population, representing every stratum of society.

When education at the University College had to be paid for and thus catered to a particular section of the community, it failed to contribute to a renewal of indigenous Ceylon culture 'nor did it become a centre of Western culture'. In fact, as a Ceylonese sociologist observes, the 'foreign content of curricula oriented towards London University examinations resulted in retardation of indigenous languages and the stultification of scientific development'.

Today, with the doors of university education opened to all, critics have observed that the fusion of indigenous and Western cultures which the pioneers of the university movement expected has not been realized owing to the increasing Westernizing influences on the classes now availing themselves of university education. Perhaps it is not unfair to say that on the university campuses there is a clash of cultures; the undergraduate who comes from a home where the old traditions are cherished and customs die hard, enters a new way of life and often finds himself uncomfortably suspended between two worlds: sometimes a stranger in his own land. His future as well as the progress of the country depends on how he faces this problem and on the answer that he finds to it.

Some of the factors that nurture and sustain the alien values and attitudes even in the face of deliberate attempts to resuscitate national culture through educational reorientation are inherent in the school system itself which has for long remained impermeable to the impact of socio-cultural and economic revivalist changes of the recent years. Others are due to the fact that the student population of the city are brought into daily contact with a wider variety of influences than are their counterparts in the rural areas.

Within the city of Colombo are to be found (a) the centre of the cultural and aesthetic life of the country – theatres, social and cultural activities, libraries, well-maintained sports fields (b) headquarters of the administration and nerve centre of the country's commercial and economic activities (c) the country's main sea port. Therefore, it is inevitable that the young people in the city have become far more receptive to the enthusiasms and affectations of lively urban life; group activities centring round fashions in music, dress, games, mannerisms and a host of other such fads that are a feature of urban life. Since schools cannot function as institutions isolated from the community, these influences are not only reinforced in the school but tend to permeate the institutions outside the city as well, for urban schools still have much to offer that other schools lack.

A Few Significant Problems

The continued process of urbanization has naturally given rise to a number of problems – some of a general and others of a specific character.

The explosive growth of the population has led to overcrowding in most parts of the city. Particularly since the end of the World War II, slums and shanties have made their appearance, though there are references to people living in sub-standard conditions even in Dutch times. In 1922, Mr Reid, the Chairman of the Municipal Council, declared that 'Nine-tenths of the dwellings of the poorer classes are overcrowded . . . there is a shortage of houses for the poor.' In a census of poverty in the city of Colombo, published in 1926, it was reported that in Kochchikade 30 per cent of the families lived in conditions 'below the requirements for the maintenance of bare physical efficiency'. There are now well over a thousand acres of congested residential areas in Colombo where the density of the population is sometimes as much as 500 persons per acre or more. The presence of these shanty towns and slums constitute a threat to the health of the city and has aggravated the problem of the housing shortage and the provision of educational facilities where they are most needed. The Alif Report on Housing, published in 1963, pinpoints the explosive growth of slums:

TABLE 6

Year	Number of shanties
1953	1,347
1960	13,332
1963	16,500

Of a total of 69,500 dwellings, 30,500 are in slums and nearly half the total population lives in slums. It would be true to say that this inward growth of the city's population has been due to the better services, the better facilities for education, and the better economic opportunities that the city has to offer, and which the suburbs do not possess.

The lack of sufficient accommodation in schools is a reflection of the lack of housing of a suitable type all over the city. There is hardly any open space left in the city for building and the first signs of its upward expansion are now to be seen in the present trend of multi-storied buildings for schools, offices, and residences. Another limiting factor is the prohibitive cost of bare land, building materials, and labour which is a result of the rise in the cost of living. Shortage of accommodation is one of the most acute problems that all schools are faced with today. Of the present total population of the city roughly one-third (200,000) are between the ages of 5 years and 18 years. The present school population for Colombo is approximately 165,000.

This indicates that a considerable number of children who are expected to be in school do not attend school. Investigations carried out by social workers and the Charity Commissioner of the Colombo Municipality point to the fact that most of these children are the children of slum dwellers, living in sub-standard conditions on the fringe of destitution, and their non-attendance at school is chiefly because of poverty.

At the beginning of every year, for the last few years, there has been a rush for admission to Grade I in schools in Colombo. The larger schools, particularly, which can offer a little over one hundred Grade I places, are overwhelmed with applications that run into thousands. In an effort to control this situation the government has directed that admission to elementary schools should be made according to proximity – those residing nearest to the school having a first claim. In spite of this, the applications for admission, especially to the long-established prestigious 'superior' schools, is far in excess of the vacancies. This state of affairs implies that the facilities provided and the quality of instruction are not uniform; the schools are unevenly distributed throughout the city; the older assisted schools with well-established traditions are preferred by the parents.

Moreover, while admission to state elementary schools is restricted by the proximity rule, the availability of a particular medium of instruction and the need to maintain the 'religious ratio' in certain schools vested in the government since 1960, the few schools that have opted to remain private observe certain other priorities for admission:

(1) they are obliged by Statute to admit only children who belong to their own denomination;

(2) the children of past students are given preference;

(3) the socio-economic status of the parents is taken into consideration.

In addition to the difficulties discussed in the preceding paragraphs, the problem of finding housing in the neighbourhood of schools makes it necessary for both children and parents to travel daily from home to place of work or school. In recent years the public transport services have had to face heavy demands upon their resources. A rough estimate puts the number of daily commuters at nearly 200,000. In recent years, the roads have been widened and improved, and the bus and train services strengthened and increased, and a special school bus service has been established, but there are several shortcomings; some of them being the natural consequence of the economic strain posed by the liberal provision of social and welfare services in a developing country. The train services seem to cater mainly for the workers in the city and are not convenient for school children. It would be true to say that the lack of adequate and suitable transport facilities has added to the problems already existing in the city in the sphere of education.

Conclusion

Under the Greater Colombo Plan an attempt has been made to find a solution to some of these problems by establishing at various centres a ring of elementary schools to feed a secondary school, and establishing on the periphery of the city a number of secondary schools with adequate facilities to which the overflow of students from within the city may be diverted as well as those from the suburbs who now seek places in the city schools.

The restructuring of the school system under the reorganization of schools introduced from January, 1968, the redesigning of the curriculum to suit present-day needs, the planning of the expansion of the secondary school on a multilateral and multipurpose basis with special emphasis on practical courses and the provision of equality in educational facilities, the improvement in quality of the instruction given, and the education of teachers in sufficient numbers, so far as this is possible, are some of the matters that are receiving the attention of the administration.

The most encouraging prospect for the future is that the Ministry of Education is aware of the magnitude of the problems caused by the rapid urbanization of the city of Colombo, and has recognized the need to take adequate measures to settle them as early as possible.

REFERENCES

Note: Demographic and other statistical data are based on information obtained from the following:

Census Reports published by the Government of Ceylon.

Annual Administration Reports of the Director of Education, The Government Press, Ceylon.

Mrs I. Kannangara, Demographic Study of the City of Colombo, Monograph No. 2, The Government Press, Ceylon, 1954.

H. A. Hulugalle, Centenary Volume of the Colombo Municipal Council (1865–1965), The Government Press, Ceylon, 1965.

Report of the Special Committee on Housing, Sessional Paper No. 23 of 1963, The Government Press, Ceylon, 1963.

34

Bangkok-Thonburi: An Urban Complex

Bhunthin Attagara and Chaloem Yuviengjaya

Bangkok and Thonburi are twin cities, situated on the banks of the Chao-Phya River, the former being on the east bank, and the latter on the west one. Bangkok has been the capital of Thailand since 1782. Prior to the foundation of Bangkok, Thonburi had once enjoyed that much-coveted status for 15 years. Bangkok is located about 25 kilometres from the Gulf of Siam, and has become the metropolitan centre proper of political, economic, cultural, and communication activities, while Thonburi is geographically its sister city, sharing those activities almost as a matter of course, though divided administratively. The two cities occupy approximately 718,708 *rai* of land (2·5 *rai* = 1 acre), and are two Changwads or provinces among the total of seventy-one provinces in Thailand. Each Changwad or province is divided into Amphurs or districts, and sub-divided into Tambols or groups of villages. The administration is placed under the guidance of a governor and a mayor of the town, and is directed through the Changwad Council and the Town Council, the members of which are elected by the general public.

General Background

Economically, Bangkok may be regarded as a predominantly commercial town, internally and internationally, while Thonburi is a town with a predominance of light industries. This does not mean that agriculture such as rice growing, fruit and vegetable farming, and animal raising, though on a smaller scale, can be entirely disregarded. For instance, the 1963 census of agriculture of Bangkok shows that 469,992 *rai* of the total 523,957 *rai* are arable land of which 89·7 per cent are under crops; and 24,303 *rai*, that is, 4·6 per cent, of the same total holdings are tree-crop land. As for Thonburi, 124,841 *rai* of the total 194,751 *rai* are arable land of which 62·9 per cent are under crops, and 49,511 *rai*, 25·4 per cent, are tree-crop land. Such is the agricultural foundation to sustain the economic development in so far as Bangkok and Thonburi are involved. The port of Bangkok and Don Muang airport, together with the city's internal network, provide other lucrative sources of economic prosperity. The adoption of a National Economic Development Plan in 1961, as well as the appointment of Regional Planning Committees for the North, the Northeast and the South coupled, in later years, with financial and technical assistance from international organizations and industrially advanced countries, has done much to speed up economic progress of the country as a whole. Bangkok and Thonburi, being in the centre of the scene of activities, seem to enjoy the benefits of priority in almost every respect, in much the same way as any metropolitan town.

From the cultural viewpoint, Thonburi and Bangkok have inherited most from their predecessor, Ayuthia: customs, social hierarchy, bureaucratic administration, literature, art, and architecture. Outstanding examples of this art and architecture are the Emerald Buddha Temple and its Bell Tower in the compound of the Grand Palace and the Temple of Dawn at Thonburi, where certain characteristics of Chinese decorative art may be also detected. Brahmanism, too, left its mark in Thai customs, art, and literature, but in a much modified form. Of all influences Buddhism seems to have had the most lasting effect on Thai cultural life. The impact of Western cultural influences has, since the long reign of Rama V (1868–1910), made itself felt in the fields of administration, education, communication, financial system, and ways of living, through the desirable results of the King's European tours and the studies abroad of his own sons and brothers. The contact with American missionaries and Western emissaries during the reigns of Rama IV and Rama V had, to a great extent, transformed the capital into the so-called 'consular Bangkok'.

Bangkok and Thonburi have undergone many phases of transition through the modification of traditional attitudes, the population explosion, economic, and social development, effective mass communication and modern tourism. Mark Jefferson has summed up the features of 'Greater Bangkok' in the following words:

It stands out alone in a different order of magnitude and significance from those of all other cities in the country . . . The finest wares are always to be found there, the rarest articles, the greatest talents, the most skilled workers in every science and art. Thither flows an unending stream of the young and ambitious in search of fame and fortune, and there fame and fortune are found. It is the kingdom's market for all that is superlative in intellectual and material production. Its super-eminence as a market runs parallel to its super-eminence in size. It is the primate city. . . .[1]

Populations

The total population of Bangkok and Thonburi in 1967 was approximately three millions, representing about 9 per cent of the total popula-

[1] In T. H. Silcock (editor), *Thailand: Social and Economic Development*, (Canberra: Australian National University Press in association with Duke University Press, Durham, North Carolina 1967), p. 45.

TABLE I

Civilian Non-institutional Population by Age and Sex: Bangkok-Thonburi Municipal Areas

Sex	Total	Age group									
		Under 11 yrs	11–14	15–19	20–4	25–9	30–4	35–9	40–9	50–9	60 yrs and over
Total	2,608,470	794,124	286,578	325,341	225,072	206,361	173,745	140,355	192,465	141,093	123,336
Male	1,302,300	420,075	156,375	157,050	96,525	92,925	33,700	69,975	95,175	74,025	56,475
Female	1,306,170	374,049	103,203	168,291	128,547	113,436	90,045	70,380	97,290	67,068	66,861

TABLE 2

Student Population by Age Group and Sex (adapted)

Sex	Total	Age group								
		11–14	15–19	20–4	25–9	30–4	35–9	40–9	50–9	60 yrs and over
Total	403,740	223,839	145,287	31,365	2,367	882	—	—	—	—
Male	239,175	135,450	85,050	16,875	1,125	675	—	—	—	—
Female	164,565	88,389	60,237	14,490	1,242	207	—	—	—	—

TABLE 3

Employed Persons by Level of Education Attainment, Age Group and Sex

Level of education	Total	Male				Female			
		Total	11–24	25–44	45 and over	Total	11–24	25–44	45 and over
Total	935,793	558,225	137,700	286,200	134,325	377,568	167,256	160,632	49,680
No formal education	199,449	115,200	7,200	41,850	66,150	84,249	16,146	34,155	33,948
Elementary and Kindergarten	517,122	290,250	93,600	158,175	38,475	226,872	127,305	88,182	11,385
Sec. and Pre-Uni. or Equiv. Academic	127,980	93,825	29,700	49,725	14,400	34,155	16,146	16,353	1,656
Higher Voc. and Techni.	6,417	5,175	1,575	2,925	675	1,242	—	1,242	—
Teacher-training	10,170	2,925	450	1,575	900	7,245	2,898	3,726	621
Short-Course Voc.	657	450	—	225	225	207	—	207	—
Other	18,477	16,200	1,350	7,650	7,200	2,277	207	1,035	1,035
Unknown	657	657	—	450	225	—	—	—	—

SOURCE: *Report of the Labour Force Survey: Bangkok-Thonburi Municipal Areas, 1966–1967*, National Statistical office, the Office of the Prime Minister, pp. 99, 101 and 103 respectively.

tion of the country. The rate of natural growth is estimated at fifty or sixty thousands a year. So far as immigration is concerned, there is an agreed immigration quota of 200 persons per annum for each friendly nation; the Chinese immigrants usually exhaust their quota almost every year, but the Indian and other immigrants seem to be well below theirs. According to the *Report of the Labour Force Survey* conducted during 1966–1967 by the National Statistical Office, the total civilian population in Bangkok–Thonburi municipal areas was 2,608,470. Of this number, there were 1,841,336 persons of eleven years of age and over, and 794,124 persons under eleven years of age. Among 852,795 'persons not in the labour force', there were 403,740 students. Tables 1, 2 and 3 give a detailed picture of the age distribution.

The Report of the Labour Force Survey for 1966–7 showed that the education levels of the labour force outside municipal areas were 'very low'. Of the 13 million persons employed in those areas, approximately 21 per cent had practically no formal education at all, 76 per cent had only primary education, 4 per cent secondary education, and only 1 per cent university education. Of the total labour force of 1·7 million persons, 19 per cent did not have any education, 15 per cent had secondary education and 2·4 per cent university education.

Population migration is due to three factors: natural labour mobility, an outflow of city-dwellers to the government-subsidized land settlements in various parts of the country, and an inflow of students from the provinces in search of better educational opportunities. On the whole, labour mobility during the present phase of industrialization is regarded by the Department of Labour as being negligible, despite the fear that the flight of many young men from their home towns to seek better job opportunities in the Bangkok–Thonburi areas would considerably drain the labour force required by agriculture in those regions. The influx of provincial students has been satisfactorily slowed down by the planned development of education in urban and rural areas.

Administration

So far as local government is concerned, it may be classified into two categories, that is, local administration and local self-government. In hierarchical order, the former concerns itself with provinces, district (Amphurs) and groups of villages, and the latter with municipalities, sanitation districts and groups of villages outside municipal areas. Each provincial government is administered by a provincial board headed by a governor (a civil servant appointed by the Ministry of the Interior), assisted by technical officers appointed by different ministries concerned such as public health officers and education officers. The provincial and district councils are responsible directly for the carrying-out of the central government's national policies. Apart from that, a provincial council is formed in each province to act as a local self-government device in order to acquaint people with democractic practice and to exercise its supervisory power over the governor's execution of local affairs. The Bangkok and Thonburi municipalities are administered by the town councils, and their administration is under the supervision of the Ministry of the Interior.

Since the end of World War II, the rapid growth of Bangkok and Thonburi has presented the local administration authorities with so many problems that they have found it hard to decide on the order of priorities. Because of the influx of migrants into metropolitan areas and the social implications of industrialization, Bangkok and Thonburi have been facing problems of housing shortage, slums, inadequate transportation and traffic congestion, overcrowded schools, and an increasing demand for power and water supply, public parks and playgrounds. Fortunately, the local administration and the two municipalities have been given some indirect help by government loans. For instance, the Public Welfare Department under the Ministry of the Interior has recently announced that, out of the twenty million *baht*[2] to be spent on housing in 1969, fifteen million *baht* will be expended on a housing project of apartment buildings to accommodate 320 families in the metropolitan areas. In addition the Department has formulated a five-year housing project, involving about two hundred million *baht*, to replace 1,700 old houses in the suburb of Huey Khwang by four hundred apartment houses in 1970. The project has already been submitted to the National Economic Development Board for approval and inclusion in the national development plan. However, the total budget for municipal expenditure in 1969 provides a good illustration of an unsuccessful attempt to balance competing exigent demands for allocations. Of the total 495 million *baht*, 44 million *baht* is to be devoted to the improvement of facilities of two municipal hospitals, and 64 million *baht* to road funds. It has been argued, in this case, that a larger allocation should be given to health facilities because the demand for them is increasing rapidly.

Transportation

Traffic congestion problems in Bangkok and Thonburi have been a much-discussed topic among the administrative officers and the public for some time, but hardly any effective or constructive measures have been taken. The main causes are the rapid increase of population concentrating in the metropolitan areas, urbanization, the lack of scientific town planning, the ill-organized bus and truck services, the inadequate road and

---

[2] 50 *baht* (approx.) = £1.

rail networks, including the need for better traffic control and regulations. In recent months, the State Railway of Thailand has admitted that fourteen level crossings in Bangkok and Thonburi frequently hold up the road-traffic flow. At a meeting between the Ministry of Communications and the State Railway of Thailand, it was agreed that fly-over bridges for such crossings and the allocation of railway terminals to the outskirts would be worth considering. It was also suggested that trucks should not be allowed to go into city centres, and goods should be transported by mini-trucks in the cities. The meeting noted that the collaboration of the Bangkok and the Thonburi municipalities is most essential in solving the traffic congestion problem. The State Railway of Thailand is now drawing up a proposed one-year plan to tackle the problem as a whole.

Trade and Commerce

During the last three decades of the nineteenth century, international trade became widespread in Southeast Asia: new markets, personal safety guaranteed by the colonial rules of European Powers and reasonable shipping rates attracted many Chinese settlers from their home towns on the coast of South China to the countries bordering the South China Sea. In most cases, they came to Thailand not to become farmers but businessmen, miners, rubber planters, and so on. Their entrepreneurial or middleman services had at one time been a great help to Thai farmers' extension of rice production. It was estimated in 1965 that there were approximately three million Chinese in Thailand, representing one-eighth of the whole population, compared with almost half of that in Malaysia. And it may be true that 'In the generation to come, the Sino-Thai will undoubtedly become increasingly absorbed by larger population, while this is not nearly probable in Malaya'.[3] The 1960 census recorded about seven thousand Indians, Pakistanis and a similar number of Europeans, Americans, and Australians in Thailand, a large proportion of whom lived in or around Bangkok. Thus Thailand obviously contains certain minority ethnic groups. It is generally accepted that the Chinese form the biggest minority ethnic group: according to G. William Skinner, 'At least one-fifth of all the Chinese in Thailand live within the limits of Bangkok's two municipalities, and about half the Chinese in the country live within fifty miles of the capital'.[4] They hold an unchallenged position as the commercial class.

Religion

Buddhism is the leading religion in the Bangkok–Thonburi area. The

---

[3] T. H. Silcock, op. cit., p. 33.
[4] G. W. Skinner; *Leadership and Power in the Chinese Community of Thailand* (Ithaca, New York: Cornell University Press, 1967) p. 17.

national 1960 census recorded just over one million Moslems, representing 3·9 per cent of the country's population, of which a number live in the two municipalities. Christians form another group. The 1960 census also recorded 461,317 believers in Confucianism, excluding a large number of Buddhist Chinese. Thai Buddhist tolerance has made it possible for different faiths to co-exist peacefully, and has afforded, in this respect, cultural assimilation, basically among Thailand-born Chinese.

Social Divisions

Social stratification cannot be strictly defined in terms of a class system. Thai society is highly centralized, and most significant policy decisions are taken in the capital. H. D. Evers and T. H. Silcock aptly commented on this point that:

> Concentrated in Bangkok are the military and civilian leaders who head the various ministries, the leading civil servants, most of the leading Chinese merchants, the leading members of the Buddhist clergy, the Privy Council, and the King. These men's decisions sometimes affect large blocks of resources directly; sometimes they influence the framework of rules, regulations, and laws which condition the behaviour of rural and urban Thais in using their own assets. The distinction between these two types of influence over economic life is, however, rather less clear-cut in Thailand than in most Western countries. Partly this arises from the way the *élites* came to be where they are. Partly it results from the fundamental structure of Thai government and authority.

In Thailand, the position of the King is one of great potential strength, despite its constitutional limitations. He is much loved and respected by people in all walks of life, and the royal patronage is a social prestige. He is also the embodiment of authority. The person of the King is undoubtedly the focus of loyalty among the bureaucrats. Next is the nobility whose derived authority is well respected. The stratification system of Thai society is not very rigid, and social mobility is taken to be quite natural. As a result of the 1932 Democratic Revolution, the ministerial administration opened a new vista for an academic merit system, by which many young and ambitious men, particularly overseas-educated graduates, moved up gradually to higher ranks and higher rungs of the social ladder. Patronage is retained to a certain extent. The Chinese community is organized on commercial lines. Apart from natural assimilation with Thai *élites*, the Chinese seek certain provision for their social welfare facilities and protection of their commercial interests through long-standing co-operation with leading bureaucrats. This kind of relationship helps considerably to engender the high mobility that characterizes the Thai-Chinese society. Despite the fact that Thai society is undergoing a rapid social change, the gradual assimilation of Thailand-born Chinese, which is beneficial to the Thai society, is expected to continue.

Teacher Education

Generally speaking, the problem of teacher education and of teacher-training facilities have their roots in various shortages and financial inadequacy, as well as in the need for a well-projected plan for teacher-training development. The ever-increasing demand from related sectors of education has evidently to be met concurrently: since 1962 the extension of compulsory primary education from four to seven years has brought in its wake the demand for more vacancies and enrolments in secondary schools, teacher-training institutions and universities. In addition, the implementation of the regular comprehensive-school project since June 1966 has made itself felt in the form of an implicit demand for particular types of teachers. On the vocational and technical aspects of education, a qualitative improvement as well as a quantitative one leads to a demand for qualified and better trained teachers to help develop enough middleman power to meet the ultimate needs of the national economic development plan in its second phase. An adequate supply of semi-skilled or skilled labour and technicians is essential to the advancing stages of the national development plan as a whole. The annual requirement of teachers is estimated at about 13,000–14,000 and the gap between the number of teachers who graduate and the actual requirement is hard to close. There are at present about forty-five teacher-training institutions, excluding four newly established sister colleges of education and the faculties of education at Chiangmai University and at Khon Kaen University. Each year, approximately 7,000 teachers qualified at different levels, graduate from training institutions under the jurisdiction of the Teacher Training Department; some two hundred graduate from the Faculty of Education, Chulalongkorn University; and over four hundred from those under the Vocational Education Department. The shortage of teachers in rural areas poses quite a persistent problem, and is accentuated by a tendency among the newly recruited teachers to prefer an assignment in a principal town, where amenities can easily be found, to that in any distant one where they anticipate hardship. As a result, there is an acute shortage of teachers in certain remote areas. According to the 1967 *Advance Report: School and Teacher Census*[5] by the National Statistical Office, there were 166,262 teachers throughout the country in 1965, 175,745 in 1966, and 183,305 in 1967; the 'per cent changes' were 4·3 during 1966–7. In the same years and the same periods as above, the total number of students in the whole kingdom were 5,162,268, 5,402,911, 5,650,996; and the 'per cent changes' were 2·6, 4·7, and 4·6, respectively. The *Report* recorded that the student-teacher ratio in 1967 was 30·8,

---

[5] It should be noted that the *Advance Report* does not include data for universities, police and military academies.

exactly equal to that of 1966 but lower than those of 1964 and 1965, that is, 31·3 and 31·1 respectively. The per cent change in the number of teachers revealed a downward trend during 1966–7.

The inadequate number of highly-qualified instructors in most teacher-training institutions and the need for more lecturers holding doctor's degrees are another crucial problem, caused by limited financial, building, and equipment facilities. Although the Teacher-Training Department has been given a reasonable share of the annual budget allocation, its operation or recurring cost and an average cost per-student are far higher than those of other Departments in the Ministry of Education; for example, during the 1960–4 period, the average recurring cost per institution was nearly 1,400,000 *baht*, while that of the Vocational Education Department was just over 400,000 *baht*; the average cost per-student was 3,316 *baht*, while those of the Vocational and the Secondary Education Departments were 2,178 *baht* and 1,273 *baht* respectively.[6] In terms of two similar averages, provision of instruction at master's and doctorate level in teacher-training institutions would, undoubtedly, involve relatively higher expenditure. The trend of events points to the fact that Thailand might have to think constructively about producing this class of personnel on her own soil, instead of sending prospective lecturers to further their studies abroad. In the case of teacher-training institutions under the aegis of the Teacher Training Department, there were, during the 1967 school and teacher census survey, 481 lecturers and teachers holding Master's or Doctor's degree, 1,242 with Bachelor's degrees and 483 with Diplomas or Certificates.

Special Problems

Certain special problems such as the influx of students from all over the country into the Bangkok–Thonburi area call for decisive action. The inflow may be caused by a belief that the twin cities could give them better educational facilities and all possible amenities. As a result, the student population is largely concentrated in the metropolitan areas. For instance, there were, in 1966, 26,354[7] students at five universities, 1,878[8] teacher students at the two colleges of education in 1968, and 7,129[9] teacher students at seven teacher-training institutions other than those mentioned above, and 656,387 students of other types of schools ranging from kindergarten up to secondary schools, including private sectors, at

---

[6] *The Department of Teacher Training, Its Work and Organization* (Ministry of Education, Thailand, 1967), Charts 1 and 2, immediately after p. 7.
[7] *Report: Universities Census*, 1966, by the office of the National Education Council, pp. 6–7.
[8] *Summary Report of the Teacher Training Department*, 1968, Table 3, following p. 2.
[9] ibid.

1,275 schools in 1967.[10] Bangkok alone has 2·4 million people or thereabout or 7 per cent of the nation's total population. A crowded community as such is inevitably facing the problems of living and breathing space, a place in the sun at school or university, transportation, and traffic congestion. Public transportation is inadequate, and school buses are few. Recreation areas are forced to give way to residential or commercial areas. Slum clearance in the municipal boundaries results in sporadic slums in suburban areas, which seem to be breeding grounds for crime and delinquency. Industrialization attracts young men to come and seek job opportunities in the capital, and at the same time causes economic dislocation. The gap between the rich and the poor seems to be widening, though not dangerously as yet. The presence of foreign armed forces has a noticeable impact upon social life of the community in certain respects: it affects people's moral values and exacerbates the high cost of living in some quarters. The flight of people in the low-income bracket to suburban areas has been a gradual movement arising mainly from the exorbitant price of land, high rents and the rising cost of living in the cities rather than from the policy of a planned urbanization by local governments. Government hire-purchase housing projects and municipal apartment-house programmes prove inadequate on account of limited funds, and private hire-purchase units on a profit-making basis seem to concern only the middle-income bracket. As a result, adequate housing for most urban low-income families is still a remote dream. Many suburbanites live in substandard dwellings and are without adequate schooling, water supply, and sewers. The plight of older suburbanites is often reflected in the behaviour of their children. Some of the wealthy communities have slummy enclaves in close proximity.

Plans for the Future

As the demand for skilled or semi-skilled manpower is pressing, Thailand has begun to plan an expansion of professional, technical, and vocational education both at secondary and higher levels, especially in the fields of engineering, agriculture, and medical science. Also, particular emphasis has been given to extending compulsory primary education and improving teacher training. The Regular Project for Compulsory Education Extension, aiming at extending compulsory education from four to seven years to all 4,900 districts in the whole kingdom within ten years, has made good progress since 1966. Efforts to lessen wastage due to a considerable number of failures in examination of grade one pupils, as well as absenteeism, have proved successful. In the field of secondary education

---

[10] *Advance Report: School and Teacher Census*, 1967, by the National Statistical Office, Office of the Prime Minister, Thailand, pp. 38–9.

an experimental Comprehensive School Pilot Project, implemented as part of the Regional Education Development Project including Higher Education (REDPHE) since 1960, became a regular Project in the 1966 academic year. The Project has been progressing rather satisfactorily, and its aim to prepare students for changing ways of living due to social and economic advancement seems to be discernable. Thailand has realized that the improvement of technical and vocational institutions is urgent if an adequate supply of skilled labour and technicians is to be obtained to meet a forthcoming demand from industrialization: the improvement of training facilities in technical and vocational institutions has been achieved through internal means as well as international co-operation; for instance, some vocational schools with rapidly decreasing enrolment have recently been merged into well-established secondary schools in the same neighbourhood to form comprehensive schools under the Secondary Education Department, and a loan for improvement of instructional and training facilities has been sanctioned by the International Bank for Reconstruction and Development on recommendations of the UNESCO Educational Investment Programming Mission. Decentralization of higher education as part of the Regional Education Development Project including Higher Education has so far counterbalanced the influx of students into the metropolitan areas: in 1964 Chiengmai University was established in the North, in 1965 Khon Kaen University in the Northeast, and in 1968 Songkhla Nagarindra University in the South. So far as teacher training is concerned, a new college of education was established at Pisanuloke in 1967, and another one at Mahasarakam in 1968. The Teacher Training Schools at Petburi and Nakorn Sridhar-maraj were raised to the status of teacher colleges in May 1969. Another college of education was opened at Songkhla and Bangkok in June 1969. Moreover, the Rural Teacher Training Programme, assisted by UNESCO for some years, has proved fruitful since its initiation in 1956: its activities to improve teaching quality and to relieve shortage of teachers in rural and remote areas with practice-teaching combined with voluntary help in community development have produced satisfactory results. Its coverage in 1968 involved 189 village elementary schools, 51,950 pupils, 1,614 school teachers, 309,324 village population, and 5,680 student teachers.

According to the 1967 *Advanced Report: School and Teacher Census*, there were, in the Bangkok–Thonburi area, only 147 municipal schools with 108,983 pupils and 3,168 teachers, and 257 local schools with 91,291 pupils and 2,294 teachers. It is estimated that the Bangkok Municipality alone has to accommodate another 38,361 pupils of a compulsory-education age group in the coming academic year. The Ministries of Education and of the Interior, as well as the two municipalities, have planned to provide an additional number of schools, including suitable annexes to the existing school buildings in the areas.

The expansion of higher-learning institutions has gradually been taking place since 1961: Chulalongkorn University has offered a number of postgraduate courses; Thammasat University has established a Faculty of Liberal Arts; the University of Mahidol Faculties of Tropical Medicine and of Medical Science, together with a Graduate School for Medicine; Kasetsart University has extended its Faculty of Engineering and established a Faculty of Arts and Science. Both Thammasat and Kasetsart Universities have planned extensions in the outskirts of the metropolitan areas. Silapakorn University has already established another college at Nakorn Prathom, not to mention those of universities in the provinces. With the support from such a general expansion, the National Education Council sees its way clear to increase enrolment in higher-education institutions in the coming academic year. Furthermore, the Department of Teacher Training has recently proposed the Project of Elementary-Education Teacher Preparation in teacher-training institutions under its jurisdiction between 1967 and 1971 and the Project of Secondary-Education Teacher Preparation in the College of Education during the same period. The first project aims at preparing at least 10,000 certificated teachers a year for elementary schools from 1971; and in 1987, at raising the standard of elementary education through preparation of only Bachelor's-degree teachers for elementary schools. The second aims at preparing 3,000 Bachelor's-degree teachers each year, and at raising the standard of secondary education through adequate provision of Bachelor's-degree teachers for secondary schools.

35

*China — In Search of an Anti-City Education**

R. F. Price

On a number of criteria China can be rated as a developing country. With a quarter of the world's population, but only 7·8 per cent of the world's cultivated land, the pressure on the food base is enormous. Coupled with this, only about 15–17 per cent of people live in towns, and methods of farming have reached a peak of productivity at the traditional, non-mechanized stage of technique. Like other developing countries, China is undergoing an industrial revolution, and her educational system has expanded enormously during the past twenty years. These changes have set up the typical surge of population from the villages into the towns.

While China can be classified as a typical peasant-agricultural country, cities have always played an important administrative and commercial role, and city and village have been linked by close social ties.[1] Traditional Chinese cities became centres for trade and handicrafts, but Confucian values did not allow the merchants to develop into a European-type city bourgeoisie, nor was it possible to accumulate capital for industrial development. The majority of cities remained areas of 'concentrated human residence' rather than productive centres.[2] The European powers which forced concession areas out of the Chinese govenment in the latter half of the nineteenth century did little to alter this. Based on foreign trade huge cities like Shanghai, Hong Kong, Tianjin and Hankou arose, and what industry did develop, served foreign interests in the main.[3] Shanghai became infamous for its enormous population of criminals and 'entertainers' whose eradication in the 1950s was to be a major triumph of communist re-education. The Japanese encouraged the development of a number of new cities in Manchuria which became the main industrial area in pre-1949 China.

---

* Throughout this article the author has used the preferred spelling system for Chinese names and words known as *hanyu pinyin*.—Editors.

[1] Franz Schurmann, *Ideology and Organization in Communist China* (Berkeley: University of California Press, 1966), p. 366.

[2] Schurmann, op. cit., p. 399.

[3] Arthur G. Ashbrook Jr., 'Main Lines of Chinese Communist Economic Policy', in: U.S.A. 90th Congress Joint Economic Committee, *An Economic Profile of Mainland China*, vol. I and II. (Washington, D.C.: U.S. Government Printing Office. 1967), pp. 15–43, p. 24.

When the communists came into power in 1949 they embarked on an industrialization programme. In April 1945 Mao Ze-dong described the future as they saw it then: '. . . additional tens of millions of peasants will go to the cities and enter factories. If China is to build up powerful national industries and many large modern cities, there will have to be a long process of transformation of rural into urban inhabitants'.[4] During the period 1952–57, which included the First Five-Year Plan, China relied heavily on importing know-how and plant from the U.S.S.R. Old industry was brought back into full production, and a number of new industries were started. Thousands of skilled and semi-skilled industrial workers were trained and special schools were established for administrators. The years 1957–61 saw a setback, the Great Leap Forward being coupled with the departure of the Soviet specialists and the abandonment of the promised 300 inter-locking industrial plants when only about half had been completed, and a series of disastrous harvests. In December 1961, the Central Committee of the Chinese Communist Party ordered a stop to basic construction,[5] the closing of factories which were operating at a loss, and an embargo on the recruitment of labour from the rural areas for a period of three years. During the whole period 1958–65 the economy showed no signs of growth, though from 1960 onwards there was steady recovery towards previous production peaks, and a number of special fields made important advances. Resources were concentrated in the fields of petroleum, fertilizers, small tractors and farm equipment, and nuclear and other weapons. Textiles and food processing were reduced.[6] This was in line with a new policy decision that agriculture was to be the base, and industry the 'leading factor'.[7]

The great expansion of education which has taken place since 1949 has been largely in the towns, and town-orientated. During the early years the emphasis was on training scientists, technical personnel and administrators to man the developing industry. The number of students graduating from third-level institutions rose from 21,000 in 1948–9 to 170,000 in 1964–5. Of these the number graduating in engineering rose from 4,752 to 60,000, and in the natural sciences from 1,584 to 10,000.[8] With all but a handful of the full-time secondary schools concentrated in the

---

[4] Mao Ze-dong, 'On Coalition Government: a Report to the 7th National Congress of the Chinese Communist Party', April 24th, 1945, in *Selected Works of Mao Tse-tung*, vol. III. (Peking: Foreign Languages Press, 1965).

[5] Tu-chung Liu, 'The tempo of economic development of the Chinese Mainland', 1949–65, in *An Economic Profile of Mainland China*, op. cit., pp. 45–76, p. 74.

[6] Liu, op. cit., p. 75.

[7] John S. Aird, 'Population Growth and Distribution in Mainland China', in *An Economic Profile of Mainland China*, op. cit., pp. 389–90.

[8] Leo. A. Orleans, 'Communist China's Education: Policies, Problems and Prospects', in *An Economic Profile of Mainland China*, op. cit., pp. 499–518, p. 511.

urban areas and the subject-matter taught concerned with urban life, these schools became a siphon drawing talent and ambition from the rural areas.

Rural Change

Turning briefly to the rural community, we find far-reaching social changes combined with rather little change in the basic way of life. Immediately after 1949 the villages were swept by the land reform which distributed the land of the bigger landowners and classified the peasants into categories: landlord, rich peasant, middle peasant, poor peasant and labourer. Mutual-aid teams were then organized to help the poorer peasants, and gradually during the middle 1950s the land was re-grouped into co-operative farms. In 1958 these were grouped into communes in a movement which sought to combine local government with production.

All these changes destroyed the old village *élite* and attempted to replace the old individual and family mores by a new collective spirit. But much remained as before. The old home life, and in a majority of cases the old production methods with their hard handwork in the fields from dawn till dusk, went on unchanged. In place of the bitter exploitation of former days, liberated peasants found themselves expected to work on huge water-conservation or tree-planting schemes during the slack seasons which they had formerly lazed through undisturbed. Cultural life was enlivened by a simple reading room, and occasional visits from travelling cinema and opera, now given a strong political message. And for the first time many villages found themselves in possession of a clinic and a primary school.

The social changes drove a number of people to seek a living in the towns. Former landlord families, and those who already had some commercial connexions were the first to leave. As co-operation progressed the more individualistic members of other strata followed. At times of disaster by flood or drought the numbers fleeing the village increased dramatically, e.g. 1954 and 1956. On a small scale, but of great significance, was the steady flow of youth climbing the educational ladder.

The Urban Attraction

The Chinese distinguish three types of urban settlement: *shi*, the cities or municipalities; *gong-kuang-qu*, the industrial and mining districts; and *zhen*, or towns.[9] The first of these are normally places with populations of over 100,000 and have the administrative status of either a province (Peking, Shanghai and Tianjin) or a *xian* (i.e. a county: all the rest). The number of places designated as cities rose from 163 in 1953 to 180 in 1958.[10]

[9] Theodore Shabad, 'The Population of China's Cities', *The Geographical Review*. XLIX, January 1959, pp. 32–43, p. 33.

[10] Shabad, ibid.

China's cities vary considerably in character. In the former treaty ports the European-style buildings remain, the prestige banks and hotels, and the villas of the well-to-do, in areas sharply contrasting with the narrow alleys, markets and small workshops of the traditionally Chinese quarters. In cities like Peking or Xi'an one-storey houses in walled courts dominate the crowded centre. Modern factories, research and teaching institutes tend to lie in the suburbs, each surrounded by blocks of flats and dormitories for workers and students. The bigger cities include large areas of farm land within their jurisdiction. Scattered throughout the cities are the cinemas, theatres, eating houses, parks, zoos and other places of entertainment. While the facilities do not match the demand, they provide possibilities for occasional diversion and expand the mental horizon, especially of the youth.

While all social services are under population pressure, housing is perhaps the biggest problem. A survey of 166 cities in 1955 showed that 50 per cent of residential buildings were unfit for occupation, and in spite of replacement and new building since then, the position remains bad. Living space is rationed on a scale which allows teachers some 6 m^2 per person, and those not employed by government or factory only just over 3 m^2.[11]

In spite of the pressure of numbers, 6-year primary education had become almost universal by the early 1960s, although there remains a shortage of crèches and kindergartens. Secondary schools, with places for about one-tenth of the primary school leavers, remain highly selective. Both primary and secondary schools operate a half-day system in order to make the best use of scarce buildings and other facilities, but the supply of urban teachers is sufficient to allow separate teachers for the morning and afternoon shifts. During 1964–5 there was a sharp increase in the number of part-work schools in the cities, mostly technical secondary or third level institutions attached to factories and other enterprises. A national conference held in 1965 saw these schools as one way of preparing the majority of school leavers for going to 'the mountains or rural areas'.[12]

In addition to the attraction which city life and the promise of an easier and more exciting life presented to the rural population, definite invitations were extended at times during the 1950s. Various industrial enterprises which needed workers recruited direct from the farms, especially during the Great Leap Forward when capital-starved enterprises saw inputs of labour as their only chance of fulfilling the unrealistic output targets set.

---

[11] Kang Chao, 'Industrialization and Urban Housing in Communist China', *Journal of Asian Studies*, XXV. May 3rd, 1966, pp. 381–396.

[12] New China News Agency, December 5th, 1965, translated in *Selections from the China Mainland Press*, 3598.

Urban Population Figures

At this point it will probably clarify the argument if we examine the available figures for the growth of the urban population. Attempts to record this during the last two decades have taken place on two occasions. From 1949 through 1953 municipal departments of public security attempted to keep urban population registers. In 1953 a national population census was taken under the general direction of the Ministry of the Interior. In both cases a number of factors made the accuracy of the result questionable. Leo A. Orleans comments, 'even if the census had only a low degree of accuracy in comparison with modern counts in other leading countries – it still stands as the most reliable count ever made of all of China's population'.[13] But J. S. Aird warns that 'the actual urban proportion of the mainland population, now or at any time in the past, is indeterminable for lack of reliable data'.[14] Figures for changes in the populations of urban areas are based on projections from the census figures, and on a sample of towns from the north-west and north-east, areas whose population figures would not, according to Orleans, compensate each other to give a representative total.[15] Published by the State Statistical Bureau in 1957[16] these figures are presumably the basis for those which appear in the *People's Handbook for 1958*.[17] According to this *Handbook* the total urban population rose from 57,650,000 in 1949 to 89,150,000 in 1956, and two-thirds of the increase was due to immigration from the rural areas.[18] An article in the *Guangming Ribao* in 1963 gave a figure of 38·9 per cent as the increase in the urban population between 1953 and 1957. This would mean a total of 99·5 million at the end of 1957, considerably higher than other estimates.[19] Economic Minister Bo Yi-bo used the much higher figure of 130 million, but did not give it a date.[20] A government survey of fifteen cities revealed an increase of one million, (28 per cent) in the 'basic population' (productive workers) between 1953 and 1956, together with a 5 per cent rise in the 'service population' and 2·5 million (70 per cent) rise in the 'dependent population'.[21] During 1956 Shanghai reported an increase in the registered population of 700,000, of which 'more than 500,000' were said to be from the rural areas.[22] During the period of the First Five-Year Plan some eight million people appear to have migrated from the rural areas, while at the same time two million people were added to the urban population through natural

---

[13] Leo A. Orleans, 'The recent growth of China's urban population,' *The Geographical Review*, XLIX, January 1959, pp. 43–57, p. 44.
[14] Aird, op. cit., p. 378.
[15] Orleans, *The Recent Growth . . .* op. cit., p. 47. [16] Aird, op. cit., p. 380.
[17] Schurmann, op. cit., pp. 380–2. [18] ibid. [19] Aird, op. cit., p. 381.
[20] Aird, op. cit., p. 382. [21] Schurmann, op. cit., pp. 381–2. [22] Aird, op. cit., p. 384.

increase.[23] Figures for the 1960s are unobtainable, but it would seem that while pressure on the towns continues it has abated somewhat.

During the years since 1949 the number of people employed outside agriculture has grown considerably, but at a decreasing rate. The total rose from 25·3 million in 1949 to 36·8 million in 1952,[24] an increase of 40 per cent in three years, but only reached a total of 39·4 million in 1957 after the completion of the First Five Year Plan. By the end of 1958 it shot up to 56·9 million, but rapidly fell again as economic difficulties set in, and the figure had stabilized to about 46 million in 1964–5.

Problems of Employment

The non-agriculturally employed population is, of course, not the same either as the urban, or the urban employed population, though it is nearer to the latter. But it is the population which has to be taken into account when considering the employment of graduates of the school system. According to one estimate the 26·3 million graduates of the secondary and third level education institutions produced during the sixteen years from 1949 to 1965 would have served to staff an urban labour force of twice the existing size.[25] Figures for unemployment, or under-employment are not available, but there is no doubt that both remain serious problems, and that finding suitable employment for school graduates is an important part of the whole question.

At the time of the Great Leap Forward of 1958–60 an abortive attempt was made to reorganize life in the cities and rapidly expand production. A government survey had shown that in fifteen cities, some 60 per cent of the population consisted of dependents, not employed in any productive process. Lui Shao-qi expressed the mood of the moment when he said: 'If everyone works, work hours can be shortened; all will have time to study, to rest.'[26] The aim was to set up integrated units which would combine production, distribution and consumption with educational, cultural, militia and police activities. At its peak in June 1960 there were reported to be some 1,027 urban communes with a total population of 52 million. Some, like the Zhengzhou Textile Factory Urban People's Commune, begun in June 1958, were based on an existing factory. Others, like that in Guiyang City begun in August 1958, were largely the work of housewives who set up small factories, kindergartens, communal eating places and other social services. All these attempts appear to have been

[23] Aird, op. cit., pp. 385–6.

[24] John P. Emerson, 'Employment in Mainland China: Problems and Prospects, in *An Economic Profile of Mainland China*.' op. cit., pp. 403–470, p. 438.

[25] Edwin F. Jones, 'The Role of Development Policies and Economic Organization in Innovation and Growth: Communist China', in *An Economic Profile of Mainland China*, op. cit., pp. 677–684, p. 682.

[26] Schurmann, op. cit., p. 383.

destroyed by conflicts over administration, shortages of raw materials, poor remuneration for effort expended, and even male objection to female involvement outside the home. After 1961 the term urban commune no longer appeared in the press or in official statements.

Halting Urban Expansion

Already in 1952 the Chinese government began to be worried about the 'blind drift' to the towns and since then various ways have been used to reduce the urban population. The first attempts were aimed at expanding rural employment by means of water conservancy projects and the development of various subsidiary handicrafts. Then in 1953 and again in 1957 urban factories were urged to use local labour rather than to recruit direct from the farms. Rural co-operative leaders were instructed not to issue travel documents to people wanting to leave the villages. An attempt to cut off the food supply from illegal urban residents was made by measures to strengthen the rationing system and limit the free market in foodstuffs.

In January 1958 the National People's Congress published new regulations governing the population registers to be maintained by the various public security authorities. These stated that

Citizens may apply for movement from rural to urban areas with the agencies for the administration of population registers in their respective localities of permanent residence only after obtaining a certificate of employment from an urban labour agency, a certificate of acceptance from a school, or a certificate of approval for movement from an urban agency for the administration of population registers.[27]

There have been a number of campaigns to expel people from the cities. In 1955, a year of good crops, large numbers of rural immigrants were returned to their native villages. 558,000 were expelled from Shanghai alone.[28] The *xia fang* movement by which urban cadres were 'sent down' to work in the villages was justified on grounds of administrative efficiency, eliminating bureaucracy, reducing administrative expenditure, but it also had the effect of freeing a certain amount of space in the cities. By September 1958 about one million cadres were affected.[29] Another campaign which has reduced the city population is the one to persuade graduates of the second and third level schools to go 'to the rural and mountainous areas to build socialism'. A combination of administrative pressure in the form of work permits, offers of employment, and of propaganda, this has produced an annual outflow of some hundreds of thousands. A slightly different movement was that begun in April 1962. Under the name *hui-*

---

[27] Orleans, *The Recent Growth* . . . op. cit., p. 53.   [28] Aird, op. cit., p. 383.
[29] Aird, op. cit., p. 386.

xiang it returned people to their native villages, largely by such administrative devices as closing small factories, and dismissing immigrants employed after 1958. It was claimed that some 20 million people returned to their former homes as a result.[30] The result of all these measures was described by one observer: 'The urban population of Mainland China is probably declining now in relative if not in absolute terms, and there is no immediate prospect for a return to rapid urban growth.'[31]

Looking Ahead

The Great Proletarian Cultural Revolution which began in 1966 and ran through two and a half stormy years has raised a number of old problems and attempted to redefine communist aims. Many of the youth who had formerly been sent out to work in such places as Xinjiang returned to their homes in the cities, and a mixture of administrative control and persuasion was used to try and get them out again. Students whose graduation from secondary and higher education had been postponed two years were recently faced with the demand to volunteer for the 'mountains and frontier regions'.[32] While it is clear that the policy is to attempt an all-round development of industry and agriculture, the emphasis is equally clearly still to be on the village.

Education, which has received increasing attention, is seen primarily in moral-political terms, in terms of relating school to the needs of the community and ensuring that those who go to school are not educated away from their worker and peasant parents. Pre-1966 schools are criticized for inculcating ideas of careerism and of 'becoming an official'. The alternative of service to the community (Mao's 'serve the people') and willingness to go 'where the Party sends me' are to be encouraged by greater emphasis on part-work schooling, and on the administration of schools by committees drawn from worker and poor peasant ranks.

While training for urban industry continues to be developed, the main attention is being given to the problem of finding an educational pattern which will adjust the youth to a future in which the great majority will have to work in the rural areas.[33] Chinese leaders see their problem not as adjusting the schools to suit the needs of the cities, but rather as fostering in the urban youth an understanding of the over-all needs of the country and a desire to carry the best skills and values of city life into the vast area of farms and villages which is China.

---

[30] Schurmann, op. cit., p. 366, footnote.   [31] Aird, op. cit., pp. 390–1.

[32] Wen hui bao, May 25th, 1968, translated in *Selections from the China Mainland Press*, 4207, June 27th, 1968.

[33] New China News Agency, December 5th, 1965, translated in *Selections from the China Mainland Press*, 3598.

36

Manila

Aprodicio A. Laquian

The City of Manila ceased to be the capital of the Republic of the Philippines in 1948, when neighbouring Quezon City was made the official capital. However, ever since it was granted a royal charter by the Spanish Crown in 1571, Manila has continued to be the economic, political, cultural and educational centre of the country. Manila is the only provincial level government in the Philippines which is 100 per cent urban. It has a population density of 307·25 persons per hectare, as compared to the next ranking Rizal province which has 8·45 and the national population density of only 0·97 persons per hectare. The city, however, has reached near saturation with a population of 1·5 million. Since 1960, its annual population growth has been less than 2 per cent, as compared to the national growth rate of 3·3 per cent per year.

Manila is the core of a metropolitan area with a population of more than three million – about 10 per cent of the Philippine population. Within the metropolitan area's 36,220 hectares are located 90 of the country's top 100 corporations, all but one of the major banks, all of the major newspapers, most of the radio and television stations, and fully one-third of manufacturing establishments. Manila and nearby Rizal province consume 81·9 per cent of all electric energy generated in the country. In 1962, while only 15·3 per cent of all Filipino families earned ₱10,000 and over per year, 35·9 per cent of the residents of Manila and suburbs earned this much.

From a politico-administrative viewpoint, the main source of Metropolitan Manila's difficulties is the fragmentation of the area into fifteen local governments which are independent of each other. Four cities (Manila, Quezon, Pasay and Caloocan) have their own charters while eleven towns (Malabon, Navotas, Mandaluyong, San Juan, Marikina, Pasig, Taguig, Cainta, Makati, Paranaque and Las Pinas) are all municipalities within the province of Rizal. No metropolitan wide government exists. Each city or municipality is supreme within its territory, with the result that such services as education, traffic, crime control, fire-fighting and others are poorly coordinated.

Another major problem is the metropolitan area's rapid population growth. This is primarily due to migration from lesser urban places and the countryside, which has jacked up Metropolitan Manila's population from 1·3 million in 1948, to 2·1 million in 1960, and 3·5 million in 1969. The immediate impact of this rapid growth is to put a strain on the city's services. Manila suffers from water shortage during the summer and floods during the rainy season, as its waterworks system originally designed for 700,000 persons has not expanded fast enough. Only one-third of the city has sewers. There is only one policeman for every 45,000 residents. Housing is tight, with close to one-third of the population living in colonies of squatters and slum dwellers.

The most recent survey of squatters and slum dwellers in Metropolitan Manila (April 1968), revealed that 183,759 households or 1·12 million people belong to this category. Of these, 80,436 families (43·8 per cent) are in the City of Manila proper. Most of the squatters are on public lands: about 17,680 families are living on the right-of-way of the railroad tracks, 6,000 families are on reclaimed lands on the shores of Manila Bay, and about 5,000 families occupy the national park site in Quezon City.

Life in Manila's slums and squatter colonies is mean and harsh. In a survey of railroad squatters, less than 60 per cent of the family heads were regularly employed. Average monthly income per family was less than ₱200 (about $50 U.S.). Average family size was six, with more than three-fourths of the children below the age of 18, and therefore dependent. Another survey of squatters on the waterfront revealed that 37·2 per cent of the children were of school age (ages 7 to 18). Of these, 11·9 per cent were out of school. Educational attainment of family members was quite low, with about 25·1 per cent reaching grades 1 to 4, 16·4 per cent reaching grades 5 to 6 and 12·2 per cent reaching high school. However, only 0·4 per cent had gone to vocational schools and only 1·46 per cent had reached college.

For the city of Manila as a whole, the demographic picture is much better. The city's population is young but it tends to be older than the national population, as shown in the fact that Manila's median age is 18 while the national median age is 16. Of people 10 years old and over, 91·4 per cent in Manila are literate, as compared to the national literacy rate of 72·0 per cent. However, 27·4 per cent of Manila's population is under ten years old, indicating that heavier investments in education are required. Furthermore, Manila has a greater proportion of people between the ages of 20 to 29 (21·3 per cent in Manila as against 16·3 in the whole Philippines belong to this category). The presence of these young adults may be explained by the fact that many Filipino students flock to Manila to get their college education, and many of them stay in the city to work after finishing college.

Administration and Finance

The Filipinos put a high value on education. The country's Constitution makes primary education (grades 1 to 4) compulsory and universal. The national government is primarily responsible for primary and intermediate education but local governments usually provide for education above the sixth grade. In the City of Manila, the city prides itself on the fact that it provides public education free, from the primary to collegiate levels.

Manila's educational bureaucracy in 1968 was made up of one superintendent, two assistant superintendents, 110 supervisors, 68 principals, and 9,823 classroom teachers. Technically, the superintendent of schools is under the Department of Education of the national government. However, he is also under the general supervision of the city Mayor. Since almost all funds for the public schools including part of the superintendent's salary are appropriated by the city, the supervisory power of the Mayor is almost tantamount to administrative control.

In its budget for 1967–68, the city allocated ₱47,464,937.00 for the city school system. The amount represented the largest slice of the budget and made up about one-third of the total city appropriations. This went to the operation of 70 primary schools (₱10,721,050·00), 48 intermediate schools (₱13,344,257·00), 26 high schools (₱22,747,278·00), and two vocational schools ₱652,252·00). School enrolment in Manila in 1968 totaled 131,691 for primary grades, 57,185 for intermediate and 115,815 for high school (97,109 for day classes and 18,706 for evening classes).

Although most people in Manila are satisfied with the educational system, there are certain problems calling for immediate attention. The fact that the educational bureaucracy is both under the national and the city government supervision and control sometimes results in friction between national and local officials. Since the national government provides funds for the city school system (especially for primary and intermediate grades) this is sometimes used by the central government to exact political concessions from the city. National-local government problems also enter into the hiring, promotion, discipline and retirement of school personnel. The Philippines, as a whole, has an abundance of teachers. Most of these want to teach in Manila where pay and fringe benefits are higher and where they have the chance to pursue higher education. Finally, making education in Manila completely free has swelled the city's school population. Many pupils from the suburbs and the provinces come to Manila and through some devious means get into the schools. The result is overcrowding, which many classes having more than 50 pupils and students alternating in morning, afternoon and evening shifts to maximize use of physical plant. Each opening day of classes in June, cries of a 'school crisis' are heard in Manila, and many students are turned away because of limited facilities.

Manila's public school system is greatly augmented by the private schools which have an enrolment almost three times that of the former. Almost half of the 281 private schools in Manila are run by the Catholic Church. Private schools have a monopoly on kindergarten teaching and on collegiate and university instruction in the City of Manila.

Numbers of Private Schools in Manila

Type of School	Catholic	Protestant	Non-Sectarian	Total
Kindergarten	30	3	13	46
Elementary	50	10	40	100
Secondary	37	7	35	79
College & University	16	1	39	56
	133	21	127	281

Enrolment in the private schools in Manila in 1968 totalled 342,987, broken down as follows: 9,805 for kindergarten, 42,976 for primary, 18,136 for intermediate, 57,929 for secondary, 206,415 for collegiate and 7,726 for vocational schools. For the other local units in the metropolitan area, a total of 328 private schools have a total enrolment of 144,434. Of the private schools, 158 are run by Roman Catholic institutions, 21 are Protestant and 156 are non-sectarian. The total enrolment of private schools in the metropolitan area (except Manila) is broken down as follows: 8,101 for kindergarten, 36,513 for primary, 11,463 for intermediate, 71,012 for secondary, 13,354 for collegiate and 3,911 for vocational.

While the private school system in Manila plays a big role in education, it is faced with serious problems. For one, the great number and variety of private schools in the city make it difficult for the Bureau of Private Schools, a national agency under the Department of Education, to supervise them effectively. No private school is supposed to be operated in the city if it is not 'recognized' by the government. However, because of the great demand for education which makes it a big business, some so-called 'diploma mills' are able to escape the government's control. Even in some of the respectable private schools, the need for profit often results in shoddy teaching, large classes, professors paid on an hourly basis giving old lectures, lack of library resources and books, etc. A survey of private colleges and universities in 1967 revealed that professors tend to have five to six classes per week on the average, are usually underpaid, and they have neither the time nor the motivation to do research and writing. There are exceptionally good private schools such as the Jesuit-run Ateneo University, the Dominican Order's University of Sto. Tomas,

De la Salle College, and San Beda College. However, many schools and colleges still leave much to be desired in terms of scholarship and academic excellence.

Racial, Religious and Social Problems

Manila is racially homogeneous, although it has the greatest number of aliens among all urban areas in the Philippines. The main alien group is the Chinese, who concentrate in 'Chinatown' within the central business district. Though some racial integration has occurred in the country, the Chinese in Manila still maintain their own culture. They run their own schools, celebrate their own holidays, operate their own theatres, and generally concentrate on trade and commerce, which they largely control.

Because of language and other difficulties, the Department of Education finds it extremely difficult to supervise Chinese schools. Filipino nationalists have agitated against the Chinese schools and certain concessions have been made. Thus, the course of studies in such schools has been revised to include Philippine history, cultural life and languages. Filipino teachers have also been employed in courses taught in English. However, the Chinese schools are still quite separate and not integrated into the national school system.

Schools run by the Roman Catholic orders and Protestant sects also constitute an educational problem. Under Philippine laws, schools run by religious organizations enjoy tax-free status. Considering that many such schools reputedly enjoy large profits, many people advocate taxing them. The curriculum in many of the religious schools has also been questioned. Naturally, courses in theology, moral philosophy and ethics are emphasized in religious schools. There are also charges that books used in the Catholic schools do not reflect true Philippine history, especially as regards the role of Spain in the Philippines. Nationalists, 'modernizers' and anti-clerical elements continually criticize the exclusiveness of the religious schools and brand them as reactionary.

Socially, there are charges that Manila's private schools foster the wide cleavage between the rich and the poor. The high tuition fees, especially in the religious exclusive schools, tend to make it impossible for poor children to attend them. Many children of poor parents coming to Manila for an education, therefore, often find themselves in the lower quality schools and even 'diploma mills' wasting their time and money and generally frustrating their ambitions. With only five public colleges in Metropolitan Manila, there is not enough room for bright but poor youngsters. The lack of vocational schools also work against these people because they often get degrees in the arts and the humanities in second-rate schools and then find that their education is of little use in finding a job.

Teachers, Theories and the Educational Establishment

Teaching as a career is very popular in the Philippines because it entails high prestige and promises steady employment in the government. An ambitious youngster from a poor family can finish the two-year normal school course, pass the civil service examination for teachers, find a job as a classroom teacher, and then proceed to a higher degree during summer or on study leaves. The abundance of teachers creates more teachers, in that many private schools regularly offer education courses in their curriculum. With some exceptions, however, teacher training in these institutions leaves much to be desired.

Education in the Philippines is made quite difficult by the language problem. During the American colonial period, English was used as the medium of instruction at all levels in Philippine schools. The high rate of school drop-outs (6·07 per cent for primary schools, 6·34 per cent for intermediate and 7·61 for high schools) made it obvious after independence that the English-language education of many Filipinos was not useful to them. In 1935, it was decided that a national language based on Tagalog would be introduced in Philippine schools. Several years ago, it was decided that the first two years of school would be conducted in the local language; the national language, Pilipino, should be introduced in the third grade, and that English should be used as a second language at this time. It is hoped that later on Pilipino will be the main medium of instruction and that English will be used as a second language. However, until the experiments in language teaching and the determination of a Philippine language policy finally come up with an answer, education in the country is made more difficult by the language issue.

Traditionally, education has always been regarded as the means for gainful employment. The fact that unemployment rates in the Philippines have rarely fallen below 6 per cent of the labour force has worried many educators. The so-called '2-2 Plan' has therefore been initiated. Under this system, a high school student can choose, in his junior year, if he wants to pursue a vocational or an academic curriculum. The plan has been in operation for about ten years, but already certain shortcomings have been noted. For one thing, many schools are not equipped with aptitude testing and guidance counselling facilities and personnel, so that many students who take the vocational courses eventually proceed to college, aspiring for an academic degree. The vocational school curriculum also emphasizes 'white-collar' work because the students prefer these courses. Facilities and equipment for a real vocational education are lacking and skilled teachers are also hard to find.

The city of Manila, however, has pioneered in stressing vocational education for young adults. Classes are held in the evening, using the physical plant of the high schools which would otherwise be idle at this time. In spite of the limitations cited above, these schools are working out and many youngsters who have dropped out are attending them, thus improving their chances for economic and social mobility.

In an attempt to improve the quality of urban life, the city school system in Manila has an Adult and Community Education Services unit, complete with supervisors and Teacher Community Coordinators in each school to help achieve the goals of the community school movement. The concept behind the community school is to make the teacher and the students take the role of change agents. Thus, the teacher is not confined to the classroom. He is also expected to elicit community participation, teach adults to read and write and to learn about their civic duties, introduce recreational programs to fight juvenile delinquency, and establish a bridge between the school and the community at large.

In an aspiring democracy like the Philippines, the ideal of the community school is an excellent one. Since Filipinos value the education of their children, they express ready concern for the public schools and are quite willing to assume financial and other responsibilities for the improvement of public education through Parent-Teacher Associations or other community organizations. Most community organization programmes for the improvement of slum and squatter areas, therefore, find it beneficial to work through the schools. Teachers, especially those promoted as Community Coordinators and volunteer instructors for adult classes are accorded great respect even in the toughest slum communities.

One drawback of the community school programme, however, is the fact that it puts additional burdens on the already overworked teacher, with no commensurate compensation for his efforts. There have been many complaints from teachers who are asked to initiate meetings of parents and teachers, conduct recreational activities, visit parents, attend community functions, etc., all this to be done during weekends or after office hours and with no overtime compensation! Community leaders have also been wary of the teachers' active participation in community affairs, fearful that the school system is becoming politicized and that the teachers might be used by political officials to boost their stock. Finally, many teachers asked to perform community functions are not trained for these activities. The curricula of many teacher-training schools is often confined to pedagogy and does not include social work and community development skills which are necessary to effective community work.

Finally, with such a great demand for schooling and the influx of young people to the urban area for education, school buildings and facilities are often sub-standard. The City of Manila, for example, pays a huge amount each year for rental of buildings used as school houses. Because such buildings are privately built and owned, they are rarely suited for classroom instruction. Laboratory and other facilities are grossly inadequate, with the result that botany, biology and other natural science courses are mostly taught through lectures and many students graduate without thorough laboratory work.

Prospects and Solutions

The main educational goal for Metropolitan Manila is clear: to provide educational opportunities for all its citizens, including the more than a million squatters and slum dwellers that reside in it. To achieve this, it is also clear that education has to go beyond the classroom and the campus. To educate the recently rural migrants who have flocked to Manila and to integrate them into urban civic life, new and imaginative programmes are needed. The night high school, evening vocational schools (known as opportunity classes) and adult education classes have been initiated by the city government to extend educational opportunities to the under-privileged. However, expanded and better coordinated programmes are needed for better results.

So long as Manila provides free public education and the other local governments in the metropolitan area do not, the city will find it difficult to provide quality education. One possible solution to this is educational administration on a metropolitan scale. Under this system, resources may be pooled and rationally allocated, with curriculum, salaries, personnel procedures and other aspects of educational administration standardized.

Because a large part of the educational system in Manila is made up of private schools, general reform in this sector is urgently called for. Already, private colleges and universities have set up their own organiza-tions to set educational standards and agree to keep them up. The task of improving private schools, however, cannot be entirely left to private initiative. The government must set up higher educational standards and a stricter supervisory machinery to make sure that they are met. More public institutions, like the City University of Manila, may also be set up to provide other avenues for students. In the end, a combination of government supervision and self-policing among the private educational institutions would be the best way of improving the quality of education they give.

Finally, the fact that a full one-third of Metropolitan Manila's popula-tion is made up of squatters and slum dwellers should be considered in the planning of the city's educational programmes. More vocational schools are called for. Community schools in the vicinity of depressed areas should be opened. More teachers trained in community organization and social work techniques must be hired and assigned to such schools. A pre-school programme may be started in the slums, not only to instil the need for education among children but to acquaint their parents with the benefits from education as well. Certainly, adult education, going beyond literacy classes to include lessons in civics, community life and the need for community participation, should be pursued on a greater scale. Education, after all, should not be regarded solely as a means for gaining employment, as it is customarily thought of in the Philippines. It must become the key to personal success, social well-being and fruitful civic and spiritual life.

37

Kuala Lumpur: a Primate City

Ruth H. K. Wong

Introduction

In the process of colonialism, the growth of towns and cities reflected the economic power and aims of the colonial masters. The places which developed most rapidly were those which afforded the most ready access to means of communication. These same places, chosen for their strategic importance in trade, became centres of dominance as colonial administrations made them their seats of government, from which they could command the resources of the hinterland. In them, political and economic hegemony met and merged. Because of the considerations determining their selection and development, these cities were generally coastal; their population was polyglot because labour, indentured or otherwise, had to be sought from non-native sources to compensate for the *naïveté* of the indigenous peoples in respect to economic goals, an attitude which rendered them economically unproductive.

Cities of developing countries, which have in the main only recently shaken off the shackles of a colonial era, are generally of the type described above. With the advent of industrialization, considerations regarding transportation and communication facilities, adequacy of public utilities, favourable market availability, trained and competent labour and so on, tend to draw industrial activities to these same locations. Furthermore, limited resources do not permit a spread of industrial endeavour to too many places at a time, and, more particularly, because initial investment in industrialization is heavy. Thus the number of towns and cities does not rapidly multiply in newly emergent countries even after independence from foreign rule.

This chapter suggests, therefore, that there is a general difference between the pattern of urbanization in Western advanced societies and that in developing countries. In the former, it is usual to find towns and cities liberally dispersed over the country. As industrialization and 'technification' spread, clusters of these locations, having certain common or interdependent activities, tend to merge as their size and population density increase with time, thus forming larger and larger megalopolitan areas around central metropolises. This process homogenizes town and country so rapidly that rural–urban distinctions disappear.

Urbanization in developing countries, on the other hand, tends to become centred around single cities within areas as large as entire provinces. Here, growing urbanization 'eats' gradually into the surrounding countryside and is a slow outward-moving process from one central city or town of each province or state. Also the urban–rural distinction clearly persists with the one city gaining prominence out of proportion to the rest of the province. Sometimes only a single city develops, leaving almost all the rest of the country lagging behind, as it were, in the modernization process. The position of Bangkok with respect to Thailand is a case in point. For many years before the development of the northern town of Chiengmai, Bangkok was synonymous with Thailand. In the same way, many cities in developing countries are the focal points of state or national development and of individual aspirations.

For the purpose of this chapter, it is proposed to refer to a city, having the peculiar position of dominance described above, as a primate city. The nature of such a city is characterized by a degree of indefinite urbanism though the criterion of population concentration applies.[1] Particularly useful would be Reiss' reference to the city as a 'distinct form of human community',[2] with all that this implies in terms of expertise, activity, organization and even 'slumminess'.

History

The city of Kuala Lumpur, capital city of Malaysia, is situated between latitudes 3 degrees 05 minutes and 3 degrees 11 minutes north of the Equator. It began its existence near the confluence of the Klang and Gombak Rivers in what is now the State of Selangor. Here the first settlers were Chinese who discovered a vast deposit of tin near Ampang, about four miles away.

In the early years of its history, Kuala Lumpur was twice razed to the ground by fire and then rebuilt. With the turn of the present century, the development of the town rapidly gained momentum. In 1957, Kuala Lumpur was declared capital of the independent Federation of Malaya and later in 1963, she became the capital city of Malaysia.

The built-up area of Kuala Lumpur today covers the undulating region of the Kenny Hills to the west and the irregular tectonic basin of Kuala Lumpur to the east. Simultaneous with Kuala Lumpur's growth, a ring of satellite towns formed, the inhabitants of which mined the rich

---

[1] In Malaysia, 'urban areas' are statistically defined as towns with a population of 10,000 to 75,000 – Vide Vital Statistics Yearbooks of W. Malaysia.

[2] A. J. Reiss Jr., 'The Nature of the City', *Cities and Society* (P. K. Hatt & A. J. Reiss Jr., eds.) (Glencoe, Ill., 1957), pp. 17–21.

tin deposits in the environs of the trading post and availed themselves of the services it offered for the export of their product. Such towns were Batu, Jinjang and Setapak in the north, Sungei Besi and Serdang in the south, Ulu Klang and Ampang in the east. Today, these have merged with the central city of Kuala Lumpur. The spread of urbanization outwards and around from Kuala Lumpur as a centre is clearly the pattern, and just beyond the ring of her immediate satellite towns, of which the more recent are Pantai and the industrial town of Petaling Jaya, others have taken shape. Initially, the royal town of Klang and the busy port, Port Swettenham, had their lifeline with Kuala Lumpur via the Klang River.

Several important factors have aided in the growth of Kuala Lumpur.[3]

(1) Its slightly higher elevation over the rest of its environs secured it against the floods of the River Klang. Hence the earlier Chinese merchants chose to build their stores here.

(2) In the earlier days, its proximity to the sea-port of Klang made it easy for the miners not only to ship their ore down the river for export, but also to replenish their supplies at the stores. The entrepreneural services offered at Kuala Lumpur and its position in the heart of the mining country enabled it to become an important trading post, where provisions were bartered for tin ingots.

(3) When the British came, Kuala Lumpur was made the administrative centre for the whole of the State of Selangor. Thus it became both the economic hub of the Klang Basin and a political centre. This was particularly assisted by its location as the pivotal centre of transportation as lines of communication developed over more and more extensive areas of the country. Out from Kuala Lumpur today radiate roads to north, south, east and west. It is also roughly midway between two very busy ports – Singapore and Penang. No other town in Malaya is in such an advantageous geographical position.

(4) Later on, in the early years of the present century, its development was assisted by the demand for rubber. Millions of acres of jungle in the coastal lowlands of West Malaysia were cleared and turned over to the cultivation of rubber, a boon to Kuala Lumpur since its position in the foothill country west of the Main Range also made it a centre for the north-south coastal rubber belt. Kuala Lumpur's economy throve, therefore, on the availability of tin and rubber, two primary products much in demand by the rest of the world.

The growth of Kuala Lumpur can be gauged by the population statistics available. In 1884, its population was estimated at 4,054 persons, increasing to 25,000 in 1896, a sixfold increase. The rate of increase was doubled

---

[3] Vide Tsou Pao Chun, *Urban Landscape of Kuala Lumpur*, Institute of S.E. Asia, Nanyang University, Singapore, 1967, pp. 16–20.

within the ensuing sixty years, so that by 1956 the figure was close on 300,000. By 1964, a bare decade later, it was nearly 400,000. Even then, the density of population in the most crowded, business centre of the city, was around 300,000 per square mile with the average density of the whole city as 11,000 per square mile.

The growth in Kuala Lumpur's population had a series of specific spurts.

(1) From the early 1890s to the late 1920s, population growth was brought about by a heavy influx of immigrants who entered the country: Indians, to supply indentured labour on the railways and the roads; Chinese to work in the tin mines and rubber estates; Indonesians and others to seek their fortunes in a new country. Most of the Indians and Chinese chose to settle in Kuala Lumpur and the other towns, where they engaged themselves chiefly as small-scale shopkeepers and money-lenders, building up their businesses over the years.

(2) There was an artificial acceleration of urbanization in Malaya following the Emergency which began in 1948. About half-a-million scattered rural dwellers were resettled.[4] Many of the rural population moved into Kuala Lumpur, particularly the Chinese.

(3) With the 1950s, came a new trend in urbanization. The enforcement of laws against unimpeded immigration was attended naturally by a decline in the inflow of the non-indigenous population, but a continuing upward trend has become increasingly discernible in the in-migration of indigenous rural folk in more recent years. If the figures of a survey of address changes,[5] based on a five per cent sample of the total population, can be taken as supplying a rough indication of population shifts, then within the years 1960–66, an average rate of 34·6 per cent of all those taking up residence in Kuala Lumpur came from strictly rural areas populated almost exclusively by Malays (see Table 1). It is also interesting to note that in 1960, there was no such in-migration from rural areas, most families moving into Kuala Lumpur having come from other towns of West Malaysia. But by 1966, the percentage reached was 55·1.

TABLE 1

PER CENT OF RURAL-URBAN IN-MIGRATION INTO KUALA LUMPUR, 1960–66

1960	1961	1962	1963	1964	1965	1966	Average
0·0	41·2	36·1	34·9	37·8	37·3	55·1	34·6

[4] Sendut Hamzah 'Urbanisation' in *Malaysia, a Survey* (Wang Gung Wu ed.) (London: F. A. Praeger, 1964), p. 87.
[5] Statistics extracted and compiled from figures supplied by the Dept. of Statistics on a study of 'Change of Addresses from Identity Cards – a 5 per cent Sample, 1966'.

One important reason for this new trend may be the identification of Kuala Lumpur with the hopes and aspirations of the Malays – a status symbol of their progress. For, increasingly of late, with the implementation of legislation regarding Malay as sole official language and the declared policy of the Government with respect to protection of the special rights of the Malays, more and more of the Bumiputras (literally 'Sons of the Soil') are participating in Government and in business. Kuala Lumpur, being the Federal, financial and political capital of the whole of Malaysia naturally has a stronger drawing power for the rural Malays than other towns.

Administrative Problems of Development

In Malaysia there is in every state one urban centre (usually associated with the sultan's royal and local rule), which receives particular attention in development, but Kuala Lumpur, as primate city in Selangor and Federal capital of the whole of Malaysia, easily outstrips all other towns in the pace of economic development, population growth, commercial activity, urban renewal and educational expansion. At the same time, as source of the legislative-executive process and nerve centre of the commerce-communications networks, decision-making tends to be highly centralized in Kuala Lumpur.

In so far as education is concerned, such centralization has its problems. Ostensibly, it may be expected to make control more easily manageable over a wide area, to effect educational development more evenly throughout the country, and to enable the implementation of the national objectives of education to be more predictably assured. Under this form of administration, then, delegation of authority takes the form of the transmission of the established decision rather than the exercise of initiative in new situations and circumstances. Thus, the local education department in each state, headed by a Chief Education Officer, appointed at Kuala Lumpur, merely serves as the local link with the central authority. Fresh decisions outside the given frame of reference have to be referred to the Federal Ministry in Kuala Lumpur. Bureaucratic red tape has a tendency to increase over the years and, what was not noticeable within a small system, can exercise a stranglehold on action within a vastly expanded system. The burden of responsibility with regard to decision-making becomes unnecessarily heavy at Kuala Lumpur, with a consequent slowing down of the process of communication. The drawing up of curricula and syllabuses, the 'hiring and firing' of teachers, the deployment of specialist staff are all directed from the centre.

In a recent report[6] it was pointed out that 'the administrative functions

---

[6] Report of the Royal Commission on the Teaching Services, West Malaysia, July 1968 (Dato Abdul Aziz Mohd. Zain, Chairman), p. 28.

are too centralized at Ministry level to be efficient. There seems to be insufficient delegation of responsibility and authority even on routine administrative matters to officers at the lower and State levels ... some decisions are unnecessarily delayed giving rise to frustration and dissatisfaction amongst teachers.'

Within the administrative service in Kuala Lumpur, the practice has also grown whereby an officer can move from responsibility to responsibility without particular training for specific positions. At the same time, certain responsibilities have been artificially distinguished as administrative or professional, where there is no real separation possible between the two sets of responsibilities. This has called forth a request in the same report[7] for the 'traditional distinction between activities and roles called "administrative" and those called "professional" ' to be reassessed. For the benefit of the country as a whole and for the qualitative improvement of education, a necessary step which has to be taken is decentralization of administration, while, at the same time, more effective communication has to be fostered between all levels of the administrative hierarchy.

Social Problems

Because of the multi-racial composition of its population and the uneven economic development of the indigenous group as compared with the once immigrant groups, potential causes of intergroup tensions are inherently present and easily surface in urban conditions of overcrowding and limited job opportunities. The Bumiputras seek participation in commerce and industry on an equal basis with other groups, but prove themselves less versatile and experienced with regard to entrepreneural skills, and thus are less successful. This has prompted the Government to devise certain protective measures for them such as reserving to them the monopoly of special activities in the transport business. In the public sector, scholarships for training in specialist fields, whether offered at local tertiary institutions or abroad, and the offer of appointments in the civil service are made on the basis of a ratio, stipulated by legislation, of three Bumiputras to one other. This has been introduced as a corrective device to adjust the inbalance of opportunity in the past between the indigenous and the immigrant groups. Yet, in many cases, this has not improved achievement motivation, while it raises the level of material expectations rather unrealistically in proportion to the work effort made. The real answer must lie in providing the Bumiputra with the proper skills through education, that is planned with the specific objectives of economic uplift in view. Such an education should have an affective and attitudinal dimension as well as its cognitive content, so that children of

---

[7] Aziz Report, ibid.

Bumiputras may not grow up to regard those of other racial origins as intruders in a country to which all, irrespective of ethnic connections, have made valuable contribution.

The main responsibilities of education with regard to Kuala Lumpur's social problems may be considered to be the following:

First, the education provided should enable children of the various races to understand one another despite their varying cultural, religious and ethnic backgrounds, and to inculcate in these children an attitude of loyalty to the country, based on an appreciation of common goals.

Secondly, education should help to raise the level of aspiration of the average city Bumiputra so that he may have higher occupational expectations and achievement orientation within an increasingly mobile society. If he is too easily satisfied, he will continue to be at a social disadvantage by comparison with members of the other ethnic groups who have had a history of struggle and achievement.

Thirdly, the education that is made available to all children of school-going age who demand a place in schools, must have both a relevance and a qualitative content, particularly since the resources that are available are limited and therefore should not be carelessly wasted. Since the system of education is highly competitive and examination-dominated, drop-outs from schools occur frequently from the early adolescent years onwards, with disadvantaged children falling behind. The content of the curriculum and the examination, despite the introduction of comprehensive education, is still too heavily biased towards the academic. What began as a well-meant attempt to diversify the curriculum has begun to take on a semblance of narrow and early specialization at the end of the ninth year of school. It is therefore necessary that the curriculum and the selection procedure for each next level of education should be under constant reappraisal. This need the Federal Ministry has in fact already recognized. There now exists a Central Curriculum Planning Committee on which sit members of the Ministry staff, representatives of the teaching rank and file, as well as members of the Faculty of Education staff at the University of Malaya.

The provision of proper educational guidance in schools will help to save children, coming from an impoverished environment, from dropping out of school through sheer inability to cope with the immediate demands of schooling. In this respect, studies should be made to find out how illiterate, urban parents with low achievement motivation themselves can be simultaneously educated with their children and be drawn into a co-operative effort to prepare their children for an increasingly demanding and competitive future.

Fourthly, although slum schools as such do not exist in Kuala Lumpur, because all schools are centrally subsidized and have their pupil populations determined to a certain extent by the State Education Departments, through a system of central enrolment and pupil deployment, the tendency for certain types of schools to be associated with children of certain socio-economic groups is still strong. This is due to the practice whereby parents are allowed to specify their preference for their children's schools. In this way, the more established city schools receive the better type of pupils and, by a natural selection process, poorer pupils of poorer environment seldom gain places in schools with good teaching and learning programmes. They are most frequently sent to neighbourhood schools, where they grow up to accept the values of their own socio-economic group, seldom exposed to the more desirable values of a society which needs to share common purpose and common goals. One way of improving such a situation would be to select teachers of quality for posting to these schools. These will be specially trained to appreciate the problems of such children and learn how to place deliberately before them the models of behaviour desirable for change. This move will not pose too many administrative problems since Government teachers are centrally deployable by the Federal Ministry. Another way would be to select the best and most promising of the children of poor and disadvantaged background and place them together in one or two well-run boarding schools. This will help to take care of the problem of lack of parental support.

Fifthly, a shortage of skilled labour and a surplus of unemployable school-leavers every year shows the need for an orientation of attitude in favour of blue-collar occupations. Successful industrialization and the generation of job opportunities depend very much on how efficiently an initial pool of skills is established. Most urban parents in Malaysia still need to be weaned from the idea that the white-collar job is superior to the blue-collar one, and that it is degrading to the individual and his family if he dirties his hands. In this respect much more use could be made of education through mass media such as the radio and the television to teach new values in respect of occupational choice and success.

Two Specific Educational Problems

The role of education institutions in Kuala Lumpur is twofold. First, they have to satisfy the specific needs of urban expansion. The various services required in the city due to commercial and industrial development have led to the setting up of all kinds of training courses within government subdivisional departments, departments of statutory and quasi-government institutions, and within private institutions. Many of these courses overlap in purpose; some departments train only for the immediate, *ad hoc* needs, while others proliferate courses of little value which promise more than they really offer. In the meantime, the schools keep to a largely traditional curriculum, despite attempts to redefine needs. In these circumstances, a more thorough evaluation of the utilitarian aspects of education needs to be made. Available training courses should be assessed as to their usefulness, and those which may meet longer term goals than those of the immediate present should be strengthened by the pooling of teaching resources. The implementation of the intent and spirit of comprehensive education rather than the letter of the syllabus should be ensured.

Educational institutions in Kuala Lumpur also tend to be viewed as models for schools throughout the country. Thus they have a leadership role thrust upon them. Too commonly whatever is done in the primate city is completely copied by institutions elsewhere and in the rural areas. It is necessary, therefore, for the university and training colleges, which are mostly sited in Kuala Lumpur, to conduct research into the problems and needs of localities outside Kuala Lumpur so that their work and courses carried out may bear relevance to the demands, not only of the city, but also of the entire country.

A Concluding Word

It is hoped that this case study of Kuala Lumpur will, in fact, have addressed itself also to the problems of primate cities elsewhere in South-East Asia, for, while rates of growth in industrialization and productivity do not conform to a single, simple pattern, the problems brought on by industrial development are essentially similar.

List of Contributors

Attagara, Bhunthin, B.Sc., A.R.C.S., Hon. Ph.D., Director General, Department of Teacher Training, Ministry of Education, Bangkok, Thailand. Formerly Director, Division of External Relations, Office of the Under-Secretary of State for Education, Bangkok.

Bamberger, Michael, B.Sc.(Econ.), Ph.D. Social Psychology, Adviser on Research, Accion Comunal Urbana, Caracas. Director of Research Accion International.

Benedetti, Anacleto, Ph.D., Research Department Manager, Unione Cristiana Imprenditori Dirigenti (UCID), Rome.

Bentwich, J. S., M.A., formerly Lecturer in Education, Hebrew University, Jerusalem.

Biobaku, S. O., B.A., M.A., Ph.D., Vice-Chancellor, University of Lagos. Formerly Registrar of the University College, Ibadan; Secretary to the Premier and Executive Council of Western Nigeria; Pro-Vice-Chancellor, University of Ife.

Bjerg, Jens, cand. psych., Assistant Professor, The Danish Institute for Educational Research, Copenhagen.

Consorte, Josildeth Gomes, B.A., Lecturer in Anthropology, Catholic University of São Paulo, Research worker on a training programme for rural workers for the National Institute for Agrarian Development (INDA).

Cooper, G. Albert, B.A. (Ed.), M.Ed., Assistant Professor of Education, Memorial University of Newfoundland. Formerly Executive Director, Nuffield Council on Alcohol Problems.

Eckstein, Max A., B.A.(Hons.), Ph.D., Associate Professor (Comparative Education) and Coordinator, Foundations Sub-Division, Department of Education, Queens College of the City of New York.

Edwards, Gordon, B.L.A., M.C.P., Director, Office of Urban Affairs, Director, Co-operative Urban Extension Centre. Formerly Urban Planner, Systems Planning Division, F.A.A., Washington, D.C.

Edwards, Reginald, B.Sc., M.Ed., Professor of Education, McGill University, Montreal; President, Comparative and International Education Society. Formerly Lecturer and Visiting Professor, Universities of Sheffield, Michigan, British Columbia, California.

Ekuban, E. E., M.A., M.Ed., Lecturer in Education, University College, Cape Coast.

Fantini, Mario D., M.A., Ph.D., Program Officer, Ford Foundation. Formerly Director, Madison Area Project; Staff Director of Special Projects, Syracuse City School District.

Georgeoff, Peter J., M.A., Ph.D., Professor of Education, Chairman, Foundations Section, Department of Education, Purdue University, Lafayette, Indiana.

Grandia, J. H. N., Doctor of Social Sciences, Social-pedagogical Adviser of the Council of Rotterdam.

Hall, Peter G., M.A., Ph.D., Professor of Geography, University of Reading.

Harding, Roy P., B.Sc., Chief Education Officer, Buckinghamshire County Council.

Hausmann, Gottfried, Dr.phil., Professor for Education Ordinarius Seminar für Erziehungswissenschaft. Formerly Head of the Department for Education, Radio Hessen, Visiting Professor, University of Ankara.

Havighurst, Robert J. A. B., Ph.D., Professor of Education, Director, National Study of Indian Education, University of Chicago.

Holmes, Brian, Ph.D., A.Inst.P., Reader in Comparative Education, University of London, Institute of Education.

Ianni, F. A. J., B.S.(Psychology), M.S., Ph.D., Director, Division of Educational Institutions and Programs, and Director, Horace Mann-Lincoln Institute, Teachers College, Columbia University. Formerly Associate Commissioner for Research, United States Office of Education.

Jansen, Mogens, cand.psych., Department of Educational Experiment Research Director, The Danish Institute for Educational Research, Copenhagen.

Laquian, Aprodicio A., B.A., Ph.D., Deputy Director, Local Government Center, College of Public Administration, University of the Philippines. Formerly Senior Specialist, East West Center, and Visiting Associate Professor of Political Science, University of Hawaii.

Larrea, Julio, Ed.D., Professor of Comparative Education, University of La Plata. Formerly Professor of Comparative Education in American universities and many Latin-American universities.

Leerskov, Anders, cand.psych., Assistant Professor, The Danish Institute for Educational Research, Copenhagen.

Lowinger, Lea, B.Sc., Research Associate, Child Development Research Unit, University of Nottingham.

Migunov, A. A., Cand. Pedagogical Sciences, Research Institute of the Theory and History of Pedagogics, Academy of Pedagogical Science, Moscow.

Miller, S. M., Ph.D.(Sociology), Professor of Education and Sociology, New York University, and Consultant, The Ford Foundation, New York. Formerly Professor of Sociology, Maxwell Graduate School and Senior Research Associate, Youth Development Center, Syracuse University, New York.

Mukherjee, K. C., Ph.D., M.A., Lecturer in Comparative Education, University of London Institute of Education.

Mylov, Peer, cand.psych., Assistant Professor, The Danish Institute for Educational Research, Copenhagen.

Newson, John, Ph.D., Senior Lecturer, Department of Psychology and Joint Director, Child Development Research Unit, University of Nottingham.

Oad, L. K., M.A., M.Ed., Ph.D., Reader in Education, Vidya Bhawan G.S. Teachers College, Udaipur.

Price, Ronald F., Ph.D., B.Sc., M.I.Biol., Lecturer in Education, University College of Cape Coast. Formerly Teacher, 2nd Foreign Language Institute, Peking.

Raum, O. F., B.A.(Hons.), Ph.D., Professor Emeritus, University College, Fort Hare, Cape Province.

Rinott, M., Ph.D., Director of Educational Studies, Haifa University College. Formerly Director, Department of Education, Haifa Municipality.

Roby, Pamela A., M.A., National Science Foundation, Graduate Fellow, Department of Sociology, New York University. Formerly Research Assistant, Department of Sociology, New York University; Instructor, Department of Educational Sociology, New York University; Research Assistant, Youth Development Center, Syracuse University.

Sirisena, U. D. I., B.A., M.A.(Lond), Dip. in Ed.(Cey), Dip. in Ed.(Lond), Director of Education (Secondary Education), Ministry of Education and Cultural Affairs, Ceylon. Formerly Assistant Director of Education (Central Region), Ceylon.

Smith, Randall, B.A., Lecturer, Centre for Urban and Regional Studies, University of Birmingham. Formerly Research Officer Acton Society Trust; Lecturer in Applied Sociology Department of Social and Economic Research, University of Glasgow.

Sturm, Rudolf, Absolutorium (Master's degree), Charles University, Prague, Ph.D., Professor of Italian and Slavic Literatures, Skidmore College, Saratoga Springs, New York.

Variş, Fatma, B.A., M.A.E., Ed.D., Associate Professor of Education, Faculty of Education, Ankara University. Formerly Member of the National Board of Education.

Watts, Hilstan Lett, B.A., B.A.(Hons.), Ph.D.(Rhodes), Director Institute for Social Research, University of Natal. Formerly Senior Lecturer, Department of Sociology, Rhodes University, Grahamstown; Senior Research Officer, and Head of Demographic Research Division, National Institute for Personnel Research (S.A. Council for Scientific and Industrial Research) Pretoria.

Wong, Ruth H. K., Dip.Ed.(Malaya), B.A.(Hons.)Belfast, Ed.M., Ed.D.(Harvard), Director of Research, Ministry of Education, Singapore.

Yuviengjaya, Chaloem, M.A., Cert. in International Studies, Education Supervisor, Department of Teacher Training, Ministry of Education, Bangkok. Formerly External Relations Officer, Division of the External Relations, Office of Under-Secretary of State for Education, Ministry of Education, Bangkok.

List of Tables, Charts and Maps

Index